Exploring and Engaging Spirituality for Today's Children

Exploring and Engaging Spirituality for Today's Children

A Holistic Approach

Edited by
LA VERNE TOLBERT

WIPF & STOCK · Eugene, Oregon

EXPLORING AND ENGAGING SPIRITUALITY FOR TODAY'S CHILDREN
A Holistic Approach

Wipf and Stock
An Imprint of Wipf and Stock Publishers
199 W. 8th Ave., Suite 3
Eugene, OR 97401

www.wipfandstock.com

ISBN 13: 978-1-4982-6778-6

Manufactured in the U.S.A.   05/12/2014

Portions of the chapter, Children Learning the Faith in the Middle Ages: Learning from Past Practices for Present Needs, by Kevin E. Lawson are adapted from: Lawson, K. E. "Learning the Faith in England in the Later Middle Ages: Contributions of the Franciscan Friars." *Religious Education* 107.2 (2012) 139–57. Reprinted by permission of Taylor & Francis (http://www.tandfonline.com).

To my grandsons Josiah, Judah, and Jeremiah
And grand-nieces Zahrah and Zailia
May you grow and become strong,
And be filled with wisdom,
And the grace of God.

Contents

Section Four: Exploring Children At-Risk, Child Porn, Social Justice, Intercultural Contexts and Abstinence Education

Illustrations and Tables

Foreword

It all started at a picnic bench in a green space of England's University of Chichester. Three or four of us conference presenters were enjoying the warm summer night and debriefing on the International Children's Spirituality Conference we were attending. The members of our picnic-table bunch had all come from the States for this conference. We knew each other through our writings—books, articles, editorials—and were happy to exchange ideas face to face. From that conversation grew a strong desire to host a Children's Spirituality Conference stateside and to focus it specifically on Christian spirituality.

That was July 2000. By fall 2000 we had a location (Concordia University Chicago), an identified source to underwrite the conference, a volunteer to write the grant proposal, and a growing committee of leaders in the field willing to help plan a conference. The Children's Spirituality Conference was conceived and on its way to being birthed.

The birthing happened in June 2003—a three-day conference with the leaders in children's faith formation and spirituality serving both as the committee and presenting at the conference. I looked around and discovered that I was meeting and working with many of the authors who were listed on the bibliography of a book I had recently edited on the topic!

Since 2003, we have held three more Children's Spirituality Conferences, one every three years. Each conference has been followed by a book put together from many of the seminar presentations at that particular conference. That brings us to today. The conference from which this book has grown was held in June 2012.

As you walk through the chapters you are holding, you will have a sense of vicariously attending a most exciting conference, complete with plenary sessions, breakouts, poster sessions, worship, prayer, great food, good weather, and a pleasant campus for sessions and for overnight stays. If you have attended one or more of these four conferences, you will be treated to reruns of both the sessions you attended and those that just couldn't fit into your schedule. All of you who are interested in the spiritual formation of children will be blessed by your travels through this book.

If this is your first introduction to the Children's Spirituality Conference still held at Concordia University Chicago, enjoy the blessings we have prepared for you. And think seriously about joining us for the fifth triennial conference in June 2015. I don't need to tell you of the importance of the spiritual formation of children.

The planning committee has now organized itself into the Society for Children's Spirituality: Christian Perspectives. Kevin Lawson served as chair for the first two conferences and he and Holly Allen led our third conference. La Verne Tolbert, our first president, led our fourth conference. We are blessed to have her strong leadership and commitment. As a further blessing, La Verne is the editor of this book that takes its content from our 2012 conference.

Exploring and Engaging Spirituality for Today's Children: A Holistic Approach includes four major sections for your exploration and contemplation. A quick journey through the table of contents gives you a view of both the breadth and the depth of our work at this conference. And now we share that work with you, the reader. Those of us who plan these conferences consider our work a labor of love and an opportunity to offer this important focus on the emerging faith of young children to each of you. May you be blessed by your reading and study! And may your thoughtful invitation to the Holy Spirit's message bring blessings to those you serve in the name of Jesus Christ our Lord.

Shirley K. Morgenthaler, Ph.D.
Distinguished Professor of Education
College of Graduate and Innovative Programs
Concordia University Chicago
River Forest, Illinois 60305

Acknowledgments

Children—with hearts receptive of God, minds curious to learn, and imaginations eager to wonder—inspire us to *teach*. I am grateful to the parents, pastors, teachers and church leaders who allow us to examine faith practices so that we can enhance our efforts in the academy as well as in the congregation.

Those who serve on the board of the Society for Children's Spirituality: Christian Perspectives do so with great passion for this work—Holly Allen, Jennifer Beste, Chris Boyatzis, Elizabeth Jeep, Shirley Morgenthaler, William Summey, and Karen-Marie Yust. Our founding board members, including those who continue to serve today, provided the vision along with the Society's educational framework—Holly Allen, Jerome Berryman, Marcia Bunge, Ronald Cram, Kevin Lawson, Scottie Mae, Marcia McQuitty, Shirley Morgenthaler, Beth Posterski, and Catherine Stonehouse. Shelley Campagnola, Lisa Long, and Gene Roehlkepartain, served on the board over the years. Thank you all for your role as iron sharpening iron.

It is impossible to nurture others unless we, ourselves, are in a spiritually nurturing environment. I am grateful for my husband, Irving, who is always so supportive, patient, and encouraging. I appreciate you my love! The women who surround me with prayer and listening ears allow me to blossom: My Mom Anna, my dear Olga, my sweet La Nej, my sister Ruth, and my Odette, along with my prayer team: Annette, Bennie, Claire, Diane, Dorothy, Gail, Kathleen, Nancy, Rosalind, Sharon, Sheila . . . and Minnie. Thank you!

Thank you, too, to Christian Amondson and Matt Wimer at Wipf & Stock for guidance with this edition from our 4th Triennial Conference. And I am very grateful to Ariel Sweet for her excellent proof-reading. Thank you, Nathan Lawson, for help with formatting.

Finally, thank you to the conference attendees who traveled to Concordia University in Chicago during the summer of 2012 to participate or to present research. To those who submitted their work for this book (I thoroughly enjoyed my editorial tasks because each chapter is so thoughtfully crafted with insights that are rich and instructive), may your diligence be rewarded as we present this tool to clergy, laity, students, and professors who are committed to serving our Lord Jesus Christ in the spiritual formation of the least of these . . .

La Verne Tolbert, Editor

Introduction

Researchers, students, professors, practitioners, and presenters descended on Concordia University's campus from nine countries—Venezuela, Netherlands, South Korea, Canada, Uganda, Nigeria, Australia, Guatemala, and Ecuador—twenty-one states, forty-four churches, thirty-four universities, ten mission and ministry organizations, and six publishing companies for the 4th Triennial Conference of the Society of Children's Spirituality: Christian Perspectives. This gathering of scholars examines factors that contribute to the spiritual development of children with the goal of impacting families, churches, schools, and communities in concert with this working definition:

> Children's spirituality is the child's development of a conscious relationship with God in Jesus Christ, through the Holy Spirit, within the context of a community of believers that fosters that relationship, as well as the child's understanding of—and response to—that relationship.

When theory informs practice, fostering spiritual formation during the critical years of a child's development becomes more effective. We understand why we are doing what we are doing. The diversity of Christian faith traditions provides the right environment for a rich exchange of ideas founded upon the Word of God and our Savior, Jesus Christ. It is therefore a great honor to gather this research into a volume that will equip students and be a useful tool for professors and ministry workers for years to come.

The brief biographies at the end of this book provide a glimpse into the scholarship of the women and men who have taken the time to question, research and write. You are surrounded by the best, not because their work is in this book, but because each has a heart for God demonstrated by a love for His children, the least of these. Modeling Christ's example to honor and esteem the child means we recognize that around our nation and, indeed, around the world, there are many children who are broken, abandoned, neglected, and abused. For them, too, spiritual formation is critical, and we must be intentional about positively impacting their lives for heaven's sake. This is our goal . . . our purpose.

Along the way, we lost a champion of children—Tina Lillig. We applaud her memory by introducing at our 2012 conference the Tina Lillig Best-Practices

Scholarship for excellence in children's ministry to be awarded to a student in good standing who is enrolled in a masters or doctoral program. We also have a scholarship honoring former board members Catherine Stonehouse and Scottie May. Benjamin Espinoza was the first recipient of the Stonehouse/May Scholarship for excellence in children's spirituality research. Our goal is to encourage students to be innovative and creative in applying principles to their ministries and to be leaders in researching children's spirituality.

In this volume, we present a holistic approach to exploring children's spirituality as we engage the learner in the process of Christian formation. *Section One* begins with an exploration of the theological and historical foundations of children's spirituality to provide a basis for this exploration, and it centers on the fundamental, foundational practice of prayer. Shirley Morgenthaler, who has graciously hosted our conference at Concordia since its inception, partners with her students and planning team members, Jeffrey Keiser and Mimi Larson, to present various prayer models for children. To help us communicate about faith in ways that are especially meaningful, Rebecca Jones explores the narratives of Robert Coles. Joel Green's chapter follows with an overview of the Gospel of Luke as we focus on Jesus and his refreshingly welcoming approach to children. In the next chapter, we are transported to how children learned the faith in the Middle Ages with Kevin Lawson which provides examples for us today, followed by Benjamin Espinoza as he examines the works of Bushnell and Westeroff to assist us in nurturing children's faith in the twenty-first century. This section concludes as we explore child-centered studies of children and religion with Susan B. Ridgely.

Section Two recognizes that the home and church provide the foundations for children's spiritual formation. Trevecca Okholm guides us through the Christian church year to focus families on reforming a kingdom worldview. Gary McKnight recognizes the value of equipping parents for the spiritual formation of their children, and Christopher Hooton encourages parents to be their children's spiritual directors. Since life begins at conception, James Estep and Mariana Hwang explore the foundations and practices of prenatal ministry for congregations. Barbara Fisher has interactive age-specific strategies for children who are beginning to read the Bible. Dana Kennamer Pemberton invites us to welcome children to holy ground by exploring contemplative practices which she has experienced with first through fifth graders. And we "listen" as children reflect on their own spiritual lives in the chapter by Pamela Caudill Ovwigho and Arnold Cole. Robert Keeley and Laura Keeley inform us of the sacred value of the Psalms in the faith formation of children and teens. Sharon Warkentin Short's chapter concludes this section with the value of teaching children of all ages about the Second Coming of Christ.

Section Three launches us into methodologies that help us engage children along the journey of spiritual formation. Holly Catterton Allen, Robin Howerton, Will Chesher and Hannah Brown explore the role of the body and physical movement in children's spiritual development. Mark Borchert takes us through the lens to examine the role of film and ethnography in children's ministry, and Gary Newton presents innovative strategies that help us engage children at their deepest level. Andrew Kereky builds on this idea by adapting the Ignatian spiritual exercises for children, and in the following chapter, Sandra Ludlow reviews literature and applies childhood theory to the process of children's emergent spiritual awareness. This section concludes with Catherine Posey's research on early adolescents who define spirituality through their writing, artwork, and conversations.

We explore children at-risk, confront child pornography, champion social justice for children, engage intercultural contexts and discuss abstinence education in *Section Four*. Susan Hayes Greener begins with spiritual formation for children who are at-risk around the world, and Jennifer Beste exposes us to the uncomfortable dark reality of child pornography. Rebecca Loveall, Kelly Flanagan, Chelsey Morrison, and Morgan Sorenson contextualize social justice and the process of spiritual formation within culture. Continuing this cultural exploration is David Csinos who challenges us to nurture a spirit of interculturalism through ministry with children. This section concludes with a discussion of abstinence education for inner-city African-American teenage girls based upon my years of research.

As you read *Exploring and Engaging Spirituality for Today's Children: A Holistic Approach* may God birth questions in your heart that only scholarly research may address, and may he inspire you with creative solutions to help solve the spiritual crises in our communities, cities, countries, and world. Most of all, may you be encouraged with a gentle, persistent nudge to keep on keeping on in your practice, study, research, and teaching of children's Christian spiritual formation.

La Verne Tolbert, PhD
President, Society for Children's Spirituality: Christian Perspectives

SECTION ONE

Exploring Theological
and Historical Foundations

Chapter 1

Engaging, Expressive and Experienced-Based Prayer Models with Children

Shirley K. Morgenthaler, Jeffrey B. Keiser, Mimi L. Larson

God asks us to come to him in prayer. We all know this and we all pray with varying degrees of success. Defining prayer is an elusive activity but we may all agree that prayer involves communication with God. Our task in this chapter is to talk with you about praying with children, about children praying, and about praying like children even as adults. As we struggled with all this, we realized that we needed to begin with ourselves, to talk about our own personal prayer experiences.

Prayer is not a model. It is an experience (Miller, 2009). It is the communion with God that Adam and Eve experienced in the Garden. When the Garden was closed to them, they began to struggle with their communion with God. However, it is quite likely that they had an easier time than we of communing with a God and Father who is both infinite and personal because they had had the ideal communion with God in the Garden. They could think about those memories and find ways to recapture them on the other side of the Garden wall.

So it is with children. For children, prayer is an experience that is natural and spontaneous. They can come to their heavenly Father much as they come to Daddy or Mommy. They intuit that God is infinite, but they talk with him as uniquely and completely personal. The task of teaching children to pray is not really a task at all. It is a journey of experiencing prayer with children in an honest way. It is a journey that requires understanding our own prayer journey with God. It is that self-understanding that allows us to be real and transparent with young children, to join in their journey of prayer and fellowship with God. As a way of inviting you to join this journey with us, we begin with our own stories.

OUR STORIES

Living a Prayer-Filled Life

Jeff's Story

As a young child, I cannot remember a time when I was discouraged from praying. In fact, we, as a family, seemed to pray nearly continually. Since my father was a pastor, and my mother a church secretary, it appeared to me that wherever we went and whatever we did, my father, especially, was being called on to pray: at the hospital, at the funeral home, in the prison cell, before eating at the wedding feast, or with one who was grieving the loss of a loved one. Others saw this as something that the pastor did. I witnessed it as something my father did, and being his youngest child, I imitated what he did for many years.

Now I realize the significance of his prayer life upon my own prayer life, which is still in many ways the prayer life of a child. I love reading the book of John, and a single word caught my attention recently. That word was children. I am referring to the story of Jesus appearing to some of the disciples after the resurrection. The exact phrase is this: "Children, do you have any fish?" (John 21: 5 ESV). It suddenly came to me: The endearment that he felt for these grown men who were still boys to him. Also, what I realized in this story is that this is the way that the Father, Jesus, and the Holy Spirit want it. We are all children, and in our childhood (no matter our age) they want us to come to them. The way that we experience relationship with them is through prayer.

Every night when I went to bed, my father came into my room and we prayed together. I started out by reciting a prayer, one which I used over and over for many years, then I prayed from my emotions (hurts, fears, joys, worries, wants, desires), and then my dad added his contribution with a voice that sounded peaceful and patient, blessing me and asking for the protection of our heavenly Father. Then he said good night.

I remember that one time shortly before my tenth birthday, I was at my aunt's house, and I called dad from my bed to pray with me. He came eagerly for our nighttime routine. Then I heard my aunt questioning my mother about this since I was nearly ten years old. I felt just a little embarrassed, but at the same time felt so close to my father and my heavenly Father in those moments that I didn't want to give them up. I am glad that I didn't because my father was gone from this earth before my twenty-second birthday.

What my father showed me in those moments of prayer together was that even though he was in his seventies, he was still a child of his heavenly Father, and his prayers showed that he was still a boy to Jesus. He was still a boy who could come to his Father and ask for anything; he could come to his Father and tell him anything; he could come to his Father and share his sadness or anger; and he could come to his

Father when he was filled with joy. What I saw in my own earthly father's prayers was his own boyhood of exploration, wonder, and need.

Unfortunately, I drifted from this way of praying which is rooted in the concept that we are children of God no matter our age and need to pray like that. But three or four years ago a friend told me about a book called *A Praying Life* (Miller, 2009). When I read it, it was like coming home to prayer. Miller (2009) reminds the reader that most of us have been taught that we must do prayer right, which is a fallacy. We are to come weary and heavy-laden, not alert and perky with all the proper words. No, we are to come in the chaos and confusion of our lives to have relationship with our Father. If we wait until we have it right, we'll never come. Miller (2009) is right when he says that as children of God, we have to come in our mess as real as possible in prayer to ask whatever we want, to believe and play like a child.

I now look at the young children around me for guidance in my own prayer life. Jesus understood that they got it. So I've begun to look at prayer as a journey and as a story that I document. When I watch carefully in prayer and make notes, I get to see the Father, Jesus, and Holy Spirit working in ways that leave me with a sense of anticipation, wonder, and gratitude.

Colorful Playing in Prayer

Mimi's Story

For many years, I ran after an illusion of the proper prayer method. The requirements included a certain amount of time, highly recommended Bible study tools and journals, and a specific chair in my home set aside just for my conversation with God. When all this was assembled, then I could do the right "method" of prayer and have this formal prayer time with God. And sadly, that is what it was—formal. Dare I say also dull, stiff, and fake? I became easily distracted and was frustrated at my lack of authenticity with myself and more importantly, with God.

After a while, I had no desire to show up anymore. I mean, honestly, who wants to meet and have a conversation with a friend who isn't honest with you or themselves? Or puts on airs and needs to be seen in the right restaurant by the right people? If we are being honest here, you wouldn't want to have met with me either.

The beautiful and gracious thing is that God still wanted to meet with me. Slowly desire to spend significant time in prayer began to grow. But something had to change. What I was doing wasn't working. So ultimately, I had to change my mindset. I needed to let go of my need to achieve something and seek out transformation. My prayer time wasn't about getting through a book or saying the appropriate words. It was about being—being with God, listening to him, sharing intimately what my heart was feeling, carrying, or struggling with.

Around that time, I experienced a devastating loss. I came to God heartbroken, in deep grief, with so much to say and no words or way to express it. Just like a child who, when he or she trips and falls, needs to be held in a parents' arms and just cry, I emotionally crawled up into my Abba Father's lap and cried. During this season of grief, my husband gave me Sybil MacBeth's book, *Praying in Color*. In it, she writes, "*Praying in Color* is an active, meditative, playful prayer practice. It . . . involves a re-entry into the childlike world of coloring and improvising" (MacBeth, 2007, 5).

Embracing with a new box of crayons and this basic concept of praying and doodling, I entered into this "childlike world" with God. I kept a journal, but it morphed into visual diary of my conversations with God. Along with writing out my prayers, it included words or images that came to mind or pictures and photos that represented something meaningful. Or sometimes, there were just doodles that were drawn as I talked with God. This journal became a visual expression of my prayer time, a visual picture book of my journey and conversations with God.

Intimacy deepened and soon I found there was no need for words. It was just important to be with God. Doodling random shapes, writing a name or heart's desire on paper while adding details and color began to focus my prayers. And for someone who months earlier could not sit still and focus for five minutes, I started finding myself praying for forty-five to sixty minutes at a time. And the time flew by! When done, these images became a prayer icon of some sort that I carried in my mind, reminding me to continue praying with God throughout the day.

This style of praying may not be for everyone. But it allows me, as I have uniquely been created, to focus my mind, calm my spirit and meet with my Abba Father.

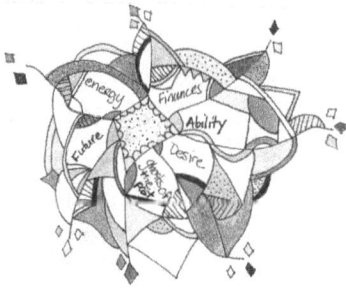

Praying through Song

Shirley's Story

Every night when I was a child, my mother would sit on the side of my bed and we would sing a series of bedtime prayers: Now the Light Has Gone Away; Dear Father in Heaven, Look Down from Above; I Am Jesus's Little Lamb; Jesus Loves Me. Some of these, most of these, had already been used as lullabies as I was sung to sleep as an infant and toddler.

There was always music in my home as I was growing up . . . not recorded music but real music that we made. We sang, we played instruments, we sang together, we harmonized. It was a way of life in my extended family. When we gathered for family events, there was always a piano, usually a fiddle (that's a down-home violin), an accordion or two, sometimes a guitar, sometimes even a German dancing-jig doll that my father would manipulate in time to the music. But the most important part of the gathering was the people: Grandparents, aunts, uncles, cousins, parents, and siblings. People of all ages gathered to make music and to enjoy each other's company. We sang folk songs, camp songs, Christian songs, and hymns—the whole gamut.

I'm remembering now that we sang as we prepared meals and as we cleaned up after a meal. One or more of us could be found humming a favorite tune as we played with toys on the floor. Most of our play took place in the living spaces of the family. Our bedrooms were upstairs and just too far away for comfortable playing. So songs during play were a group event. It might be only one child humming a tune, but everyone else participated by listening and enjoying.

Over the years I have tried to pray by a formula: the right place, the right words, and the right time of day. But after a season of attempting this, I would give up in frustration and guilt, assuming that there was something wrong with me that I couldn't follow the advice of the prayer gurus whose books I amassed and read. Then I'd find a new book and start the process all over again. And again it didn't work. I would find my brain singing the simple songs of childhood rather than focusing on the praying that I should be doing. Then it hit me. I really was praying! I was praying through song.

I realized that I had always prayed through song, but I hadn't named it praying. It was just something I did, and something that I couldn't help doing (Palmer, 2000)!

Now I allow myself to sing my prayers. It's not the only way I pray. But it's the way I connect with my Abba throughout the day. The first prayer—a spoken one—that I remember being taught was learned sitting in my high chair. "Abba, lieber Vater. Amen." That's German for "Daddy, beloved Father. Amen." That's the mealtime prayer I said even as I learned my first words. It's a mealtime prayer I said for several years, then taught younger siblings and prayed it with them.

For me, bedtime is still the time that I expect to have time with my Abba. When I was a child, my mother sat at my bedside and sang with me or listened to me sing.

Then we would have a time of talking—quiet and peaceful talking. Sometimes, maybe oftentimes, we would end with spoken prayers that grew out of that quiet discussion. Since my sister Estelle, only fifteen months younger than I, shared my double bed, we were a trio—mother, Estelle, and I—singing and praying . . . praying and singing joys, worries, and concerns among the three of us.

It has occurred to me recently that my prayers oftentimes are still a trio—my husband, me, and my Abba. I can feel him joining into the conversation with my brain singing and a sense of peace. I can visualize Jesus as my brother supporting me in those prayers. And when the prayer is difficult and doesn't want to come, I feel the Holy Spirit groaning for and with me into a song or hymn of my childhood. My best and most precious praying happens when I come to my Abba as a child, his child.

LOOKING AT OUR STORIES TOGETHER

For each of us, our prayer life has been a journey. That journey has included a time of frustration, of attempting to "get it right." Our prayer journeys have also involved discovery of the simplicity of prayer, of coming to God authentically. Those journeys have taken us back to a child-like relationship with God, a relationship that is messy (Miller, 2009), that is honest enough to come to God as we really are (Palmer, 2000), that comes as children who need to doodle prayers (MacBeth, 2007).

For each of us an Abba or Daddy is an important way to think about God. When Shirley walked the streets of Jerusalem five years ago, it was powerful to hear small children call their fathers Abba. It was a reminder that the relationship between father and child is simple and authentic. The child can ask anything of his or her Abba (Luther, 1986). The Abba answers in the way that is most helpful for the child: "Yes," "No," "Maybe later."

Our Abba may also answer with, "No, I have something better in mind. Prayer is putting your life fully into my hands, into my control, into the possibility of the impossible. Are you ready for that? My miracles always make the impossible a fact, an event, a reality. In fact, I have no impossible! I simply want you to put all of your 'impossibles' into my hands and into my timing."

Another theme that runs through each story is a willingness to put oneself into the hands of a loving Father, to be formed and transformed by a real and authentic relationship with God. Prayer must be a journey, not a destination (Modi & Merritt, 2013). An authentic relationship with God is transformational. It is a journey with God in which the destination is unknown. The important component of prayer is a faith-filled walk with God in which we allow God to be in charge, to make and mold us as he wills. This is a childlike journey where the destination is unimportant; it is the trip in relationship that is significant. As Klaus Issler (2001) writes, "To deepen our relationship with God, we must become comfortable in new ways of connecting with God, in 'wasting time' with God" (30). Another vital component of prayer is the willingness to rest in God, to be refreshed by crawling into His lap to be comforted, to sing the simple prayer songs of childhood, to truly talk and walk with God in every moment of the day.

Each of us has experienced a transformation in our relationship with God that keeps us coming back for more. It's like a runner's high. The high is not experienced the first time the runner goes on a run. It takes persistence and repetition to get to the high. When the runner gets that high, he or she wants to run again in order to get the high again. Prayer, our relationship with God, is similar. It takes persistence and repetition to get to the connection with God. When the "pray-er" gets that connection, he or she wants to pray again in order to get the connection with God again. The more we engage in prayer as a child of God, the more that we crave it. The "pray-er" looks forward to time with God, time that is transformational and encouraging, time with that special friend, our Abba Father, who always listens, always loves.

Transformation is something we receive. It is done within us, but not by us. Our relationship with God, our Abba Father, is a trust in him that the transformation he will do within us is good, and is for our good, and results in good for us and those we love. Transformation means change. Transformation means being willing to be put into the impossible knowing that our redeeming God will make it good in ways that we cannot see. Living into the impossible is expecting a miracle: every day, any day, in us and in those we love and pray for.

Real prayer is experiencing prayer in such a way that we cannot live without it. We know our prayer is real when to miss it is to miss an important aspect of the day. When we are worrying about "getting it right," we are missing or messing with the relationship aspect of prayer. Getting it right doesn't matter. In truth, trying to get prayer 'right' takes us out of the present and divides us from our Father. Prayer relates to who we are and whose we are.

THE CHILD'S STORY

We all know that children can pray. Just as they ask their earthly parents for something, they can ask their Heavenly Father as well. Children watch and imitate the adults and caregivers in their lives. They do what we model. And this brings a sense of identity and belonging for children. As research has shown, through a connection to their faith community or family, "the sense of identity which was associated with communal acceptance" (Mountain, 2005, 302) is a common experience for children who pray together as part of a community.

Pray before meals. Pray at bedtime. Pray for other people. Pray for a friend who is sick. Unless the parent or caregiver is intentional about taking time to pray with a child, that child will miss the experience of prayer. Children miss prayer when it is absent. Every preschool or kindergarten teacher in a Christian school has stories about children who teach their parents to pray before meals. Shirley's granddaughter stopped a buffet meal at her grandparents' home by reminding Grandpa that everybody forgot to pray!

Prayers with children form the foundation for the expectation of prayer in children's lives. Prayers with children lead to prayers that children initiate and lead. Prayers with children grow into a life of prayer and a relationship with God. Children walk with God in prayer to a similar degree that they experience their parents' walk with God.

Children learn to connect with God by experiencing that connection, by being *in* prayer rather than learning how to *do* prayer. Children will pray with honesty, openness, and a trust that often surprises adults. Sometimes we are taken aback at how to-the-point children will pray. They pray expecting an answer, a miracle. We all have stories of children or new Christians praying within a group in such a way that we are surprised by the honesty and confidence of that prayer. Children know that God is real and that he is their Heavenly Father, their Abba.

Prayer is learned through experiences. It is learned through relationships. It is learned through the invitation to visit their Abba. It is learned in the everyday, every day. Children know better than adults that prayer is a relationship, not a job. They delight in their visits with Abba. They delight in telling stories of answered prayer.

Prayer is not about the hours spent to achieve something, but the hours spent to become the Father's exact creation. It's about being in prayer and not doing prayer. We are not teaching children how to pray, not giving them a formula about how to pray, or even showing them how to pray. We are praying with them and welcoming them into an experience with God, a shared experience with God as a child of the king.

Our challenge in working with children is to honor their honesty and nakedness in prayer. This is honoring "the interior life of the child" (Mountain, 2005). If we start telling children their prayers are right or wrong, we are destroying the trust between them and their Father. What was powerful about the most recent Child Spirituality Conference is that we did pray, we didn't just talk about it. We did it. We honored the interior life of the conference participants. On the last session we asked participants to pray for each other in small groups asking, "How may I pray for you today?"

Our challenge as adults is to live and walk in prayer with God and with children, to honor their honesty, to encourage them to watch for answered prayer, to trust in and claim the power of prayer in the child's petitions and requests, and to praise God in prayer as a way of being sure that children learn about prayer as life, not as telling God what we want. Children don't put on an act. They are genuine and just bring themselves. Our challenge as adults who are concerned with children and their ongoing spiritual development is to trust the experience of prayer without making it a recipe or a roadmap. The challenge in working with children is to honor their prayers and take them seriously no matter how simple or how audacious. How could you think God would answer that prayer? But a child who is in relationship with God trusts God as a loving parent and knows that God will do what is right and good.

The child isn't worried that God will judge him on the words or how the prayer is presented. He knows God will understand his heart. It is a heart-to-heart relationship with that most-important person in his life.

Relationship is the key to prayer. The voice of love of the Father is heard in prayer (Nouwen, 1993, 23). Christ's own life example was one that was bathed in prayer. He prayed to his Father for others, for himself, and for the kingdom. The example that is left for us in the Lord's Prayer is one that is prayed as a child of God: Heaven, holiness, kingdom authority in eternity and among mortals, sustenance, forgiveness, deliverance. These are lofty ideas but left to the simple lips of children of all ages. As Christ modeled for us, so we must model for children.

We use the word, model, here carefully. It was chosen over the word "teach." The reason for this is that prayer is an experience in relationship. Because it is a relationship, teaching or instructing can yield poor results with prayers becoming stilted or formulaic which may not further a strong relationship with God. At least that has been our experience most of the time. It is through modeling and encouragement that children's prayer lives develop. It is no coincidence that Billy Graham, a man known for prayer, said in a recent interview that he wishes that he had spent more time in prayer (as cited in Van Susteren, 2010). So it is our view that children cannot easily be taught to pray, but the community around them must model a strong prayer life.

In many ways it is the child that models a prayer-filled life for the adults in their midst. Children have a great sense of the significance of the present. They are ecstatic when they can play with friends for seemingly unending amounts of time catching fireflies on summer nights, playing kick the can or lying down on a grassy hillside watching the clouds go by overhead. They remember being startled when their mother calls them home for dinner because it had been hours since they thought about what time it was. It is that Pooh Bear within us that wants to count the honey jars endlessly, and share the excitement of how many there are with our Father (Milne, 1979). Child-like gratitude is legitimately prayer that is experienced in the here and now.

But adults are limited many times because, as Henri Nouwen (1994) says, "we allow our past, which becomes longer and longer each year, to say to us: 'You know it all; you have seen it all, be realistic; the future will just be another repeat of the past. Try to survive it as best you can,'" (16). Children are not bound by such artificial limits. They take great joy in living here and now. Their prayer lives of singing, playing, and communing attest to the idea that this moment is only here one time, and how we treat it shows whom we trust. Children trust their heavenly Father without the baggage of the past or the worries of the future. R.C. Sproul says it this way, "Our Father is the self-existent One, the Creator, who made all things. That's our dad. How could we do anything but trust?" (Sproul, 2012, 37).

YOUR STORY—ANOTHER . . . TOGETHER

Now you need to fill in your story. The challenge for us is to discover what Nouwen describes, "'what is my way to pray, what is the prayer of my heart?' just as artists search for the style that is most their own, so people who pray search for the prayer of their heart," (Nouwen, 1999, 37).

Use some of the tools that we've suggested here or lay hold of other ones. The choice is yours. We together have discovered that our prayer lives did not have the same path, and yet they each served to build a relationship with our heavenly Father. When you are discovering this path, be sure that you share it with others, not suggesting it as their way, but sharing it as the discovery of one who has found a way to great treasure (Isaiah 45:3 NIV) and wants to share it with his brothers and sisters. As God's prayerful family of all ages "We are bound together by faith" (Bonhoeffer, 1954, 39).

REFERENCES

Bee, V. E. *Dear Father in Heaven*. Public domain, 1901.

Bonhoeffer, Dietrich. *Life Together*. San Francisco: HarperSanFrancisco, 1954.

Bradbury, William B. *Jesus Loves Me*. Public domain, 1862.

Havergal, Frances Ridley. *Now the Light Has Gone Away*. Public domain, 1869. http://openhymnal.org/Gif/I_Am_Jesus_Little_Lamb-Weil_Ich_Jesu_Schaflein_Bin.gif

Issler, Klaus. *Wasting Time with God: A Christian Spirituality of Friendship with God*. Downers Grove, IL: InterVarsity Press, 2001.

Luther, Martin. *Luther's Small Catechism with Explanations*. St. Louis, MO: Concordia Publishing House, 1986.

MacBeth, Sybil. *Praying in Color: Drawing a New Path to God*. Brewster, MA: Paraclete Press, 2007.

Miller, Paul. *A Praying Life: Connecting with God in a Distracting World*. Colorado Springs, CO: NavPress, 2009.

Milne, Alan Alexander, and Ernest Howard Shepard. *The House at Pooh Corner*. London: Methuen Children's Books, 1979.

Modi, Kunai, and Laura Merritt. "Class Day, 2013: Kunal Modi, MBA 2013, and Laura Merritt, MBA 2013." Harvard Business School. Retrieved from http://www.youtube.com/watch?v=uoU-jRYtKeI. May 29, 2013.

Mountain, Vivienne. (2005). "Prayer is a Positive Activity for Children: A Report on Recent Research." In *International Journal of Children's Spirituality*, 10, no. 3 (2005): 291–305.

Nouwen, Henri J.M. *Here and Now: Living in the Spirit*. New York: The Crossroad Publishing Company, 1994.

Nouwen, Henri J.M. *The Only Necessary Thing: Living a Prayerful Life*, ed., W. Wilson Greer. New York: The Crossroad Publishing Company, 1999.

Palmer, Parker J. *Let Your Life Speak: Listening for the Voice of Vocation*. San Francisco, CA: Jossey Bass, 2000.

Sproul, Robert Charles. *The Call to Wonder: Loving God Like a Child*. Carol Stream, IL: Tyndale House Publishers, 2012.

Susteren, Greta van. "Interview with Billy Graham." On the Record [Television broadcast].
    New York: Fox News Channel, December 21, 2010.
von Hayn, Hentrietta L. *I Am Jesus's Little Lamb*. Public domain, 1724–1782.
Warner, A.B. *Jesus Loves Me*. Public domain, 1892–1915.

Chapter 2

Exploring the Narratives of Robert Coles and Seeking Meaningful Communication with Children About Faith

Rebecca A. Jones

Had it not been for his ability to be at the right place at the right moment, just as historic events unfolded, Robert Coles's life might have been very different. Trained in medicine and child psychiatry, Coles told of a chance encounter early in his career that helped influence his life's work. In 1960, Coles witnessed history unfolding in New Orleans as public schools began court-ordered desegregation. On his way to a professional meeting, Coles saw angry protests as six-year old Ruby Bridges entered the formerly all-white William Frantz School for the first time (Coles, 1990). On that day, Coles watched as Bridges walked to school accompanied by armed federal marshals. Later portrayed by Norman Rockwell's 1963 painting, *The Problem We All Live With*, the scene is now etched in the cultural mindset (Doyle, 2011). Coles was intrigued by the little girl and curious about her mental state after experiencing the mob's rage. He wanted to understand how the child was coping with her circumstances, and after approaching judicial officials and then appealing to the NAACP, Coles was granted permission to talk to Bridges by Thurgood Marshall, chief counsel for the NAACP (Coles, 2008).

Coles interviewed Bridges many times over several months. He was surprised by how well she held up despite the difficulty of her daily experiences, and he questioned her often on her thoughts about the protesters. Coles suspected she was experiencing fear, anxiety, and a lack of understanding, yet conversations with Bridges led him away from these suspicions. He asked Bridges what she thought of the people who screamed at her as she walked to school. He was surprised by the little girl's response, and in a 2008 lecture, he recounted her comments, "She said, 'well, I pray for them.'" Coles reflected on his reaction to the statement:

> I said, *you* pray for them? Silence. I thought, I have to help her out. She's praying for them. I know that she must be furious; she must be anxious; she must be all the shrink things that people like me come up with, and she's praying for them? So, I said to her that way, *you're* praying for them, *Ruby*? . . . All you hear; all that's said—you're praying for them? She looked at me oh a moment and she said, "Well don't you think they need praying for?" That was the end of me—deservedly.

> . . . And then she came up with something that was remarkable. She said, "You know, Jesus went through a lot of mobs. He had a lot of trouble and he wasn't very popular, and a lot of people didn't like him. So I think that what we're doing is sort of like what Jesus did and would want us to do." That was new to me—to think that way. I was stunned, but that's what she said and felt and got from her parents too—very devout Christians—church all the time and prayers. (Coles, 2008)

As an adult, Bridges (now Bridges Hall) explained that her mother influenced her to consider prayer as the best response to her circumstances. Ruby's mother accompanied her to school the first few times she went, but later was unable to make the trip because she needed to be home with younger children. Mrs. Bridges assured her daughter she would be well cared for by the federal marshalls who would be with her as she entered the school building, but if she was afraid, she could pray. "You can pray to God anytime, anywhere. He will always hear you" (Hall 2000). Bridges Hall continued, "That was how I started praying on the way to school. The things people yelled at me didn't seem to touch me. Prayer was my protection" (Hall, 2000).

Years after the desegregation events in New Orleans, Coles (1989a) recalled an experience with Bridges's mother. He described his interaction with the family, suggesting it took time and effort to build trust in the relationship. On one occasion after their relationship had solidified, Mrs. Bridges delicately questioned Coles about an area she felt lacking in his conversations with Ruby. "You're the doctor, I know. I shouldn't be asking you questions. You know what to ask children. But my husband and I were talking the other night, and we decided that you ask our daughter about everything except God" (135). Coles, startled by the question, fumbled for something to say and asked Mrs. Bridges for clarification. She said, "God is helping Ruby, and we thought you'd want to know that" (137). Coles changed the subject and did not revisit it. In his mind, he rationalized that his work was focused on children's psychology not their spirituality, which were distinctly separate and unrelated in his thinking at the time.

In spite of Coles's early trepidation over entering the spiritual realm of children's lives, Ruby Bridges pushed him in that direction. Her reliance on God and use of prayer and forgiveness offered a transcendent moment for Coles that enlarged the window through which he would view children's inner lives. It also offered professional opportunities that led him to research and write prolifically about children involved in "crisis and social upheaval" (Coles, 2008). Eventually, almost three decades after first meeting Bridges Hall, Coles's work led him to write extensively on the subject of children's spirituality in his book, *The Spiritual Life of Children*.

As Coles moved to study the spirituality of children, he had to determine his own thoughts about the interaction of the spiritual and psychological. Trained in psychoanalysis, the conception of Freud and others who believed God to be an "illusion" or mental disorder created in the minds of humans to help them manage "life's mysteries," Coles wrestled with ideas, read extensively, and criticized some of Freud's positions on God and religion (Coles, 1990, 2–3). Coles ultimately made the case that his method of interviewing children to find their thoughts on spiritual matters was a "psychoanalytic approach toward religious and spiritual thinking" (21).

Coles concluded that he could use Freud's psychoanalytic tools to allow the children he interviewed to tell him their thoughts about God and their spiritual beliefs. Coles found a way to combine his training with his questions about spirituality in children, and he used his version of Freud's methods to gain access to children's thoughts on spiritual matters. It was actually Freud's daughter, Anna Freud, a noted psychoanalyst in her own right, who suggested this approach to Coles. While visiting with Ms. Freud, Coles posed questions to her about religion and his intended research into children's spirituality. She said, "Let the children help you with their ideas on the subject" (quoted in Coles, 1990, xvi).

Coles took Anna Freud's advice and, along with his wife and sons, conducted more than 1,000 interviews with hundreds of children around the globe (Hubbard, 1990). Using a large and diverse group of children, Coles was able to look closely at their inner lives, to illustrate their thoughts on spirituality, their religious beliefs, and their questions about life and death, heaven and hell. Drawing on his background in medicine, psychiatry, sociology, and literature, Coles used a qualitative process whereby he asked children to tell and show him their stories and thoughts. He compiled and narrated his research in *The Spiritual Life of Children*, which was the third book in a series examining the inner lives of young people. The book is frequently cited and served as a turning point in American scholarship on children's spirituality.

Coles came to the belief that spirituality is a vital consideration of children's inner lives. He poetically described the spiritual space that exists within children and its interaction with the other components that make up a child. "The child's 'house has many mansions'—including a spiritual life that grows, changes, responds constantly to the other lives that, in their sum, make up the individual we call by a name and know by a story that is all his, all hers" (Coles, 1990, 308).

Coles presented his findings through a narrative lens that provided specific stories of interactions with individuals and groups of children. Rather than making generalizations, his work allows readers to gain a sense of the nuances he encountered and helps readers gain perspective on the spiritual in children and the beliefs they hold sacred. Perhaps because of his lifelong appreciation for the stories of classic literature, Coles used narratives to capture the essence of selected conversations. Coles employed narrative structure in other works, but it is especially significant that he chose to write in this way for this book because of the spiritual impact stories had on his life. He pursued a lifelong exploration into the connection between literature and spirituality and was inspired by the work of writers such as Tolstoy, Dickens, O'Connor, and others (Cox, 2005).

Also influential to the research for *The Spiritual Life* was the approach he developed early in his medical career for working with psychoanalytic patients. His methodology required him to carefully listen to the stories his patients told. Coles realized as a medical resident that he could enable his patients to tell their stories and could gain insight about the patient's lived experiences as well as their fears, troubles, and resulting psychological symptoms. Instead of relying too heavily on psychoanalytic theory and classification systems, he chose to become a listener looking to better understand "the unfolding of a lived life rather than the confirmation such a chronicle provides for some theory" (Coles, 1989b, 22). Coles was encouraged by a mentor to present cases of patients he encountered by "err(ing) on the side of each person's particularity" and to offer his "version of their version of their lives" rather than classify symptoms and rely too heavily on jargon (27). Coles took this advice and adopted an appreciation for the stories he heard from patients and later from the children he met.

In a seminar on storytelling, Coles shared his insights on the "power of narrative" (Giles 2004, 3). Coles "describ(ed) the transformative power of stories, (and) remind(ed) us how stories about others can lead us to discoveries about ourselves and how they absorb the reader into the emotions of the characters" (3). Coles used stories in *The Spiritual Life* to help readers become absorbed in the lives of children. He also used language to connect readers to the lived experiences and inner worlds of children because he felt this was the most effective, natural way to communicate the sometimes surprising messages he found through his research. "I think we are born storytellers. We're creatures of language, who can tell about ourselves and tell about others . . . . I think at times, when I've heard from children, my surprise and awe measure an initial loss of understanding on my part just who they are and what they are capable of doing" (Cox, 2005, 569).

Coles's stories of children enable readers to gain perspective on "who (children) are and what they are capable of doing" (Cox, 2005, 569). His narrative approach connects readers to the children who talked with him about their spiritual experiences. From the stories Coles presented, it is possible to consider and analyze communication with children about matters of spirituality and faith.

Key among Coles's (1990) discussion is his characterization of children as spiritual "pilgrims," journeying alongside adults in search of meaning in life and a greater understanding of God and the universe (322). Coles borrowed his definition of a spiritual pilgrim from his wife, who conceptualized pilgrims in this context as "travel(ing) on a road with some spiritual purpose in mind" (322). Dorothy Day, founder of the Catholic Worker movement, which included a soup kitchen in New York where Coles volunteered, added to his idea of the spiritual pilgrim (Forest). "To me," she said, "a pilgrim is someone who thinks ahead, who wonders what's coming—and I mean spiritually. We are on a journey through the years—a pilgrim is—and we are trying to find out what our destination is, what awaits us when the bus or train pulls in" (quoted in Coles, 1990, 326).

To fully appreciate the conceptualization by Coles of children as pilgrims seeking a spiritual purpose and wondering what is coming, it is helpful to reflect on an experience from his childhood. When he was a young boy, Coles's mother took him to a Boston art museum where he saw a painting by Paul Gauguin, which included questions written into the work and depicted in the imagery: *Where Do We Come From? Who Are We? Where Are We Going?* Coles reflected on these questions and said his own spiritual development was influenced largely by the art and literature his parents presented to him as a child (Cox, 2005). In *The Spiritual Life of Children*, Coles found that many of the children he met dealt with existential questions similar to those that haunted Gauguin and Day, and that philosophers and theologians have pondered throughout human history (Ostling, 1991).

Coles presented a number of specific instances when his discussions with children led him to characterize them as pilgrims co-journeying through life and wrestling with big questions. He said children, like adults, are eager to understand things that occur in their lives. "Children try to understand not only what is happening to them, but why; and in doing that, they call upon the religious life they have experienced, the spiritual values they have received, as well as other sources of potential explanation" (Coles, 1990, 100).

Coles met a classroom of young pilgrims in their school in Massachusetts. The questions, beliefs, and explanations given by the fifth graders illustrated the wonder and uncertainty they felt. Coles began a discussion with the students by asking them to describe themselves emphasizing one unique characteristic. One boy's thoughts sparked a dynamic group interaction. In his description, the student said, "I don't know what to say. I was put here by God, and I hope to stay until He says OK, enough, come back. Then, I'll not be here anymore. By the end I hope I'll find out why I was sent down, and not plenty of others. There must be a lot waiting. God decides" (quoted in Coles, 1990, 312).

Realizing his classmates were confused by his statement, the boy clarified, ". . . it's up to God—He decides who's born. He puts us here, and then He's the one who says we should go back and be with Him." (quoted 312)

Another student responded:

> Well, how does He decide? How can He possibly keep track of everyone? I asked our priest, and he said all kids want to know, and you just have to have faith, and if you don't then you're in trouble, and besides you'll never know, because that's God's secret. He can do things, and we think they are impossible, but He does them, anyway. But I still can't see how God can keep His eyes on everyone, and my uncle says it's all a lot of nonsense. (quoted 312)

Other students reacted and continued the discussion with the following comments (quoted 313–16):

> " . . . We'll never know about God, until we die."

> "True, but we know something: he did come here once!"

> "Yes, but that was a long time ago. What has he been doing since he died and left?". . .

> "If you go to church, he'll be there. "

> " . . . I believe in God, but it's hard to know whether you're doing the right thing, what God wants, or the wrong thing . . ."

> "I still say, everyone here can try to be good and God will notice—whether you go to church or not. It's up to you whether you go."

The conversation continued with many students voicing their thoughts about prayer, the role of priests and ministers, and of church attendance. When the conversation subsided, a student commented on its value, "We should do this more often. You think a lot when you're listening, and then you say what you're thinking, and you don't forget what you've heard—when it's this kind of talk" (quoted 316).

Another student agreed and talked about overhearing adult family members discussing the sacred and spiritual, particularly in difficult times. She noted that her family pondered what they should do in light of their beliefs. The student cited her grandfather's concept that people have to "march through life" and that they should "remember God and how he had his bad times, too," but the march goes on for "a long time . . . if you're lucky" (quoted 316). As the conversation continued, the same student added " . . . we should try to be as good as our parents, as good as the best person we know. God will help us if we try. He's sent us here, and we've got a good chance to get to see Him in heaven, if we're good in our life" (quoted 318).

This conversation offers insight into the thoughts, worries, and questions of young people. Coles gave children the opportunity to speak freely without fear of censure or judgment. Because of his conversations with children and willingness to give them voice through his writing, readers can better understand the depth of spiritual searching that may go unnoticed. Those interested in communicating with children about faith and spirituality benefit from the knowledge of Coles's conversations with children and from his communicative model.

Beyond this, just as children's spiritual searching may go unnoticed, it could be easy to dismiss the notion of children as pilgrims on life's spiritual journey, as people who are filled with questions about life and death and the meaning of it all. Coles was struck by what he saw in children and found the things he learned from them fascinating, surprising.

> I've been stunned by what they told me about God. . . . In trying to figure out how the planet came into being, how man as a species came into being, how long this all will last, they call upon God for an answer. And if there is no specific answer in their particular religion, they are willing to venture a guess. (Wingert, 1990, 74)

Coles's ideas pose a communication challenge for those who seek to interact in meaningful ways with children about faith and spiritual matters. His work invites us to engage in conversations of depth with children, to pose questions to them about God and his role in our lives and in the universe, to listen to children's thoughts and share ours, to seek answers together, and to co-create meaning as a result of our dialogues. Coles endorsed the value of this type of communication.

> So it is we connect with one another, move in and out of one another's lives, teach and heal and affirm one another, across space and time—all of us wanderers, explorers, adventurers, stragglers and ramblers, sometimes tramps or vagabonds, even fugitives, but now and then pilgrims: as children, as parents, as old ones about to take that final step, to enter that territory whose character none of us here ever knows. Yet how young we are when we start wondering about it all, the nature of the journey and the final destination. (Coles, 1990, 335)

Among those with the greatest opportunity to interact with children about spiritual matters are parents, grandparents, and other family members. Coles cited dozens of examples of children who were influenced by their families and looked to them for wisdom, information, and encouragement. The children Coles met listened intently to what they had been told by their families about God. Many of them internalized conversations and adopted the beliefs of family members or fashioned their own ideas from those they were taught.

Betsy, a Massachusetts fourth grader, commented on her idea that God has moods because people have moods. "If God knows you, He knows of your good days and your bad days. Granny says she has both, and she's sure God watches her all the time. It may be tiring a little, but He's God" (quoted Coles, 1990, 43).

Martha, aged twelve, discussed frightening dreams she experienced and her belief that God helped her to stop feeling scared. She attributed God's help to something she learned from her grandmother. "My gramma used to tell me that when you need God, He'll show up; He'll come and touch you, and you'll be alright afterwards" (quoted Coles, 1990, 48).

Haroon, a child of Muslim descent, talked about "special messages he felt privileged to have, messages he pointedly directed" toward Coles (Coles, 1990, 70). Coles later learned that Haroon's method of sharing his spiritual life closely resembled that of his parents.

Gil, a Jewish child, talked about adopting his father's methods for interpreting spiritual questions. "My father doesn't try to push religion on us, the way his father did on him. It's different. But dad has told me he used to ask himself a lot of the questions I do, and he couldn't find the answers, and probably I won't. I don't ask questions anymore. I just try to listen, and some of what I hear I believe, and the rest I don't believe" (quoted Coles, 1990, 145).

As a final example, Coles (1990) presented a moving story of Leah, a Jewish teenager who battled acute leukemia. Coles regularly visited the hospital as Leah went through treatment and eventually died. He witnessed Leah's response and that of her parents to the circumstances of her illness; he observed the family's reliance on "the only hope they knew—God's ultimate wisdom" (275). Coles described his impressions,

> I saw in Leah a child intensely attached to a family's religious and spiritual life
> . . . its spoken acknowledgment of the Lord, its remembrance of his words of
> what he and his people had experienced together in the past and were still, in
> that hospital room, in our time, undergoing together. "I'd like to go to that 'high
> rock,'" Leah told her dad just before she slipped into a final coma. (p. 276)

After that time, Leah's father was often heard reciting Psalm 61 in Hebrew. "'Hear my cry, O God; attend unto my prayer. From the end of the earth will I cry unto thee, when my heart is overwhelmed; lead me to the rock that is higher than I.' The rock for Leah, for her family was Judaism that would not break or yield, even at the death of a young girl" (276).

These examples illustrate the influence families have on the spiritual lives of children. Coles said in an interview about his book that he believed a child's spiritual life begins "when the parents begin telling the child about God or their belief in God, or their lack of belief in God, or aspects of a religious story" (Wingert, 1990, 74). He also found that "all children wonder about finitude; space and time are natural questions for all of us . . . They (children) bring it around to themselves in the form of moral and spiritual reflection" (Wingert, 1990, 74). Whether they encourage spiritual development and belief, serve as a model for the child, discourage spiritual searching, or create the "rock" the family clings to in times of crisis, Coles's work indicates that the teachings families share with their youngest members can take hold and even become cornerstones of faith and spirituality.

One concern Coles had when talking with children was that they simply repeated what they heard from family members. While he did hear them talk about things they learned at home, he also detected in many children their own faith, one that had been influenced by family but made the child's own. Sometimes children's comments even reflected cynicism when they perceived that what they were taught in their homes or churches differed from the actions they witnessed.

> They (children) have pointed out to me that the churches and synagogues and mosques can betray the original spirit of the faiths those children have been brought up in. Lots of children have commented on how Jesus lived, his association with outcasts and unpopular people, his poverty, the fact that he was a carpenter and his friends were peasants, that he didn't go to college and get fancy degrees, didn't have a lot of money, didn't associate with big-shot people. (Ostling, 1991, 16–17)

Coles found that children have the ability to identify authenticity and to know when things they have been taught do not ring true with the experiences they witness in their lives. Sometimes this is shaped by parents who lodge complaints within the family about ministers, priests, or churches. At other times, it had to do with the behaviors they witnessed within their families. Whatever the source, Coles found that children possessed a hunger for knowing about the spiritual and for understanding what was happening within their lives and families.

Coles's work in this area provides added support to the centrality of family in the spiritual development of children and can be considered in the context of communicating with children about faith. Coles endorsed the idea that parents should use their relationships with their children to pass values to their children. "Parents need to use the emotional connectedness they ought to have with their children as a means of transmitting values, acceptable ways of behaving, and a sense of responsibility to rules and regulations" (Ryan and Jenkins, 1997, 14).

A final consideration from Coles's work involves what he calls the "moral imagination" of children, their mental ability to move beyond the stories they have been taught, to transform them into applicable, relevant ideals they can integrate into their lives. Coles's comments about Gil (referenced earlier) clarify this concept. Gil wondered extensively about God's "experiment" with creating earth and humanity. Based on what his grandfather told him, Gil understood the experiment to be God's creation of humanity and his decision to allow humans to have "freedom to live as best we can or to be as bad as possible" (quoted Coles, 1990, 146). Gil reasoned that because humans had been both good and evil, God would be left to determine the outcome of the experiment. Gil questioned his grandfather about how God might decide. Puzzled, his grandfather told him his questions were "too big" and that "all you can do is try to be good and let God take care of the rest" (quoted 146).

Coles reflected on Gil's discussion, his questions, and the exchange with his grandfather. He explained that "Gil was trying to comprehend the universe and the religion of his ancestors" (146). According to Coles, he believed Gil was referencing what he had learned from family and teachers as well as . . .

his imagination, and, not least, his mind's intellectual, contemplative capacity; the ability he has with the rest of us to learn symbols and use them, to borrow metaphors or similes or images used by others, to create some of his own—all for the purpose of doing what philosophers have traditionally done over the centuries. Like them the boy was searching for an explanation of what is, of reality as he saw it, heard, felt it, both palpably and within his mind. . . . He was trying to pull together what he had observed, learned, read, heard others espouse—to make, thereby, his own 'system,' his own set of principles. . . . He most certainly was trying to assemble what he had learned in a narrative of his own, which he could offer to others. (146)

Gil and many children took what they learned, created their own questions, and worked to understand, as much as possible, the spiritual in their lives. They used their moral imaginations to craft narratives of their beliefs in God and their comprehension of spirituality. Coles observed children who demonstrated, a "sometimes urgent determination to define God, to locate Him in time and place, to know Him as precisely as possible, to explain (to themselves and others) who and what He is . . ." (Coles, 1990, 147).

Understanding that children have an intense, "urgent" desire to know God opens the way for meaningful communication about faith within families, churches, schools, etc. Coles's work points out that children are imagining and working to craft their stories of God whether or not adults enter the conversation. As co-pilgrims on life's journey, it is thought provoking and motivating to realize the potential significance of co-creating meaning with younger pilgrims on the journey.

Based on his work, Coles offered insights on the value of communicating with children about spiritual concepts, and he warned of the potential danger of not embarking on conversations of this sort. Rather than focusing on the needs of the world around them, children can become obsessed with self. Coles said, "I just worry about what children are asked to believe in, if anything these days—other than themselves. The 'culture of narcissism' appears to be what they're asked to believe in" (Ryan and Jenkins, 1997, 6). If families take the opportunities they have to communicate with children about spirituality, Coles infers that there are opportunities to help children focus on the needs of others and to move their attention away from themselves. Helping children consider the questions of God and teachings available through religious systems enables children to become less self-centered and to potentially accomplish what Coles felt was a most worthy pursuit, "Children need to recognize that world (outside themselves) and to become committed to it, heart, mind, and soul" (Ryan and Jenkins, 1997, 6).

Ruby Bridges Hall has spent her life focusing on the world outside of herself. The teaching she received as a child and her own spiritual pilgrimage influenced her to focus on the needs of others and trying to bring people together. She offers seminars and speaks to school children about racism and ways to bring it to an end. Using her story of forgiveness and faith, she seeks to inspire others to turn away from prejudice and toward reconciliation. She is committed to making a difference in the world and sharing her faith in God with others (Hall, 2000).

In addition to the difference she has personally made, Bridges Hall's action of praying for the people who persecuted her impacted Coles and his life's work. One of the legacies of that impact is a children's book Coles wrote in 1995, *The Story of Ruby Bridges*. In it, he recorded the prayer the little girl said twice each day on her way to and from school. "Please, God, try to forgive those people. Because even if they say those bad things, they don't know what they're doing so you could forgive them, just like you did those folks a long time ago when they said terrible things about you" (23). One cannot help but imagine that in writing this book after completing his work on children's inner spirituality, that perhaps Coles hoped to create a narrative tool that would be helpful to children on their spiritual pilgrimages, and also to the parents, grandparents, and others who would seek to communicate with those children about God, the universe, and the meaning of it all.

REFERENCES

Coles, R. *Harvard Diaries.* New York: The Crossroad Publishing Compan, 1989a.

———. *The Call of Stories.* Boston: Houghton Mifflin Company, 1989b

———. *The Spiritual Life of Children.* Boston: Houghton Mifflin Company, 1990.

———. *The Story of Ruby Bridges.* New York: Scholastic, 1995.

———. Children Consider Human Conflict. Lecture presented at Harvard University Extension School: Lowell Lecture, 2008. http://vimeo.com/2713153 (accessed June 10, 2010).

Cox, J. "A Life in Psychiatry and Literature: An Interview with Robert Coles." *Christianity and Literature* 54, no. 4 (2005):563–575.

Doyle, J. Rockwell & Race, 1963–1968. *PopHistoryDig.com*, 2011. http://www.pophistorydig.com/?tag=ruby-bridges-norman-rockwell (accessed June 25, 2013).

Forest, J. n.d. "A Biography of Dorothy Day." *Catholic Worker Homepage.* http://catholicworker.com/ddaybio.htm (accessed July 31, 2010).

Giles, B. "'Thinking About Storytelling and Narrative Journalism: At a Seminar with Robert Coles, the Topic is Stories and How They are Best Told." *Nieman Reports* 3, (2004).

Hall, R. B. "The Story." *Ruby Bridges:Official Site,* 2000. http://www.rubybridges.com/story.htm (accessed July 30, 2010).

Hubbard, K. "After 30 Years Plumbing Children's Hearts and Minds, Robert Coles Writes an End to His Life's Greatest Chapter." *People Weekly* (December, 1990), 84–86.

Ostling, R. N. "Youngsters Have Lots to Say About God." *Time,* January, 1991.

Ryan, K., and C. B. Jenkins. "Robert Coles—On the Loose: An Interview." *Journal of Education* 179, no. 3 (1997):1–15.

Thurgood Marshall College: UC San Diego. *Thurgood Marshall, Supreme Court Justice.* http://chnm.gmu.edu/courses/122/hill/marshall.htm (accessed June 2013, 25).

Wingert, Exploring Childhood. *Newsweek,* (1990), December, 74.

Chapter 3

Hospitality for Kids
A Lukan Perspective on Children and God's Agenda

Joel B. Green

To readers of the Gospels, Jesus's engagement with children is well-known (e.g., Francis, 1996, 72–79; Gundry-Volf, 2000; May, Posterski, Stonehouse, and Cannel, 2005, 39–43; Balla, 2003, 114–56), but nowhere in the New Testament are children more at center stage than in Luke's Gospel. The Lukan narrative opens with happy celebrations at the conception and birth of two children, John and Jesus, and the third evangelist devotes a further scene to Jesus as a youth engaging in learned conversation with Israel's teachers. In Luke's Gospel, Jesus presents children — indeed, infants — as models for his disciples and observes that how people respond to children is a barometer of their dispositions toward God. At several points in Luke's narrative, Jesus heals children.

Luke's interest in children is on display already in the opening scene of the third Gospel, when the Lord's angel announces to Zechariah that he and his wife Elizabeth, as old as they are, will be blessed with a child (1:6–25). "He will be a joy and delight to you," Zechariah is told (1:14), and Elizabeth responds to her pregnancy by affirming, "This is the Lord's doing. He has shown his favor to me by removing my disgrace among other people" (1:25). What is more, Luke's account of the annunciation to Zechariah has it that John's agenda will be:

> to turn the hearts of fathers toward their children, and the disobedient toward righteous patterns of thought and life (1:17; my translation).

The parallelism of these two phrases is devastating in its representation of fathers, who are paired with the disobedient, but startlingly positive in its affirmation of children, who are paired with those characterized by righteous patterns of thinking, believing, feeling, and behaving (φρόνησις, *phronēsis*). If such patterns are indeed characteristic of children, then it is no wonder that, elsewhere in the narrative, we find that children are "paradigm[s] of greatness and authority" (Carroll, 2008, 188–91; cf. Luke 9:46–48; 18:15–17; 22:25–27).

Our familiarity with such stories may threaten to mask how much Luke's portrait of Jesus and his mission uses images and textures that stand out in sharp relief on the mural painting of children in the ancient Mediterranean world. In truth, innovations in child development theory can fail us here, too. For example, attention to developmental stages might cause us to overlook the degree to which children in Luke's Gospel are not so much subjects (or actors) with their own crises and questions as they are objects of comparison and recipients of positive (as well as unwanted) attention by characters, both human and otherwise, within the narrative. Attention to developmental stages might also eclipse the ways in which Jesus's attention to children in Luke's Gospel contravenes deeply held dispositions toward children. Again, contemporary commitments regarding children might result in our overlooking how deeply embedded in the culture of Roman Palestine Luke's portrait of Jesus actually is. Children might feature in Jesus's teaching (e.g., Luke 7:31–35), but his teaching is nowhere explicitly directed *to* children. Jesus might present children as object lessons to his followers, but Luke's Gospel does not participate in any way in what might be regarded as the modern-day romanticizing of children.

In what follows, then, I want to work with some of the relevant Lukan material from the perspective of cognitive science as a basis for suggesting how topsy-turvy a narrative Luke has provided us, not least with respect to its portrayal of children. My first step will be to introduce a cognitive linguistic approach to metaphor, which I will then illustrate with reference to Zacchaeus — a well-known, surprisingly child-like character in Luke's Gospel. After this test case for my approach to conceptual metaphor, I will turn to a few Lukan texts concerned with children. Taking this path, I hope to convince you that it is not enough that Luke's audience would regard his presentation of children as counterintuitive. The more pressing question would be, What would be the effect of putting into practice this message?

MAPPING GOD'S AGENDA IN METAPHOR

Among the claims shared by almost all recent Lukan scholars is that the label "programmatic for Jesus's ministry" belongs to Luke's account of Jesus's sermon in Nazareth, Luke 4:16–30: "The Spirit of the Lord is upon me, because the Lord has anointed me. He has sent me to preach good news to the poor . . ." Without denying the pivotal character of Jesus's pronouncement at his hometown synagogue, I want nevertheless to urge that we hear in the earlier words of Mary a kind of heading for or description of the character of salvation as this is portrayed in the Third Gospel. I refer, of course, to Mary's Song, and especially to these words celebrating God's work:

> He has pulled the powerful down from their thrones
>   and lifted up the lowly.
> He has filled the hungry with good things
>   and sent the rich away empty-handed. (1:52–53)

Here are images of the reversal or transposition that will characterize the good news — not only throughout Luke's account of Jesus's ministry, but already in his presentation of John's prophetic ministry in Luke 3: "Every valley will be filled, and every mountain and hill will be leveled" (3:5).

Up, down — images of upward and downward movement dot the landscape of Luke's narrative, so much so that we can justifiably speak of a Lukan *verticality schema*. Let me illustrate this claim with a series of examples.

- Sometimes, of course, up-down language is simply transitional, as when people sit down to eat (e.g., 9:14–15; 12:37) or get up in order to depart (e.g., 1:39).

- The instances are numerous where down is correlated with inactivity or, more pervasively, with illness or disorder, and up is correlated with renewed health. A demon might throw someone down, for example (4:35; 9:42). Or someone might be weighed down with sleep, excessive partying, drunkenness, or the worries of this life (9:32; 21:34). After Jesus rebuked her fever, Simon's mother-in-law "got up and began to serve them" (4:39). Jesus told a man being carried on a bed on account of his paralysis to stand up and walk, and he does (5:18–19, 24–25). A bent-over woman was able to stand up straight (13:11–13). That most pitiable of persons in Luke's narrative for whom the status of "expendable" make sense is Lazarus, who was laid at the gate of a stupendously wealthy man (16:20).

- Similarly, to destroy something is to tear it down, as in the case of the temple: "The time is coming when no stone will be left on another; all will be thrown down" (21:6, my translation; cf. 12:18). The same can be said of unproductive trees: they will be cut down (3:9; 13:7, 9).

- The most extreme set of examples related to health and healing would include announcements pertaining to rising from the dead. The corpse of a widow's son is being carried on a stretcher; Jesus directs him to be raised up, and the dead man sat up (7:12, 14–15). The queen of the South will rise at the judgment, as will the people of Nineveh, both to exercise judgment over others (11:31–32). Jesus himself is laid in a tomb (23:53) but is declared to have risen (24:5). Indeed, Jesus had anticipated that the humiliation of his passion would be a way station on the path to his being raised up in glory (e.g., 9:22; 18:31–33; cf. 24:7, 46).

- Heaven is up, so it is not surprising that Jesus looks up (ἀναβλέπω, *anablepō*) when he blesses the loaves and fish (9:16), Jesus anticipates his ascension (ἀνάλημψις, *analēmpsis*, 9:51), and at the end of the Gospel Jesus is carried up (ἀναφέρω, *anapherō*) into heaven (24:51). Nor is it surprising that God's voice speaks from above (3:22; 9:35), or that God himself is known as the Most High (1:32, 35, 76; 6:35; 8:28). In his humility, the tax collector would not even look up to heaven (18:13). Contrariwise, ᾅδης, *hadēs*, the netherworld, the place of the dead, is the underworld — as in Jesus's pronouncement of judgment: "And you, Capernaum, will you be raised up to heaven? No, you will be cast down to Hades" (10:15, my translation).

- Reflecting widespread usage, both in Israel's Scriptures and beyond, mountains are places of revelation, where one draws closer to God. Thus, Jesus goes up to pray, sometimes taking others with him (e.g., 6:12; 9:28; 22:39, 41).

- Reflecting usage from the days when geographical sensibilities were drawn more explicitly from judgments about importance than from compass orientation (Lindstromberg 2010, 191), movement to Jerusalem is a journey up and those who travel away from Jerusalem are going down (e.g., 2:51; 10:30; 18:31; 19:28). Similarly, Jesus tells the story of a Pharisee and a tax collector, two men, who "went up to the temple" (18:10).

- Honor is associated with the head of the table, so that guests of lower status are seated at the lowest seats and guests of higher status are told, "Move up higher" (14:7–10). Similarly, scribes are known for seeking seats reserved for those of high status both at the synagogue and at banquets (20:46).

- Attitudes of deference and dispositions of submissiveness are embodied through kneeling or sitting at one's feet — as in the cases of the Simon Peter (5:8), a Gerasene man from whom demons had gone (8:35), Mary (10:39), or the one leper who had seen that he had been healed (17:15). On the Mount of Olives, Jesus knelt to pray (22:41).

- Reflecting the polarity present already in Mary's Song, on two different occasions Luke reports Jesus's words, "For all who exalt themselves will be humbled, and those [*or* all] who humble themselves will be exalted" (14:11; 18:14).

These texts exemplify what I have earlier called a Lukan *verticality schema*.

Up—down — we known them as prepositions, but, as we have begun to see, they can function as powerful metaphors. In fact, I have gathered examples of what the cognitive linguist Joseph Grady referred to as primary metaphors (1997). By referring to Grady as a cognitive linguist, I mean to associate my interest in metaphors with the cognitive linguistic approach to metaphor — that is, with conceptual metaphor theory. Conceptual metaphor theory operates from the basic premise that metaphor is not linguistic decoration or an unnecessary but ornamental stylistic feature of language, but is characteristic of thought itself. Semantic structure mirrors conceptual structure, as we conceive the world around us by projecting patterns from one domain of experience in order to structure another domain. The one is a source domain, the other a target domain, and studies have shown that where these two domains are active simultaneously, the two areas of the brain for each are active (e.g., Posner and Raichle, 1997, 115; Ramachandra, 2004, ch. 4; Feldman, 2006; Gibbs, 2006, 158–207). Borrowing a principle from the neuropsychologist Donald Hebb, known as Hebb's Rule, we know that *neurons that fire together wire together* — with the result that conceptual metaphor theory is grounded in the actual embodiment of the conceptual patterns by which we make sense of the world, which we share with people across cultures, and which drive our responses to the world around us. In short, primary metaphors derive directly from our experiences and are predicted to be universal among humans (Yu, 2010, 248). Essentially all of our abstract and theoretical concepts draw their meaning by mapping to embodied, experiential concepts hardwired in our brains.

Cognitive scientist Jerome Feldman puts it like this: "In a general way, the embodied basis for abstract meanings can be seen as inevitable. A child starts life with certain basic abilities and builds on these through experience. Everything the child learns must be based on what she or he already understands" (2006, 199). In this case, a child observes the rise and fall of levels of piles or fluids as more of a given substance is added or some is subtracted. That part of her brain concerned with vertical orientation is activated, and is correlated with the subjective experience of modulating quantities. In this way, her experience provides a physical basis for an abstract understanding of quantity. That is, she learns that Up Is More and Down Is Less — a primary metaphor lying behind scores of phrases that dot the landscape of everyday conversations:

> The stock market has taken a dive.
> Gas prices are on the rise again.
> She got a high score for that routine.
> Could I get a raise?

In time, this child will understand dozens of corollaries of this primary metaphor, as she expands her ability to activate novel conceptual linkages (cf. Lindstromberg, 2010, 191–202):

Up Is Happy

Up Is More Powerful

Up Is More Important

Up Is Active

Up Is Healthy

Up Is Good

And the converse would also be true: Down Is Sad, Down Is Ill, and so on.

Conceptual metaphor theory predicts that primary metaphors transcend culture since they have to do with universal human experience. Whether the orientational schema predicted by the primary metaphor Up Is More is true of all cultures, we have already begun to see that it is certainly true of Luke's narrative world. What is more, we cannot escape the ease with which we grasp Luke's use of his verticality schema—a schema that requires no explanation from us. In fact, I doubt that most of us have given Luke's up-and-down language a second thought. Why should we? After all, primary target concepts relate to subjective responses and operate at a level of cognitive processing to which we have low conscious access. Primary target concepts are responses and evaluations that derive from background operations in our brains. We conceptualize the world according to such patterns without even thinking about them.

Conceptual metaphor theory, then, takes as its point of departure and at the same time underscores both the embodiment of our thought processes and the significant degree to which the patterns by which our everyday, situated cognition takes place at a preconscious level. Accordingly, we conceptualize and evaluate sensory data, and formulate responses, without conscious thought. I emphasize this not in order to condemn the human race to its prejudices: once formed, always formed — as though, once those neural pathways are in place there would be no possibility of their transformation. Rather, I emphasize the embodied character of everyday, situated cognition in order to highlight how difficult it might be to see things in any other way. If a verticality scheme is operative at a preconscious level, so that we intuitively make sense of the world according to its terms, then it will require conscious, critical reflection to see things any other way.

My real point, of course, is that Luke's narrative, if taken seriously, would already push us in the direction of transposing our deeply ingrained conceptual patterns. Among the variety of possibilities to which I might draw attention, let me suggest two ways in which Luke's narrative inculcates alternative conceptual patterns. The first is the way the third evangelist undermines the verticality schema in the story of Jesus's encounter with Zacchaeus in Jericho (19:1–10). The second is the way he not only overturns the verticality schema but actually urges the (re)formation of persons with topsy-turvy conceptual patterns in his presentation of children. We turn first to the story of Zacchaeus.

THAT "WEE LITTLE MAN," ZACCHAEUS

Persons with any exposure at all to childhood Christian education will know that the chief characteristic of Zacchaeus is that he was "a wee little man, and a wee little man was he." Actually, this characterization is unfortunate insofar as it leads too quickly to a particular reading of Luke 19:1–10. To be sure, we find in this textual unit images of verticality: Zacchaeus was "short in stature" (τῇ ἡλικίᾳ μικρός, *tē hēlikia mikros*), he "climbed" (ἀναβαίνω, *anabainō*) a sycamore tree, Jesus "looked up" (ἀναβλέπω, *anablepō*) and told Zacchaeus to "come down" (καταβαίνω, *katabainō*), and Zacchaeus "came down" (καταβαίνω, *katabainō*) before standing (ἵστημι, *histēmi*) to address Jesus. However, we would be mistaken to imagine that Zacchaeus's height per se was the problem he had to overcome. Zacchaeus does not suffer from dwarfism (*pace* Parsons, 2006, 97–108), but he does suffer from the ailment accompanying those who are shorter than their peers, those for whom diminutive stature is correlated generally with diminutive status. Indeed, twenty years of psychological research has demonstrated that height is a metaphor for power and status, with those who are taller more likely to acquire respect and influence (e.g., Egolf and Corder, 1991; Judge and Cable, 2004; Schubert, 2005; Giessner and Schubert, 2007). For our purposes, we should not overlook the way Luke has associated Zacchaeus in ch. 19 with the little kids of ch. 18 — smaller than those around them (19:3) and shunned either by the disciples or more generally by those standing-by (18:15; 19:7), but nonetheless acknowledged as exemplary and blessed by Jesus (18:16–17; 19:9–10).

Read within the Lukan narrative as a whole, the most noticeable aspect of Luke's portrait of Zacchaeus is his mixed status (*contra* Parsons, 2006, who fails to account for perspective in his exclusively negative assessment of Zacchaeus's status). Within Luke's Gospel, tax collectors and sinners are negatively assessed by people but consistently respond well to the gospel (e.g., 5:27–32; 15:1–2). Conversely, within Luke's Gospel, rulers and the wealthy are highly regarded by people but find themselves on the wrong side of God's good news (e.g., 1:52–53). Zacchaeus is all four of these: a ruler, but a ruler of tax collectors, rich but regarded by unnamed observers as "a sinner." Both for characters within Luke's narrative and for Luke's readers, the usual categories fail in this instance, their paradoxical complexity undermining one's ability to prejudge Zacchaeus's character on the basis of the usual descriptive labels. Even the vertical images compete with one another — profoundly and humorously so. Zacchaeus elevates himself in his quest to see the one whom he addresses with the even more elevated title, "Lord" (κύριος, *kyrios*). Zacchaeus may be a ruler, but his throne appears to be a sycamore tree. In the end, none of these qualities is decisive for Luke's presentation of Zacchaeus. This is because Jesus himself provides the definitive descriptor. He refers to Zacchaeus as "son of Abraham," asserting that salvation — Jesus himself — has this very day come to this household.

In this way, Luke adds to his verticality schema variations on another orientational metaphor, this one related to the experience of being *in* or *out*. That is, he uses correlates of a primary metaphor grounded in the experience of something's or someone's presence or movement in or out of a container, or even in or out of familial intimacy. What is at the center? What is at the periphery? Spatial experience maps onto relational concepts (see Johnson, 1987, 30–40) — and so: Closeness Is Belonging.

In fact, each of the labels used in Luke's account can be cast as "containers," with each representing a subset of a particular kind of person. There are sinners and there are rulers. There are tax collectors and there are the wealthy. There are children of Abraham and there are little people. Importantly, within the Lukan narrative, some of these subsets have overlapped, while others have been quite distinct. We can imagine a rich ruler, for example (18:18–23), and we have seen tax collectors and sinners together as a group (5:30; 7:34; 15:1). Zacchaeus is enigmatic, though, because he belongs to a series of subsets that otherwise do not overlap in Luke's Gospel.

Up or down? In or out? From the crowd's perspective, Zacchaeus, this "wee little man," is "down" and "out." Indeed, Zacchaeus's inability to see Jesus is not simply a matter of his diminished height. Rather, Luke writes that he was unable to see Jesus "because of the crowd" (ἀπὸ τοῦ ὄχλου, *apo tou ochlou* — using ἀπό, *apo*, in its causal sense). Just as the disciples constructed a barrier between Jesus and babies in 18:15, so the crowd has formed a barrier between Jesus and Zacchaeus. Just as those who headed the parade coming into Jericho blocked the blind man's access to Jesus in 18:39, so the crowd has blocked Zacchaeus's access to Jesus. From the perspective of the unnamed observers, Zacchaeus does not belong — he is a sinner; he is an outsider. Yet Zacchaeus takes extraordinary initiative to seek Jesus out and happily extends hospitality to him. Zacchaeus does more than meet Jesus in the streets and share a meal with him (cf. 13:26); through his customary practices of restitution and sharing with the poor, his behavior puts on display a life oriented toward God's purpose (cf. 3:7–14). From Jesus's perspective, then, Zacchaeus is not a ruler, not a tax collector, not a rich man, and not a sinner. He is not even a wee little man. He is a son of Abraham. He belongs to God's family.

If Luke's account of the encounter between Jesus and Zacchaeus dismantles those conceptual patterns inherent to the verticality schema, the instruction regarding children he narrates inculcates topsy-turvy conceptual patterns; indeed, if taken seriously by Luke's audience, this material would lead to the formation of communities in which children might learn different patterns altogether. This is because Luke's narrative would call for human formation that contravenes those developmental patterns predicted to be universal by conceptual metaphor theory.

WELCOMING CHILDREN, CARING FOR CHILDREN

Chances are we find ourselves stunned by the disciples' behavior as this is recounted in Luke 18:15. There, parents are bringing their newborn babies (βρέφος, *brephos*) to Jesus in order that he might bless these little children, and the disciples respond by scolding the parents. Given our child-valuing, child-celebrating proclivities, this might seem to be bizarre behavior indeed. Read against the backdrop of Luke's cultural horizons, however, the disciples' reaction is not at all extraordinary. To the contrary, it makes good sense to reprimand parents for taking up Jesus's time; after all, as the narrative quickly reveals, a wealthy ruler is waiting in the wings to seek Jesus's counsel (18:18).

We might be tempted to sentimentalize "children" in terms of "innocence" or "trusting," or, tearing a page from Carl Jung's archetypal theory, we might even think of the child in terms of "futurity," that is, a child's openness to the future (Via, 1985, 130). However, these are not the social scripts generally associated with children in Roman antiquity (e.g., Rawson, 1986, 1991, 2003, 2011). Luke's observation that people brought "*even* newborn babies" (καὶ τὰ βρέφη, *kai ta brephē*, my translation) underscores the dire situation faced by these little ones, including the high mortality rate among young children and the widespread practices of infanticide and "exposure," or "child abandonment." More generally, children occupied the bottom rung in a world preoccupied with social status and the conventions accompanying relative honor. Children were "not adults." Though perhaps valued for their present or potential contribution to the family business, especially if this entailed agribusiness, children possessed little by way of intrinsic value as human beings. Like slaves, they occupied society's periphery. Children might be signs of divine blessing, but this only acknowledges further their instrumental role — that is, they are the means by which honor accrued to their mothers (e.g., Luke 1:25; 11:27; Gen 30:13; 49:25; *2 Apoc. Bar.* 54:10; cf. Petronius, *Satyricon* 94.1: "How blessed is the mother who gave birth to such a one as you"). To parody the title of a recent publication on children's spirituality (May, Posterski, Stonehouse, and Cannel, 2005), children did not matter, and their place in the world was not celebrated.

Against this backdrop, even the relatively passive and objectified role of children in Luke's Gospel stands in sharp relief. We may note, for example, those occasions in which Jesus's mission is realized in the healing of children — his raising back to life the twelve-year-old daughter of Jairus and his wife (8:41–42, 51–56) and his expelling an unclean spirit from the son of an unnamed "man from the crowd" (9:38–42). Each of these accounts is framed in terms of Jesus's response to a parent's request, a pattern also found in Jesus's healing of a centurion's slave (7:1–10) and, by implication, his raising to life a widow's only son (7:11–17).

Perhaps more telling are those Lukan accounts where Jesus positions children as exemplars of greatness and authority. Thus, in Luke 9, we read of the disciples that an argument arose among the disciples about which of them was the greatest. Aware of their deepest thoughts, Jesus took a little child and had the child stand beside him. Jesus said to his disciples, "Whoever welcomes this child in my name welcomes me. Whoever welcomes me, welcomes the one who sent me. Whoever is least among you all is the greatest" (9:46–48).

Again, it is doubtful that adults in the Greco-Roman world would have been baffled by the disciples' behavior, as Luke recounts it here. Concern with relative social position, however implicitly, would have characterized any Roman gathering, so natural were questions of relative status and behavior appropriate to one's station. Jesus's response is to place a child in an honorable position at his side, and then to articulate a claim that struck at the root of conventional dispositions and behaviors concerning social rank and social relations. That these dispositions and behaviors drew their legitimacy from pervasive views about God's will (or, in the larger Roman world, about the will of the gods) and from widely held views about the nature of things (see Balla, 2003, 70–73, 97–104) only highlights what must have been the bewildering character of Jesus's word and deed.

The force of Jesus's message may be startling enough in an adult-centered world, but it comes into even sharper focus when we recall that "welcoming," or "showing hospitality" (δέχομαι, dechomai), is shorthand for receiving someone as an honored guest. What might this entail? Earlier in his Gospel, Luke illustrates appropriate hospitality through his description of the behavior of a sinful woman from the city. Simon the Pharisee and householder had invited Jesus to a meal, but he had failed in his role of host. Though an unwelcome guest, the sinful woman nevertheless put hospitality on display through such practices as the washing of feet, the kiss of greeting, and anointing with oil (7:44–46). Jesus's message to his disciples, then, would be to take up the role of the sinful woman, not the householder Simon. And rather than negotiating with one another along conventional lines regarding who might be first, then second, and so on in terms of honor, disciples would instead regard children as their social betters — and treat them accordingly.

Put sharply, whereas children might be called upon to perform acts of hospitality, such as washing feet, so now Jesus's followers are called upon to do so. Moreover, they are called upon to perform such acts on behalf of those of the lowest position. According to Luke, Jesus thus turns the social pyramid on its head, pulling the rug out from under the very conventions that would have fueled the interests in relative greatness initially expressed among the disciples. In a more didactic fashion, Paul puts it like this in his letter to the Philippians: "With humility think of others as better than yourselves. Instead of each person watching out for their own good, watch out for what is better for others" (Phil 2:3–4). These transformed patterns of thinking, feeling, believing, and behaving might be difficult enough to cultivate with reference to adults. How much more so, then, the transformation necessary to reckon little children as one's superiors.

What is more, Jesus identifies this child, this infant (παιδίον, *paidion*), with himself. The honor shown to this child is actually honor shown to Jesus. Conversely, we might say, the honor shown Jesus is the measure of honor appropriate for a little child. When we recall the honor shown Jesus as a newborn (2:1–20), this is no small thing. To honor children is to honor Jesus, and to honor Jesus is to honor God.

A second Lukan text presses the same message. Thus, in Luke 18 we read:

> People were bringing babies to Jesus so that he would bless them. When the disciples saw this, they scolded them. Then Jesus called them to him and said, "Allow the children to come to me. Don't forbid them, because God's kingdom belongs to people like these children. I assure you that whoever doesn't welcome God's kingdom like a child will never enter it." (18:15–17)

The significance of this exchange between Jesus and his followers lies in part in the overlap of this text with the one from Luke 9 we have just considered. Perhaps even more so, its importance is signaled by its immediate context, set as it is between Jesus's Parable of the Pharisee and the Tax Collector (18:9–14) and Jesus's famous encounter with a rich ruler (18:18–23). That is, in the surrounding context, Jesus emphasizes the status transformation characteristic of his ministry. As he himself summarizes, "All who lift themselves up will be brought low, and those who make themselves low will be lifted up" (18:14). The ramifications of this proverb are far-reaching. Indeed, immediately on the heels of Jesus's interaction with his disciples regarding children, with no break in the narrative at all, a rich ruler wonders what he must do to inherit eternal life and is told he must divest himself of his wealth and identify with the marginal. We can hardly visualize this scene without thinking of Mary's Song:

> He has pulled the powerful down from their thrones
> and lifted up the lowly.
> He has filled the hungry with good things
> and sent the rich away empty-handed. (1:52–53)

Recall that, in Luke 9, Jesus had informed his disciples that they embody the gospel when they extend hospitality to little children. To welcome children is to welcome Jesus and, in turn, God. Now, however, we find that, rather than extending to these little ones an honorable welcome, the disciples actually refuse them access to Jesus. The disciples effectively and rudely close the door in their faces. Jesus's response is to correct his disciples, teaching them that God's kingdom is inhabited by these little ones.

Luke's wording of v. 16 underscores what is at stake here, namely, our grasp of the nature of God's royal rule. Consider the parallelism between the phrasing in Jesus's Sermon on the Plain (6:20) and here:

| "God's kingdom belongs to you who are poor" (my translation) | "God's kingdom belongs to people like these children" (CEB) |

ὑμετέρα [i.e., οἱ πτωχοί] ἐστὶν ἡ
βασιλεία τοῦ θεοῦ

*hymetera [i.e., hoi ptōchoi] estin hē
basileia tou theou*

τοιούτων ἐστὶν ἡ βασιλεία τοῦ θεοῦ

toioutōn estin hē basileia tou theou

Clearly, for Luke, children, these little ones, exemplify those who are aligned with God's royal rule; we see in them the politics of God's kingdom. Here we have on display the dispositions of those whose lives are at significant remove from the corridors of conventional power and prestige — indeed, whose identification with God's ways brings with it misunderstanding, disappointment, and even harassment from those who have not yet embraced God's kingdom. When Jesus wants to speak of God's royal rule, in Luke's Gospel he points to the poor, including newborn babies. Their place in the world serves to fill out a definition of the life-world revealed in Jesus's coming. It is a strange world, to be sure, where the poor can be declared "happy" rather than "down on their luck," and where a child is to receive an honorable welcome instead of having the door slammed in his or her face. But this only emphasizes the eschatological character of Jesus's mission and message — not a vision of life relegated to a future bliss, but the present revelation of the way God does things. To put it differently, Jesus sketches the way things really are, if only we had eyes to see it clearly.

Let us turn to another possibility for framing Jesus's message to his disciples, this time in 18:17. English translations generally have it that Jesus remarked, as the CEB puts it, "Whoever doesn't welcome God's kingdom like a child will never enter it." Accordingly, we would hear Jesus call his followers to become like children, which, in Roman antiquity, would entail their setting aside their status in the community and embracing the marginal location of children who reside at the bottom of the social ladder. Jesus's words could be heard to say even more, however, if we hear an ellipsis in his phrasing. In this case, we might translate, "Whoever doesn't welcome God's kingdom *in the way that one welcomes* children will never enter it." In this case, one would go further than to embrace the lowly status of a child; instead, one would humble oneself even further, to the extent that even children would be viewed as higher in terms of privilege and prestige. So fully would disciples embrace the topsy-turvy system of values and practices proclaimed by Jesus that they would extend respectful service to that most marginal and overlooked of social groups, children.

According to this way of putting the world together, God's kingdom deconstructs those worldly systems, conventions, and practices that lead to the devaluation of little ones like these newborn babies. And according to this way of putting the world together, the disciples' behavior is self-incriminating. Just as they have censured parents bringing their infants to Jesus, so their behavior is now censured by God's own valuation system, in which the lowest are held in the highest regard.

Finally, toward the end of Luke's Gospel, at the Last Supper, we read:

> An argument broke out among the disciples over which one of them should be regarded as the greatest. But Jesus said to them, "The kings of the Gentiles rule over their subjects, and those in authority over them are called 'friends of the people.' But that's not the way it will be with you. Instead, the greatest among you must become like a person of lower status and the leader like a servant. So which one is greater, the one who is seated at the table or the one who serves at the table? Isn't it the one who is seated at the table? But I am among you as one who serves." (22:24–27)

Here is Jesus's final attempt to reconstruct his followers' patterns of thinking and behaving regarding relative importance. He does so in a way that is representative of the way Luke's narrative itself has been working on this question. That is, he uses typical expectations, then reverses them. Conventional canons are represented by Gentile kings; they are the rulers, they have authority, they dominate, they are the great ones. Yet Jesus himself is Lord and his presence makes present God's royal dominion. He is the great one, but he exercises his lordship through service, through behaving toward others as though they were the persons of highest honor. We might better translate the beginning of v. 26 this way: "The greatest among you must become like the youngest [νεώτερος, *neōteros*]." In this way, the one who first found his bed not in a guest room but in a feeding trough (2:7), whose first visitors were not rulers but shepherds (2:15–16), and whose parents offered on his behalf the sacrifice allowed for the impoverished (2:24) is seen to embody his own message about honor. As in Luke 12:37, so here, Jesus is the L/lord (κύριος, *kyrios*) who fastens his belt, has the slaves sit down to eat, then comes and waits on them at the table. Truly, to show hospitality to a child is to show hospitality to Jesus, for Jesus comports himself as "the youngest." He comes to us as a child.

CONCLUSION

There is more to the story of children in Luke's Gospel, but perhaps we have seen enough to appreciate how far Luke goes to counter pose an alternative reality — an alternative not simply to the Roman world of Luke's Gospel, but also to the worlds of Luke's readers, both historical and contemporary. That is, his narrative counters the conceptual patterns structured around the primary metaphors, Up Is More and Down Is Less. If it seems only natural to us that Up Is More Powerful and Up Is More Important, then the attention Jesus directs toward children and his identification of these little ones as exemplars should strike us as odd, somehow against the natural order of things.

I want to suggest, though, that Luke's narrative wants more from us than a recognition that Jesus's message is baffling when compared with the taken-for-granted values and practices of the Roman world. It is not enough that Luke's audience would regard his presentation of these little ones as counterintuitive. The more pressing question would be, What would be the effect of putting into practice this message? That is, what if Luke's audience were to honor children in this way, to allocate to them the importance counseled by Luke's narrative? What would happen if their everyday embodied experience was one in which Little Is Important? Little Is Better? Little Is More? In this case, would it not be that Luke's narrative counters what we can hardly help but imagine is the natural order of things, that Up Is More and Down Is Less? Would Luke's narrative not at the same time urge the (re)formation of persons with topsy-turvy conceptual patterns?

REFERENCES

Balla, Peter. *The Child-Parent Relationship in the New Testament and Its Environment.* Peabody, MA: Henrickson, 2003.

Carroll, John T. "'What Then Will This Child Become?': Perspectives on Children in the Gospel of Luke." In *The Child in the Bible,* edited by Marcia J. Bunge, Terence E. Fretheim, and Beverly R. Gaventa, 177–194. Grand Rapids: Eerdmans, 2008.

Egolf, Donald B., and Lloyd E. Corder. "Height Differences of Low and High Job Status, Female and Male Corporate Employees." *Sex Roles* 24 (1991): 365–73.

Feldman, Jerome A. *From Molecule to Metaphor: A Neural Theory of Language.* Cambridge, MA: The MIT Press, 2006.

Francis, James. "Child and Children in the New Testament." In *The Family in Theological Perspective,* edited by Stephen C. Barton, 65–85. Edinburgh: T. & T. Clark, 1996.

Gibbs Jr., Raymond W. *Embodiment and Cognitive Science.* Cambridge: Cambridge University Press, 2006.

Giessner, Steffen R., and Thomas W. Schubert. "High in the Hierarchy: How Vertical Location and Judgments of Leaders' Power Are Interrelated." *Organizational Behavior and Human Decision Processes* 104 (2007): 30–44.

Grady, Joseph. "Foundations of Meaning: Primary Metaphors and Primary Scenes." PhD Diss., University of California, Berkeley, 1997.

Gundry-Volf, Judith M. "To Such as These Belongs the Reign of God: Jesus and Children." *Theology Today* 56 (2000): 469–80.

Johnson, Mark. *The Body in the Mind: The Bodily Basis of Meaning, Imagination, and Reason.* Chicago: University of Chicago Press, 1987.

Judge, Timothy A., and Daniel M. Cable. "The Effect of Physical Height on Workplace Success and Income: Preliminary Test of a Theoretical Model." *Basic and Applied Social Psychology* 89 (2004): 428–41.

Lindstromberg, Seth. *English Prepositions Explained.* Rev. ed. Amsterdam: John Benjamin, 2010.

May, Scottie, Beth Posterski, Catherine Stonehouse, and Linda Cannel. *Children Matter: Celebrating Their Place in the Church, Family, and Community.* Grand Rapids: Eerdmans, 2005.

Parsons, Mikeal. *Body and Character in Luke and Acts: The Subversion of Physiognomy in Early Christianity.* Grand Rapids: Baker, 2006.

Posner, Michael J., and Marcus E. Raichle. *Images of Mind.* New York: W.H. Freeman, 1997.

Ramachandra, V.S. *A Brief Tour of Human Consciousness*. New York: Pi, 2004.

Rawson, Beryl. *Children and Childhood in Roman Italy*. Oxford: Oxford University Press, 2003.

———, ed. *The Family in Ancient Rome: New Perspectives*. Ithaca, NY: Cornell University Press, 1986.

———, ed. *Marriage, Divorce, and Children in Ancient Rome*. Oxford: Oxford University Press, 1991.

———, ed. *A Companion to Families in the Greek and Roman Worlds*. Malden, MA: Wiley-Blackwell, 2011.

Schubert, Thomas W. "Your Highness: Vertical Positions as Perceptual Symbols of Power." *Journal of Personality and Social Psychology* 89 (2005): 1–21.

Via Jr., Dan O. *The Ethics of Mark's Gospel — In the Middle of Time*. Philadelphia: Fortress, 1985.

Yu, Ning. "Metaphor from Body and Culture." In *The Cambridge Handbook of Metaphor and Thought*, edited by Raymond W. Gibbs Jr., 247–61. Cambridge: Cambridge University Press, 2010.

Chapter 4

Children Learning the Faith in the Middle Ages
Learning from Past Practices for Present Needs

Kevin E. Lawson

The medieval church time period has been viewed by many as an era of declining effectiveness in church practices with children and adults, leading to lay ignorance of the key tenets of the faith, reduced piety, and increased superstition. Certainly several reformers, Catholic and Protestant alike, shared this view, including Erasmus, Philipp Melanchthon, and Martin Luther (Roest, 2004, ix). With the decline in the catechumenate following the institution of infant baptism in the early church era, the church's teaching efforts, especially with children, have been viewed as increasingly limited in extent and effectiveness. However, the following historical review challenges these perceptions.

EXPLORING THE NEGLECTED MEDIEVAL ERA

While many Protestants found little to learn from the church's practices in this pre-Reformation time period regarding fostering genuine Christian faith among children, recent scholarship is challenging this viewpoint, painting a portrait of a vital faith experience, especially in the later middle ages (thirteenth-to-fifteenth centuries) (Duffy, 2005). There may indeed be more to learn from this era than many of us who care about the spiritual life of children had thought.

In general, the Protestant study of the history of Christian religious education has not given the time period of the middle ages adequate attention. Perhaps that is because of our own commitments to the study of the Scripture for nurturing faith and the apparent limited access by the medieval laity in general, and children in particular, to the Bible. While this is indeed a significant limitation of the time period, it may have obscured our understanding and appreciation of a wide range of other ways that people were indeed learning the faith the church desired to pass on. Duffy, in his well-received book, *The Stripping of the Altars*, (2005) challenges the perception of spiritual apathy and ignorance in the later middle ages and encourages us to give closer attention to the ways that faith was learned and nurtured. For those who work with children today, if we shift our focus from *how the faith was taught* in this time period to *how children learned the faith*, it may encourage us to better consider how our own children are actually learning the faith today and how our teaching efforts may fit within a larger ecology of spiritual nurture.

What did children experience during the medieval era? What was their religious involvement in their families, schools, and churches like? What religious instruction did they have access to? How else were they formed in their faith? This chapter explores these questions.

HOW CHILDREN LEARNED THE FAITH THROUGHOUT THE MIDDLE AGES

Throughout the medieval era (600–1500 AD), the three main ways children learned the Christian faith were partly formal instruction and partly informal socialization. These included: (1) the formative power of experiencing the liturgical year, (2) basic instruction by parents and godparents, and (3) hearing sermons preached at church.

1. Celebrating and Living into the Story—The Liturgical Calendar

The liturgical calendar in the Western Church formed slowly over the centuries, with major events developing after the official acceptance of Christianity within the Roman Empire under Constantine. Over the centuries that followed, a fairly standard calendar cycle evolved, impacting the lives of all who grew up following it. Beginning with Advent and ending with Pentecost, every year brought a flow of activities, celebrations, fasts, feasts, and teachings that recalled the story of the promise of a Savior (Advent), the birth and baptism of Christ (Christmas and Epiphany), His ministry on earth, His crucifixion and resurrection (Holy Week, Easter), and His ascension into Heaven (Pentecost and Ascension) (Talley, 1991). Through these events, and many others, the salvation story was rehearsed every year through church celebrations and family practices, ensuring a basic grounding in the faith. It also encouraged times for reflection on one's sin (e.g., Lent), the need for forgiveness, and the grace and love of God in Christ.

Through these events, children experienced the life of faith of their families and their congregations well before they were taught the faith in more formal ways. These practices, shared each year, were a strong experiential grounding in the basics of the faith, especially the life and ministry of Christ. This on-going cycle of the life of faith is the foundation stone upon which all other instruction in the faith rested.

2. Introduction to the Basics of the Story—Godparents and Spiritual Kinship

In the early church, baptism followed instruction, with a sponsor giving testimony of the transformed nature of the person preparing for baptism. With the development of the doctrine of the sin nature and inherited guilt for Adam's sin came greater concern about the status of infants who died without baptism (Lawson, 2011). The development of a repeatable penance to address the impact of sin after baptism opened the opportunity for baptism at an earlier age. These two developments led to a change of church practice to infant baptism before instruction. The role of sponsor shifted to the parents who brought their children for baptism, with a focus on their responsibility to instruct the infant in the faith. This new role became a shared one, with parents selecting "godparents" who agreed to assist with the instruction of the child, particularly in the event of the death of the parents, and be moral examples and guides to the child. This kind of "spiritual kinship" had social dimensions as well, but the primary emphasis was on ensuring that the child was raised to know, accept, and be confirmed in the faith when he or she came of age.

In the 800s, under Charlemagne, those desiring to be godparents had to know the Apostles Creed, Lord's Prayer, and the Ten Commandments in order to serve in this role (Lynch, 1986, 305). Throughout the medieval era, godparents worked with parents to instruct children in the basics of the faith, particularly as confirmation became more separated in time from baptism. In some settings the godparents instructed the child and presented him or her for confirmation. As with many other practices, this instruction could be carried out with great integrity, or haphazardly. Not all children received careful instruction in the faith from their godparents, but this practice was established and carried out with that purpose in mind, and many benefited.

3. Hearing the Story—The Ministry of Preaching

Preaching in the early middle ages was mainly the task of bishops with other church leaders, particularly in monastic settings, preaching and teaching within their communities. Parish priests carried out the sacrament of the Mass as a retelling of God's salvation in Christ and as a means of grace for addressing the impact of ongoing sin. Hearing preaching through the Scriptures on a weekly basis was not a common experience.

An emphasis on popular preaching (in the vernacular language) by clergy other than the bishop dates to Caesarius of Arles in the sixth century, was reemphasized at the synod of Arles in the early ninth century, and was promoted under Charlemagne in the late eighth and early ninth centuries. For those children growing up in communities where popular preaching was carried out on a regular basis, this would have been one of the few ways that they would have been instructed in the message of the Scriptures. While this was not a common, regular experience for many parishes in the early middle ages, this changed in the later Middle Ages as renewed emphasis was placed on instructing both clergy and laity in the faith. A key turning point came early in the thirteenth century, as church leadership gathered to address concerns throughout the Western church.

THE FOURTH LATERAN COUNCIL AND EDUCATIONAL RENEWAL IN THE LATER MIDDLE AGES

In 1213, Pope Innocent III (1198–1216) announced the upcoming Fourth Lateran Council to be held in 1215. In addition to addressing issues regarding the church's continuing involvement in developments in the Holy Land, the bulk of the resulting constitution of the council dealt with aspects of pastoral care. In particular, concerns were expressed with how to better form and reform the moral life of the laity, how to counter false teaching, and how to strengthen the faith of the people. Out of this council came two major decrees that stimulated renewed educational efforts within the church. The one with arguably the greatest impact was Canon 21 regarding the necessity of all Christians receiving communion at least once a year at Easter.

> All the faithful of both sexes shall after they have reached the age of discretion [i.e., fourteen] faithfully confess all their sins at least once a year to their own [parish] priest and perform to the best of their ability the penance imposed, receiving reverently at least at Easter the sacrament of the Eucharist, unless perchance at the advice of their own priest they may for a good reason abstain for a time from its reception; otherwise they shall be [barred from entering] the church during life and deprived of Christian burial in death. (Shinners, 1997, 9)

This seemingly simple requirement had great implications. To partake of the Eucharist one must first make confession to the local parish priest. In order to make a good confession, one must know what God requires and what He considers to be sin. To know this, one must be taught God's laws and the basics of the faith and how to confess. The decision of the Fourth Lateran Council to require annual communion led church leaders to take initiatives to strengthen and extend their teaching ministry to better equip secular clergy for the cure of souls, and to teach the laity both through public preaching and private instruction in the context of confession.

The second canon that greatly impacted the religious education of the laity was Canon 9 regarding the appointment of preachers to minister the Word of God and to hear confession.

> It often happens that bishops by themselves are not sufficient to minister the word of God to the people, especially in large and scattered dioceses. . . . We therefore decree by this general constitution that bishops are to appoint suitable men to carry out with profit this duty of sacred preaching, men who are powerful in word and deed and who will visit with care the peoples entrusted to them in place of the bishops, since these by themselves are unable to do it, and will build them up by word and example. . . . We therefore order that there be appointed in both cathedral and other conventual churches suitable men whom the bishops can have as coadjutors and cooperators not only in the office of preaching but also in hearing confessions and enjoining penances and in other matters which are conducive to the salvation of souls. If anyone neglects to do this, let him be subject to severe punishment. (Leclercq, 1910)

These two decrees regarding communion, preaching, and confession, led to a major overhaul in the ways lay people, including children, were instructed in the faith and what was expected of them and their parish priests. This renewal of concern for the instruction of the laity sparked a major creative effort to communicate the faith and reach the hearts and minds of the laity with the story of salvation. The earlier ways of learning the faith continued; preaching grew under the friars, but new initiatives had a major impact on what children experienced and how their faith was formed. These newer ways included: (4) vernacular poetry and music, (5) increased use of the visual arts, (6) religious drama, and (7) development and use of a catechism.

4. Learning the Story through Poetry and Music

The writing of religious poetry and song lyrics grew during this time period. These short poems were variously referred to as prayers, meditations, or treatises (Woolf, 1968, 1). Verse was incorporated into preaching to capture attention, make the message memorable, and give affective power to the message being preached. In England, the friars have been noted as the first to use vernacular verse in their sermons (Jeffrey, 1975, 184). The great number of lyrics in the *pastoralia* written by Franciscans in England shows they were used extensively. In some cases, such as in the *Red Book of Ossory,* religious words were put to secular tunes (Caldwell, 1991, 104). In other cases, popular poetic forms were used to make the gospel message appeal to the laity. Given how well children enjoy verses and songs, this growth had an impact on their access to instruction in the faith and their ability to recall what they were taught.

Two types of poems can be identified from the literature that is available to us today: devotional/meditative and didactic.

Devotional/Meditative Lyrics. A major theme of the poetry of this time period is the Passion. John Grimestone's preaching book provides an example of this emphasis. While its 150 pages include poems on about 100 topics, about one-fifth of them relate to the Passion, many of which had been in circulation for generations (Woolf

1986, 20). This focus on the passion was to arouse a response of love and contrition, both essential in preparing the way for repentance of sin and a good confession. It also illustrated the growing emphasis on a personal relationship with and response to God characteristic of Carthusian and Cistercian spirituality, which was embraced and promoted by Franciscans in their ministry of preaching.

Didactic Lyrics. Much of the curriculum of instruction of the laity was set to verse to capture attention during the preaching event and to aid remembrance of the sermon after the fact. The *Speculum Christiani,* a preaching manual, provides examples of how poems were used to illustrate and expound doctrinal and creedal teaching as well as to effect devotion and contrition. Roest writes about the Franciscan use of verse in teaching:

> An overwhelming number of English religious lyrics has (sic) an outright didactical catechistic message. This catechistic message comprises poetic explanations of basic theological doctrines on original sin, the act of redemption, the tenets of faith and the acts of charity. Such teachings were found in poems on the ten commandment (*sic*) the *Pater Noster* and the *Ave Maria* prayers . . . (Roest, 2004, 291–292)

While the use of poetry and music to teach the faith was beneficial for people of all ages, particularly those who could not read, it was especially appropriate for instructing children in the faith, making what they were learning memorable and enjoyable.

5. Seeing the Story in the Visual Arts

Church buildings in the later Middle Ages were highly decorated, and much of the artistic display had a didactic motivation. For example, Miriam Gill, citing Rosemary Woolf (1986, 57), describes the use of wall paintings common in the church in the middle and later medieval period:

> Medieval apologists sometimes described monumental art such as wall paintings as "*muta predicatio*" or "silent preaching." Meditating on a religious image was presented as "synonymous with reading and hearing God's word." The high level of didactic material found in wall paintings suggests that they were a favoured medium of religious instruction. Like sermons, they addressed a large and diverse audience, transcending the barriers between illiterate and literate. (Gill, 2002, 155)

What Wolf and Gill describe regarding wall paintings can also be applied to other art media used in the church, including stained glass and sculpture. In many cases, the subjects mentioned in sermon collections of this era can be seen illustrated in church artwork of all kinds of media. While Lollards attacked the use of images out of concern for possible idolatry, John Mirk, writing in his *Festial,* defended the practice of using images to teach when he wrote:

> There are many thousands of people that could not imagine in their heart how Christ was treated on the cross, but as they learn it from the sight of images and painting. (Erbe, 1905, 171)

In particular, the growing emphasis that priests preach and teach their congregants the basic elements of the catechetical curriculum a few times a year seems to have led to certain didactic themes being incorporated into church architecture. For example the following curricular elements are frequently depicted in painting, stained glass, and sculpture in English medieval churches:

- *Apostles Creed:* Images of the Apostles, each with a scroll with one element of the Creed written on it

- *Seven Deadly Sins and Seven Principal Virtues:* Trees with images on branches representing these sins and virtues

- *Lord's Prayer:* Often taught in relation to the Seven Deadly Sins, as an antidote to them

- *Seven Corporal Works of Mercy:* Illustrated by images of people doing these good works

- *Ten Commandments:* Images of characters from *exempla,* or stories illustrating the consequences of breaking one of the commandments

- *Last Judgment:* Doom paintings visualizing the last judgment to warn sinners of their need to receive God's mercy in Christ and through the sacraments of the church

- *Seven Sacraments:* A collection of images/reliefs carved into the baptismal font

In addition to these more common didactic themes, other images were used to depict important doctrinal beliefs, including the crucifix (emphasizing Christ's suffering and death for sinners), images of the Eucharist (emphasizing transubstantiation), the fragility of life (shown in the wheel of fortune images), and the importance of other sacraments. Stories from the life of Christ and the Virgin were also often portrayed in paintings and in stained glass.

Caiger-Smith, in discussing the strong connection between the educational agenda of church leaders and the development and use of art in the early Gothic period, concludes:

> Thus it was appropriate, and perhaps inevitable, that the range of subjects in provincial wall-paintings in the great age of popular instruction should be fairly restricted. The appealing decorativeness and simplicity of the provincial paintings thus became an important virtue, enabling people to identify and

memorize the principal features of pictures and to connect them with the verbal instruction of the parish priest's sermons. (Caiger-Smith 1963, 22)

For children attending church worship services with their parents, these artistic displays provided concrete images of the key elements of the faith about which they were learning. The passion of Christ for their sin, the examples of the saints, images of the "fruit" of sin and virtue, and many other images provided emotionally powerful lessons without anyone saying a word.

6. Experiencing the Story through Religious Drama

Religious drama developed throughout the thirteenth to early sixteenth centuries in England. Four basic types can be identified. *Liturgical Plays* developed within the worship setting, giving added life to the reading of Scripture and portrayal of biblical events. *Biblical Plays* developed as public presentations of key events in the biblical story of redemption. The York "Mystery Plays" are an example of this type of drama with over fifty stories from creation to Christ's second coming portrayed annually on Corpus Christi Day on wagons which stopped at several stations on their way into the central market area of the city. *Saints Plays* depicted the life, conversion, and sometimes suffering and martyrdom of various biblical saints (e.g., Paul, Mary Magdalene) and historical saints important to the church in England. Finally, *Morality Plays* provided ethical teaching and exhortation to obedience to God and resisting temptation.

For children living in areas such as York, England, where cycle plays of biblical stories were put on annually, the salvation story of Scripture, from Genesis to Revelation, was vividly presented, providing images and greater understanding of the events of Scripture. To experience these dramatic presentations each year would have impacted their understanding of what they heard from sermons and learned from parents and godparents throughout the year.

7. The Renewal of the Catechism and its Use in Church and School

In light of the requirements for communion and confession stated in the canons of the Fourth Lateran Council, church leaders became more convinced of the need for parishioners to be instructed in the faith. This led to the development of sets of catechetical materials and their use in the preaching of the church.

In England, 1281, at the Council of Lambeth, Archbishop John Peckham's vision for the educational needs of the church was detailed in the chapter known as *Ignorancia Sacerdotum*. Peckham's syllabus for the church's teaching ministry was more extensive than those that had preceded, including the Creed (fourteen articles), the Ten Commandments, the Seven Works of Mercy, the Seven Vices, the Seven Virtues, and the Seven Sacraments. These were to be taught by the parish priests to the laity four times a year in the vernacular. This curriculum became the model for the teaching expectations of diocese across the country, influencing the development of catechetical resources for pastoral use. For example, Bishop John Stafford of Bath and Wells had Peckham's decree translated into English and a copy placed in every church in his diocese.

Peckham's decree impacted the scope of instruction of other major works that followed, including John Mirk's *Instructions to Parish Priests* (Bryant and Hunter, 1999), and Archbishop Thoresby of York's development of a catechism in the vernacular for lay use in 1357 AD (the so-called "Lay Folks Catechism") (Simmons and Nolloth, 1901). This marks the first officially sanctioned written catechism in England in the vernacular, and it bears the imprint of Peckham's vision of instruction. Others followed in the later fourteenth and fifteenth centuries, prior to the Reformation.

The story of the growth of different kinds of schools, and who benefited from them, is too complicated to explore here, but one thing that developed in the later medieval era was the use of the catechetical curriculum that Peckham and others developed as a focus of instruction. Children first learned to spell and to write by studying and copying the catechetical materials—the Apostle's Creed, Lord's Prayer, and Ten Commandments. What was taught nonformally in the church and home became part of the formal curriculum of the school.

REFLECTION ON LESSONS WE MIGHT LEARN FOR MINISTRY WITH CHILDREN TODAY

For me, this review of ways that children learned the faith during the medieval era sparks a lot of questions and ideas. Are there insights from the past that might be helpful to those who seek to nurture the spiritual life of children today? Here are a few initial thoughts to consider.

1. Experiencing the Salvation Story through the Cycle of the Year

Many families today live life by the school calendar with a layer of the sports calendar on top along with a sprinkling of national and religious holidays. Children growing up in the medieval era learned to see life through a lens of salvation history. The annual cycle of feasts and fasts associated with the events in Christ's life, and the traditions that went with these celebrations in the church and in the home, provided a storyline for understanding life. Children were participants in these events, celebrating with the church what God had done for them out of His great love and grace. This helped shape their sense of purpose and identity.

Some churches and families today make good use of the church calendar to revisit important aspects of God's story. Others can become more intentional in promoting and celebrating the church calendar as part of their experience of the year together.

Using the cycle of the year to tell the salvation story provides a spiraling curriculum in which children can both grow in their understanding of what these celebrations mean and in their depth of personal experience and participation in them. Both in the congregation and in the home, intentionality in involving children in the celebrations of God's unfolding story of redemption can be deeply meaningful.

2. Fostering Spiritual Kinship

Medieval parents understood that they were not to be the sole providers of religious instruction for their children. They turned to others to come alongside them, serving as "spiritual kin" in the raising and instruction of their children. Some denominations today still have godparents identified when children are baptized, but this often is more of a social honor, with little follow through. Where god-parenting is carried out, those who agree to be godparents need careful instruction in their tasks, resources to assist them, and role models to show the way. This can be a rich and rewarding ministry.

Even in churches where god-parenting is not the norm, parents can develop friendships with other families where the parents can serve as role models of people who seek to know and follow God. Intergenerational ministry opportunities in churches can help foster this as well. Children can get to know other adults who can be examples to them, share their spiritual journeys with them, and model what it means to live for Christ. There may be times in the future when the children, now grown, will want to talk with someone other than their parents about important issues of faith and life. Intergenerational ministries and formal mentoring programs can both provide those opportunities.

3. Renewing the Vision of Preaching as Teaching for All Ages

Not all churches have children participate in their worship services with the adults. Where this is done, those who design the worship experience need to be diligent to look for ways to make these services meaningful experiences for children, not just something to be endured.

Where children are in separate worship services from the adults, any message shared needs to be viewed as an opportunity to both inform and to shape the growing faith of the children. These need to be designed to intentionally teach key aspects of the faith, not just an interesting Bible story. This requires careful thought and translation work to bring the foundational aspects of the Christian faith into forms that children can both understand and take to heart. One of my previous pastors was very intentional in this whenever he preached, and it had a positive impact with children and adults alike. Combined with opportunities to talk with parents about what they heard and exploring where and how God might use it to impact their lives, these messages can have a deep impact in a child's growing faith.

4. Employing the Power of the Visual Arts, Music, and Drama

Children in the medieval era learned about the Christian faith through a variety of arts, both oral and visual. Hearing poetry and music made instruction memorable and enjoyable. Seeing the stories of Scripture and images of sins and virtues made instruction more concrete, easier to take in, understand, and recall. Having the Bible stories come to life in dramatic presentations was powerful and memorable.

In our churches today, investing in creative arts in worship and instructional times can help children grow in their understanding and deepen the affective impact of what they are learning. In education, we're familiar with the concept of learning styles and this has helped us move away from a heavy reliance on auditory teaching. We need to bring this into the church and home, too, stimulating us to find ways to use the various arts as means of both experiencing learning more fully and for children to express their growing faith. This applies to music, visual arts, and drama—all can become rich expressions of faith, both for those "receiving" them as well as for those offering them.

5. Renewing the Use of a "Catechism"

In the later medieval era, there was recognition that there were certain key elements of the faith that everyone ought to know, young and old alike. While we may have different ideas of what belongs within the scope of that "catechism" compared with the church leaders of that time, it is helpful for us to think carefully about what we believe all children ought to learn. What belongs in our core curriculum, or "catechism?" What is worth investing time to teach and to "test" to assure the children's knowledge and understanding? When we have examined this, we may need to redevelop our teaching ministries in our homes and churches to confirm that this core curriculum is being covered well and often.

In too many cases, children in our churches receive instruction on a variety of Bible stories, perhaps with moralized applications, but not on the broad scope of the essentials of our faith. We must think carefully about what we want our children to receive and ensure that our teaching ministries and resources are helping us achieve those goals. If not already the case, it may be helpful to consider particular ages and ministries where a more carefully designed "catechetical" curriculum may be used to ensure that all children entering the church's ministries have an opportunity to be well grounded in the essentials of the faith.

CONCLUSION

When we ask the question, "how did the church teach the faith" during the medieval period, we may struggle a bit to identify much we can learn from. But asking "how did children learn the faith" during this period helps us see a richer range of ways that the Christian faith was expressed and intentionally shared, and in turn learned by children and adults alike. Asking that same question, "how do children learn the faith today," may help us better attend to ways in which children learn outside of our formal teaching efforts and may identify ways for us to be more intentional in using nonformal and informal means to inform and shape their faith. Our time period is different and our resources are different, but there is much we can learn from this era to stimulate our ministry development today. I hope this review stimulates your own thinking and helps you see new ways to design ministry efforts with the children God entrusts to your care.

REFERENCES

Bryant, Geoffrey F., and Vivien M. Hunter. *"How Thow Schalt Thy Paresche Preche": John Myrc's Instructions for Parish Priests, Part One, Introduction and Text.* Barton-on-Humber Branch, UK: Workers' Educational Association, 1999.

Caiger-Smith, Alan. *English Medieval Mural Paintings.* Oxford: Clarendon, 1963.

Duffy, Eamon. *The Stripping of the Altars*, 2nd ed. (2005). New Haven, CT: Yale University.

Erbe, Theodor. *Mirk's Festial: A Collection of Homilies.* Early English Test Society Extra Series, 96. London: Early English Text Society, 1905.

Gill, Miriam. "Preaching and Image: Sermons and Wall Paintings in Later Medieval England." In *Preacher, Sermon, and Audience in the Middle Ages,* edited by C. Muessig, 155–180. Boston: Brill, 2002.

Lawson, Kevin. "Baptismal Theology and Practices and the Spiritual Nurture of Children, Part I: Early and Medieval Church." *Christian Education Journal* 8 (2011): 130–145.

Leclercq, Henri. "Fourth Lateran Council (1215)." In *The Catholic Encyclopedia.* New York: Robert Appleton, 1910. No pages. Online: http://www.newadvent.org/cathen/09018a.htm

Lynch, Joseph H. *Godparents and Kinship in Early Medieval Europe.* Princeton: Princeton University, 1986.

Orme, Nicholas. *Medieval Children.* New Haven, CT: Yale University Press, 2001.

Roest, Bert. *Franciscan Literature of Religious Instruction before the Council of Trent.* Boston: Brill, 2004.

Shinners, John. *Medieval Popular Religion, 1000–1500: A Reader.* Orchard Park, NY: Broadview, 1997.

Simmons, Thomas Frederick, and Henry Edward Nolloth. *The Lay Folks' Catechism, or the English and Latin versions of Archbishop Thoresby's Instruction for the People; Together with a Wycliffite Adaptation of the same, and the Corresponding Canons of the Council of Lambeth.* London: C. Scribner & Co., 1901.

Talley, Thomas J. "Calendar, Liturgical." In *The New Dictionary of Sacramental Worship,* edited by Peter E. Fink. 150–163. Collegeville, MN: The Liturgical Press, 1990.

Woolf, Rosemary. *Art and Doctrine: Essays on Medieval Literature.* London: Hambledon, 1986.

Chapter 5

Bushnell, Westerhoff, and Nurturing Children's Faith in the Twenty-First Century

Benjamin D. Espinoza

The works of Horace Bushnell and John Westerhoff III have laid critical theoretical foundations for understanding the way people grow in the life of faith. Of Bushnell, historian Robert B. Mullin (2002) notes, "*Christian Nurture* bears the unmistakable traits of the tinkerer's handiwork. It was intuitively bold . . . decades later scholars would acknowledge that Bushnell had touched on many facts developmental psychologists later discovered about how children learn" (2002, 119). Similarly, Westerhoff continues to be a vital voice in conversations related to Christian formation. Westerhoff is referred to as a theologically moderate successor to Bushnell (Gangel and Benson, 2002, 281). Charles Foster (1982) writes, "Thanks in particular to the work of . . . John Westerhoff, the insights and categories of sociology and anthropology have come to be increasingly explored and appropriated by Christian educators" (58). Moreover, Bushnell's *Christian Nurture* (1847) and Westerhoff's *Will Our Children Have Faith* (1976) are still foundational textbooks in college and seminary classes related to children's Christian education.

This chapter analyzes Bushnell's concept of Christian nurture and Westerhoff III's community of faith enculturation paradigm for the purpose of identifying key themes in their work that prove helpful for ministry with children today. From an analysis of Bushnell and Westerhoff's works, three themes for children's ministry emerge: (1) the need to critically reflect upon current ministry practices while imagining new possibilities, (2) the necessity of fostering a child's religious imagination, and (3) the importance of a vital faith community that nurtures the faith of children. This chapter aims to be a valuable contribution not only to the literature on Bushnell and Westerhoff, but also to help practitioners envision fresh ways of ministering to children in light of Bushnell's and Westerhoff's ideas.

HORACE BUSHNELL AND CHRISTIAN NURTURE

Horace Bushnell, whose commitment to Christ was based on "a simple and profound desire to be and do right, rather than to have a personal relationship with God" (Adamson 1966, 19), is best known for his 1847 work, *Christian Nurture*. Bushnell wrote the work against the backdrop of the Second Great Awakening in New England (early to mid-nineteenth century), which centered on the belief that a "single experience . . . would lead each believer to greater devotion and more conscientious study of Scripture" (Gonzalez, 1985, 228). This renewed emphasis on a personal conversion experience led to division within Bushnell's own Congregational denomination. Whereas the "New Lights" embraced the Second Great Awakening's popularization of the instantaneous conversion experience, the "Old Lights" thought this emphasis was unhealthy, and instead favored a position akin to Bushnell's described notion of Christian nurture (Lawson 2011, 156).

The implications of these two schools of thought became increasingly evident. Old Lights favored the view that "as parents taught and guided their children in the light of the gospel, the children would confirm this faith as their own when they reached an age of discretion" (Lawson, 2011, 156). However, New Lights expected parents to inform their children of their inherent sinfulness, and thus lead them to recognize their need for a visible, experiential, and attestable conversion experience later in life (Lawson, 2011, 156). According to Gangel and Benson (2002), the push for conversion stemmed from two components of predominant Calvinist theology: the seriousness of humanity's depravity, and the radical nature of Christian faith (279). Gangel and Benson (2002) describe the implications of New Light theology in practical terms:

> Based on a strong Calvinistic theology, the revivalists taught that a young child could not possibly be a Christian. Rather, the task of the parent was to teach his children that they could in no way please God. A young child was to be taught that he could not pray, that he could not read Scripture, and that he could not possibly please God in any way. (279)

Thus this environment did little to nourish the faith of developing children, as "it was the parents' duty continually to point out the sinfulness of the child to him and to prepare him for conversion at a later date" (Gangel and Benson 2002, 279). Contrary to the prevailing fanaticism of revivalism, Bushnell sought to produce a generation that was "ardent without fanaticism, powerful without machinery" (Mullin 2002, 119). In speaking against revivalism, Bushnell (1847) writes:

> The aim, effort, and expectation should be, not, as is commonly assumed, that the child is to grow up in sin, to be converted after he comes to a mature age; but that he is to open on the world as one that is spiritually renewed, not remembering the time when he went through a technical experience, but seeming rather to have loved what is good from his earliest years. (10)

Bushnell sought to stimulate the religious potential of children by challenging parents and revivalists to expose children to the spiritual realm from early on.

Bushnell and Christian Nurture

In *Christian Nurture*, Bushnell (1847) famously posited the notion that "the child is to grow up a Christian, and never know himself as being otherwise" (10). Though this may be the central thesis of Bushnell's work, several components merit mention, namely Bushnell's emphases on the organic connection of the family, his belief in the child's potential to overcome sin through nurture, and the nonlinear spiritual development of the child.

A foundational idea of Bushnell's nurture theory is that of the "organic" connection which exists between parents and children. This organically connected family is to be "the primary medium by which the grace of God could be transmitted" (Reed and Prevost, 1998, 316). In articulating this notion to parents, Bushnell vividly noted, "Your character is a stream, a river, flowing down upon your children, hour by hour" (1847, 74). He elaborates:

> So, if there be an organic power of character in the parent, such as that of which I have spoken, it is not a complete power in itself, but only such a power as demands the realizing presence of the Spirit of God, both in the parent and the child, to give it effect. As Paul said, 'I have begotten you through the gospel,' so may we say of the parent, who, having a living gospel enveloped in his life, brings it into organic connection with the soul of childhood. But the declaration excludes the necessity of a divine influence, not more in one case than in the other. (Bushnell, 1847, 32)

In describing Bushnell's description of this organic connection, Reed and Prevost note "He argued that. . . one generation is the natural offspring of another. At birth an exerting power over the infant exists. With no capacity of will, the child forms impressions from his or her surroundings. As character forms from nurture, the child grows in the likeness of the parents, especially the mother" (1998, 316). In this sense, there is a spiritual connection between the parent and the impressionable child that symbiotically connect the two in spiritual harmony. The moral and spiritual character of the parents necessarily influences the child. This made the spiritual environment for the child all the more significant in Bushnell's thought.

Bushnell supposedly believed that depravity was present in children, and that in order to increase the chance of them coming to saving faith in Christ, they must be exposed to a godly environment at an early age. However, as Downs (1983) suggests, ". . . as his doctrine is traced more fully, it becomes evident that he also saw within man the potential for good which does not allow for *total* depravity" (48–49). Downs cites the writings of Charles Hodge, John W. Nevin, and William Alexander Johnson as evidence for Bushnell's adherence to partial depravity, at best (1983, 48–49). Bushnell did hold to a form of depravity, but a form that allowed for the possibility of goodness to arise from within the child, a form of depravity that was not *total*. If Bushnell held to total depravity, *Christian Nurture* would have sought to bridge the gap between Old Light theology and New Light theology, as both contained elements of truth pertinent to the nature of sin in children. From the Old Lights, he would have maintained his emphasis on nurture, but from the New Lights, he would have been more forthright in asserting that children, from an early age, should have an awareness of their depravity and need for redemption. Regardless, Bushnell's theology led him to emphasize the religious potential of the child against the prevailing revivalism of his day.

According to Bushnell, children need to be developed from birth eliminating the need for them to *have* to be converted later.

> Brought up in their society, under their example, baptized into their faith and upon the ground of it, and bosomed in their prayers, there ought to be seeds of gracious character already planted in them; so that no conversion is necessary, but only the development of a new life already begun. Why should the parents cast away their privilege, and count their child an alien still from God's mercies? (1847, 372–373)

There is no need for conversion for Bushnell since the Christian life comes naturally through the process of nurture, a belief that distraught the revivalists. Bushnell (1847) describes spiritual development as a nonlinear process of moral tension which was not marked by conversion:

> The growth of Christian virtue is no vegetable process, no mere onward development. It [a child's development] involves a struggle with evil, a fall and a rescue. The soul becomes established in holy virtue, as a free exercise, only as it is passed round the corner of fall and redemption, ascending thus unto God through a double experience, in which it learns the bitterness of evil and the worth of good, fighting its way out of one, and achieving the other as a victory. (23)

The circular nature of a child's development is one of the hallmarks of Bushnell's theory. Within the context of this cyclical process of moral and spiritual development, Bushnell advocated a style of nurture that sought to inculcate an orientation toward goodness in children. That is, all instances should be regarded as learning experiences that form children spiritually for a lifetime of Christian faithfulness.

Bushnell sought to provide a model of Christian education to the offense of many who took issue with his unsettling view of depravity and optimism of the religious potential of the child. Many of Bushnell's ideas are less offensive to evangelicals today, but there are still concerns related to his view of depravity. Regardless, Bushnell brought many important ideas into the conversation on children's faith development. As we will later see, Bushnellian thought continues to exert an influence on the way scholars conceptualize children's spirituality.

JOHN WESTERHOFF III AND COMMUNITY OF FAITH ENCULTURATION

In *Will Our Children Have Faith?* (1976), noted Duke scholar and Episcopalian priest John Westerhoff III contends that the Deweyan schooling-instructional model pervasive within public education and the church had rejected informal means of education and embraced professionalization and cultural transmission, isolating several components in the Christian formation process, particularly the community of faith. Westerhoff interpreted this as a "broken ecology," and proposed a restored ecology of education composed of home, church, community, and other institutions which sought to wed formal and informal educational practices in order to bring a fully-orbed scope to Christian education practice.

Westerhoff argues that the schooling-instructional model of education based on the work of John Dewey has infiltrated the church, making the church susceptible to isolating "the process of socialization from our consideration" (2000, 15). That is, since the informal curriculum in our churches is often more influential than the formal curriculum of church, "the schooling-instruction paradigm will always be less than inadequate for the evaluation and planning of Christian Education" (2000, 15). For Westerhoff, the schooling-instructional model often served as a vehicle for control:

> Another example results from the unfortunate fact that the schooling-instructional paradigm encourages adults to be with children in ways that assert their power over them. The language of teaching, learning, behavioral objectives, and subject matter tend to produce a mind-set that results in the tendency to inflict on children adult ways of being in the world. It is difficult for us simply to be with the neophyte in song, worship, prayer, storytelling, service, reflection, and fellowship. We always seem to want to do something to or for them so they will be like us like what we would like to be. (2000, 64)

Westerhoff also argued that religion, not faith, could be taught in the traditional schooling-instructional model. He notes, "We can know about religion, but we can only expand in faith, act in faith, live in faith. Faith can be inspired within a community of faith, but it cannot be given to one person by another" (2000, 17). Thus Westerhoff proposed a community of faith enculturation paradigm that brought together the home, the church, and the community as a whole into conversation with one another for the purpose of nurturing and fostering the faith of children.

Westerhoff posits that "Enculturation emphasizes the process of interaction between and among persons of all ages. It focuses on the interactive experiences and environments within which persons act to acquire, sustain, change, and transmit their understandings and ways" (2000, 74). He elaborates that, "In enculturation one person is not understood as the actor and another the acted upon, but rather both act, both interact, and both react" (2000, 74). Bickford (2011) has summarized several components of Westerhoff's community of faith enculturation paradigm. His summary is worth mentioning here:

1. Community defined as being a group of people who share a common memory, have a clear identity, is small enough to have meaningful interactions, and includes at least three generations.

2. Worship exists at the center of community life.

3. Experience is seen as an essential and normative aspect of faith life.

4. The community is a testing community; it does not just accept what is, it tests held truths and beliefs in an effort to always grow.

5. Belief in tradition and the Bible is to be seen as "poetry plus" rather than as "science minus."

6. Persons are seen as unique children of God whose goal is to fully become who God has already created them to be.

7. The goal of a mature faith is social transformation that brings liberation, justice, and peace. (92–93)

In order to fully understand this paradigm, one must understand that Westerhoff relies heavily on liberation theology. Bickford (2011) notes that Westerhoff "saw [liberation theology] as the best approach to move beyond a focus on nurture, which at best can bring an individual into the life of the Church, and to one that emphasizes both nurture and conversion, the process whereby the person goes from having a faith that was given and develops a faith that is owned" (93).

Westerhoff's enculturation paradigm includes both nurture and conversion, a contrast to Bushnell's model which only emphasized nurture. Westerhoff lays out his concerns of nurture: "We have expected too much of nurture, for at its very best, nurture makes possible institutional incorporation . . . The Christian faith by its very nature demands conversion. We cannot gradually educate persons through instruction in schools to be Christian" (2000, 35).

For Westerhoff, nurture led to a transmitted institutional faith, while enculturation led to an "owned" faith. An emphasis on conversion is what sets Westerhoff apart from Bushnell. However, one cannot read *Will Our Children Have Faith?* without seeing the influence that Bushnell played into Westerhoff's understanding of children's Christian education.

Westerhoff built on the foundation of Bushnell, and proposed an alternative solution to the problem of the schooling-instructional model of Christian education. Unfortunately, many of our churches today still operate within the schooling-instructional model. Evangelical churches would do well to engage Westerhoff's work and apply his concepts to their educational ministries, children's ministries in particular.

BUSHNELL, WESTERHOFF, AND CONTEMPORARY CHILDREN'S MINISTRY

Bushnell and Westerhoff posited models of children's Christian education that sought to bring all components of a child's life into conversation with one another. For Bushnell, the organic connection of the family environment and the church was a key component in the process of nurture. For Westerhoff, the church school was to be only one component of a child's Christian education, as all formal and informal learning was vital to fostering a child's life of faith. Three themes emerge from Bushnell and Westerhoff's writings which merit further exploration; many scholars have latched onto these themes and developed their own concepts and models for children's Christian education. In our postmodern world, we will do well to emulate these models of Christian formation for they mesh well with the priorities of postmodernity. These three themes emphasize the need to critically reflect upon current ministry practices while imagining new possibilities—the necessity of fostering a child's religious imagination—and the importance of a vital faith community that nurtures the faith of children.

Critical Reflection on Current Ministry Practices with Imagination

Bushnell and Westerhoff both wrote to counter a perceived problem in children's Christian education. For Bushnell, emphasizing conversion at the expense of meaningful Christian nurture disallowed children from any formative spiritual experiences which they desperately needed in order to nourish their young souls. For Westerhoff, the schooling-instructional model framed church as a "school" by which to obtain objective facts as opposed to a vital community of faith. Bushnell and Westerhoff not only critiqued the theory and practice of those within their contexts but also creatively imagined ways to counter the assumptions of these contexts.

Groome (1980) proposes a shared-praxis approach to Christian education that challenges us to critically reflect on our present action and "our whole engagement in the world, our every doing that has any intentionality or deliberateness to it" (184). Groome explores the importance of this critical reflection:

> In reflecting upon the source of our activity, we come to know our own story and to name our constitutive knowing, that is, the knowing which arises from our engagement with the world. Without this our own stories are forgotten, and the world is named for us. But critical reflection is incomplete if it rests only on reason and memory. The purpose of naming our present and knowing our story is that we may have some freedom to imagine and choose our future. (1980, 186)

In keeping with the spirit of Groome's theory, I offer several questions which we must answer before retooling or formulating any other children's ministries:

- Are our ministries reflecting cultural trends or theological underpinnings?

- Are we engaging children's "present actions"?

- Do our ministries recognize the explicit shift from modernity to postmodernity?

- What barriers to children's spiritual growth are we putting in the way?

- Are we seeing progress in these ministries?

Once we have engaged in critique of our ministry practices, it is essential that we imagine new ways of living and ministering within our contexts. It is not enough to obliterate the theological, philosophical or anthropological assumptions of our contexts but through an imagination empowered by the Holy Spirit, it is imperative that we imagine new ways of creating space for children to flourish in the life of the faith as Bushnell and Westerhoff attempted.

Fostering a Child's Religious Imagination

The second implication that emerges from Bushnell and Westerhoff is that any effort to stifle the child's religious imagination neglects the true nature of a child's spirituality; that it is active, imaginative, creative, emotional, and needs adequate space in order to grow. Bushnell, against the tide of conversionism, proposed that children need to be active in the life of faith, and that they naturally had a faith that *could* be nurtured and fostered in a hospitable environment. Westerhoff (2000), contrary to the prevailing schooling-instructional paradigm, posited that children need to be exposed to the entirety of congregational life, not simply the church's "school," in order to fully explore, test, create, and "recreate" their faith (89). Thus Bushnell and Westerhoff sought to bring children into a special place filled with space for wondering and pondering over the vastness and richness of God.

Several scholars have followed this trend and have expanded on the proposals of Bushnell and Westerhoff. Cavalletti (1992) posits, "Wonder. . . attracts us with irresistible force toward the object of our astonishment," and leads us to be become "immersed in the contemplation of something that exceeds us" (138–139). Catherine Stonehouse (1998), nuances this idea by noting,

> To say that children are spiritual beings does not assume that they are ready
> for spiritual disciplines or that they can be expected to consider what pleases
> God in all their interactions. Often children experience God in fleeting mo-
> ments of awareness and may not be fully conscious of the encounter. Such
> glimpses of God, however, are real, and the joy, peace, and insight of those
> glimpses germinate within the child and someday may come into the full
> bloom of conscious love for God. (Stonehouse, 1998, 182)

Karen Marie-Yust (2004), in a manner similar to Stonehouse, contends that children's environments shape their perceptions for a lifetime, and thus it is necessary
for parents to create a spiritual environment for their children to identify with in the
midst of broader society (21–40). Yust follows the spirit of Bushnell's organic family
connection theory, by noting "the cultivation of our own spiritual awareness means
that we are better prepared to supply some of the religious information that our children need for their own development of a spiritually reflective life" (2004, 136).

In our contemporary evangelical churches, we must ask ourselves if we are doing
everything we can to foster a child's religious imagination. Children do not naturally
have an adult-like inclination toward knowing objectively and rationally. Instead, they
need to have space in order to thrive in their faith, to wholeheartedly make their faith
their own, and to experience God on their own terms. It is common in our American
churches to simply assume that the recitation of certain doctrinal truths on the part
of children equals spiritual growth. These practices are necessary in inculcating faith
in children, but we must provide space for children to learn how to worship and love
God on their own. Reflective engagement models posited by Cavalletti (1992), Stewart and Berryman (1989), and Berryman (1995; 2009) seek to bring children to a place
of religious exploration and engagement with God's story.

A Vital Faith Community that Nurtures

Both Bushnell and Westerhoff affirmed a belief in an empowering faith community
that nurtures children for spiritual growth. Bushnell did little to distinguish between
the roles of family and church in the process of nurture, as he believed these two institutions enjoy an organic relationship. Westerhoff's emphasis on the community of
faith seeks to bring the generations together for the purpose of meaningful interaction
and learning. In the vein of Bushnell and Westerhoff, Barnhill (2007) notes, "Rather
than seeing children as somehow unfinished and unable to participate in the life of the
church until they have learned something, we can encourage children to contribute to
the community" (56).

Several scholars not only affirm this essential component in children's Christian
education, but have built upon the foundation of Bushnell and Westerhoff. Richards
(1988) posits fives processes that directly affect a child's faith development based on
nurture concepts in the Old and New Testaments: Communicating belonging to a

vital faith community, participation in the life of a vital faith community, modeling of members of the faith community, biblical instruction as interpretation of life, and encouraging growing experience of personal choice (76).

May, Posterski, Stonehouse, and Cannell (2005) explore five gifts children receive in community, as well as the gifts they offer a community. I would like to explore these five components and discuss why children do need the nurture of a faith community.

First, children receive true belonging in the faith community. The authors note,

> "A sense of belonging grows as children build relationships with adults and other children in the church, as they receive love and in turn love others . . . The church will be a positive influence in the development of its children to the degree that they are seen *as part of* the church . . . Children need churches committed to the nurture of the whole of childhood. (pp. 139–140)

In the intergenerational relationships churches seek to build, a genuine sense of belonging will inevitably develop among members of the lifespan, particularly children. Too often, children are viewed as being of lesser importance than adults simply because they do not understand the faith in the cognitive manner adults do. Bringing children into the community of faith will give them assurance that their faith is valid and worthy of the community's attention, engagement, and nurture.

Second, children offer meaningful participation in the faith community. The authors indicate, "Growth is healthiest when children participate in these meaningful activities along with persons who have developed understanding and skill in the practices and are able to guide and teach the children" (2005, 140). That is, children should participate in the ministries of the local church, from reading Scripture aloud to the congregation, to serving the marginalized in the local community. The act of allowing children to serve in ministry validates their membership in the faith community, and only adds to enriching their spiritual experiences as children.

Third, children are able to become formed through experience and education in the faith community. When children are exposed to a vibrant, worshipful faith community, their sense of religious imagination is sparked as they "sense the joy, wonder, and awe of those around them as they worship together" (2005, 142). Children who experience the life of the church firsthand are not only exposed to a community of people worshipping the Lord , but also to the stories and teachings of Scripture. Adults in the church have the opportunity to shepherd children into understanding the character of God through ministries that seek to teach children the entirety of Scripture. Moreover, children learn what it means to be a Christian from the adults. May et al. exhort us to critically reflect upon our practices: "What are children in our congregation observing, experiencing, and learning? Are they seeing Christian character, the life God desires Christians to live?" (2005, 142–143).

Fourth, children vitally need community, but the community also vitally needs children. "We see faith in fresh ways when we invite children to process their experiences with us, and we experience grace as God ministers to us through them" (2005, 143). As Christ exhorts his disciples to emulate the ways of a child, so we must acknowledge the example of children in our faith community. Children engage faith in a way that adults regularly do not. They are able to provide insights into the spiritual life of which we may neither engage nor be cognizant. To allow children the safe space to share their thoughts, feelings, and ideas about the life of faith is to not only enrich their relationship with God, but also enrich ours as well.

Finally, children benefit from the mystery of formation in community.

> How does God meet children in the faith community? . . . God meets children in the same way God meets adults—through the mystery of the Holy Spirit's work, through relationships among the people of God, through the revelation of God's will and purpose in Christ and the Scriptures. (May, Posterski, Stonehouse, and Cannell, 2005, 144)

We will never comprehend the mystery of community all Christians share, that many people from a multiplicity of different backgrounds and life circumstances can come together to witness the awe and wonder of God. We will never completely understand how God uses the Scriptures to speak to us, nor will we fully discern how the Holy Spirit moves. However, though these questions will always be shrouded in mystery to us, we can have the faith that when we come together and worship with children, we all somehow grow in the knowledge and love of Christ.

CONCLUSION

In this chapter, Bushnell's nurture theory and Westerhoff's community of faith enculturation paradigm have been analyzed and themes have been identified that are relevant to ministry with children today. It is important that we never forget to review the past and allow it to inform our present. Harold Burgess (2000) wrote, "If you don't know history, you don't know anything. You're a leaf that doesn't know it's part of a tree" (19).

As we plough through Christian history and Christian education history in particular, we see a group of people forging ways of forming believers to exemplify Christ in a "crooked and perverse generation" (Phil 2:15). However, as we move forward, we must be critically reflective of our ministry practices. Changes in society and in the church directly impact the effectiveness of our ministries. To ignore these changes is to marginalize groups of people who desperately need the gospel of Christ. The revivalists of Bushnell's day marginalized children by withholding an open space for children's faith exploration. The schooling-instructional model Westerhoff opposed failed to expose children to a loving community of faith. These movements were the result of a people who may have been unwilling to critically reflect on their practices, and Bushnell and Westerhoff took it upon themselves to imagine new and better ways of ministering to children.

Lawson (2011) advises that everyone in the congregation shares the responsibility of educating children "toward spiritual vitality and a faithful response to the God who has both created them and called them to relationship with Himself in Jesus Christ," (p. 130). Yes, it is the responsibility of children's ministers and Christian educators to imagine and envision new ministry possibilities that respect the spirituality of children as we seek to nurture their imaginative, engaging, and heart-felt spirituality.

REFERENCES

Adamson, W.R. *Bushnell Rediscovered*. Cleveland: United Church Press, 1966.

Barnhill, Carla. "The Postmodern Parent: Shifting Paradigms for the Ultimate Act of Recreation." In *An Emergent Manifesto of Hope*, eds. Doug Pagitt and Tony Jones, 51–58. Grand Rapids: Baker, 2007.

Berryman, Jerome. *Godly Play: An Imaginative Approach to Religious Education*. Minneapolis: Augsburg, 1995.

Berryman, Jerome. *Teaching Godly Play: How to Mentor the Spiritual Development of Children*. Rev. and expanded ed. Denver: Morehouse, 2009.

Bickford, Michael S. "John H. Westerhoff III: A Humanistic and Historical Analysis of His Impact on Religious Education." Ph.D. diss., Fordham University, 2011.

Burgess, Harold William. *Models of Religious Education: Theory and Practice in Historical and Contemporary Perspective*. Nappanee, IN: Evangel, 2001.

Bushnell H. *Christian nurture*. General Books LCC, 1847.

Cavalletti, Sofia. *The Religious Potential of the Child: Experiencing Scripture and Liturgy with Young Children*. 2nd English ed. Chicago: Liturgy Training Publications, 1992.

Downs, Perry. "Christian Nurture: A Comparison of Horace Bushnell and Lawrence O. Richards." *Christian Education Journal* 4 (1984): 43–57.

Foster, Charles. "The Faith Community as a Guiding Image for Christian Education." In *Contemporary Approaches to Christian Education*, eds. Jack L. Seymour and Donald E. Miller, 53–71. Nashville: Abingdon, 1982.

Gangel, Kenneth O., and Warren S. Benson. *Christian Education: Its History and Philosophy*. Eugene, OR: Wipf and Stock, 2002.

González, Justo L. *The Story of Christianity*. 2nd ed. New York: HarperOne/HarperCollins, 2010.

Groome, Thomas H. *Christian Religious Education: Sharing our Story and Vision*. San Francisco: Jossey-Bass, 1999.

Lawson, Kevin. "Baptismal Theology and Practice and the Spiritual Nurture of Children, Part II: Reformation to the Present." *Christian Education Journal* 8, no. 1 (2011): 146–163.

Lillig, Tina. *Catechesis of the Good Shepherd: Essential Realities*. Oak Park, IL: Catechesis of the Good Shepherd, 2004.

May, Scottie, Beth Posterski, Catherine Stonehouse, and Linda Cannell. *Children Matter: Celebrating Their Place in the Church, Family, and Community*. Grand Rapids: Eerdmans, 2005.

Mullin, Robert Bruce. *The Puritan as Yankee: A Life of Horace Bushnell*. Grand Rapids: Eerdmans, 2002.

Reed, James E., and Ronnie Prevost. *A History of Christian Education*. Nashville: Broadman & Holman, 1993.

Richards, Larry. *Children's Ministry: Nurturing Faith within the Family of God*. Grand Rapids: Ministry Resources Library, 1988.

Stewart, Sonja M., and Jerome Berryman. *Young Children and Worship*. Louisville: Westminster John Knox, 1989.

Stonehouse, Catherine. *Joining Children on the Spiritual Journey: Nurturing a Life of Faith*. Grand Rapids: Baker, 1998.

Westerhoff, John H. *Will Our Children Have Faith?* Harrisburg, PA: Morehouse: 2000.

Yust, Karen. *Real Kids, Real Faith: Practices for Nurturing Children's Spiritual Lives*. San Francisco, CA: Jossey-Bass, 2004.

Chapter 6

Beyond Sunday School
How Child-Centered Studies of Religion are Transforming Our Understandings of Children and Their Traditions

Susan B. Ridgely

I recently taught an upper-level seminar on children and religion at UW-Osh, a large comprehensive state university. At the beginning of the class I asked the students to write a short paper that set out their definition of "a child." The results reflected many common assumptions about children. All twenty-five students, for example, included something about childhood being a happy or carefree time of innocence. One student captured the class' understanding when she wrote, children are "innocent and they need to be protected by the adults around them."

Along with a universal belief in childhood innocence and the necessity of adults to act in children's best interest, my students also had little appreciation of children's capacities. For the most part they wrote that children would do and believe whatever their parents taught them. Elizabeth, for instance, argued, "religions were practiced the exact same way [across generations] . . . because of the mimicking children do." While Elizabeth was certain that children could understand more than adults usually acknowledged, she was also clear, although less overt in her argument, that they did nothing original, creative, or of their own making with that understanding. Child-rearing literature that talks of parental modeling and media outlets that inform us all that children are impressionable beings in constant need of adult care and surveillance reinforce Elizabeth's and her classmates, shared assumptions. These everyday reminders of who children are supposedly, are buttressed by legal decisions that do not recognize children's consent as legally binding and that privilege parental desires over those of young people.

With little evidence to counter these adult statements about children, my students had no means of entre into thinking about children as stakeholders who are actively engaging in the world around them. To point out the gap in my students' understanding, I asked them, "Why are you here? If children only mirror adults' religious beliefs and practices why not simply study the adults?" The students had no answers. My answer to them was that children not only parrot adults, they also push adults to new understandings; they don't just mimic adult actions, they also create meaningful rituals of their own.

It took fourteen weeks for me to convince my students that the work scholars are doing to "let the subaltern speak," as Spivak says, is important and useful, not as a means to control children, but as a means to free them from the constraints of societal assumptions (Spivak, 1988). These studies allow adults to see the agency children already have in the world and work to give them a seat at the decision-making table, particularly when their present and their future is at stake.

To move in this direction I had to get my students to shift their thinking from the ideal or imagined child and childhood, to actual children who are currently living in this world where they negotiate friendships, navigate their neighborhoods, and find a place for themselves in their churches and schools. None of these tasks are simple. Nor can adults accomplish them on children's behalf. So, I pushed the students to think of the children they knew both ordinary and extraordinary—who run through sprinklers, suffer from cancer, preach at their church, have children of their own, start protest movements small and large, and yes, even murder.

All of these children challenge the stereotype of the mimicking, innocent child. All of these examples display children's knowledge and capabilities rather than emphasize their deficiencies. To look at religions from the perspectives of actual children, I asked my students to adopt some of the recent child-centered approaches to ritual and belief. To do so, they had to contend with the fact that children are simultaneously theoretical and actual beings, both current participants in religious life and placeholders for the future of communities. The contributions of children stem as much, if not more, from their current standing as from the adult believers they will become.

Many of these most recent efforts to attempt to view religious traditions from children's points of view have been informed by work spurred by the U.N. Convention on the Rights of the Child. Although the U.S. has not signed the convention, it has promoted a great deal of work in Europe seeking to access children's thoughts on politics and education. Under Article 12, the Convention insists that courts and political agencies solicit the children's opinions about policies that will affect them. The U.N. Convention and its attendant scholarship challenges the assumptions articulated by my students by stressing the ways in which children participate capably in the world around them, rather than simply live innocently in a world apart. Instead of ending discussions about children with the sentiment that their desires with respect to serious adult topics will forever be obscured—because of power differentials between children and adults or the inabilities of children to understand the world in which they live—researchers in signatory countries have begun to seek ways to provide children with the support and information necessary to make informed decisions.

Traditionally the work conducted in childhood studies, both in the United States and in Europe has centered on children in schools, court houses, streets, and shopping centers, almost everywhere except churches, synagogues, temples, and other places of religious engagement. For instance, substantial volumes such as *The Children's Culture Reader* (1998) and *An Introduction to Childhood Studies* (2004) make no significant references to religion. That does not mean, however, that this absence has gone unnoticed. After all, we are all here working to understand children's roles in religion.

Using a child-centered approach to religion in which scholars listen to children and attend to the complicated situations that they negotiate today and have negotiated in the past—in their schools, homes, places of worship, and elsewhere—has seemed threatening to many scholars and believers alike that I have encountered because it reveals the limited amount of control adults have over children's lives and acknowledges children's agency in the world. It has been a struggle to apply this approach to research with children in the arena of religion where discussions of children coincide most frequently with ideas of socialization and the transmission of a static, sometimes God-given, culture, rather than of creation and innovation.

In terms of religion, as American religious historian, Robert Orsi emphasizes, "Children signal the vulnerability and contingency of a particular religious world, and of religion itself" (p. 77). Along with exposing the fragility of sacred worlds many believers understand to be secure, it seems that children's religion has struggled to be included in academia because adults tend to see childhood as a transitory phase meant to prepare young people for the world they will encounter as teens and adults. If this view of childhood is true, then childhood is a time of acquiring culture, but not using it.

In this chapter, I use two snapshots from my research, one with Catholic first communicants and the other with evangelical youth, as well as work done by historians using similar theoretical approaches, to counter these assumptions. I argue that analyzing children's lived religion enriches current understandings of religious traditions on the level of individual ritual and local community as well as on the level of theory and meta-narrative. Although my examples may seem disparate, together they illumine the potential transformations that including young peoples' religious practice from a child-centered perspective might cause in the study of religion as well as in religious education.

The following examples demonstrate how focusing on children's religion forced me to wrestle with the importance of attending to the material qualities of religion and how critical it is to acknowledge children as co-creators of their traditions, rather than measure their practices against established adult norms. Finally, these examples reveal how children's practices go beyond maintaining parallel youth congregations to help to constitute the religious, social, and political world for people of all ages.

CHILDREN AS CURRENT PRACTITIONERS, NOT THE FUTURE GENERATION

Adopting a child-centered approach is quite difficult because to be child-centered means to see children's worlds, as much as possible, as they are or as they were. Thus scholars must account for differentials in power, vocabulary, and experiences between themselves and their young consultants. Moreover, researchers must contend with the ways in which children always point toward tomorrow. Like my students, Americans of all ages typically view young people with an eye toward the future, toward the knowledgeable and capable adults we hope they will become. For instance, when I asked nine-year-old Alison what it was like to take the Eucharist three months after her First Communion, she replied, "[I]t's like a memory to me . . . of when I was a kid."

Surprised by this answer, I inquired further, "So you're not so much of a kid now?" "Well, kind of," she said hesitatingly, as if she wasn't sure she how to put what she felt into words. So I tried one more question: "How do you think you're different now?" "I used to not know a lot of stuff about the Church, but I do now." "Kid" for Alison and for many adults was strongly correlated with not just innocence, but also ignorance. This ignorance, of course, is facilitated by adults who withhold information from children, often under the auspices of protecting them. In so doing, the adult congregation created in Alison and her classmates a sense that, although they felt they belonged in their religious community, they were not true members of their church.

While some might claim that this stance is particular to Catholicism and other traditions that delay full participation, virtually all churches discuss children as "the next generation" of believers. Thus, congregations position young people as future, rather than current, practitioners of their traditions even as they actively engage in Sunday school and services, even if it is just to protest their forced presence in these places. Despite their often obvious efforts to embrace, thwart, or transform their communities' traditions, young people are overlooked in practice and in scholarship because of the overwhelming concern with childhood as a time to build the skills children will need for "real life." Of course, however, children currently live a real life and all of us are in some sort of transitory phase—assistant professors moving to full, young couples becoming parents, older adults preparing for retirement.

Nonetheless, when discussing children, the developmental trajectory seems to overshadow other ways of analyzing the interactions that parents, religious educators, scholars, and peers have with young people. As a result, the bulk of scholarship on children in religious studies has sought to understand how religious traditions socialize children into their communities—sometimes centering on the ethical issues surrounding a tradition's stance on childhood and other times working to discover the best practices of rearing the next generation of believers.

Studies on the religious formation of children emphasize the complicated interplay between theology and lived religion. This work has been a springboard for more child-focused work in pastoral theology (Miller-McLemore, 2003; Mercer, 2005; May and Posterski, 2005) and church history (Horn et al., 2009; Bakke, 2005), as well as for the more collaborative works, such as those generated by previous conferences. These approaches reveal new and important information about adult concerns surrounding children and their faith (often leading to the posing of fruitful new theological questions).

Many studies continue to underplay the ways in which young people shape their beliefs as they enact and create religious practices in their everyday lives. Developmental psychologist Chris Boyatzis and others, however, are working to explore how children are co-creators of their religious traditions, working both with and against their many caregivers to navigate their own spiritual path (2003, 2006a, 2006b). In his recent work, Boyatzis (2011) studies parent-child conversations about faith, attending to the way children both influence parents' thinking on religion and are influenced by it. Although these studies on the religious formation of children offer readers an opportunity to hear children's voices; these voices are heard primarily in the service of adult concerns, particularly the concern that children flourish within their parents' faith. We have much more to learn about what young people do with what they learn from their engagement with their religious communities, friends, and the media.

Christian Smith's monumental survey National Study of Youth and Religion (2001–2010) offered a glimpse at young peoples' perceptions of their religious practices. Using teens' answers to survey questions about how they create and live out their religious beliefs, Smith and others in his research team were able to challenge many assumptions about a growing distance between teens' religious practices and those of their parents, as well as revealing teens' belief in Moralistic Therapeutic Deism. In these areas and others, the survey opens up many promising areas for more sustained and in-depth research that might continue to re-shape religious studies.

Pushing the interest in children and religion further would mean shifting from an adult-centered research design, like the one used by Smith, to a child-centered one. This shift would entail allowing teens to construct the survey themselves. Religious studies scholar Ruqquay Khan demonstrated the differing results researchers can achieve by using or excluding children from the survey design process in her recent work with high school students in Bosnia Herzegovina. Khan worked with Muslim students in Bosnia on an open-ended pilot survey and then used those responses to construct some of her forced-choice answers for the larger multiple-choice survey (Khan, 2011).

Comparing the questions on which she used the student feedback and those she did not revealed areas of inquiry that had been obscured primarily because the survey questions came solely from a place of adult concern or curiosity. Referring to an adult-centered question on interreligious interaction, she stated, "given the recent history of war and genocide in the region, I, as an adult scholar of religion, deemed it salient and significant to poll Bosniak students on their relations with members of other faiths, but maybe Bosniak *youth* do *not* perceive their Catholic or Orthodox or Jewish peers in terms of the 'other.'" Unfortunately, creating this question without the children's input means we will not know how these young people define themselves or use religion to make community.

Khan's child-centered work demonstrated, for instance, that young Bosniaks viewed their Muslim identity primarily in terms of pride and ethics rather than the actions and beliefs the adult survey creators had originally assumed (Khan, 2011). Had Khan chosen not to involve the children in the survey creation questions reflecting emotions and values would have been absent and the key areas of the youth's interest in their own religion would have been ignored.

Even with the wonderful work that has come from the National Study of Youth and Religion, we are still left to wonder how might the questions and the answers the children developed from their own sense of the key issues in religious practice, for instance, compliment and challenge the ones asked in a survey in which religiosity is defined by adults. What would a child-centered survey reveal about young people's definitions of religion, tradition-specific practices, and theological questions? While few surveys like this have been conducted, scholars have been working to include not only children's voices in their discussions of religion, but also children's input in the design and implementation of the studies that center on them.

For my part, I have sought to explore questions about how children create and interpret their religious worlds using the tools provided by anthropology, folklore, and childhood studies. Coming from this perspective, my work differs from the pioneering work done in childhood and religion by Marcia Bunge, Christian Smith, and others because I am not concerned with the children's religious or spiritual development. Instead I come to issues of children and religion convinced by much of the childhood studies work done outside of religious studies that demonstrates children's abilities to use the knowledge they glean from both adults and peers to shape their religious beliefs and practices.

I wonder what it would mean if we took seriously the position posed in Article 14 of the U.N. Convention on the Rights of the Child which states that "state parties shall respect the right of the child to freedom of thought, conscience, and religion" (U.N. Convention, 1989). While many conservative groups in the U.S. are outspoken in their opposition to the Convention and any other political action that "might give children the right to object to their parents' religious beliefs or training" (Blanchfield, 2009), children do, of course object as well as conform to their parents' religious beliefs and training, whether or not adults choose to recognize it.

Letting children speak for themselves carries the risk of undermining many of our assumptions about young people, childhood, and the role of adults in relation to both. But then, it is these very assumptions that should be challenged. Whether the U.S. ever signs the convention, the conversation it engenders has forced many to see that children's religious practices and understandings matter now.

Between 1997 and 2001 I attempted to hear children's perspectives on religious practice and how they were simultaneously informed by what adult taught them and transforming those teachings to meet their own needs. I spent four years immersed in an ethnographic project with seven, eight and nine year-old Catholics in North Carolina as they prepared for and celebrated their First Communion.

To hear what the children said about their experiences with the wine and the host, I had to maintain a child-centered approach throughout my research. I analyzed and wrote about my interviews with the children using my fieldwork to help me understand the interpretations that the young people shared. Before coming to any tentative conclusions, I asked what had they been told by teachers, parents, friends, siblings, the media, and the marketplace about the issues we were discussing. Then I tried to bring only this information to bear on my analysis in my book, *When I was a Child* (Bales, 2005).

For a researcher to remain in a child-centered mindset once she leaves "the field," I soon learned was not the norm. While transcripts are full of children's views, as childhood-studies scholars Pia Christensen and Alison James note, they are "generally analyzed and interpreted in terms of more abstract questions, which as a rule, reflect the beliefs and priorities of the researchers, rather than the children" (Christensen and James, 2008).

As I worked to put the children's priorities before mine, it became clear that the host, far from being a bland piece of bread, seemed to be the receptacle of the children's thoughts about transubstantiation. A child's comment that the host tasted like cardboard, when taken out of context, might be viewed as another example of a "the cute things kids say" moment. However, when put in the context of the great degree of anticipation that the child had about how *consecrated* bread would taste, the comment might be understood to express unfulfilled expectations and tremendous disappointment that Jesus's body did not taste like something more delicious and magical—these children approached transubstantiation as a sensual rather than an intellectual experience.

For adults, who have received the Eucharist hundreds of times, the sensual aspect is often less pronounced, and seems insignificant. However, the attention the children give to the taste, texture, and the cultural meaning of the elements reminds scholars of the meaning that these elements give to ritual events. Through drinking wine, in American culture, one becomes an adult. In tasting the host, a mystery is solved. By performing the gestures correctly, one demonstrates the ability to be a part of a religious community.

This work of interpreting the religious world from a child-centered perspective can be fruitful for historians as well as ethnographers. Religious studies scholar, Philipa Koch's work with Puritan children's literature, for instance, exemplifies what applying this theory to historical sources can reveal (Koch, 2011). In her re-examination of this much studied realm, Koch attempted to analyze these stories using only the information about theology and society that children of the period would have possessed. She sifted through the documents created by both the adult authors and contemporary scholars demonstrating the adults' many investments in this material. The authors hoped to shape Puritan children to live in a Calvinist world centered on predestination, while later scholars sought to demonstrate the progress of their brand of Christianity over and against the dark days of Puritanism.

Viewing these sources apart from these adult concerns, Koch offers a convincing reading of this literature as a source of hope and help to the children who read them, rather than the typical modern read which casts these sources as another indication of the abuses of Puritan childhood. Although the children's voices were not literally audible in this study, nor are they easily heard in any child-centered work, this archival study emphasizes the new discoveries that can be made when researchers work carefully to understand the networks within which children's interpretations of their religious lives are created and attempt to see those lives (and hear those stories) from the children's perspective.

These networks developed from inter-personal relationships, the exchange of information, and, importantly, emotional connections to visual culture as well as adult co-religionists and peers. The importance of these sensual and emotional aspects of ritual and religious education may change over time, lessening for those children who continue to practice and serving as a touchstone, perhaps, for those who leave the church.

CHILDHOOD CHOICES AND THE CONSTRUCTION OF RELIGIOUS PRACTICE

Some innovations of childhood practice, however, may be sustained across the lifespan. The lasting influence of childhood practice became clear to me as I listened to interviews I had done with evangelical children and their families about how they use Focus on the Family's prescriptive literature. In this case it was attending to the disjuncture that I noticed between the children's and their parent's answers that made me question what a child-centered study of religion might reveal about established theories in the study of American religion.

When I asked thirteen-year-old Rose and ten-year-old Chip what made their Evangelical Christian family different than other families, for instance, Rose began to answer by explaining that her family prayed together and her parents monitored what she watched on television. Then, Chip quickly shifted from his family to the public school he attends outside Philadelphia, Pennsylvania. He explained that "the different religions are a big part of our school, for me, in my class a lot of kids don't have any religion at all. The most common thing that I've heard about is a kid with a Jewish dad and a Christian mom and they celebrate both, but really they celebrate nothing. Yeah, people have different names for themselves, the 'Christian Kids' and the 'Jew Crew.'"

Rose continued, "[Although kids of each religion mostly stick together], I am friends with the really dedicated Jewish kids. So there is sort of a separation [based on] the levels of practice." Then her brother jumped in explaining that these divisions disappeared to some extent on the sports field where children of all religions were members of the same team. Chip and Rose's mother, Tina, listened intently as her children described how they navigated their religiously diverse public school.

Moments later, I asked Tina, their mother, what she wanted her children to learn about being Christian. She replied, "[my husband and I both want our children] to really have a relationship with Jesus. And to know that there is something more out there. . . . It's kind of like they are in training now, so that when things do go wrong the things that they've stored up will help them get through these crises, these problems later in life . . . tough times are going to come and they are going to be able to get through those times with their faith." As she answered I began to wonder if she had heard her children discuss the role of their faith in their lives at school.

While Tina's answer looked toward their future struggles with dating, marriage, money, and other adult issues, the children had spent nearly five minutes discussing how they used religion to help them negotiate problems, secure friendship groups, and form their identities currently in their daily lives. Listening to Tina's views about childhood as a training ground and way station prompted me to think about the consequences of overlooking the role of religion in children's present lives, be it the present experienced by children in 2011, 1820, or 1680.

What if we remained as fully in the children's present as possible, carrying with us only the concerns for the future that they expressed to us? How might our understandings of trends in religious practice shift on the institutional and theoretical levels not just on the local and personal ones? I recalled Rose stating that she went to the bar mitzvahs of some of her orthodox Jewish friends. What if we took this seemingly mundane childhood experience seriously?

Given the current understanding of religion in the U.S., these alliances along the lines of religious dedication, rather than affiliation, seem quite normal. In 1988, sociologist Robert Wuthnow wrote *The Restructuring of American Religion,* in which he argued that the conservative/liberal split was more significant than denominational affiliation. In his groundbreaking analysis he attributed this realignment to the important place of social issues, such as abortion, in American culture.

Listening to Rose, however, made me wonder whether studying children's lived religion might have led him to a slightly different conclusion. If, as Wuthnow argues, interreligious marriage had become much more accepted by 1975, this is not only significant for what it tells us about the level of tolerance in adult culture in the U.S., but also significant because of the changes occurring in the lives of American children as a result. Many children for the late-1960s and beyond, unlike their parents before them, were born into an interreligious family or had a friend who was. Thus, their loyalty to denominations might have already been softening. These children and their friends, who grew up to be the adults Wuthnow surveyed, might have been less inclined to see denominational identity as a firm boundary marker because they had deep affection for someone outside of their religious community.

Further, many children, who as adults might have been part of this restructuring, would have been going to public schools like Rose's, which, since the Bible-reading court cases of 1963 and the change in immigration laws in 1965, would have become increasingly religiously diverse. Away from adults who might enforce religious beliefs that dictate converting rather than embracing the "other," these children may have developed inter-religious friendships based on their own decisions about the most salient characteristics in friendships. Having made close bonds outside of their denominations may have made these children look for different markers around which to build their identities than their parents, who most likely grew up in the religiously and ethnically segregated neighborhoods of the 1920s and 30s.

These children, then, as they became adults might have continued to value alliances across religious lines, and to use the identity markers they created in grade school—including, perhaps, level of religious commitment, modesty in dress, taste in music, and acceptable conduct around the opposite gender—to define themselves. Of course, it would take a great deal of work to prove such a theory, but it is certainly plausible that the restructuring of adult religion in America that was noticed in the late 1980s began on the playgrounds of the late-1960s, not by means of division, but through the creation of new social groups.

In many ways, then, Tina, Chip and Rose's mother, is correct: childhood is a time of training for the future, but to some degree that is true of every life stage. It seems, however, that when adults study people their own age they can see how their subjects are both working toward future goals and acting in the present.

Work on children often reveals, however, that adult concern for the future eclipses whatever is happening in the present, both in its findings and in the amount of scholarship done on preparation for the future versus children's daily life. This unexplainable pull toward viewing children as "the next generation," rather than as current participants, leaves many unanswered and undiscovered questions in the field of religious studies.

Following the strands of youth religious practice might push child-centered scholars to move beyond denominational boundaries. In investigating these religious worlds, scholars might discover that the recent trend toward religious hybridity in America, noted by the latest Pew research poll, began with childhood religious practices as children pragmatically pieced together religious traditions that could answer questions and help negotiate problems that their parents and their priests never faced.

American Religions scholar, Kristy Nabhan-Warren's work with Latino gang members is instructive here (Nabhan-Warren, 2011). These cholos and cholas frequently witness, and sometimes commit, murder and live in the midst of great family and financial stress. Many of these young people state that they joined the gang because the members are supportive and loyal in ways that their families are not.

Surprisingly, perhaps, the Cholas told Nabhan-Warren that the only people more loyal than their homies were Jesus and Mary. Nabhan-Warren's analysis of the religious lives of these gang members argues that working with youth necessitates letting go of one's presuppositions about both adolescents and religious practice. Otherwise, the hybrid religious worlds that teens actively create and inhabit are obscured. This community of teenage gang members, for instance, seemed to transform the Eucharistic theology of Jesus's actual presence to give meaning to their tattoos of Jesus and the Virgin Mary, tattoos that allowed these guardian/sacred figures to be physically present in the teenagers daily lives. For Nabhan-Warren, accepting the teens' definitions of "sacred" meant attending to tattoos, violence, and pressured sexual encounters with as much care as they attend to the sacraments of the Catholic Church. Otherwise, scholars will miss some of what the teens see as their most important avenues of religious expression.

To understand the effects of young peoples' choices in friends as well as religious practices, scholars need to do all they can to view these worlds as the children do, to respect the decisions the children make, to learn the meanings that the children give their religious symbols and practices, and to take those meanings seriously. And, not simply weigh them against the traditions' official doctrine to see how children are progressing toward full membership, full adulthood in the community.

Instead, recent work on children and religion has revealed that scholars interested in child-centered views of religions need to put equal, if not greater weight, on material expressions of religion over the theological or some might say "spiritual" aspects of it. As we have seen, the religion of young people has a dynamic quality to it that seems to be less pronounced in adult lived religion.

Sometimes contrary to adult desires, children do more than imitate the older generations' practices. Children sort through the networks of support and influence in their lives in an attempt to find meaningful ways to express their religious beliefs and to develop practices that synthesize adult teachings with their own interpretations and needs. We realize that the meaning of a sip of wine is not the same for an adult as it is for an American child in a Catholic Church. Similarly, understanding premarital sex from the perspective of these gang members transforms this traditionally sinful act into what they feel is a Christ-like sacrifice that unites their community to each other and to God.

REFERENCES

Anderson, Priscilla. "Researching Children's Rights to Integrity." In *Children's Childhoods: Observed and Experienced,* edited by Berry Mayall. Washington, D.C.: The Flamer Press, 1994, 33–44.

Bado-Fralick, Nikki and Norris, Rebecca. *Toying with God: The World of Religious Games and Dolls.* Waco, TX: Baylor University Press, 2010.

Bakke, Odd Magne. *When Children Became People: The Birth Of Childhood In Early Christianity.* Brian McNeil, trans. Minneapolis: Fortress Press, 2005.

Bales, Susan Ridgely. *When I Was a Child: Children's Interpretations of First Communion.* Chapel Hill: The University of North Carolina Press, 2005.

Bartkowski, John P. "Spare the Rod . . . or Spare the Child? Divergent Perspectives on Conservative Protestant Child Discipline." *Review of Religious Research* 37, no. 2 (1995): 97–116.

Bartkowski, John P., and Christopher G. Ellison. "Discipline and Cherish: Conservative Protestant Perspectives on Children and Parenting." In *Children and Childhood in American Religions,* edited by Don S. Browning and Bonnie J. Miller-McLemore. New Brunswick, N.J.: Rutgers University Press, 2009, 42–55.

Bartkowski, John P., and W. Bradford Wilcox. Conservative Protestant Child Discipline: The Case of Parental Yelling. *Social Forces* 79, no.1 (2000): 265–290.

Blanchfield, Luisa. "The United Nations Convention on the Rights of the Child: Background and Policy Issues" (Congressional Research Service, December 2, 2009).

Bluebond-Langner, Myra. *The Private Worlds of Dying Children.* Princeton, NJ: Princeton University Press, 1978.

Boyatzis, Chris. "Agency, Voice, and Maturity in Children's Religious and Spiritual Development. In *Children and Religion: A Methods Handbook.* Edited by Susan B. Ridgely. New York: University Press. 2011, 19–32.

———."Unraveling the Dynamics of Religion in the Family and Parent-Child Relationships" [Special issue]. *The International Journal for the Psychology of Religion* 16, no. 4 (2006a).

———. Dollahite, D. C., & Marks, L. D. "The Family as a Context for Religious and Spiritual Development in Children and Youth." In *The Handbook of Spiritual Development in Childhood and Adolescence,* eds. Eugene C. Roehlkepartain, Pamela E. King, Linda Wagener, & Peter L. Benson (2006b). 297–309.

———.and Janicki, D. Parent-Child Communication about Religion: Survey and Diary Data on Unilateral Transmission and Bi-Directional Reciprocity Styles. *Review of Religious Research* 44, (2003): 252–270.

Bunge, Marcia, ed. *The Child in Christian Thought.* Grand Rapids: William B. Eerdmans Publishing, 2001.

Calvert, Karen. *Children in the House: The Material Culture of Early Childhood, 1600–1900.* Boston: Northeastern University Press, 1992.

Capps, Donald. *The Child's Song: The Religious Abuse of Children.* Louisville: Westminster John Knox Press, 1995.

Christensen, and James, A. eds. *Research with Children.* London: Routledge, 2008.

Fowler, James. *Stages of Faith: The Psychology of Human Development and the Quest for Meaning.* San Francisco: Harper and Row, 1981.

"Convention on the Rights of the Child," (accessed August 7, 2013) http://treaties.un.org/Pages/ViewDetails.aspx?mtdsg_no=IV-11&chapter=4&lang=en

Greven, Philip. *The Protestant Temperament: Patterns of Child-Rearing, Religious Experience, and the Self in Early America.* New York: Alfred A. Knopf, 1977.

———. *Spare the Child: the Religious Roots of Punishment and the Psychological Impact of Physical Abuse.* New York: Alfred A. Knopf, 1991.

James, Allison, Chris Jenks, and Alan Prout. *Theorizing Childhood.* New York: Teachers College Press, 1998.

James, Allison and Alan Prout. *Constructing and Reconstructing Childhood: Contemporary Issues in the Sociological Study of Childhood.* London: Falmer Press, 1997.

Jenkins, Henry, ed. *The Children's Culture Reader.* New York: New York University Press, 1998.

Jenks, Chris. *Childhood.* New York: Routledge, 1996.

Koch, Phillipa. "God Made this Fire for Our Comfort: Puritan Children's Literature in Context." In *Children and Religion: A Methods Handbook*, edited by Susan B. Ridgely. New York: New York University Press, 2011.

May, Scottie and Beth Posterski. *Children Matter: Celebrating their Place in the Church, Family, and Community.* Grand Rapids, MI: Wm. B. Eerdmans Publishing, 2005.

Mayall, Berry ed. *Children's Childhoods Observed and Experienced.* Washington, D.C.: The Falmer Press, 1994.

Mercer, Joyce Ann. *Welcoming Children: A Practical Theology of Childhood.* St. Louis, MO: Chalice Press, 2005.

Miller-McLemore, Bonnie J. *Let the Children Come: Re-imagining Childhood from a Christian Perspective.* San Francisco: Jossey Bass, 2003.

———. and Don S. Browning. *Children and Childhood in American Religion.* New Brunswick, N.J.: Rutgers University Press, 2009.

Mintz, Steven. *Huck's Raft: A History of American Childhood.* Cambridge, MA: Harvard University Press, 2004.

Nabhan-Warren, Kristy. "What Mexican American Gang Members Can Teach Us About Researching and Writing About Religion." In *Children and Religion: A Methods Handbook* edited by Susan B. Ridgely. New York: New University Press, 2011.

Nandy, Ashis. "Reconstructing Childhood: A Critique of the Ideology of Adulthood." In *Traditions, Tyranny and Utopias: Essays in the Politics of Awareness.* Delhi: Oxford University Press, 1987.

Orsi, Robert A. "Material Children: Making God's Presence Real for Catholic Boys and Girls and for the Adults in Relation to Them." In *Between Heaven and Earth: The Religious Worlds People Make and the Scholars Who Study Them.* Princeton: Princeton University Press, 2005.

Palmer, Susan J. and Charlotte E. Hardman, eds. *Children in New Religions.* New Brunswick and London: Rutgers University Press, 1999.

Ridgely, Susan B., ed. *Children and Religion: A Methods Handbook.* New York: New York University Press, 2011.

Roehlkepartain, Eugene C., Pamela E. King, Linda Wagener, & Peter L. Benson (eds.). *The Handbook of Spiritual Development in Childhood and Adolescence.* Thousand Oaks, CA: Sage, 2006.

Smith, Christian with Melissa Lundquist Denton. *Soul-Searching: The Religious and Spiritual Lives of American Teenagers.* Oxford and New York: Oxford University Press, 2005.

Spivak, Gayatri. "Can the Subaltern Speak?" *Marxism and the Interpretation of Culture*, (1988): 271–313.

Wilcox, Brad. *Soft Patriarchs and New Men: How Christianity Shapes Fathers and Husbands.* Chicago, IL: University of Chicago Press, 2004.

Wuthnow, Robert. *Growing Up Religious.* Boston: Beacon Press, 1999.

Wuthnow, Robert. *The Restructuring of American Religion: Society and Faith Since World War II.* Princeton: Princeton University Press, 1988.

Yust, Karen Marie and Eugene C. Roehikeartain. *Real Kids, Real Faith: Practices for Nurturing Children's Spiritual Lives.* San Francisco: Jossey-Bass, 2004.

Yust, Karen-Marie, Aostre Johnson, Sandy Sasso, and Eugene Roehlkepartain, eds. *Nurturing Child and Adolescent Spirituality: Perspectives from the World's Religious Traditions.* Lanham, MD: Rowman and Littlefield Publishers, 2006.

SECTION TWO

Engaging Parents and Congregations

Chapter 7

Re-Forming a Kingdom Worldview
Exploring Spirituality with Families Through the Christian Church Year

Trevecca Okholm

Those of us who have served in church ministry long enough have been witnesses to a monumental paradigm shift for ministry with children, youth and families. From the waning years of the twentieth century to the dawning of the twenty-first we have paddled fast to keep up with the bombardment of cultural values that have buoyed the evangelical church along with the shifting tide of secularization.

An examination of the spiritual lives of the children, youth and families that make up many North American congregations demonstrates the influence of a culture saturated with consumerism, individualism, rights and entitlements, confusion over marriage, and the breakdown of community relationships. One might say that too many of the families in our church communities are *dis–oriented, dis–tracted and dis–integrating* despite our best ministry practices. The best practices of the twentieth century that seemed to serve us so well are proving impotent in the face of the current North American cultural ethos.

In order to begin to understand this monumental paradigm shift in families and in ministry, perhaps we need to begin with a brief historical overview and a couple of questions: (1) When did the church begin to *accommodate* the surrounding culture? and, (2) In what ways has a secular worldview formed us more profoundly than a *Christian* worldview?

By the mid-twentieth century, North America had successfully moved out of WWII with new prosperity, a new rise in technology with new media influences we had never encountered before, new theories in human development, influences from the social sciences, and educational expectations including age-segregated classrooms and age-appropriate curriculum. The local church no longer found itself in the favored position of impacting and influencing the surrounding culture but rather found itself competing with the cultural ethos for the hearts, minds, and attention even of the *non*-nominal Christians.

This historical paradigm shift in the culture also brought a plethora of ministry shifts in the way the church functioned within the surrounding culture. These paradigm shifts are explored at length by Thomas Bergler (2012) and C. Ellis Nelson (2008). However, for our purposes in this chapter we will deal primarily with: (1) a shift away from the parent's role as spiritual educators in the home and, (2) the formation—or lack of formation—of a biblical worldview *lens* through which we see ourselves and the surrounding culture.

One result of the mid-twentieth century's new prosperity, new theories in human development, and influences from the social sciences on the way the church competed with and at times accommodated the surrounding culture has been to take spiritual formation out of the hands of the parents and give it to *professionals,* which included directly or indirectly *selling* the perspective that Christian education could be done best with flashy, well-designed, age-appropriate and age-segregated, published curriculum.

Another result of church accommodation has been the shift from a *Christian* worldview to a more secularly influenced view of life. In other words we have inadvertently trained many parishioners to view Scripture through a consumerist, individualistic perspective. By the last few decades of the twentieth century the cultural accommodation by the church had unintentionally convinced parents that their responsibility was only to get their children and youth to the church building where *professional church educators and youth ministers* would do it for them.

The church had, inadvertently, *dis–integrated* the family even as the church and the para–church organizations struggled to hold the family together. Show me a church with a state-of-the-art youth and children's facility and highly visible trained staff and I'll show you too many young people walking away from faith. (For more in depth research on this phenomenon see: Bergler (2012); Smith and Denton (2009); Kinnaman (2011).

The good news is that "after decades of departmentalizing and compartmentalizing members of the family, the church [realized] that maybe it was time to start putting the family back together again," (Penner, 2003). A 1998 Barna survey discovered that 85 percent of Christian parents agreed that the spiritual nurture of their children is their job, but most also agreed that they felt inadequately prepared for the task, primarily due to the church's emphasis on specialized children and student ministries resplendent with all the latest curriculum and technology prepared to accomplish what Scripture had clearly commanded parents to do.

For the purposes of this chapter, we will now narrow our focus to practical ways that parents might be equipped and empowered by the church in this new cultural context to *re-integrate* the *dis-integrating* family, *re-align* and find balance for *distracted* lives, and *re-orient* their vision as witnesses to God's Kingdom—the practices of *seeing* life through the lens of the historical, biblical narrative.

RE-INTEGRATION: RE-MEMBERING OUR FAITH FAMILY

Integrity and integration are key components for healthy families and healthy churches and for a healthy witness to a longing world. A myriad of books, articles, surveys and studies attest to the fact that in order to *re-member* who we are as the family of God that witnesses to an individualized culture that pulls us apart, the church must be more intentional and keenly focused on this integration of ages, stages and styles, mission, and service.

However, integration is more than simply putting generations together for worship and service; to truly become authentic in our witness our integration dare not neglect the integrity of our historical metanarrative. As the church became an accommodation of the surrounding culture, we allowed ourselves and our church's children to be formed outside of that *historically informed Christian metanarrative*, risking the free-floating insecurity so prevalent in our nation today which lacks a sense of transcendent identity, purpose and direction.

By integrating Christian worship, our Christian mission, and the intentional nurture of our children within an integrated narrative greater than ourselves, we begin to form and *re-form* a community that transcends current media trends: we are held by and developed into the sort of people who are so very much needed in God's Kingdom. Although media and neo-church leaders want us to believe it, authenticity is not about the latest and newest and far removed from the "boring" past. Authenticity is *really* about something that is authoritative *and* something that has passed the test of time.

For most people worshiping in North American churches today, it is not that they actually reject the traditions, rituals and rites of passage that have existed in the church down through the centuries and have the integral power to hold us together; it is more an issue of not *understanding* the authenticity of the church's historical traditions and rituals, *why* the church has done these things and *what* bearing these things have, or should have, on our current life situation (Okholm, 2012).

So practically speaking, the parent's and the church's mandate is to: (1) integrate families and all generations into the metanarrative of the historical church practices; (2) train folks to understand why the church does what it does and how the church practices allow God's people to transcend the cultural habits that too readily form us; and (3) become formed by a different way of life and an alternative order of living. The festivals and celebrations of our Christian church year, the holy days, the liturgical seasons, the liturgy of worship and the ways in which we explain all of these to our children and youth are vital in helping families to see through a Kingdom-of-God worldview lens.

The *liturgical season* is a cyclical movement through all the biblical text—a rehearsal of the long story of God's actions in the world. (Note: *liturgy* is defined as *the work—or duty—of the people.* It comes from the Greek words *leitos* (meaning *people*) and *ergo* (meaning *to do*). Using a form of *liturgy* for our church worship service engages all present, involving folks in the *work* of worship which gives purpose and responsibility for our corporate worship as opposed to worship as a "spectator" sport in which we simply show up (too often unprepared) to be entertained by the "performers" for a *consumerist* model of worship that has taken over many of our evangelical churches in our North American culture, feeding our consumerist worldview.

Worshipping regularly as a family with all generations and finding out for ourselves as we train our children to understand *why we do what we do* helps us to know that we belong to something greater than the here and now. With today's American families so isolated from the extended family and its heritage, belonging to and connecting with a faith tradition and community takes on a radical importance in giving us and our children the ability to develop our identity, purpose and direction (Okholm, 2007).

RE-ORIENTATION: LEARNING TO SEE FAMILY LIFE THROUGH THE LENS OF THE BIBLICAL NARRATIVE

Not long ago on PBS, I watched a documentary by Ian Cheney about the effects of light pollution on humans and nature. For one example, *The City Dark* gave statistics on huge number of migrating birds that increasingly lose their navigational orientation and as a result, they fly into buildings. Another example pointed out newly hatched sea turtles that are so disoriented by the light pollution of city lights they are drawn toward them and away from the safe haven of their ocean home. In their disorientation they are easy prey, their survival dependent upon knowing where they belong and how to arrive at that destination. In a very real way, the survival of our Christian community is dependent upon knowing where we belong (our identity, our tribe), and on knowing our Christian story, even as the cultural *light pollution* disorients us and tries to pull us into a different worldview.

This all came to light for me as I began to read and listen to the messages of Bartholomew and Goheen (2004). Their book *The Drama of Scripture* reminded me that

> . . . human communities live out some story that provides a context for understanding the meaning of history and gives shape and direction to their lives. If we allow the Bible to become fragmented, it is in danger of being absorbed into whatever other story is shaping our culture, and it will thus cease to shape our lives as it should. (12)

And so I have asked myself if over the past twenty plus years as a Christian educator whether I have been guilty of fragmenting the Bible? Have our wonderful and developmentally appropriate curriculum publishers done the same? Not only that, but have we inadvertently created a personal reality in which to live out our faith? In trying to make a "life application," have I worked too hard to fit God's Kingdom message into my *personal faith* and *personal devotions* so that my *personal growth* becomes my highest goal? According to Novelli:

> In the past several decades Protestant churches in America have highlighted an individual and personal faith which points toward personal devotions, personal evangelism, and personal growth as benchmarks. This way of thinking contributes to the idea that 'God is a part of *my* story.'" (Novelli, 2008)

In the 78th Psalm, a writer named Asaph, David's music director and author of twelve of our biblical Psalms, spends seventy-two verses retelling the history and the story of the Jewish nation from the time of slavery in Egypt to David's reign. It was told over and over to each generation of the Hebrew people so they would not forget God and make the same mistakes as their ancestors. Asaph begins this historic psalm with this admonition:

> 1 My people, listen to my teaching.
> Pay attention to what I say.
> 2 I will open my mouth and tell stories.
> I will speak about things that were hidden.
> They happened a long time ago.
> 3 We have heard about them and we know them.
> Our people who lived before us have told us about them.
> 4 We won't hide them from our children.
> We will tell them to those who live after us.
> We will tell them about what the Lord has done that is worthy of praise.
> We will talk about his power and the wonderful things he has done. (Psalm 78: 1–4 NLT)

What was his purpose?

> The psalmist, Asaph, was calling the people to make a *trans–generational* commitment (verses 3–4) to remember the stories of faithfulness from their ancestors in the family of God and bind them to the present and future generations so they would know their identity and begin to think like a family member of God's Kingdom. (Kang and Perrott, 2009)

The church is responsible to encourage parents to read and reread the stories of faith with their children at home. One of the effects of reading, telling, re–reading and re–telling the biblical stories is the powerful way they speak to the human situation even in the midst of the twenty-first century North American context and to our common human condition in each generation. As I read and re–read the stories of Joshua or Judges or Kings, I am reminded of the truth of 2 Timothy:

> All Scripture is inspired by God and is useful to teach us what is true and to make us realize what is wrong in our lives. It corrects us when we are wrong and teaches us to do what is right. God uses it to prepare and equip his people to do every good work. (2 Tim 3:16, 17 NLT)

The good news for church ministry and families today is the plethora of new *storied* texts that are becoming available for home as well as church use. Among my favorites are: *The Jesus Storybook Bible* by Sally Lloyd–Jones (Zondervan, 2007); Walter Wangerin's *Book of God* (Zondervan, 2001); Berryman and Stewart's *Young Children and Worship* (WJK, 1988) and; *Following Jesus* (Geneva, 2000) which incorporates a form of instruction commonly referred to as *Godly Play* (www.godlyplayfoundation.org) and is easily adaptable by parents in the home as well as in church settings.

A paradigm shift that is beginning to take hold in churches and in families is an attitude that more than inviting Jesus into my life, to be a part of my story, I am better oriented by realizing that Jesus invites me, my family and my church community into God's story, into God's light to become a part of God's mission in the world. Reading the biblical narrative together and teaching our children from materials and story-lessons such as those available from the Godly Play Foundation provide a user-friendly means of engaging children of all ages with the biblical story. The Godly Play model uses the powerful tool of "wondering" together. Wondering questions offer a time for reflection based on the experience *of* God rather than on being told *about* God and help us avoid moralizing the story.

For example: rather than "How many times did Noah send out the dove?" or "Why did God send a flood to destroy the world?" we might ask, "I wonder how it felt to be in the ark in all that rain?" or "I wonder if Noah and his family were afraid?" or "I wonder how they felt when they saw the rainbow?" In other words, it is not just remembering facts nor finding a moral, but reliving the experience of God's participation in history. This model is easily accomplished by parents in the home without costly curriculum and training. A testimony to this is the large number of "Godly Play themed" blog sites—mainly from young moms—that are popping up on the internet.

RE-ALIGNMENT: KEEPING OUR BALANCE AND FINDING OUR PURPOSE

Last year on Memorial Day weekend, my husband and I joined a group at St. Andrew's Abbey in Valyermo, California (http://www.valyermo.com). We traveled there to attend an all day talk and poetry reading by an eighty-six-year-old monk named Brother Peter. Brother Peter was born and reared in Mainland China in the early years of the twentieth century. At the age of twelve he entered a Benedictine Monastery, but within a few years all foreigners, including the Belgian monks who ran the monastery, were deported. All of the Chinese Christians who did not swear allegiance to the state-run church were arrested and imprisoned.

From age twenty-nine until his release at age fifty-five, Br. Peter lived in prison. For most of those twenty six years he was allowed no reading or writing materials and spent many months in shackles and, at times, solitary confinement. He mentally composed over six–hundred poems that reflected on his life and his faith. He was not allowed to write them down nor even speak them aloud. Once he did recite a poem aloud and received an additional six-year sentence on top of the twenty years he was already serving.

There was much to impress me about the faith and the life of Br. Peter as I listened to his story that day. But it was a comment on the way that he marked time, remembered his faith, and rehearsed his poems that inspired me most. He was not allowed any books, especially not a Bible, and he was never allowed to write anything down. The only reading material he did receive annually for most of those years was a Chinese calendar. Because Br. Peter had been so indoctrinated with the Christian liturgical calendar in his youth, he was able to remember its rhythm well enough to mentally envision and impose the liturgical seasons and holy days onto the Chinese calendar he was given. He remembered the biblical story through the seasons of the year! He visualized the seasons of waiting: Advent (before Christmas) and Lent (preparing for holy week). He remembered the forty days following Easter up to the Ascension and counted the next ten to reach Pentecost when he secretly celebrated the gift of the Holy Spirit. He rehearsed the stories of faith through the church season that is referred to as Ordinary time and then started anew each year with the season of waiting at Advent.

It was his imposition on the cultural calendar that provided the template for remembering the passage of holy seasons and celebrations. For this reason alone I am reminded of the value of introducing families to the rhythm and balance of the church year calendar. Most evangelical ehurches threw out the church calendar (also called the liturgical calendar) along with the *Catholic bathwater,* and it has been to our detriment. The beauty of intentionally incorporating the church calendar into our daily home life is to celebrate and understand more fully the entire mystery of Jesus Christ, from his incarnation and birth until his ascension, the day of Pentecost, and the expectation of his return in glory.

During the course of a year, the paschal mystery—the passion, death, resurrection, and ascension of Jesus—is viewed from different angles, in different lights. And it has the potential power to *re-member* us to God's Kingdom and *re-form* our families to a sacred ordering of time and place. The Church calendar gives opportunity for us to create intentional traditions, habits and rituals (liturgical living)—giving order, establishing a rhythm of time, and being shaped by God's story. Following a church calendar gives focus and formation of life and purpose rather than simply giving information and inspiration, something a few choice quotes on Facebook might as easily accomplish for us. Below is a very simple model of a church calendar—the one that I have used with kindergarten and early elementary age children for many years.

The Church Year Calendar

Illustratated by Jeremy Searcy©

As you can see, even though it's not in color, the church year begins with the four weeks of Advent "waiting" season (traditionally purple or light blue). The simple act of celebrating the Christian New Year the first Sunday of Advent rather than waiting until the secular celebration on the first of January speaks clearly into our family identity as Christ-followers, not least because January is named for the Roman god *Janus*, the gate-keeper. Go ahead and celebrate the New Year beginning in January, of course, but don't neglect the Christian beginning of a new church year four weeks earlier. As

I've often told the families in my church ministry, Christians are blessed because we celebrate *two* New Year's days!

I tested this calendar last school year reminiscent of the lesson I'd learned from Br. Peter's experience when I was teaching a group of junior kindergarteners in our church's pre-school. After teaching them the stories all school year, in the month of June I pointed again to the big round church calendar on the classroom wall and asked if they could tell me any of the stories we'd learned back in the "green" *ordinary time* weeks of September.

Amazingly they could! They could also remember many of the stories of Advent, and Lent, and Epiphany just by looking at the colored squares on the calendar.

Of course, the most powerful way for families to be *re-aligned* and find rhythm and balance in daily life is to obey the fourth Commandment, "Remember the Sabbath, and keep it holy," (Exodus 20:8). This commandment not only describes how best to live in community in balance and stability, but it also serves as a prescription for the health of the community. If we don't keep the Sabbath as a day of rest from the labors of the other six days, *we will surely die* (Exodus 31: 12–18 and Jeremiah 17:19–27). In other words, if we don't live according to the rhythm of life designed by God we will kill ourselves from the stress (physical, mental and emotional) that comes from living life out of balance! There are a myriad of practical ways to accomplish this in family life (Okholm, 2012). By observing Sabbath in a regular rhythm we are reminding our families to move within a different reality. We are not human beings having occasional spiritual experiences; rather we might learn the reality of being spiritual beings having human experiences.

Defy what the culture dictates. As followers of God, we have a new name, a new identity. We have been chosen and set apart for a holy purpose (1 Peter 2:9–10).

REFERENCES

Barna, George. *The Second Coming of the Church: A Blueprint for Survival.* Nashville: Thomas Nelson, 1998.

Bartholomew, Craig and Goheen, Michael. *The Drama of Scripture: Finding Our Place in the Biblical Story.* Grand Rapids: Baker, 2004.

Bellah, Robert et al. *Habits of the Heart: Individualism and Commitment in American Life.* Berkeley and Los Angeles: University of California Press, 1996.

Bergler, Thomas. *The Juvenilization of American Christianity.* Grand Rapids: Eerdmans, 2012.

Berryman, Jerome and Sonja Stewart. *Young Children in Worship.* Louisville: Westminster John Knox, 1988.

Bolsinger, Tod. *It Takes a Church to Raise a Christian: How the Community of God Transforms Lives.* Grand Rapids: Brazos, 2004.

Castleman, Robbie. *Parenting in the Pew: Guiding Your Children into the Joy of Worship.* Downer's Grove: InterVarsity, 1993 (2002 expanded edition).

Cheney, Ian. (film producer) The City Dark. (2012) http://www.pbs.org/pov/film-files/the-city-dark-fact-sheet_press_file_2.pdf

Claiborne, Okoro, and Wilson–Hartgrove. *Common Prayer: A Liturgy for Ordinary Radicals.* Grand Rapids: Zondervan, 2010.

Clapp, Rodney. *Families at the Crossroads: Beyond Tradition and Modern Options.* Downers Grove: InterVarsity, 1993.

Garland, Diana. *Inside-Out Families: Living the Faith Together.* Baylor: Baylor University Press, 2010.

Garland, Diana. *Sacred Stories of Ordinary Families.* San Francisco: Jossey–Bass, 2003.

Kang, S. Steve and Gary Perrott. *Teaching the Faith, Forming the Faithful: A Biblical Vision for Education in the Church.* Downers Grove: InterVarsity, 2009.

Kang, S. Steve. "When Our Children Become Our Brothers, Sisters, and Friends in God's Household." Priscilla Papers, (Summer, 2009), Vol. 23, No. 3.

Keeley, Robert. *Helping our Children Grow in Faith.* Grand Rapids: Baker, 2008.

Kinnaman, David. *You Lost Me: Why Young Christians are Leaving Church and Rethinking Faith.* Grand Rapids: Baker, 2011.

Lloyd–Jones, Sally. *The Jesus Storybook Bible: Every Story Whispers His Name.* Grand Rapids: ZonderKids, 2007.

Nelson, C. Ellis. *Growing Up Christian: A Congregational Strategy for Nurturing Disciples,* Macon: Smyth and Helwys, 2008.

Novelli, Michael. *Shaped By The Story: Helping Students Encounter God in a New Way.* Grand Rapids: Zondervan/YS, 2008.

Okholm, Dennis. *Monk Habits: Benedictine Spirituality for Everyday People.* Grand Rapids: Brazos, 2007.

Okholm, Trevecca. *Kingdom Family: Re-Envisioning God's Plan for Marriage and Family,* Eugene: Cascade, 2012.

Penner, Marv. *Youth Worker's Guide to Parent Ministry.* Grand Rapids: Zondervan, 2003.

Robinson, David. *The Family Cloister: Benedictine Wisdom for the Home.* New York: Crossroad, 2000.

Smith, Christian and Melina Lundquist Denton. *Soul Searching: The Religious and Spiritual Lives of American Teenagers.* Oxford: Oxford Press, 2009.

Stewart, Sonja. *Following Jesus.* Louisville: Geneva Press, 2000.

Thomas, Gary. *Sacred Marriage: What if God Designed Marriage to Make us Holy More than to Make us Happy?* Grand Rapids: Zondervan, 2000.

Thomas, Gary. *Sacred Parenting: How Raising Children Shapes Our Souls.* Grand Rapids: Zondervan, 2004.

Thompson, Marjorie. *Family as the Forming Center: A Vision of the Role of Family in Spiritual Formation.* Nashville: Upper Room, 1996.

Wangerin, Walter. *The Book of God.* Grand Rapids: Zondervan, 2001.

Chapter 8

Equipping Parents for the Spiritual Formation of their Children

Gary McKnight

Humanity was created *imago dei*, in the image of God, to have fellowship with God, steward his creation, and reflect his likeness in the midst of that creation (Gen 1:26–28). Though the Fall marred that likeness, people still reflect God's image (e.g., Gen 9:6; Jas 3:9). Christ died so that people "should not perish but have eternal life" (John 3:16). Such life, a present possession of those who have trusted Christ (John 5:24), involves restoration of the *imago dei*, progressively in this life (Eph 4:20–24; Col 3:9–10) and fully when they will one day see him face to face (1 John 3:2). God loves all people (John 3:16) and desires that all should come to repentance and eternal life (2 Pet 3:9).

Yes, God loves all people, but it may be argued that he has a special concern for children, a concern that is distinct from the "casual view toward the life or death of children" prevalent in many ancient and some modern cultures (M. S. Lawson, 2011, 79). Not only is God concerned about the physical well-being of children, but he also greatly cares about their spiritual nurture. The institutions and practices designed by God for Israel constituted a detailed and elaborate system to educate and form from childhood those who were to constitute "a kingdom of priests and a holy nation" (Exod 19:6). Peter revealed that God has also made Christians to be

> . . . a chosen race, a royal priesthood, a holy nation, a people for his own possession, that you may proclaim the excellencies of him who called you out of darkness into his marvelous light. (1 Pet 2:9, ESV)

God cares no less today about the spiritual formation of people, ideally beginning in childhood. Spiritual formation of children is to take place in the larger community of faith (Ps 78:1–8). However, God assigns to parents a special role and responsibility in the spiritual nurture of their children (e.g., Deut 6:4–9; Eph 6:1–4).

In this chapter, we will: (a) consider the *need* to equip parents to assist in the spiritual transformation of their children; (b) delineate several *models* for children and family ministry; and, (c) suggest criteria for *evaluation* of efforts to equip parents for the spiritual formation of their children. First, let's consider the definition of *children's spirituality*. The Society for Children's Spirituality: Christian Perspectives offers this working definition:

> Children's spirituality is the child's development of a conscious relationship with God, in Jesus Christ, through the Holy Spirit, within the context of a community of believers that fosters that relationship, as well as the child's understanding of—and response to—that relationship. (K. E. Lawson, 2012, xiv)

A helpful theological definition of *spiritual formation* is:

> our continuing response to the reality of God's grace shaping us into the likeness of Jesus Christ, through the work of the Holy Spirit, in the community of faith, for the sake of the world. (Greenman, 2010, 24)

These and similar definitions emphasize the Trinity, relationship, and the believing community.

THE NEED

Recognition of the need to equip parents to facilitate the spiritual formation of their children grows first and foremost from a biblical and theological perspective. Coulter and Thompson (2011) have noted that "the role that a family plays in the growth, development, and education of children is highly influenced by one's theology, whether intentional or not" (136). Here, we will consider several key themes related to children, families, and faith formation. (*Note*: A complete treatment of the pertinent biblical and theological material is beyond this chapter's scope. Sources worth consulting are: Bunge (2001); Bunge, Fretheim, and Gaventa (2008); and Zuck (1997). Gundry-Volf (2001), M. S. Lawson (2011), and Melick (2011) are briefer treatments that discuss the biblical material within its historical and cultural settings.)

BIBLICAL CONSIDERATIONS CONCERNING CHILDREN AND THEIR SPIRITUAL FORMATION

May, Stemp, and Burns (2012) summarize the place of children in God's story as seen in the Old Testament:

> The Book of Deuteronomy instructs the people of God that children are to be taught to love, obey, and fear the Lord God in the context of life, and are

to assemble with adults to learn the things of God (Deut 6:1–3; 11:18–21; 31:12–13). Other passages describe how children were present with the whole faith community as they stood to hear from God. (p. 242)

Of special note are Deuteromy 6:4–9 and Psalm 78:1–8. The first passage teaches that there is only one God (v. 4) who his people are to love with their entire being (v. 5), keeping God's words in their hearts and diligently teaching their children (vv. 6–7). Parents are to love God passionately and deeply, with the result that they can pass the faith to their children; teaching the children is to be both planned and spontaneous (v. 7), using words (v. 7) and visual reminders (vv. 8–9). Psalm 78 reveals God's plan that parents teach their children who will then reach the next generation, and so on.

Before reviewing Jesus's view of children, the significance of his coming into the world as an infant and growing through childhood to adulthood must be considered. Stonehouse (1998) observed:

> The incarnation affirms the importance of childhood. When "the Word be-came flesh and lived among us" (John 1:14), God did not arrive as a mature adult. No, Jesus came as a baby and lived each phase of childhood. He knew the love and comfort of parents and the fears, sorrows, and joys of a child. (33–34)

The words and actions of Jesus are noteworthy. Jesus welcomed children, hold-ing them in his arms and setting a child in his midst (Mark 9:35–37). He promised rewards for those who minister to his little ones (Matt 10:42). Jesus acknowledged that spiritual truths which are hidden from those who are "wise" (and, presumably, older) are sometimes revealed to children (Matt 11:25–26). Later he used children as a model for entering the kingdom of heaven (Matt 18:2–3). When Jesus's disciples tried to stop people from bringing their children to him to be blessed, Jesus became indig-nant and told the disciples, "Let the children come to me; do not hinder them, for to such belongs the kingdom of God" (Mark 10:14). On another occasion he declared that it would be better for a person "if a millstone were hung around his neck and he were cast into the sea than that he should cause one of these little ones to sin" (Luke 17:2). The ESV Study Bible (2008) commented on this verse that, "Drowning with a millstone around one's neck has less serious consequences (because they may not be eternal consequences) than causing *one of these little ones* (who believe in Christ or who have begun to follow him in some way) *to sin*" (1992).

THE DEVELOPMENTAL NEEDS OF CHILDREN

The Commission on Children at Risk (2003) issued a landmark report, *Hardwired to Connect: The New Scientific Case for Authoritative Communities*. This group of thirty-three children's doctors, research scientists, and mental health and youth ser-vice professionals sought to "investigate empirically the social, moral, and spiritual foundations of child well-being" and "evaluate the degree to which current practice and policy in the U.S. recognize those foundations" (2). The report described a two-fold crisis: epidemiological in that "more and more young people are suffering from mental illness, emotional distress, and behavioral problems" (p. 8), and intellectual since "failures of understanding" have resulted in "our inability as a society to respond effectively to these deteriorations in child and adolescent well-being" (8). The Commission noted the limitations of pharmacological and "at risk" models, which focus on treatment (or deficit). It argued that these models are necessary, but insufficient: "Our deepest challenge today is to think and act much more ecologically—to broaden our attention to the environmental conditions creating growing numbers of suffering children" (14).

What should be done? The Commission advanced the argument that scientific evidence: (a) "shows that we are hardwired for close attachments to other people, beginning with our mothers, fathers, and extended family, and then moving out to the broader community"; and (b) "suggests that we are hardwired for meaning, born with a built-in capacity and drive to search for purpose and reflect on life's ultimate ends" (14).

> Meeting the human child's deep need for these related aspects of connected-ness—to other people and to meaning—is essential to the child's health and development.
>
> Meeting this need for connectedness is primarily the task of what we are calling *authoritative communities*—groups of people who are committed to one another over time and who model and pass on at least part of what it means to be a good person and live a good life . . . . strengthening these communities is likely to be our best strategy for improving the lives of our children, including those most at risk. (14–15)

Unsurprisingly, the Commission cites the family as "arguably the first and most basic association of civil society, and a centrally important example of what should be an authoritative community" and "usually the source of the most enduring and formative relationships in a child's life" (40).

God has so designed human beings with a need to connect to other people for moral and spiritual meaning that parents (and churches) can have a tremendous in-fluence on children and adolescents, for good or for ill. But what does this have to do with spiritual formation? Mulholland (1993) has cogently argued that "life itself is a process of spiritual development" and "the only choice we have is whether that growth moves us toward wholeness in Christ or toward an increasingly dehumanized and destructive mode of being" (24).

Childhood is a particularly important time for the spiritual formation of chil-dren, often setting the basic trajectory for the rest of their lives. George Barna re-ported (2003) that a series of studies conducted by The Barna Group showed that "the probability of someone embracing Jesus as his or her Savior was 32 percent for those between the ages of five and twelve; 4 percent for those in the thirteen- to eighteen-range; and 6 percent for people nineteen or older." The conclusion: "if people do not embrace Jesus Christ as their Savior before they reach the teenage years, the chance of their doing so at all is slim" (34). Similarly, Barna's research indicates that by age thirteen a child has formed most of his or her basic beliefs, with only 3 percent of America's thirteen-year-olds having a biblical worldview.

> The chances of seeing the worldviews of young people change to be more re-flective of biblical truth are slim . . . We find an astounding level of consistency between the religious beliefs of adults and children. This has two implications. Initially, it suggests that whatever beliefs a person embraces when he or she is young are not likely to change as the individual ages. . . . In addition, the consistency means that the average young person will encounter fewer adults or peers whose worldview is sufficiently different enough as to pose a serious challenge to his or her own existing belief system. (Barna, 2003, 37)

Recognizing the importance of these crucial early years, in recent years missiologists have emphasized the importance of reaching those in the "4 to 14 Window" (Brewster, 2005).

THE SPIRITUAL FORMATION OF CHILDREN AND ADOLESCENTS

If childhood is such a formative time spiritually and God takes the spiritual formation of children so seriously, the question to ask is, do we? The empirical evidence suggests that the answer is no, or at least not as seriously as we ought. According to the Family Needs Survey conducted by Family Life in 2007–8 with nearly forty thousand Christian parents:

- Over half of parents said that their families never or rarely engaged in family devotions.

- About 40% of parents said that they discussed spiritual matters with their children never, rarely, or only occasionally.

- Nearly one-quarter of parents never or rarely prayed with their children, and another one quarter prayed with their children only occasionally. (Jones, 2011, 27–28)

Such statistics show that many Christian parents have disengaged from their God-intended role as the primary spiritual nurturers of their children. This is despite the fact that many children and youth identify their parents as an important source of religious information and spiritual counsel. Roehlkepartain (2012,) reports explor-atory research with 6,725 youth (ages twelve to twenty-five) in eight countries in which 43 percent of the youth identified their families as the most helpful influence in their spiritual life, as compared to only 14 percent for their religious institution. In a nationally representative study of church-attending U.S. adolescents ages thirteen to seventeen, Christian Smith (2005) found that only 19 percent of the youth reported talking with a religious leader about a personal question or problem, while 81 percent stated that their families engaged in spiritual conversation together at least a few times per year. Smith's (2009) follow-up study five years later found six combinations of important factors that were likely to produce highly religious emerging adults. High parental religious service attendance and importance of faith was one of the four most critical factors, along with high teen importance of religious faith in everyday life, many personal religious experiences by the teen, and frequent prayer and scripture reading by the teen (see especially 224–229). Clearly, family valuing and practice of religious faith are significant.

However, we must not forget the importance of children's involvement with the broader faith community. M. S. Lawson (2011) pointed out the need to remove "our twenty-first-century glasses" that usually view the family as "a husband, wife, child/children, and perhaps an occasional loose relative attached for a brief time" (68). The Hebrew understanding of family was broader. Other Christians are referred to in the New Testament as "the household of faith" (Gal 6:10) and "the household of God" (1 Tim 3:15).

Yust (2004) addressed the importance of the faith community for children's spiritual formation in her book *Real Kids, Real Faith*:

> Parents are the principal guides in children's spiritual formation, yet children need a religious community within which to experience God as something other than their own friend or possession. They need the benefit of others' discoveries about divine love and others' testimonies to the challenges of faithful living. They need to rub up against different ideas about God and experience the affirmation of shared understanding. They need opportunities to be shaped by communal rituals and practices that extend beyond the narrow confines of their immediate family so that they realize their kinship with other spiritual people. They need to recognize that their own religious language belongs to many others and that they can speak this language outside the home as well as within it. Affiliation with a religious community provides children with the kind of extensive and diverse support that no one or two individuals can provide, given the limitations of human time, energy, and experience. (p. 164)

More recently, Yust (2012) has noted that, "Children need the comfort of a shared family spiritual journey and the challenge of walking with a diverse group of congregational pilgrims in a lifelong process of faith formation" (226). The recent book by Allen and Ross (2012), *Intergenerational Christian Formation*, convincingly made the case for "bringing the whole church together in ministry, community and worship" (the book's subtitle) and offered numerous practical suggestions toward that end.

What are some of the potential obstacles to parental involvement in the spiritual formation of their children? The first is parents' lack of understanding of their biblical responsibility to serve as the primary spiritual nurturers of their children. As DeBoer pointed out (as cited by Yust, 2005, 225), we live in an age in which parents often rely upon specialized coaches, tutors, and instructors when it comes to their children's advancement in areas such as athletics, academics, and the arts. Many parents take this same outsourcing approach to their children's spiritual formation, expecting the

> "religious professional(s)" at church and/or a parachurch organization to do the job. This is despite the great impact that parents can have due to their relationships with their children and the much greater time they are able to spend together. However, this tendency to outsource responsibility for children's spiritual nurture is not only contra biblical, it is contrary to what most parents know is right. (Allen, 2012, 198)

In a study sponsored by the Gheens Center for Christian Family Ministry at Southern Baptist Theological Seminary, Jones (2011) investigated the dynamics of parents' desertion of discipleship processes in their families. Jones summarized some of the key findings:

> Well over 90 percent of parents rejected the notion that professional ministers were the people primarily responsible for their children's spiritual development. When asked whether parents ought to engage personally in a discipleship process with their children, not one parent disagreed, and most strongly agreed. Fewer than 14 percent of parents expressed even the slightest agreement with the suggestion that church ministries are where children ought to receive the bulk of their biblical teaching. More than 90 percent of parents wanted to answer their children's biblical and theological questions. Only 1 percent of parents strongly identified church leaders as the persons who ought to develop their children's souls. (98)

Thus, lack of knowledge concerning their own responsibility to help disciple their own children is not a factor for most Christian parents in America. How, then, do we explain the failure of most parents to consistently engage in the positive spiritual formation of their children?

A second type of obstacle, this one very real, pertains to the spiritual nature of this task. Our flesh, meaning our capacity and tendency to sin, hinders our faithfulness in facilitating the spiritual formation of our children. Furthermore, parenting and discipling children involves us in a spiritual conflict against a deadly enemy seeking both our and our children's destructions (Eph 6:12; 1 Pet 5:8). "Spiritual forces of evil in the heavenly places are warring against parents' efforts to bring up their children 'in the discipline and instruction of the Lord ' (Eph 6:4 ESV; see also v. 12). The sole sufficient response to such conflict is to clothe ourselves in the strength of God himself (Eph 6:13–20)" (Jones (2011, 99–100).

{}{} spiritual

However, the enemy of our souls also uses earthly trends and factors in this spiritual conflict. Jones (2011) has conducted research in which 90 percent of the parents who had "disengaged from their children's spiritual development," defined as "a failure to engage consistently in any form of prayer or Bible study with children," cited lack of time (10 percent), lack of training (28 percent) or lack of both time and training (52 percent) as reasons for their inactivity (111). Thus, (perceived) lack of time and lack of training are the third and fourth obstacles.

We've established the importance of parents in the spiritual formation of their children and the contemporary failure of many Christian parents to fulfill their role in this regard. Now, we will examine types of family ministry models and several considerations in assisting children's faith development.

FAMILY MINISTRY MODELS

In an effort to ascertain healthy and effective models for family ministry, Jones and Stinson (2011) surveyed both biblical foundations for a family ministry model and family ministry models throughout church history. In programmatic ministry approaches, which predominated in the last century and are still common, ministry to families often meant "a segmented and professionalized ministry for each member of the family" which at best "trained family members separately in ways that unified them in other contexts" (171). Family ministry in this model, labeled by Anthony (2012) as "family sensitive" typically consists of intervention and training programs added to the existing collection of church programs. The addition of new, age-segmented programs typically reaches only a minority of families and fails to promote intergenerational interaction (Holmen, 2007). Most critical, according to Jones and Stinson (2011), "the church is in a state of crisis because parents have disengaged from the personal processes of Christian formation with their children" (173). In response, three new types of family ministry models have emerged in recent years.

In the *family-based ministry model* (the "family friendly model" in Anthony's terminology), the church's "programmatic structure remains unchanged," and individual ministries design programs to "intentionally draw generations together and encourage parents to take part in the discipleship of their children and youth" (Jones & Stinson, 179). The *family-equipping ministry model* (or "family empowered model," according to Anthony) retains age-targeted programs, but the church is restructured "to draw generations together" in order "to equip parents and champion their position as primary disciple makers" of their children (Anthony, 24). Finally, a *family-integrated ministry model* (which Anthony refers to as "family centered") eliminates age-segregated programs and events in favor of multigenerational ones, emphasizing the responsibility of parents to evangelize and disciple their children with modeling and with help from the larger faith community.

Although in practice there may be some overlap among the models of family ministry just described, each "represents a distinct and identifiable approach to the challenge of drawing the home and the church into a life-transforming partnership" (Jones & Stinson, 177). Thus, in all three of the new models, family ministry could be defined as "the process of intentionally and persistently realigning a congregation's proclamation and practices so that parents are acknowledged, trained, and held accountable as persons primarily responsible for the discipleship of their children" (173).

Jones and Stinson (2011), based on their study of the Scriptures and family ministry throughout church history, propose "three axioms that ought to characterize present and future family ministry models": (1) "God has called parents to take personal responsibility for the Christian formation of their children;" (2) Intergenerational relationships should be promoted so that children and youth can gain wisdom from older generations; and (3) "Family ministry models must be missional"—i.e., "family ministry must mobilize families to be on mission together" (pp. 177–178).

FROM MODELS TO PRACTICE

The movement for churches to partner with parents by equipping, supporting, and holding them accountable for the spiritual nurture of their children has resulted in conferences such as the D6 Conference (http://d6conference.com/) and a large and growing literature, for example Freudenburg (1998), Wallace (1999), Holmen (2007), Haynes (2009, 2011), Joiner (2009), Bruner and Stroope (2010), Anthony and Anthony (2011), Jones (2011), Stinson and Jones (2011), Anthony (2012), and Kimmel (2013).

One important, path-breaking initiative has been the Strong Families Innovation Alliance. In April of 2007 leaders from 14 evangelical churches gathered in Scottsdale, Arizona to launch a two-year innovation process to develop working models to make generational faith transfer a key priority for the local church. At a second meeting in November 2007, participants identified ten components they considered essential to creating "a customized strategy for church-driven, family-centered redemption." These components, taken verbatim from the session executive summaries (Bruner, 2008, 15) are:

1. Empower a Visionary Champion—If everyone owns it, no one does. Make it clear which senior leader is responsible for keeping family-centered objectives on the team's radar screen.

2. Establish New Success Measures—What gets measured gets done. Introduce simple measures that will keep family-centered strategies on the radar screen and drive continual improvement.

3. Build Upon Existing Church Vision—Do not compete with or criticize the existing vision. Build upon it to drive family-centered strategies. Don't call on the church to change everything—but to make everything more effective.

4. Build Into Existing Church Calendar—Include experiences that will drive people toward greater intentionality on the church calendar rather than try to squeeze them in as exceptions or special events. The more "autopilot" your family-emphasis game plan becomes, the easier it will be for everyone.

5. Use "Home" Lens for All vs. Creating New Silo—As a priority every area of the church must own, apply "faith at home" lenses to every department and program rather than creating another "silo" (independent, unrelated program) competing for attention and resources.

6. Define Success and Call Families to Commitment—Give families a vision of success and repeatedly call them to commit themselves.

7. Foster a Culture of Family Intentionality—Find ways to communicate the priority and celebrate the practice of families becoming intentional.

8. Customization: One Size Won't Fit All—Every family is unique due to its season in life, ages and number of children, marital health, special circumstances, etc. Provide tools that make it easy for families to customize.

9. Invest in Tools for Families—Just like we invest in curriculum for Sunday School, we need to invest in tools that will make it easier for families to do the right thing.

10. Two Degree Strategies—It is better to start small and build momentum than wait until you have a perfect plan with complete buy-in from all sectors.

One of the prime goals of the Strong Families Innovation Alliance was to help kick-start working models of innovative family ministry that could serve as models for other churches to emulate and contextualize to their own settings. The HomePointe model pioneered at Lake Pointe Church in Rockwall, Texas provides an outstanding example of such a model.

An executive summary of the model (Bruner, n. d., 2) states: "HomePointe is an integrated church strategy for creating a culture of intentional families. It exists to increase the likelihood that those attending our churches will (1) Build a life-long, thriving marriage, (2) Introduce their children to Christ, and (3) Launch their teens as committed believers." Three main strategies are employed to help create a culture of intentional families: (1) to cast a vision that God has designed the family as the primary context of faith formation, (2) to make it easier for families to become intentional at home by providing them with practical tools, and (3) to make it more likely that the families in the church will become intentional by at least three times per year coordinating campaigns in which the families are invited to create 120-day intentionality plans (Bruner and Stroope, 2010, 184–188). Further information on the model can be found in Bruner and Stroope (2010) and at the Drive Faith Home website (http://www.drivefaithhome.com).

CHURCH EVALUATION

The following questions are offered as an initial set of criteria for help in evaluating a church's efforts toward equipping parents for the spiritual nurture of their children. First, does the church provide sound teaching from Scripture about such things as the roles of church and home and have a biblical, intentional strategy for spiritual formation? Does this strategy include specific markers/targets for spiritual formation? For example, from three important passages of Scripture (the Ten Commandments in Exod 20, Jesus's Sermon on the Mount in Matt 5–7, and the "fruit of the Spirit" in Gal 5), Barna (2003) identified 24 life outcomes/goals for Christians. Haynes (2009, 2011), Holmen (2007), and Holmen and Texeira (2008) have suggested spiritual developmental milestones for children and how the church can help prepare parents to assist their children's development at different ages/stages.

Second, is equipping the home to be the primary place of spiritual nurture one church initiative among many or an integrative thrust present in all ministries? Third, is the proper strategic filter applied to all church activities and events? An initial question might be, "How will this element of our ministry equip families to function as the foundational unit of discipleship?" Follow-up questions might include: "Does this activity bring families together or pull them apart? How can we intentionally connect this program or event back to what could be taking place in the home? How will this program or event resource, train, or involve parents to disciple their children?" (Strother, 2011, 257).

Fourth, has an intentional ministry design and implementation process, like those described by Strother (2011, 253–267) and Jones (2011, 123–196), been used to increase "buy in" and effectiveness? In particular: Have key faith building skills/objectives been identified? Is training available for parents at the appropriate times to prepare them when their children are ready for learning and, as much as possible, at times when the parents (and their children or youth) would already be at church? Does the training cover all three domains of learning—cognitive, affective, and psychomotor or behavioral? Fifth, does the ministry lack any of the ten essential components identified by the Strong Families Innovation Alliance as essential for church-driven, family-centered redemption?

Barna (2003) argued for the importance of evaluation in facilitating the spiritual growth of children. He suggested that outcomes can be evaluated though the following means: formal evaluation tools; self-report evaluation tools; conversation and dialogue; observable behavior or perspectives; and inferences from choices.

CONCLUSION

This chapter advanced preliminary considerations regarding the equipping of parents to facilitate the spiritual formation of their children. First, the need for this type of equipping was established by briefly examining biblical teaching in the Old and New Testaments, emerging evidence in terms of child development, and evidence that many Christian parents are not active in the spiritual formation of their children. Next, various types of family ministry models and elements for equipping parents were considered and a functioning prototype was highlighted. Finally, an initial set of evaluative criteria for ministries seeking to equip parents for the spiritual nurture of their children was suggested. It is my prayer that churches intentionally reexamine their strategies to equip parents and encourage the family in the spiritual formation of children.

REFERENCES

Allen, H. C. (with Adams, C., Jenkins, K., and Meek, J. W.). "How Parents Nurture the Spiritual Development of their Children: Insights from Recent Qualitative Research." In *Understanding Children's Spirituality: Theology, Research and Practice,* edited by Kevin E. Lawson. Eugene, OR: Cascade, 2012, 197–222.

Allen, H. C., and C. L. Ross. *Intergenerational Christian Formation: Bringing the Whole Church Together in Ministry, Community and Worship.* Downers Grove, IL: IVP Academic, 2012.

Anthony, M. *Dreaming of More for the Next Generation: Lifetime Faith Ignited by Family Ministry.* Colorado Springs, CO: David C. Cook, 2012.

Anthony, M and Anthony, M. eds. *A Theology for Family Ministries.* Nashville, TN: B&H Academic, 2011.

Barna, G. *Transforming Children into Spiritual Champions.* Ventura, CA: Regal Books, 2003.

Brewster, D. The 4/14 WINDOW: Child Ministries and Mission Strategies, August, 2005. Retrieved from http://www.compassion.com/multimedia/The%204_14%20Window.pdf

Bruner, K. Strong Families Innovation Alliance: Session Executive Summaries, June, 2008. Retrieved from http://www.mediafire.com/view/?s4736tnx0375zze

Bruner, K. HomePointe: An Executive Summary for Local Church Leaders, n. d. Retrieved from http://www.mediafire.com/view/?2a0cxxaxsc2qwtm

Bruner, K., & S. Stroope. *It Starts at Home: A Practical Guide to Nurturing Lifelong Faith.* Chicago: Moody Publishers, 2010.

Bunge, M. J. (ed.) *The Child in Christian Thought.* Grand Rapids, MI: William B. Eerdmans, 2001.

Bunge, M. J., Fretheim, T. E., & Gaventa, B. R. (eds.) *The Child in the Bible.* Grand Rapids, MI: William B. Eerdmans, 2008.

Commission on Children at Risk. *Hardwired to Connect: The New Scientific Case for Authoritative Communities.* New York: Institute for American Values, 2003.

Coulter, G. R., and ,J. W. Thompson. "A Theology of Grandparenting and Generational Faith." In *A Theology for Family Ministries,* edited by M. Anthony and M. Anthony. 135–154. Nashville, TN: B&H Academic, 2011.

ESV Study Bible, English Standard Version. Wheaton, IL: Crossway Bibles, 2008.

Freudenburg, B. (with Lawrence, R.). *The Family-Friendly Church.* Loveland, CO: Group, 1998.

Greenman, J. P. "Spiritual Formation in Theological Perspective: Classic Issues, Contemporary Challenges." In *Life in the Spirit: Spiritual Formation in Theological Perspective,* edited by J. P. Greenman and G. Kalantzis. Downers Grove, IL: IVP Academic, 2010, 23–35.

Gundry-Volf, Judith M. "The Least and the Greatest: Children in the New Testament." In *The Child in Christian Thought,* edited by M. J. Bunge. Grand Rapids, MI: William B. Eerdmans. 29–60. 2001.

Haynes, B. *Shift: What it Takes to Finally Reach Families Today.* Loveland, CO: Group, 2009.

Haynes, B. *The Legacy Path: Discover Intentional Spiritual Parenting.* Nashville, TN: Randall House, 2011.

Holmen, M., and D. Texeira. *Take it Home: Inspiration and Events to Help Parents Spiritually Transform their Children.* Ventura, CA: Gospel Light, 2008.

Holmen, M. A. *Building Faith at Home: Why Faith at Home Must be Your Church's #1 Priority.* Ventura, CA: Regal Books, 2007.

Joiner, R. *Think Orange: Imagine the Impact When Church and Family Collide.* Colorado Springs, CO: David C. Cook, 2009.

Jones, T. P. *Family Ministry Field Guide: How Your Church Can Equip Parents to Make Disciples.* Indianapolis, IN: Wesleyan, 2011.

Jones, T. P., and R. Stinson. "Family Ministry Models." In *A Theology for Family Ministries,* edited by M. Anthony & M. Anthony. 155–180. Nashville, TN: B&H Academic, 2011.

Kimmel, T. *Connecting Church and Home.* Nashville, TN: Randall House, 2013.

Lawson, K. E. "Introduction." In *Understanding Children's Spirituality: Theology, Research and Practice,* edited by Kevin E. Lawson. xi-xv. Eugene, OR: Cascade, 2012.

Lawson, M. S. "Old Testament Teachings on the Family." In *A Theology for Family Ministries,* edited by M. Anthony & M. Anthony. 66–87. Nashville, TN: B&H Academic, 2011.

May, S., K. Stemp, and G. Burns. "Children's Place in the New Forms of Church: An Exploratory Survey of These Forms' Ministry with Children and Family." In *Understanding Children's Spirituality: Theology, Research and Practice,* edited by Kevin E. Lawson. Eugene, OR: Cascade Books, 2012, 238–263.

Melick, R. "New Testament Teachings on the Family." In *A Theology for Family Ministries,* eds. M. Anthony & M. Anthony. 88–105. Nashville, TN: B&H Academic, 2011.

Mulholland, M. R. *Invitation to a Journey: A Road Map for Spiritual Formation.* Downers Grove, IL: InterVarsity Press, 1993.

Roehlkepartain, E. C. "It's the Way You Look at Things: How Young People Around the World Understand and Experience Spiritual Development." In *Understanding Children's Spirituality: Theology, Research and Practice,* edited by Kevin E. Lawson. 152–172. Eugene, OR: Cascade Books, 2012.

Smith, C. (with Denton, M. L.). *Soul Searching: The Religious and Spiritual Lives of American Teenagers.* New York: Oxford University Press. 2005.

Smith, C. (with Snell, P.). *Souls in Transition: The Religious and Spiritual Loves of Emerging Adults.* New York: Oxford University Press, 2009.

Stonehouse, C. *Joining Children on the Spiritual Journey: Nurturing a Life of Faith.* Grand Rapids, MI: Baker Academic, 1998.

Strother, J. "Making the Transition to Family-Equipping Ministry." In *Trained in the Fear of God: Family Ministry in Theological, Historical, and Practical Perspective,* edited by Stinson & T. P. Jones. 253–267. Grand Rapids: Kregel Academic & Professional, 2011.

Wallace, E. *Uniting Church and Home.* Lorton, VA: Solutions for Integrating Church and Home, 1999.

Yust, K. M. *Real Kids, Real Faith: Practices for Nurturing Children's Spiritual Lives*. San Francisco: Jossey-Bass, 2004.

Yust, K. M. "Being Faithful Together: Families and Congregations as Intergenerational Christian Communities." In *Understanding Children's Spirituality: Theology, Research and Practice*, edited by Kevin E. Lawson. 223–37. Eugene, OR: Cascade, 2012.

Zuck, R. B. *Precious in His Sight: Children and Childhood in the Bible*. Grand Rapids, MI: Baker Academic, 1997.

Chapter 9

Parents as Spiritual Directors
Fostering the Spirituality of
Early Elementary-Aged Children

Christopher C. Hooton

> Then little children were being brought to him in order that he might lay his hands on them and pray. The disciples spoke sternly to those who brought them; but Jesus said, "Let the little children come to me, and do not stop them; for it is to such as these that the kingdom of heaven belongs." And he laid his hands on them and went on his way. (Matt 19:13–15 NRSV)

Who would doubt Jesus's sincerity about wanting children to come to him? Yet the actions of some in the church may imply that children can't really access the depths of relationship with Christ. There are challenges associated with the spirituality of children, to be sure, but against these stand the very nature of God and ancient practices that assist children on the way.

CHALLENGE

When I was a teenager I was delighted to be ministering to children. I felt called to children's ministry as a child, and as a teenager I was already realizing the dream. However, one Sunday morning shook my convictions so violently that I nearly abandoned the thought of ministry to children. A new pastor had just taken over the children's ministry that I had been leading with some friends. I was helping her this particular Sunday when she invited the children to respond to a salvation message. I saw many children finding places of prayer, asking Jesus to be their Savior.

Instead of producing joy, this event rocked me to my core. Many of these children were already saved and had in the weeks and months before been finding places of prayer to deepen their relationships with God and seek the baptism in the Holy Spirit. I was immediately faced with the question: Can children understand this spiritual life? Is the richness of relationship with the triune God available to them?

Today, I am the father of five-year-old, Foster, and seven-year-old, Ella. This challenge comes home as I attempt to use all of my training as a children's pastor to help them find their own experiences with God. Ella is naturally more interested in the things of God. Foster is younger and is at a stage where "Jesus things" are boring. Exploring Foster's spirituality with him is even more challenging. I have come to believe that the wealth of spiritual relationship is for them, yet those questions from my teen years spur me on to study how that spiritual growth occurs.

Worldview

The stakes are high. The majority of people who come to faith in Christ will do so as children. At the same time, the church is facing large numbers of young adults who are abandoning their faith as they enter college. Their worldview is challenged, and for many who have made an inflexible structure of beliefs and ideas, their faith will topple.

George Barna (2003) gives a litany of statistics profiling the children of our nation. Fewer than three out of ten fourth graders read at grade level. One-in-ten teenagers report having had sex before their thirteenth birthday. One-in-ten eighth graders smokes daily and one in three were drunk within the past year. While Barna notes that these statistics don't represent a crisis and children on the whole do pretty well in spite of messy lives he says, "Our nation's children will struggle to maintain a healthy balance in life." The trajectory of statistics suggests that, "The end result of growing up in this challenging culture will be a country of adults whose standards have been lowered and whose sensitivities have been blunted" (Barna, 2003, 26). Barna suggests that the missing factor on which all these problems hinge is spiritual health.

Rational Theology

The church has wrestled with what to do with children from its earliest days. There have been many questions. Are children born innocent or guilty? What happens to an infant who dies before coming to Christ as savior? Does infant baptism redeem them? These questions have influenced the way the church has dealt with the challenge of forming faith in young ones, and the church's responses have created many challenges over the years, challenges which became stark during the enlightenment when theology and spirituality were increasingly rational.

Two Extremes

The major solution to the question posed by the church was the *age of accountability*. This idea proposed that children are in a special state of grace until such time as they can discern right from wrong. There has never been a consensus about what age this occurs, and it has been left mostly subjective. Theologians approach this idea from two perspectives: the inherent innocence or guilt of the child. The early church before the time of Augustine and his contemporaries emphasized the child's innocence (Allen, 2008) and it was this innocence that Jesus was commending to his followers as a subject of imitation. Augustine and some of his contemporaries argued for the immediate baptism of infants because their fallen nature would condemn them in death. The two extremes, then, are that children are innocent and nothing need be done for them, and that children are sinful and unbaptized children will not enter the Kingdom. In between these extremes is belief in the special status of children before the age of accountability.

The response of the church to these ideas falls on a continuum from inaction to zealous evangelism. If one holds completely to the innocence of children, the danger is that no effort or value will be placed on developing the spirituality of children. Inaction is also the possible outcome of those who, trusting in infant baptism, leave the child's spirituality alone until confirmation. The same can be said of those who rely on a Christian family environment to protect a child. On the other hand, the revivalists of the enlightenment came to see children as the objects of intense evangelism and focused on conversion, possibly ignoring spiritual formation altogether.

Revivalist Approach

During the enlightenment, revivalists were calling people to repentance and conversion. They expected that men and women would come to rational terms with their sinfulness and turn to God. As the enlightenment came to a close, revivalists came to question the practice of leaving children in their sinfulness until such a time as they could have a conversion experience because they had reached a level of mental reasoning (Anthony, 2006). D. L. Moody, Charles Finney and Edward Payson Hammond began to increase their efforts at evangelizing children. Yet the enlightenment/rationalist attitude toward children prevailed in church thought as theories of cognitive development seemed to place limits on the kind of rational thinking about God in which children were expected to engage.

Developmental Theory

For years the church followed modernist thought, birthed out of the enlightenment, that spiritual development required high-level abstract reasoning skills and was reserved for thinkers, intellectuals and academics. It was not for the average Christian, let alone the child. This thought dominated the research of children's spirituality during the cognitive period (1960–1990). Based on the work of Jean Piaget, the prevailing notion suggested that children developed in stages. The cognitive ability to reason in the abstract doesn't occur until adolescence (Allen, 2008). If this is the mark by which children are seen to have access to the spiritual richness found in Christ, then young children are excluded.

Fortunately for those interested in the spiritual development of their children, Piaget does not have the last word. Erik Erikson's stages of development offer insight into ways parents and other adults can help the child experience God. In each of Erikson's stages there is a core conflict being addressed by the individual with one of two outcomes. In infancy the conflict is between trust and mistrust. The parent aids the spirituality of the child by helping him or her learn to trust mom and dad. As the toddler begins the struggle between autonomy versus shame and doubt, the parent helps the child learn self-control without losing self-esteem. Children at this stage learn they have a will and also how to submit to the will of another. From four to six, the child struggles between initiative and guilt. Not only does she test boundaries but she also develops conscience. These are important aspects of the development of the child morally, and the parent offers guidance throughout these and every subsequent stage of life (Stonehouse, 1998).

Stage theory has its limitations, however. Many people looked to the developmental stages offered by Piaget, Erikson and others to determine how best to nurture the spirituality of children. One problem with this is that "a descriptive account of what *is* does not automatically lead to a prescriptive account of what *can* or *should be*" (Allen, 2008, 32). Building lessons and methods based on generalized ideas about the cognitive level of a group will leave children who are ahead or behind the mark feeling frustrated. On the other hand, children can often rise to a challenge set before them.

Another note is that much of the research into what children could experience spiritually was based on what they said about their spiritual experiences. This is limited by their ability to use language. Because the child's ability to express a spiritual experience is limited, this may not indicate that the experience itself is limited (Hay and Nye, 2006).

Along came the recent work of Rebecca Nye and David Hay (2006) to answer these concerns. They found that behind the language and descriptions of the children there was a common thread. The core of the spirituality of children was a *relational consciousness*. Those experiences that were spiritual in nature were times when children had a heightened consciousness of their relationship to reality. The exciting fact to note is that this is not directly tied to cognitive development. Nye and Hay's research demonstrates that the core of spirituality is available to children and can be nurtured. The challenge then is how do adults best nurture the unique spiritual lives of children? There is a wealth of material that has emerged recently about children's spirituality and the implications for formation.

THEOLOGICAL FOUNDATION

There is no better place to look for a foundation of our treatment of children's spirituality than in the very nature of God. In his breathtaking book, *The Knowledge of the Holy*, A. W. Tozer (1961) bookends his discussion of the attributes of God by drawing the tension between two chapters, "God Incomprehensible," and "The Open Secret." These two attributes will serve us well as we approach the spirituality of children.

The Incomprehensible God

God is completely other. Our minds cannot conceive of something so outside our experiences. Tozer (1961) notes, that even the mythical creatures of lore are nothing more than fanciful versions of creatures known to human experience in nature. In God, there is no such point of reference that can accurately capture who God is. We make comparisons in order to understand truths about God, but they are poor approximations of the reality of the Transcendent.

Faced with the awesome reality of God, our minds completely fail. No creative imagination of child or adult can create majesty so resplendent as to be worthy of God. No amount of logic and systematic theology can draw the outline of God's boundaries. Volumes have been written and myriad traditions guard numerous sacred truths, and yet God is not known in true fullness.

For many the idea that God is ultimately beyond our mental capacity is disconcerting. We have learned to distrust mystery and fear that which we cannot know. How can we be confident in our relationship with God if we can never fully know God? For those who wonder if children can have access to God before they have the capacity to comprehend God, however, this is good news. Children are in good company! None us can apprehend God with our minds.

Apophatic Spirituality

Words sometimes get in the way of our understanding of our experiences with God. This is true for adults as well as for children. Apophatic spirituality is an ancient way of approaching God without words. This way affirms that God cannot be apprehended by the intellect but can be apprehended by love.

The fourteenth-century English mystic who wrote *The Cloud of Unknowing*, spoke of putting all the good and valuable things under a *cloud of forgetting* and placing our naked intent before the *cloud of unknowing* (Johnston, 1973). We are invited to "beat upon that thick *cloud of unknowing* with the dart of your loving desire and do not cease come what may" (Johnston, 1973, 55). He adds:

> Try to understand this point. Rational creatures such as men and angels possess two principal faculties, a knowing power and a loving power. No one can fully comprehend the uncreated God with his knowledge; but each one, in a different way, can grasp him fully through love. Truly this is the unending miracle of love: that one loving person, through his love, can embrace God, whose being fills and transcends the entire creation. And this marvelous work of love goes on forever for he whom we love is eternal. (Johnston, 1973, 50)

I am reminded of Hay and Nye's work in children's spirituality. Words often limit the child's ability to describe the spiritual experience. In some cases, even religious language to which children retreated becomes a fallback to hide from the reality of what they experienced. Apophatic spirituality is about apprehending God with love. This resonates with the core of children's spirituality as found by Rebecca Nye's relational *consciousness*. Even without the higher, abstract, reasoning capacities garnered in adolescence, children still experience the spiritual as relationship.

For Christian children this means experiencing their love for God and God's love for them. Five-year-old Foster can say, "Do you know how much I love my whole family? As much as I love Jesus!" In that statement, he is aware of his special relationship with his family and with God through Jesus Christ. That is intensely spiritual though he and children like him may struggle with their young minds to understand the nature of that relationship.

The Constant Voice of God

While no person can apprehend God through intellect, God delights in revealing his divine nature to us. God's voice is constantly speaking, and self-revelation is almost a compulsion for God. It seems that all of creation exists so that God may express his divine nature. Scripture is the story of God with us, God's self-revelation, and also contains evidence of God's compulsion. God walks with Adam. God covenants with Abraham. God speaks to Moses as to a friend. In the ultimate act of self-revelation, God became man in the person of Jesus Christ, who is the "radiance of God's glory and the exact representation of his being," (Heb 1:3 NIV).

At the end of his chapter, "God Incomprehensible," Tozer (1961) says that while we will never know what God is like in God's self, we can know the things God has revealed. "The Open Secret" is that we each may know God in relationship.

> To know God is at once the easiest and the most difficult thing in the world. It is easy because the knowledge is not won by hard mental toil, but is something freely given. As sunlight falls free on the open field, so the knowledge of the holy God is a free gift to men who are open to receive it. But this knowledge

is difficult because there are conditions to be met and the obstinate nature of fallen man does not take kindly to them. (Tozer, 1961, 180)

The conditions that he describes are the disciplines. The voice of God is constantly speaking to us. It rolls on like a river from eternity past. The disciplines put us in a place where that grace can wash over us. The voice of God's self-revelation, as Tozer puts it, is like sunlight surrounding us and bathing us in its light. Children are constantly surrounded by the speaking voice of God. It may speak to them from the beauty of nature. It may even come when wrapped in wonder over the "water running from a tap" (Hay and Nye, 2006, 122). The voice is constantly speaking, though we may not always recognize it. Adults and children, alike, benefit from someone who will help them listen.

BIBLICAL PHILOSOPHY

> Now Samuel did not yet know the Lord, and the word of the Lord had not yet been revealed to him. And the Lord called Samuel again the third time. And he arose and went to Eli, and said, "Here I am, for you called me." Then Eli perceived that the Lord was calling the boy. Therefore Eli said to Samuel, "Go, lie down; and if he calls you, you shall say, 'Speak, Lord, for thy servant hears.'"
> (1 Sam 2:7–9a RSV)

In this account, Samuel hears the voice of God for the first time. It takes three interruptions of his sleep for Eli to realize what was happening, but he is finally able to help his young charge recognize the voice of God. Scripture repeatedly affirms that God speaks to children. To the child, Jeremiah, God says,

> Before I formed you in the womb I knew you, and before you were born I consecrated you; I appointed you a prophet to the nations. (Jer 1:5 RSV)

Jeremiah protests that he is too young to speak to the nations, but God affirms that he has placed Jeremiah even as a youth over nations and kingdoms to deliver God's word. To Timothy, Paul writes,

> But as for you, continue in what you have learned and have firmly believed, knowing from whom you learned it and how from childhood you have been acquainted with the sacred writings which are able to instruct you for salvation through faith in Christ Jesus. (2 Tim 3:14–15 RSV)

Often we exalt the testimonies of those who have dramatic adult conversions. How much more wonderful is it, however, for a person to be able to say with Samuel or Jeremiah or Timothy, I have known the voice of God since I was a child?

God's Use of The Family

Timothy was the child and grandchild of godly women. As he writes 2 Timothy 1:5, Paul is reminded of the sincere faith of Timothy's grandmother, Lois and mother, Eunice. God used Timothy's family to stir in him "a sincere faith." The family is God's chosen instrument to form the faith of little ones. In Deuteronomy 6, Moses instructs parents to pass on the commands he is giving them. The imagery he uses is continual, daily and creative. Parents are to talk when they get up and when they lay down, when they walk on the road and when they stay home. The commandments are to be written on the walls and gates and tied to their hands and foreheads. This symbolism is a constant reminder of faith formation in the context of the family.

Barna (2003) reports that, "four out of five parents (85 percent) believe that they have the primary responsibility for the moral and spiritual development of their children, but more than two thirds of them abdicate that responsibility to the church," (77, 78). God has uniquely equipped the family with constant contact and given them the tools to nurture spiritual formation. The church has never found a better way and must help families fulfill this high calling.

MODEL

How then can parents help children recognize the speaking voice of God? There is a strategy for doing just that which has been practiced for centuries: Spiritual Direction.

Spiritual direction is a relationship in which three people enter into a conversation: the person seeking direction (directee), the director, and the Holy Spirit. There is one purpose to this meeting, helping the directee recognize the voice of the Spirit. The director listens and asks questions of the directee while all the time listening to the Spirit. The directee shares experiences with life or prayer where they might be conscious of the relationship with God. The director simply helps the directee to see and hear more clearly and to pay attention to elements of richness they might otherwise miss.

Brief Overview

This relationship is different than counseling or coaching. In these contexts, two people meet before God to pursue a human goal, while in spiritual direction, the directee and God meet in the presence of a witness, the director, to pursue God's goal (Temple, 2004). The director is another set of eyes and ears, a mirror to reflect the conversation back to the directee who is experiencing God's voice.

The spiritual direction meeting, then, is a place of prayer. When I sit down with my daughter, Ella, for spiritual direction, we light a candle and spend a little time in silence to become aware of the presence of Jesus. I want to establish an atmosphere of prayer. Both the director and the person need to approach direction with this attitude of prayer. Prayer is when "the human heart discloses itself to God and is open to listen and respond" (Bakke, 2000, 39). In spiritual direction, the director is invited to listen along.

> Effective spiritual direction meetings depend on both people intending to listen attentively for the Holy Spirit, which leans more toward patient waiting than active striving to hear God. Prayer becomes a mixture of activity and passivity: an active intentionality to be available to the Spirit and a passive open willingness that invites God to set agendas for spiritual direction conversations. Directees do not need to have what they describe as an outstanding or successful prayer life. But they do need to be willing to pray regularly and explore the Spirit's invitations. The willingness of directors and directees to continue to pray and seek God even when prayer is not satisfying or comfortable is essential for spiritual direction to take place. (Bakke, 2000, 39)

The role of the director is to ask questions that help the directee recognize where God might be speaking while listening to the Spirit in order to give feedback or to ask questions that help the directee follow God's direction. The job is not an easy one. It demands the directee's full, active attention. At the same time, the director is listening with rapt attention to the stirrings of the Spirit. From the Spirit, the director may sense what parts of the directee's story are important, what to press, and where to ask questions. The director may also hear from the Spirit a special word of encouragement or direction for the person.

The director must have a high view of the directee. Thomas Merton writes, "A true director can never get over the awe he feels in the presence of a person, an immortal soul, loved by Christ, washed in His most Precious Blood, and nourished by the sacrament of His Love" (Merton, 1960, 34).

Parents as Spiritual Directors

In order to minister to children, I am convinced one must approach them with the kind of awe and humility about which Merton writes. We must be convinced that the spiritual needs of our children are as important as our own, and that the charge of nurturing that spiritual formation is a high and holy calling. Spiritual direction can be an intimate setting, as the directee and the director both lay their souls bare to receive from the Spirit. It is appropriate for parents to serve in this very intimate position.

After centering into the presence of Jesus, the director usually asks, "Where have you felt close to God this week?" However, it could be a month since the last meeting. That is common for adults, who have full hour sessions but I have found in directing my own children that weekly fifteen to twenty-minute sessions are more productive.

The child—the directee—answers with examples about where they have felt God. It may be a special time at church, or maybe they felt Jesus playing with them, or helping them with their schoolwork. Often the discussion centers on some experience of prayer. If the child doesn't have experiences from which to draw, the parent can help the child recognize these experiences throughout the week. Going on prayer journeys from *The Praying Family* (Butts, 2003) or exploring disciplines from *Habits of a Child's Heart* (Hess and Garlett, 2004) may be very helpful, too.

The parent as director listens and asks questions for clarification. Here, the parent must resist the urge to correct the experience or to interject a moral lesson. The role of the director isn't to teach but to listen and draw out from the child conclusions about where and how God is speaking.

Spiritual direction is also helpful in times of stress or crisis for the child. When Ella was having a difficult time at school, spiritual direction became a safe place for her to rest in the love of daddy and Jesus. When we found out that she was being bullied, I led her through a healing prayer meditation where she actually took her bullies to Jesus! She was imagining Jesus with her, and she asked him where he was when she was being bullied. Jesus showed her that he was right behind her, following her every step. This is an image she can take with her, and when she feels threatened or hurt she can lean into Jesus or turn and give him a hug.

For parents to become successful with directing their children, it is important to have a personal experience with a spiritual director that's separate from the sessions with their children. These direction sessions will not only help parents "hear" where God is speaking, but will also introduce and strengthen techniques and methods for being a good director. Parents may also find an experienced director to supervise the direction of their children. A supervision relationship helps the director recognize blind spots that may affect the ability to effectively direct the child. A supervisor normally listens to a recounting of the director's session with an ear to what is happening in the director and between the director and God.

A Note About the Term

There has been much discussion among spiritual directors about what this relationship should be called. Many feel uncomfortable with the term "Director" as the best spiritual direction is non-directive. Alternatives have been suggested including: spiritual friendship, spiritual father/mother, Anam Cara, soul friend, or as one colleague suggested, simply dad. Some very specific expectations come along with the term. I have in mind simply what I have described above. I am not suggesting that parents be subjected to the same rigorous code of ethics maintained by organizations such as Spiritual Directors International, nor should they be recognized as spiritual directors by the community in general.

Some issues could be difficult to navigate as well. Spiritual direction, as we have discussed it, is not a time for instruction or making assessment as to the correctness of the directee's spirituality. This is an important part of the normal role parents are to take in the lives of their children, but for the spiritual direction session this should be set aside. However, it may be difficult for a child, hungry for parental approval, to set this role aside. This brings us to another potential difficulty: navigating the power differential that exists between parent and child. I believe that these issues can be successfully navigated, particularly with the use of supervision.

CONCLUSION

The spiritual direction approach is consistent with what we have discovered about children's spirituality. Spiritual direction may well be the missing component to the spiritual development of children. They learn cognitive lessons through Sunday school, devotions, and biblical accounts, but the *relational consciousness* can be developed through conversations that take place during spiritual direction.

As we build a foundation of experience of relationship with God, we help children find that which cannot be taken away. A worldview can be challenged, beliefs may be shaken, but when a child experiences his or her own relationship with God, that story can never be denied.

REFERENCES

Allen, Holly Catterton, ed. *Nurturing Children's Spirituality: Christian Perspectives and Best Practices.* Eugene, OR: Cascade, 2008.

Anthony, Michael J, ed. *Perspectives on Children's Spiritual Formation: Four Views.* Nashville: Broadman & Holman, 2006.

Bakke, Jannette A. *Holy Invitations: Exploring Spiritual Direction.* Grand Rapids: Baker, 2000.

Barna, George. *Transforming Children Into Spiritual Champions.* Ventura, CA: Regal, 2003.

Barry, William A., and William J Connolly. *The Practice of Spiritual Direction.* New York: HarperCollins, 1982.

Butts, Kim. *The Praying Family: Creative Ways To Pray Together.* Chicago: Moody, 2003.

Hay, Robert, and Rebecca Nye. *The Spirit of the Child: Revised Edition.* Philadelphia: Jessica Kingsley Publishers, 2006.

Hess, Valerie E., and Marti Watson Garlett. *Habits of a Child's Heart: Raising Your Kids With the Spiritual Disciplines.* Colorado Springs: Navpress, 2004.

Johnston, William, ed. *The Cloud of Unknowing and The Book of Privy Counseling.* New York: Doubleday, 1973.

Merton, Thomas. *Spiritual Direction & Meditation.* Collegeville, MN: Liturgical Press, 1960.

Stonehouse, Catherine. *Joining Children on the Spiritual Journey: Nurturing a Life of Faith.* Grand Rapids: Baker Academic, 1998.

Temple, Gray. "Spiritual Direction in the Episcopal Tradition." In *Spiritual Direction and the Care of Souls,* by Gary W. Moon and David G. Benner, 78–95. Downers Grove, IL: Intervarsity, 2004.

Tozer, A. W. *The Knowledge of the Holy.* New York: HarperCollins, 1961.

Chapter 10

Prenatal Ministry
Exploring the Foundations and Practices of Congregational Ministry to the Unborn

James Riley Estep Jr. and Marianna Hwang

When does the church's ministry begin with children? Is it at birth or when children are dedicated to the Lord? While the latter is common among the churches of Korea, among Korean churches in the United States, a growing number of evangelical congregations are beginning children's ministry much sooner—at the prenatal stage.

It has been known that the mother's physical health has a direct impact on the fetus' development and postnatal health. However, mounting evidence suggests that the environment does indeed influence far more than just the physical development of the fetus, and these effects last well into childhood. "Fetal Origins," what a child learns prior to birth, is increasingly the subject of articles, studies, and books.

This chapter explores prenatal ministry in the context of local congregations based on the literature of prenatal ministry in Korea and in the United States as well as on the practices of congregations that have adopted prenatal ministry. The following dimensions are addressed: (1) Christian rationale for prenatal ministry both theology and theory, developing a praxis statement for the inclusion of prenatal children's ministry, and noting its potential and limitations; (2) a literature review of prenatal ministry in Christian education designed to introduce the major voices and works for prenatal ministry both in Korea and in the United States including a demonstration of the "textbook" model of ministering to the unborn; (3) a survey of congregational models of prenatal ministry with some of the predominant components or themes in those ministries identified, and; (4) a proposed model for prenatal ministry in the local congregation with a template or starting point for those congregations and pastors considering the implementation of a prenatal ministry.

AN INTRODUCTION TO FETAL ORIGINS AND LEARNING

Fetal origins theory is a relatively new science that has existed for twenty years. It began with British physician David Barker who suggested that the only explanation for certain health conditions in the poorest regions of England and Wales was in fact attributable to a common occurrence as fetuses (Paul, 2010b). Fetal origins suggest that learning does not begin in preschool, or with language acquisition, or when the child is held by its mother; but rather *fetal learning* begins before birth itself. Fetuses learn by three means (James 2010): (1) *Habituation* or the ability to stop responding to a repeated stimulus, (2) *Classical conditioning* when fetuses tend to respond better to situations parallel to classical conditioning than to other forms of learning (cf. Kawai, 2010), and (3) *Exposure learning* which is response to environmental factors such as sound.

Each of these indicators of learning emphasizes the significance of the environment on the child even before birth. Lollar and Cordero (2007) regard fetal origins as a matter of public health. "Environmental factors affect learning and behavior and influence children throughout their lives—even from before birth," and result from "the physical, emotional, and experiential environments to which the mother and the child are exposed," (Lollar and Cordero, 2007, 10).

Similarly and more recently, Annie Murphy Paul concluded, "The fetus treats these maternal contributions as information, as what I like to call biological postcards from the world outside," (Paul 2011; cf. Paul 2010a for treatment of maternal bonding). We are taught by daily life even before we are born. Air, food, drink, stress, and emotion all influence the child, especially if the emotion is depression (Paul 2010a).

How is a Fetus Learning?

We learn about the world or our immediate environment prior to entering it. How can someone know a fetus is "learning"? What are the indications that thought is occurring? Fetal heart rates seem to indicate levels of cognitive processing— response to a familiar voice, typically the mothers, or even a smell while still in womb (cf. Kisilevsky and Hains, 2011; DiPietro, et al. 2007; Sevelinges, Sullivan, and Messaoudi, 2008)—indicating positive reactions to auditory and olfactory stimuli. These impressions extend into the life of the newborn and even into childhood.

Some studies underscore that what is learned may be soon forgotten. The fetus's memory seems to be somewhat limited ranging from 10-minute short-term memory to about twenty-four hours of long-term memory while still in the womb (Heteren et al., 2000; Dirix et al., 2009). However, some studies indicate the opposite, that fetal memory impacts the behavior and life of the newborn. For example, a 2002 study concluded that exposure to music prior to birth changes the behavioral state of the fetus and remains present in newborns suggesting that a basic form of "fetal programming or learning" did occur (James, Spencer, and Stepis, 2002, 437–438). Other studies have had similar results, indicating "that fetal memory persists into neonatal life" (Gonzalez-Gonzalez et al., 2006, 1160). The general conclusion is that fetal learning extends into newborns and infants (cf. Hopkins and Johnson, 2005).

What is a Fetus Learning?

Annie Paul explains how such influences impact the child beyond the physiological condition. The unborn interpret such methods in terms of matters critical to their survival, such as the availability of resources, level of security, and the general emotional potential and state of existence. In short, what does their experience in the womb convey about their future life outside of womb? (Paul, 2010b; Paul, 2011).

For clarification, fetal origins/learning is not what is commonly called the "Mozart Effect." Fetuses can and do learn patterns and sequences—not music—but impressions of life. For example, in relation to brain development, maternal stress can actually have a measurable effect on learning in children (Kapoor et al., 2009; Huang, 2010). Columbia University professor, Catherine Monk, has documented how an expectant mother's mental state can influence the child's psyche (Columbia Psychiatry, 2012; cf. Paul, 2010a, 156–158). Similarly, strong correlations have been identified between maternal obesity during pregnancy and the child's later negative emotional state (Rodriguez and Walderstrom, 2008). Exposure to cigarettes not only causes physiological problems for fetuses but also has been linked to a child's later cognitive development (Mezzacappa, Buckner, and Earls, 2011; Gutteling and de Weerth, 2006). Children can even develop inborn temperaments due to environment.

Fetal origins theory leads us to two inescapable conclusions. First, and perhaps most importantly, infants are not a *tabula rasa*. When we are born, we are "not clean slates, unmarked by life" (Paul, 2011). Second, fetal learning speaks to the ideas of *determinism vs. individuality*. Fetal origins do not excuse behaviors. We are not programmed. There is no loss of free will. However, we may be more disposed to certain behaviors. "Prenatal experience doesn't force the individual down a particular path; at most, it points us in a general direction, and we can take another route if we choose," like water taking the path of least resistance (Paul 2010a, 195).

BIBLICAL-THEOLOGICAL INSIGHTS ON FETAL ORIGINS

Scripture is not silent on the subject of the unborn. In fact, surprisingly, the subject of the fetus is found in numerous passages of the Old and New Testaments as well as at the center of some early church theological controversies. First, *Scripture teaches that human life begins before birth, even prior to conception* (Luke 1:36, 57). The phrase, "conceived and bore," occurs forty-eight times in the Old Testament (e.g. Gen 4:1, Hos 1:8). Job 3:3 parallels conception and birth, not because one must precede the other, but because existence begins prior to birth. It would be remiss to overlook this truth: At onetime, Jesus was an unborn child (Matt 1:20).

Second, *Scripture describes the unborn as children* (Gen 25:22, Hos 12:3, Jer 1:5). Exodus 21:22–25 treats an unborn child as legally protected with adults (cf. discussion in Bakke 2005, 110–114; Thompson, 2008, 204–205). Third, *fetal formation and growth are in the hands of God* (Job 10:8–11). The imagery of a child being knit in his mother's womb by God (Ps 139:13) reflects the cultural context of ancient Israel. Ancient cultures believed that the baby is pre-formed in the father's body and sexual intercourse only planted the preformed baby into the mother's body for the purpose of growth vs. from God. Jeremiah and Paul both received their calling from God before birth (Jer 1:5 and Gal 1:15), as does the Servant who was foretold by Isaiah (Isa 49:1–5). Paul uses fetal images as a means of expressing his spiritual and apostolic life (1 Cor 15:8, Gal 1:15 ἐκτρώματι—paralleling Ps 139:13 and Isa 49:1, 5–6. cf. Aasgaard 2008, 249, 257–8, 274; Reidar 2008, 249).

Fourth, *Scripture describes children as being known by God and capable of knowing God* (Psa 139:13–16). As an unborn child, Samson was bound by vows (Judg 13:7). Luke describes how John the Baptist, when he was a six-month-old fetus, responded to the presence of Jesus (Luke 1:39–44). John the Baptist was filled with the Holy Spirit (Luke 1:15) and displayed this through spiritual discernment literally from the womb (Luke 1:41–44).

Finally, *parental nurture is at the heart of child care, even before birth.* Children are part of the family, even the unborn. Scripture describes that children are to be nurtured by parents and the community of faith and that this starts at a very early age (cf. Feutch, 1966).

The Fetus in Theological Context

Marcia Bunge (2008) notes that children are often the subject of significant theological dialogue and attention. More specifically, three major theological debates of the church are centered on unborn children: the *Incarnation* with implications for the deity of Christ; *Christian anthropology*, which determines the innate nature of humanity; and the *pre-existence of the soul*, which was part of neo-Platonism's influence on the early church's theology.

Incarnation: The most important unborn baby in the Bible is Jesus. It is central to the Christian faith that the eternal Word of God took human flesh and lived a human life in this world (John 1:14) which started with Jesus's immaculate conception. Issues of Christology in the early church may have reached a definitive conclusion with the Chalcedonian Definition in A.D. 451, but even it had to address the nature of Jesus in the womb, introducing the word Θεοτοκο' (Gk. *theotokos*, God-bearer) not so much to describe Mary, but Jesus's synchronistic nature as both wholly God and wholly human.

Christian anthropology: The question of humanity's spiritual default setting—depravity, innocence, or good—is accentuated with the question of childhood conversion-transformation (Estep, 2002; Estep, 2010). This debate partially fueled the question of infant baptism in the early church, serving as a theological rational for the practice that remained questioned into the fourth century A.D. (Estep, 2008). Horace Bushnell's concept of Christian nurture rested on the "organic unity of the family," which he stressed continues even after birth, implying that it existed prior to birth (Bushnell, 1846, 27, 30, 92).

Pre-Existence of the Soul: Due to the significant influence of Platonic thought on the early church, the pre-existence of the soul was the subject of frequent debate within the patristic tradition. Three options emerged within the authorities of the early church: (1) Every child gets a newly formed soul; (2) Every child inherits the soul from the parents, and (3) The soul pre-exists and it is put into the body. Augustine and Jerome discussed this at length in their letters, settling on the second option, called *traducianism* (Disney and Poston, 2010, 274–279; Greggo, 2005). This debate was not limited to the Western church tradition, but also occurred in the Eastern Church as demonstrated by Theodoret of Kyros and the Antiochian schools theologizing on the relationship of the physical and spiritual existence of individuals before birth (Crego, 1996).

TOWARD A CHRISTIAN RATIONALE ON PRENATAL MINISTRY

By integrating the insights from fetal origin theory with those of Scripture and church tradition, several affirmations may be made regarding a Christian approach to ministering to the unborn child providing a Christian rationale for prenatal ministry in the Church.

1. God values the life and individuality of the unborn child.

2. Regardless of the default setting of humanity (innocence, depravity, goodness), the child is not a *tabula rasa* at birth.

3. We can influence the life, disposition, and learning of a child even before he or she is born.

4. Parents, particularly mothers, are responsible for the nurture of children from conception through childhood.

5. Spirituality is one of the factors that should comprise a child's prenatal environment such as prenatal formation of trust which is foundational to later faith development as theorized by Erikson and Fowler.

6. General interest in prenatal health/fetal origins is a ministry opportunity for the contemporary church.

The insights of fetal origins theory embellish the affirmations of Scripture regarding unborn children and contribute a valuable perspective on the subject of the church's prenatal ministry.

PRECEDENT LITERATURE IN PRENATAL STUDIES

The importance of prenatal education was well recognized and encouraged by seventeenth-century educator Comenius (1592–1670), who in his *Pampaedia* (lifelong education) distinguished eight stages of human life and characterized eight other 'schools.' It was credited as the first classification of such in the history of pedagogy, which considered the moment of conception as the starting point of the whole human life (Gundem, 49–50).

The importance of prenatal care has also been recognized and practiced in Korea for thousands of years. Sajudang Lee (1739–1821), a Korean mother of four children, wrote *The Mystery of Prenatal Education*, which is recognized as the world's first book on the subject. Lee wrote from information that had been orally transmitted and practiced by Korean people for thousands of years as well as from her own experiences raising children. Amazingly, the book also describes not only the mother's roles and responsibilities for her unborn baby but also the father's involvement as well.

In recent years, a number of scientists have investigated the importance and effects of prenatal care based on scientific results. And those studies agree that prenatal care/education is science and it must be practiced by all expecting mothers. For instance, Soo Yong Kim (2011), a Korean neuroscientist, specifically investigated the relationship between prenatal care and brain development. He concluded that an unborn baby's brain—the cerebral cortex development—is deeply related to the love that the unborn baby receives from the mother and father. In other words, the brain of an unborn baby who is loved by parents develops faster than one who is not loved by his/her parents. Also, the cerebral cortex of the infant who is loved is much thicker compared to the child who is unloved. Kim asserts that the love of parents is the foundation of prenatal education (Kim, 99).

Frederick Wirth, a neonatologist, agreed with Kim and wrote, "your love work is more effective before birth than after your child is born because your brain chemically communicates with him/her directly," (Wirth, 2001, 47). Wirth also investigated how the emotion of the expecting mother affects the development of the unborn infant's emotional well-being.

> When the infant's mother enjoys her partner's rendition of what happened, her brain is secreting neuropeptides that make her feel content, loved, and safe. The neuropeptides produced by her brain flow out into the bloodstream

> and cross the placenta to bathe the developing baby's brain. The infant's brain is affected by this experience and after twenty-eight weeks of pregnancy he will remember the emotions he passively experienced while hearing his parents' laughter and conversation. This is the beginning of the child's emotional development and the early simple experiences are the foundations for later reactions to similar stimuli. This is how your infant prepares for the emotional world he/she will greet after birth. (41–42)

In fact, both authors agree about the importance of mother's emotional well-being, especially the feeling of being loved. Annie Murphy Paul (2010), a science reporter, in her book *Origin*, affirmed that the mother's health and well-being has a crucial impact on the unborn infant. A fetus can hear the sound of the mother's voice by the fourth month in her womb; by the seventh month, a fetus can learn language and, at birth, the baby cries with her mother's native accent. A fetus can learn taste and smell from his mother's foods and flavors.

Effectiveness of Prenatal Education

Several studies investigated the effects of prenatal education/care. David Olds (2008) conducted a thirty-year longitudinal study to research the effects of the nurse-family partnership program which was designed for low-income mothers during their first pregnancy. Results indicated that the program outcomes were positive and cost-effective. Babies were healthier mentally and physically eliminating costs usually set aside to care for weak or sickly newborns.

Larisa Duncan and Nancy Bardacke (2010) developed a curriculum called "Mindfulness-based Childbirth and Parenting Education (MBCP)," and practiced it with fifty-nine groups of expectant couples. MBCP focuses on family health and well-being during pregnancy and childbirth and early parenting through meditation, stress coping, and emotion control. The result was also positive. Couples who practiced the mindfulness during pregnancy exercises showed less pregnancy anxiety, depression, and negative effects related to pregnancy.

The importance of prenatal care is getting more attention as growing number of infants are born with some sort of disabilities. According to USA Today, one in six children (about 17 percent of children) have some sorts of developmental disabilities (Szabo, 2011). In fact, mother's antenatal anxiety explained 22 percent of the variance in ADHD symptoms and 9 percent of anxious symptoms in eight to nine-year-old children. Another study demonstrated that significant anxiety in late pregnancy was associated with a doubling of the risk of having a child with ADHD, anxiety, depression or a conduct disorder at four and seven years of age (Mann et al., 2008, 19).

In order to find ways to help release maternal anxiety, a number of studies have been conducted to investigate the effect of religion or spirituality in mental and emotional illness or anxiety; however, the studies showed mixed results regarding the effects of religion in maternal anxiety treatment. Some studies showed a positive effect of religion on maternal anxiety (Mann et al., 2008; King et al., 2005; Baetz et al., 2006; Shreve-Neiger and Edelstein, 2004); while others showed reverse effect (Smith et al., 2003; Dailey and Stewart, 2007). Also, the studies conducted by Koenig (2009) and Baetz et al. (2006) showed mixed results on the relationship between religiosity/spirituality and mental disorder. Below is the summary of those findings:

- Participation in non-organizational religious activities were significantly associated with lower occurrences of moderate to severe anxiety symptoms (Mann *et al.*, 2008);

- Religious attendance and intrinsic religious orientation (viewing religion as the framework in which all of life is understood) were generally associated with lower levels of anxiety (Smith et al., 2003; Shreve-Neiger and Edelstein, 2004);

- Worship attendance was significantly inversely associated with mental illness (including panic disorder and social phobia, though generalized anxiety was not assessed) and substance abuse in Canadian adults, while endorsement of spiritual values was not a protective for most conditions (Baetz et al., 2006);

- A few studies found that certain aspects of religiosity (most notably extrinsic religiosity, which views religious activities as means to an end rather than being worthwhile for their own sake) were associated with increased anxiety (cited in Mann et al., 2008);

- High worship frequency was associated with fewer psychiatric disorders. In contrast, those who considered higher spiritual values important (in a search for meaning, in giving strength, and in understanding life's difficulties) experienced more psychiatric disorders (Baetz et al., 2006).

The implication is that for those who have faith in some religions or practice some sort of spiritual rituals, spirituality can help lower levels of anxiety. On the contrary, for those who do not have faith in any religion, some religions or religious practices may have a negative effect resulting in increased stress levels.

PRACTICES AND PRINCIPLES OF PRENATAL MINISTRY

Prenatal education is widely practiced in Korea in both church and non-church settings especially, by OBGYN facilities. A number of Korean Christian higher institutions and seminaries offer a prenatal education certificate program as part of continuing education. Churches provide a prenatal education class once or twice a year as a part of Christian education program and in conjunction with community outreach. Most churches offer a four to twelve week series related to prenatal care.

The focus of the prenatal program is centered on the unborn baby's physical, intellectual, emotional, and spiritual well-being, and churches usually invite experts on the subjects to fulfill the objectives of the program. Some of the topics that are taught in prenatal schools include: becoming a parent and its biblical perspectives; the mystery of life and the process of giving birth; pregnancy and mothers' psychology, especially the importance of mothers' emotional well-being; the prenatal care for the unborn baby's character development; the prenatal care for the unborn baby's brain development; music in relation to the prenatal care; storytelling in relation to the prenatal care; foods in relation to the prenatal care; physical exercises in relation to the prenatal care; the role of father in relation to the prenatal care.

Prenatal education is also practiced in Korean churches in the USA as well as non-church settings although it is not as commonly recognized and practiced as it is in Korea. In the states, the focus of prenatal education centers on how to meet the emotional and physical needs of expecting mothers. Some of the prenatal care programs that are practiced include childbirth education, doula, meals for new families, mentoring, new parent support, lending library, and supply closet.

In the church settings, the prenatal ministry is largely conducted by volunteers with some necessary training instead of by specialists. Although a legally recognized standard for training is not required for church volunteers in America to provide the prenatal education, such as a doula or childbirth, formal training is highly encouraged. Various Christian organizations, such as Birthing Naturally, Apple Tree Family, and First Birth Ministries, offer prenatal educational programs and resources, including Teaching Christian Childbirth, the Christian Childbirth Workbook, the Christian Childbirth Handbook, the Lord of Birth, and 40 Weeks. These organizations promote and support prenatal education by providing resources and information, by helping churches to set up a prenatal education program, or by offering small group Bible study programs or mentoring programs in order to help expecting mothers apply the principles of Christianity to their pregnancy and birth, drawing them closer to God.

Public organizations also offer prenatal educational programs such as La Leche League Model, AA Model, and Couple to Couple League. Monthly or bi-weekly small group meetings among participants are common practice for these programs, and the foci of the programs are to educate and support the pregnant mothers' emotional and physical well-being.

A MODEL FOR PRENATAL MINISTRY

We are not limited to only educating a child once she is born, but we can begin to influence a child months before birth. The church's ministry to children has traditionally extended to the time of birth but the insights gleaned from Fetal Origins Theory suggest that it could begin much earlier. We already have birth rituals in the church, but many of these "birthing rites" have not been inclusive of or affirming of the expectant or new mothers. Enzer-Probst (2004) identifies "secular rites," referring to medical attention to the mother and unborn child, advocating that the church should do the same. The prenatal ministry of the church is one designed not only for the unborn child, but also for the parents, siblings, and family as a whole.

Four-Fold Model for Prenatal Ministry

The following template for a four-fold integrative model of prenatal ministry emerges from a survey of prenatal ministry church websites:

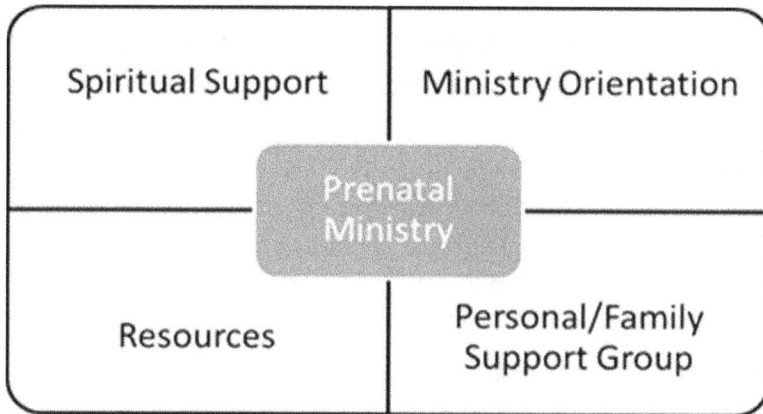

Spiritual Support	Ministry Orientation
Prenatal Ministry	
Resources	Personal/Family Support Group

Spiritual Support may include such items as a parents commitment service (Eph 6:4), prayer for the child, mother, and family during pregnancy, or engaging in rituals such as a parent dedication prior to the birth of the child (cf. Estep, 2002). Encouraging a mother and family to keep a personal reflection and journal of their experience has likewise proven beneficial to the family during pregnancy. Also, read, speak, and listen to the child to have a positive impact on their development even prior to birth.

Churches can do a *Ministry Orientation* for new parents, who have probably not had a previous occasion or reason to enter the nursery. Giving tours and providing expectant parents with opportunities for parental instruction and orientation is a common practice in Korea. Sharing with parents the opportunities for them and their family helps build relationship between the church, the family, and ultimately the unborn child.

Resources may be provided to the family for both the care of the unborn child and for themselves. Information, guidance, and child development from the church would be very beneficial, as would food and nutritional resources for those less fortunate. In Korea, health care is a common component and physicians are often invited to speak to the congregation about nutrition and exercise. Perhaps most unique is the provision of prenatal and natal tools such as a speaking tube, music, and reading material.

Personal/Family Support Group also contributes to the prenatal ministry. Conducting prenatal support groups of peers is especially helpful in light of single parenting. Emotional support is also crucial to lower the emotional stress for any pregnancy where there is the unfortunate loss of a child through miscarriage/still born birth.

Here is opportunity to discuss birthing options, deal with unexpected pregnancies, or provide counsel and support when there are serious complications.

CONCLUSION

In 1932 Aldous Huxley, famed author and humanist, released his book *Brave New World*. In it, he describes a world based entirely on a manufacturing paradigm, wherein even embryos are preprogramed to fulfill a particular function and place in society, from the high achieving Alphas to the subordinate Epsilons. Neither Fetal Origins Theory nor Prenatal Ministry claims to offer such exaggerated promises.

Prenatal Ministry is based on the affirmations of Scripture and church tradition that value the life and potential of the unborn child and supports the findings of the recently developed theories of Fetal Origins regarding the learning capacity of children prior to birth. It has not only the potential of improving the life of the child before being born, but also of ministering to the expectant family while building a congregational ethos that actively values mothers, families, and the unborn, as well as challenging Christian educators to make the most of every possible opportunity to advance ministry.

REFERENCES

Aasgaard, Reidar. "Like a Child: Paul's Rhetorical Use of Childhood." In *The Child in the Bible*, edited by Marcia J. Bunge. Grand Rapids: Eerdmans Publishing Company, 2008, 249–277.

Baetz, Marilyn, Rudy Bowen, Glenn Jones, and Tulay Koru-Sengul. "How Spiritual Values and Worship Attendance Relate to Psychiatric Disorders in the Canadian Population," *Canadian Journal of Psychiatry* 51 (2006): 654–661.

Bakke, O. M. *When Children Became People: The Birth of Childhood in Early Christianity*. Minneapolis: Fortress Press, 2005.

Bunge, Marcia J. Bunge (eds.) *The Child in Christian Thought*. Grand Rapids: Eerdmans Publishing Company, 2001.

Bushnell, Horace. *Christian Nurture*. Grand Rapids: Baker Books, 1846.

Centers for Disease Control. "Mothers Beginning Prenatal Care in the First Trimester by Race/Ethnicity, 2005." Accessed February 24, 2012. http://mchb.hrsa.gov/.

Columbia Psychiatry. 2012. "Christine Monk." Accessed February 24, 2012. http://asp.cumc.columbia.edu/facdb/ profile_list.asp?uni=cem31&DepAffil=Psychiatry&view=research

Crego, Paul. "Theodoret of Kyros on the Relationship of the Body and the Soul before Birth." Greek Orthodox Theological Review 41 (1996): 19–37.

Dailey, D. E. and Stewart, A. L. "Psychometric Characteristics of the Spiritual Perspective Scale in Pregnant African-American Women." *Res Nurs Health* 30 (2007): 61–71.

DiPietro, Janet A.; Costigan, Kathleen; Bornstein, Marc H.; Hahn, Chun-Shin; Achy-Brou, Aristide. "Fetal Heart Rate and Variability: Stability and Prediction to Developmental Outcomes in Early Childhood." *Child Development* 78 (2007): 1788–1798.

Dirix, Chantal E. H., Jan G. Nijhuis, Henk W. Jongsma, and Gerald Hornstra. "Aspects of Fetal Learning and Memory." *Child Development* 80 (2009): 1251–1258.

Disney, Lindsey, and Poston, Larry. "The Breath of Life: Christian Perspectives on Conception and Ensoulment." *Anglican Theological Review* 92 (2010): 271–296.

Dobinson, C. H. (Ed.). *Comenius and Contemporary Education.* A Paper Presented at an International Symposium for Commemoration of the Tercentenary of the Death of Comenius. Published by UNESCO Institute for education, Hamburg, 1970.

Duncan, Larisa. G. and Nancy Bardacke, N. "Mindfulness-Based Childbirth and Parenting Education: Promoting Family Mindfulness During the Perinatal Period," *Journal of Child Family Studies* 19 (2010) 190–202.

Enzer-Probst, Brigitte. "Waiting for Delivery: Counseling Pregnant Women as an Issue for the Church." *International Journal of Pastoral Theology* 8 (2004): 185–201.

Estep, James Riley. "Christian Anthropology: Humanity as the Imago Dei." In *Christian Formation: Integrating Theology and Human Development* edited by James Riley Estep and Jonathan H. Kim. Nashville: Broadman and Holman, 2010, 9–36.

————. "The Christian Nurture of Children in the Second and Third Centuries." In *Nurturing Children's Spirituality: Christian Perspectives and Best Practices* edited by Holly Catterton Allen. Eugene, Oregon: Cascade Books, 2008, 51–77.

————. "Childhood Transformation: Toward an Educational Theology of Childhood Conversion and Spiritual Formation." *Stone-Campbell Journal* 5 (2002): 183–206.

Feucht, Oscar. "Place of the Family in the Church's Educational Ministry." *Concordia Theological Monthly,* 37 (1966): 340–354.

Gonzalez-Gonzalez, N. L., M. N. Suarez, B. Perez-Piñero, H. Armas, E. Domenceh, and J. L. Bartha. "Persistence of Fetal Memory into Neonatal Life." *Acta Obstericia et Gynecologica* 85 (2006): 1160–1164.

Greggo, Stephen P. "Soul Origin: Revising Creationist and Traducianist Perspectives in Light of Current Trends in Developmental Psychology." *Journal of Psychology and Theology* 33 (2005): 258–267.

Gundem, Bjorg. B. "Vivat Comenius: A Commemorative Essay on Johann Amos Comenius, 1592–1670," *Journal of Curriculum and Supervision* 8 (Fall, 1992): 43–55.

Gutteling, Barbara M.; de Weerth, Ca. "Prenatal Cigarette Exposure and Infant Learning Stimulation as Predictors of Cognitive Control in Childhood." *Journal of Abnormal Child Psychology* 34 (2006): 787–796. (EJ748600)

Heteren, Cathelijne F. van, P Focco Boekkooi, Henk W. Jongsma, and Jan G. Nijhuis. "Fetal Learning and Memory." *The Lancet* 256 (2000): 1169–1170.

Hopkins, Brian and Scott Johnson. *Prenatal Development of Postnatal Functions.* Westport, Connecticut: Praeger, 2005

Huang, Hao. "Structure of the Fetal Brain: What We Are Learning from Diffusion Tensor Imaging." *Neuroscientist* 16 (2010): 634–649.

James, David K. "Fetal Learning: A Critical Review." *Infant and Child Development* 19 (2010): 45–54.

James, D. K. and C. J. Spencer, and B. W. Stepsis. "Fetal Learning: A Prospective Randomized Controlled Study." *Ultrasound Obstet Gynecol* 20 (2002): 431–328.

Kapoor, Amita, Alice Kostaki, Christopher Janus, and Stephen G. Matthews. "The Effects of Prenatal Stress on Learning in Adult Offspring is Dependent on the Timing of the Stressor." *Behavioural Brain Research* 197 (2009): 144–149.

Kawai, Nobuyuki. "Towards a New Study on Associative Learning in Human Fetuses: Fetal Associative Learning in Primates." *Infant and Child Development* 19 (2010): 55–59.

Kim, Soo Yong. 뇌과학이 밝혀낸 놀라운 태교 이야기 (*Amazing stories on pre-natal education revealed by brain science*). Seoul, Korea: 종이거울사 (Paper Mirror), 2011.

King, Dana. E., D. Cummings, and L. Whetstone. "Attendance at Religious Services and Subsequent Mental Health in Midlife Women." *Int. J Psychiatry Med* 35 (2005): 287–297.

Kisilevsky, Barbara S., and Hains, Sylvia M. J. "Onset and Maturation of Fetal Heart Rate Response to the Mother's Voice over Late Gestation." *Developmental Science* 14(2011): 214–223. (EJ941760)

Koenig, Harold G. "Research on Religion, Spirituality, and Mental Health: A Review." *Canadian Journal of Psychiatry* 54 (2009): 283–291.

Lollar, Donald and José F. Cordero. "Prenatal and Perinatal Factors in Child Development: A Commentary." *School Psychology Quarterly* 22(2007): 8–12.

Mann, Joshua R., Robert E. McKeown, Janice Bacon, Roumen Vesselinov, and Freda Bush. "Do Antenatal Religious and Spiritual Factors Impact the Risk of Postpartum Depressive Symptoms?" *Journal of Women's Health* 17(2008): 745–755.

Mann, Joshua R., Robert E. McKeown, Janice Bacon, Roumen Vesselinov, and Freda Bush. "Religiosity, Spirituality and Antenatal Anxiety in Southern U.S. Women." *Archives of Women's Mental Health* 11 (2008): 19–26.

Mezzacappa, Enrico, Buckner, John C., and Earls, Felton. "Prenatal Cigarette Exposure and Infant Learning Stimulation as Predictors of Cognitive Control in Childhood." *Developmental Science* 14(2011): 881–891. (EJ929761)

O'Connor, Thomas G., Heron Jonathan and Vivette Glover. "Antenatal Anxiety Predicts Child Behavioral/Emotional Problems Independently of Postnatal Depression." *Journal of the American Academy of Child and Adolescent Psychiatry* 41 (2002): 1470–1477.

Olds, David L. "Preventing Child Maltreatment and Crime with Prenatal and Infancy Support of Parents: The Nurse-Family Partnership." *The Journal of Scandinavian Studies in Criminology and Crime Prevention* 9 (2008): 2–24.

Paul, Annie Murphy. "What Babies Learn Before they are Born." 2011 TED Global Conference, (Edinburgh, Scotland). Accessed February 24, 2012. http://www.cnn.com/2011/12/11/opinion/ paul-ted-talk/index.html.

_____. *Origins: How the Nine Months before Birth Shape the Rest of Our Lives*. New York: Free Press, 2010a.

_____. "Origins: How the Nine Months before Birth Shape the Rest of Our Lives." *Time* 176 (2010b). Accessed February 24, 2012. http://www.time.com/time/magazine/article/0,9171,2021065,00.html.

Rodriguez, Alina, and Waldenstrom, Ulla. "Maternal Pre-Pregnancy Obesity and Risk for Inattention and Negative Emotionality in Children." *Journal of Child Psychology and Psychiatry* 49 (2008): 967–976. (EJ808056)

Sevelinges, Yannick; Sullivan, Regina M.; Messaoudi, Belkacem. "Neonatal Odor-Shock Conditioning Alters the Neural Network Involved in Odor Fear Learning in Adulthood." *Learning & Memory* 15 (2008): 649–656. (EJ809449)

Shreve-Neiger, Andrea K. and Barry A. Edelstein. "Religion and Anxiety: A Critical Review of the Literature," *Clinical Psychology Review* 24 (2004): 379–397.

Smith, Timothy B., Michael E. McCullough, and Justin Poll. "Religiousness and Depression: Evidence for a Main Effect and the Moderating Influence of Stressful Life Events." *Psychological Bulletin* 129 (July 2003): 614–636.

Szabo, Liz. "One in Six Children have a Developmental Disability." *USA Today,* May 22, 2011. Accessed February 1, 2013. http://usatoday30.usatoday.com/news/health/story/health/story/2011/05/One-in-six-children-have-a-developmental-disability/47467520/1.

Thompson, Marianne Meye. "Children in the Gospel of John." In *The Child in the Bible*, edited by Marcia J. Bunge. Grand Rapids: Eerdmans Publishing Company, 2008, 194–214.

Wirth, Frederick. *Prenatal Parenting: The Complete Psychological and Spiritual Guide to Loving your Unborn Child.* New York: HarperCollins, 2001.

Chapter 11

Interactive Age-Specific Strategies for Introducing Beginning Readers to the Bible as Authentic Text

Barbara Fisher

In 2011, the King James Version celebrated its 400th anniversary! Since 1603, this amazing and ancient publication has had significant influence on great western literature, art and music. It is the only book that has been consistently published since the invention of the printing press. It is the most translated book in the world, and it is still the best-selling publication of all time (Ball, 2011). This ancient text continues to inspire writers in the twenty-first century as demonstrated by the movie, *The Passion of the Christ* and the popular book, *The Da Vinci Code.*

If this ancient text is such a valuable and unique book, why is current research pointing to a noticeable decline in Bible reading and biblical literacy among Christians from all age brackets (Morris, 2008)? Why is there such a lack of knowledge regarding this important ancient book and its message? Even though there is a proliferation of contemporary Bible translations, easy accessibility to personal electronic Bible devices and increasing Bible affordability, why has the decline in biblical literacy continued? Peterson (2003,) wants to know, "How has it come to pass that the enormous success in achieving mass literacy so that everyone can read the Bible and the technological invention that revolutionized printing so that everyone can have a Bible to read has resulted in such widespread biblical illiteracy?" (11).

Cole and Ovwigho's research (2010,) exploring children's personal scripture engagement, found that, "less than one-fifth" of the children surveyed in their study "reads or listens to the Bible with their family at least four days a week" (111). If the next generation is going to reverse the current negative trend and embrace Christian values and biblical truths in a meaningful and purposeful way then we need a generation of Christians who from infancy have been taught to know and love the scriptures.

One program that is actively addressing the problems of biblical illiteracy among children is *Bible Reading 4 Beginner Readers*. This program teaches non-readers and beginner readers to read and positively interact with the Bible. It aims to nurture and develop positive Bible reading habits in five and six year-olds because Barna's research indicates that the habits we form in our impressionable years are the behaviours that define us as we grow older (The Barna Group, 2004). "You have been taught the Holy Scriptures from childhood, and they have given you the wisdom to receive the salvation that comes by trusting in Christ Jesus," (2 Tim 3:15).

RECOGNIZED BENEFITS OF BIBLE ENGAGEMENT

The Bible is central to a Christian's daily faith formation and experience (Ps 119:105) and it informs our understanding of who we are and who God is (Peterson, 2003). It is a living book. According to Hebrews 4:12, "The word of God is alive and active." Reynolds (2003) states that when we engage with God's word we can look into the heart of God. Age or intellectual ability is inconsequential declares Dewey (2001) because, "The simplest soul and the youngest child, if they are open to God, can get as much as anyone else from reading the Bible," (7). It is the great lesson book, says White (1943), and children should have access to its pages so that they can learn to know God. Peterson (2003) argues that, "It is not a difficult book that only 'smart' people can get" (13). According to White (1943), angels are sent to impress the mind and enlighten our understanding.

One important aspect of biblical literacy that is rarely mentioned is the intellectual benefits it affords the reader. Jeynes's (2009) research on the relationship of Bible literacy to academic achievement and behavior found that the students with the highest level of biblical literacy also ranked the highest in academic achievement and displayed the best behavior of the three groups in the cohort. Interestingly, those with the lowest level of biblical literacy also had the lowest academic scores and worst behavior of the three groups.

Other benefits of Bible engagement include a balanced life style, a resilience of character and the discernment of truth (White, 1943). Cole and Ovwigho (2012) discovered that both adults and children who read the Bible at least four times a week engaged in less risk-taking behavior and experienced less personal issues. Second Timothy 3:16 reminds the reader that, "All Scripture is God-breathed and is useful for teaching, rebuking, correcting and training in righteousness."

If children are to discover the dynamic nature of God's Word then they need to interact individually with the Bible so that the Word of God can speak to them and teach them (Castle, 1993). Children live in a fast-moving, stimulating, electronic and instant-gratification age, so Bible teaching needs to be innovative, creative and activity-based if it is going to be seen as relevant, informative and important.

Current practical Bible teaching resources mention relevant ways of teaching Bible stories, how to have innovative Bible lessons, ways of engaging in lively and relevant discussions and many more ideas which are all necessary. However, there is a noticeable lack of a variety of resources actually showing how or where to use the Bible in a Bible lesson. Many of the resources appear to talk about teaching the Bible and Bible stories, but excluded are suggestions of actual hands-on experiences that encourage young children to individually interact with the Bible.

While it is true there are parts of the Bible that only adults can comprehend the following thoughts need to be considered.

> Our Heavenly father, in giving His word, did not overlook the children. In all that men have written, where can be found anything that has such a hold upon the heart, anything so well adapted to awaken the interest of the little ones, as the stories of the Bible? (White, 1952, 185)

Perhaps we are missing out on the most impressionable years of children's lives. Why not use the Bible as an authentic reading text in the teaching of early language literacy skills?

AN EARLY LITERACY INTERACTIVE BIBLE READING PROGRAM

It is a fact, credited to the work of the Bible Society, that the Bible can be used to teach literacy. If the Bible can be used to teach literacy to the illiterate in a variety of non-English speaking countries surely the Bible has a place in early literacy education where English is the primary language. If we believe that Bible reading brings the reader into "contact with the thoughts of the Infinite" (White, 1952, 124), why have we traditionally waited until children are competent readers before introducing them to the experience of personal Bible reading? By waiting are we wasting some of the most important years of children's lives? The author of the following *Bible Reading 4 Beginner Readers* program believes that a love for engaging with and reading the Bible can be fostered and developed in impressionable young children by engaging them in age-appropriate, interactive, supported Bible reading experiences.

Bible Reading 4 Beginner Readers (BR4), an original Bible literacy program, was designed, created, developed and trialled by this researcher. Its primary goal is to encourage five to six year-olds, both readers and non-readers, to interactively experience the Bible on a personal level. Like any early literacy program engagement, nurture and success are important considerations at this stage of early development. The BR4 program emphasises interaction with the Bible rather than information about it or how to use it. There are no pre-requisite Bible reading skills for this program. It is a non-threatening early literacy program that nurtures and encourages children to interactively read a known Bible story. Once children's literacy skills are more developed, specific Bible reference and navigation skills are then introduced in BR4 Stage Four. This biblical literacy program can be used in a variety of settings:

1. as a stand-alone program, or

2. as an addition to any Bible story time at home, or at school, or as part of the Children's Ministry church program.

Competent reading ability is not a pre-requisite for this program. The program has been developed so that all children can experience success and achievement at all stages.

THE BIBLE READING 4 BEGINNER READERS (BR4) PROGRAM STRUCTURE

The BR4 program, currently being taught as part of a Christian pre-service elementary teacher degree program in Australia, is an interactive Bible reading program that is divided into four sequential stages. It begins with an introductory exploration of the Bible as the sacred text before developing word, sentence, and verse location skills in a supportive and nurturing environment. The structure is as follows:

- *BR4 Stage One Bible Exploration*: The beginning stage encourages an initial exploration of the Bible as a sacred book and encourages mastery of page location skills.

- *BR4 Stage Two Word Level*: The next stage introduces early literacy Bible word recognition, Bible word identification and Bible word isolation skills and strategies.

- *BR4 Stage Three Sentence Level*: This stage continues to develop the skills from BR4 Stage Two but introduces the more advanced skills of early literacy repeated Bible reading, Bible sentence rhythm patterns, and scripture songs.

- *BR4 Stage Four Verse Level*: The final stage is the most advanced stage and continues to develop the skills from BR4 Stage Three while adding the more complex skills of Bible navigation and verse location.

BIBLE READING 4 BEGINNER READERS (BR4) PROGRAM DETAILS

BR4 Stage One: Bible Exploration Explained

Bible exploration is the introductory stage where children explore the Bible as a sacred book. For children at this early stage of the program, discovering Bible page numbering, contents, maps etc. are all relevant experiences. Mastering page location skills and the skill of placing a bookmark in a specific page are extremely helpful at this stage.

These skills can save a lot of frustration if the Bible is accidently closed or the specific page inadvertently lost. If the introductory lessons are conducted in a classroom or group setting, it is advisable to use the same Bible version for the entire class. The particular version is not significant at this stage but a personal copy of a large print Bible is recommended with verse numbers easily identifiable on the margin. When the children have mastered the skill of finding the correct page, it's time to move up to BR4 Stage Two.

BR4 Stage Two: Word Level Explained

The next stage introduces the children to interactive early literacy Bible word recognition, Bible word isolation, and Bible word identification strategies. To facilitate positive initial experiences with the Bible, it is expeditious to begin with the book of Genesis. It is the first and easiest book of the Bible to find and Genesis 1 has several repetitive words and phrases suitable for the beginner reader. The word "God" appears at least fourteen times from Genesis 1:1 to Genesis 1:14 and the repetitive phrase, "the first day . . . the second day," appears throughout the chapter.

Daily revision of previously encountered words, before new words are introduced, is a valuable teaching technique for this stage of the program. By learning a minimum of one new word a day the beginner reader can recognise at least five new words within a week. By the end of two weeks the children may be able to recognise ten words and the beginner reader will now have the skill to independently read a small number of specific words found in the Bible. When the children are comfortable with finding, identifying and remembering about twenty words such as Bible characters, places and objects, they are ready for the next step in the BR4 program.

Word Level Interactive Group Bible Reading Strategies

As the adult reads a stated Bible passage:

1. The children listen for a specified word, such as God, and clap each time they hear it read aloud from the passage.

2. Groups of children listen for a specified word, for example, Group One: God; Group Two: Adam; and Group Three: Eve, and then perform a designated action for example, Group One: clap; Group Two: stamp, and Group Three: thumbs up each time they hear the word read aloud from the passage.

3. The children look for a written word such as God in their Bible and raise their hand every time they hear the word read aloud from the passage.

4. The children look for a written word such as fish or sheep and do the actions or make a sound every time they hear the word read aloud from the passage.

5. The children look for several words such as Jesus, sheep or shepherd, in their Bible, which are written on cards and given to different class members. Every time a word is read the children hold up their card.

Word Level Lesson Plan

The Lesson Plan in Table 1 illustrates the BR4 program as an integral part of a Bible story time. It demonstrates how children can interactively read the Bible when word recognition and sound identification skills are applied in a supported learning environment.

TABLE 1: Stage Two word level lesson plan

Stage Two: Word Level Lesson Aim:	
At the end of the lesson the children should be able to retell the main points of the Bible story and recognise the written name of God in Genesis 1:1.	
Procedure:	
Step 1	At the conclusion of telling the creation Bible story the adult opens her Bible to Genesis 1:1 and writes the page number on a 6 x 8 inch card and displays it to the class. The children are assisted with finding this page in their Bible.
Step 2	The children place their book mark in the correct page.
Step 3	The adult writes the word "God" on a 6 x 8 inch card and then reads the written word "God" aloud. This activity associates the sound of the Bible character's name with the Bible character's written name. This is developing word and sound identification skills.
Step 4	Collectively the children say the Bible character's name that is written on the 6 x 8 inch card before individually looking for it on the specified Bible page.
Step 5	The children say the written name aloud as they point to the Bible character's name in their Bibles. Individually they repeat it aloud again several times while pointing to their Bibles.
Conclusion:	
Individually the children point to the identified Bible character's name in their Bible, and read it aloud to several children in the class. Finally, the children leave the bookmark in the specified page. This is done to assist the children in finding the Bible story, and the relevant Bible character's name, when the Bible is next opened.	

BR4 Stage Three: Sentence Level Explained

This stage continues to develop the skills from BR4 Stage Two but now includes more advanced early literacy skills of repeated readings, rhythm patterns and scripture sentence songs. Specific Bible sentences are selected for repeated readings, sentence rhythm patterns are introduced to assist in reading and memorising the selected Bible sentences, and the selected Bible sentence is set to music. Once children are comfortable finding ten or more Bible sentences independently it is time to move to BR4 Stage Four.

Sentence Level Interactive Bible Reading Strategies:

There are three sequential strategies for Stage Three:

Strategy A: Bible Sentence Songs Commercially Available

Strategy B: Scripture Sentences Set to Public Domain Music

Strategy C: Bible Sentence Rhythm Patterns

     Following is an explanation of each strategy.

Strategy A: Bible Sentence Songs Commercially Available

Table 2 lists three commercially available scripture songs. The music may often be found on the Internet.

TABLE 2: Commercially available scripture songs

Bible Text	Bible Sentences using Scripture Songs
Psalm 118:24	"This is the day the Lord has made; Let us rejoice and be glad in it."
Rev 3:20	"Behold I stand at the door and knock. If anyone hears my voice and opens the door I will come in."
Nehemiah 8:10	"The joy of the Lord is your strength."

Strategy B: Scripture Sentences Set to Public Domain Music

Table 3 illustrates how three scripture sentences can be set to well-known, traditional, public domain music. The lyrics in the following examples have been specifically written to fit the rhythm of the music.

TABLE 3: Scripture sentence songs set to public domain music

Bible Text	Bible Sentence Lyrics	Traditional & Public Domain Music
Genesis 1:27 "So God created man in his own image."	So God created man in his own image, his own image (Repeat 2x) So God created man In his own image, So God created man in his own image.	Music: *If you're happy and you know it*

Genesis 1:1 "In the beginning God created the heavens and the earth."	In the beginning God created, God created, God created. In the beginning God created the heavens and the earth.	Music: *Mary had a little Lamb*
Psalms 119:105 "Your word is a lamp unto my feet."	Your word is a lamp unto my feet. (Repeat 4x)	Music: *Skip to my Lou*

Strategy C: Bible Sentence Rhythm Patterns

The five examples of rhythm patterns in Table 4 illustrate how to use rhythm patterns to read and interact with a Bible sentence.

TABLE 4: Bible sentence rhythm patterns

BIBLE SENTENCE: Psalms 119:105 NIV, "Your word is a lamp unto my feet."									
Words	Your	word	is	a	lamp	un-	to	my	feet
Example 1 Clap as you say each syllable	clap	clap	clap	clap	clap	clap	clap	clap	clap
Example 2 Clap plus stamp on major words as you say each syllable	clap	stamp	clap	clap	stamp	clap	clap	clap	stamp
Example 3 Clap plus hold up pictures of major words as you say each syllable	clap	Picture of a Bible	Clap	Clap	Picture of a lantern	Clap	Clap	Clap	Picture of feet
Example 4 Clap plus actions for major words as you say each syllable	*Action:* Point to God in heaven	*Action:* Hands open like a book	clap	clap	*Action:* Pretend to hold a candle in the palm of your hand	clap	clap	clap	*Action:* Point to your feet
Example 5 No words but actions and clapping of the entire rhythm pattern	*Action:* Point to God in heaven	*Action:* Hands open like a book	clap	clap	*Action:* Pretend to hold a candle in the palm of your hand	clap	clap	clap	*Action:* Point to your feet

Sentence Level Repeated Reading Lesson Plan

This lesson plan (Table 5) demonstrates how to use the repeated reading strategy to learn to read a Bible sentence.

TABLE 5: Sentence level repeated reading lesson plan

Stage Three: Repeated Reading Lesson Aim:	
At the end of the lesson the children should be able to independently locate and read a Bible sentence.	
Procedure:	
Step 1	With adult assistance, the children locate the allocated Bible page and sentence. A bookmark is placed in the open page.
Step 2	As the adult reads the entire sentence, the children listen and follow along by placing their finger under each word in their Bible.
Step 3	The children place their finger under each word in their Bible and read along with the adult.
Step 4	Repeat Step 2 twice.
Step 5	The children attempt to read the Bible sentence unaided. If the children still need assistance to read the sentence, repeat Step 2 & 3 again. It is crucial at this stage that the children experience success with this new skill.
Conclusion:	
The children read the sentence unassisted to two other people. If this can be accomplished without any adult intervention then the children have clearly demonstrated that they have successfully learnt to read this Bible sentence.	

Sentence Level Music and Repeated Reading Lesson Plan

The Lesson Plan in Table 6 demonstrates how to use the early literacy skill of repeated reading and music to assist learning in a stand-alone lesson.

TABLE 6: Sentence level music and repeated reading lesson plan

Stage Three: Music and Repeated Reading Lesson Aim:	
At the end of the lesson the children should be able to independently read, locate and sing the Bible text found in Nehemiah 8:10, "The joy of the Lord is your strength."	
Procedure:	
Step 1	The children are assisted by an adult to find Nehemiah 8:10. They place their bookmark in the open page.
Step 2	The meaning of the text is discussed. The text is read as the children place their finger under each word.
Step 3	The children repeat the words of the Bible text after the adult.
Step 4	The children are then taught a song using these Bible words set to music.
Step 5	The words, "The joy of the Lord is your strength," are highlighted or underlined in their Bible.

Conclusion:
The children sing the Bible text while pointing to the words in their Bible. Finally, to assist finding Nehemiah 8:10 in the future, the children leave the bookmark in its place. The Bible has now become their Bible Songbook as well as their Bible Reader.

BR4 Stage Four: Verse Level Explained

This is the most advanced BR4 stage. Bible verse location skills are introduced for the first time. BR4 Stage Two and Three skills continue to be developed. Repeated reading strategies will still assist the reading of entire Bible verses. Bible location skill development in BR4 Stage Four is a significant step toward assisting and encouraging the child to become an independent Bible reader.

When the children have mastered verse location skills, then the BR4 program has achieved its goal and the children can be moved on to programs that cover more sophisticated knowledge about how to use the Bible. The advanced skill of learning about the structure and history of the Bible is intentionally kept until the children are comfortable with independently locating Bible verses.

Upon completion of BR4 Stage Four there are a variety of available resources that can strengthen and extend the Bible skills already established. (See Appendix A)

Verse Level Strategy Using Rhyme

Rhyme is a strategy that can assist children while they are learning the skill of finding a specific Bible reference. The following example of a reference rhyme in Table 7 can be found in the book *Follow the Bible: 52 Bible Lessons for Beginner Readers Ages 6–8.*

TABLE 7: Reference Rhyme

Reference Rhyme
"First I find the book or page number of the book.
Then I find the chapter; the big number's where I look.
Last, I find the verse; the small number is the one.
I've got it now!
Finding verses is such fun!" (Ford, Spence, & Stoker, 2003, 36)

Verse Level Lesson Plan- Introducing Bible Location skills

This lesson (Table 8) is adapted from *My Volcano Adventure: Discovering the Bible's Power* (2004, 30). It teaches children how to locate a specific Bible verse.

TABLE 8: Bible location skills lesson plan

Stage Four: Introducing Bible Location Skills Lesson Aim:	
At the end of the lesson the children should have an introductory knowledge of how to locate a Bible reference or a Bible address.	
Procedure:	
Step 1	The adult explains that a Bible text has an address so that we can easily find a specific Bible verse. Our home address lets our friends know where they can find us so a Bible address lets us find a Bible location. Our home address = Town + Street + House Number A Bible address = Book + Chapter + Verse Number
Step 2	Children check the contents list at the front of the Bible to assist them in finding the names and correct order of the 39 Books of the Old Testament and 27 Books of the New Testament.
Step 3	The adult explains the Bible address for Psalms 119:105. The first part of the address is the book's name (e.g. Psalms). The second part is the chapter number (e.g. 119). -Most books are divided into chapters. -Chapters are the big numbers on each page. The third part of the address is the verse number (e.g. 105). -Every chapter in the Bible is divided into verses. -Verses are the small numbers on every Bible page. Most Bible references use a colon (:) to separate the chapter from the verse (e.g. Psalms 119:105).
Step 4	The children use their Bible to explore the selected given text with adult assistance.
Step 5	The children explain and demonstrate, to the adult or other children, how to find a Bible text. If children can do this without any prompting then it shows that they have grasped the skill of Bible navigation and verse location.
Conclusion:	
Play a game of "Bible Seek" where one person chooses a Bible text and the other player has to locate it. Once located they change roles and the game is started again.	

PERSONAL OBSERVATIONS

After several years of implementation, I've noted the following anecdotal results:

1. It was discovered that when the BR4 program was sequentially implemented with 5 to 6 year-old beginner readers that positive attitudes toward the Bible and Bible interactions were developed.

2. Some children chose to read the Bible in preference to other books available to them when they were given a choice of reading material.

3. Reading skill development was given a boost when the children engaged with the living word.

4. Interaction with the Bible became a regular and normal activity for the children and it extended beyond the classroom. Some parents commented that their child independently read the Bible at home.

CONCLUSION

It is my prayer that all children will have the opportunity of engaging in positive, age-appropriate and interactive experiences with the Bible while still young and impressionable. Perhaps if these early habits are nurtured and continually developed by significant adults in these young children's lives they will continue to be Bible reading and Bible practicing Christians in their teenage years. I believe, that with God's help, the BR4 program has the possibility of starting and nurturing a creative and positive biblical literacy trend.

APPENDIX A-ANNOTATED BIBLIOGRAPHY

PARENT/TEACHER AND CHILD BIBLICAL LITERACY RESOURCES:

1. Davis, Mary, ed. *Big Book of Bible Facts and Fun: Cool Stuff about the Bible (Ages 6–12)* Reproducible. Ventura, CA: Gospel Light, 2005.

    A useful reproducible resource that includes, (as listed on the back cover): "Bible maps, fun cartoons, a kid-friendly time line, Bible study pages, Bible book cards, puzzles, and a Bible dictionary."

2. Ford, Linda, Christine Spence and Bruce E. Stoker, eds. *Follow the Bible: 52 Bible Lessons for Beginner Readers Ages* 6–8. Cincinnati, OH: Standard, 2003.

    This resource provides fifty-two reproducible lessons written for readers aged 6 to 8 that, "build enthusiasm for reading Bible stories" (p. 8) and provide skill-building ideas especially for using the Bible.

3. Lale, Tim. *We can Trust the Bible: Helping Children Understand where the Bible Came From.* Nampa, ID: Pacific Press, 2012.

    This book, as it says on the back cover, is "A kid's-eye view of how we got the Bible." It is written in language 6 to 8 years-olds can understand and includes valuable teaching tips and "behind-the-scene glimpses of how the Bible came into existence."

4. Volcano Adventure Team. *My Volcano Adventure: Discovering the Bible's Power.* Fort Collins, CO: Through the Bible, 2004.

    This book is about, "the Bible's origin, authority, message, and purpose," as stated on their website and provides valuable age-appropriate activities. There is a child's book and a Teacher's Guide on-line http://www.discipleland.com

CHILDREN'S BIBLICAL LITERACY RESOURCES:

1. Holmes, Andy. *If You Give a Girl a Bible.* Grand Rapids, MI: Kregel Kidzone, 2005.

This delightful picture book includes comical drawings but a very serious message: If you give a girl a Bible, her faith will grow and she'll want to give her friend a Bible too. There is a similar book available for boys: *If you Give a Boy a Bible.*

2. Thomas, Jerry, D. *Detective Zack: The Secret of Blackloch Castle.* Nampa, ID: Pacific Press, 1998.

This well written children's mystery, chapter book, involves Zack and Stef who seek answers to the mystery of the Blackloch Castle. In the process they discover the story of how we got the Bible. It appeals to those who are aged eight or older.

PARENT/TEACHER BIBLICAL LITERACY RESOURCE:

Fisher, Barbara J. *Developing a Faith-based Education: A Teacher's Manual.* Terrigal, NSW: David Barlow, 2010.

This book offers a comprehensive and balanced view to support the nurturing of spirituality and faith formation for children zero to twelve years of age. It includes strategies for purposeful interactive reading of the Bible with children, fun ideas for memorising Bible texts, and suggestions for personal Bible study programs that are appropriate for children.

REFERENCES

Ball, Bryan. *Can We Still Believe the Bible and Does it Really Matter?* Warburton, VIC: Signs, 2011.

Castle, Tony. "Introduction." In *Teaching the Bible to Children.* ix–x. London, UK: Marshall Pickering, 1993.

Cole, Arnold and Pamela Caudill Ovwigho. "Bible Engagement as the Key to Spiritual Growth: A Research Synthesis." Center for Bible Engagement (2012) 1–9. Online: http://www.centerforbibleengagement.org/images/stories/pdf/Research_Synthesis_Bible_Engagement_and_Spiritual_Growth_Aug2012.pdf

Dewey, David. *The Bible Unwrapped: Developing Your Bible Skills.* Bletchley, England: Scripture Union, 2001.

Ford, Linda, Christine Spence and Bruce E. Stoker, eds. *Follow the Bible: 52 Bible Lessons for Beginner Readers Ages 6–8.* Cincinnati, OH: Standard, 2003.

Jeynes, William H. "The Relationship between Bible Literacy and Academic achievement and School Behaviour." *Education and Urban Society* 41 (2009):419–436.

Morris, Linda. "Confession: Fewer know their Bible." *The Sydney Morning Herald,* September 10, 2008. No pages. On-line:http://www.smh.com.au/news/national/confession-fewer-know-their-bible/2008/09/09/1220857547474.html

Ovwigho, Pamela Caudill and Arnold Cole. "Scriptural Engagement, Communication with God, and Moral Behavior among Children." *International Journal of Children's Spirituality* 15 (May 2010):101–113.

Peterson, Eugene. "Forward." In *Reading the Bible for the Love of God*, Alan Reynolds, 11–13. Grand Rapids, MI: Brazos, 2003.

Reynolds, Alan. *Reading the Bible for the Love of God*. Grand Rapids, MI: Brazos, 2003.

The Barna Research Group. "Faith has a Limited Effect on Most People's Behaviour." *The Barna Update May 24, 2004*. No pages. On-line: https://www.barna.org/barna-update/article/5-barna-update/188-faith-has-a-limited-effect-on-most-peoples-behavior

Volcano Adventure Team. *My Volcano Adventure: Discovering the Bible's Power*. Fort Collins, CO: Through the Bible, 2004.

White, Ellen. *Counsels to Parents, Teachers and Students*. Mountain View, CA: Pacific Press, 1943.

———. *Education*. Mountain View, CA: Pacific Press, 1952.

Chapter 12

Welcoming Children to Holy Ground

Exploring Contemplative Practices with 1st Through 5th Graders in a Multi-Age Context

Dana Kennamer Pemberton

As many churches are embracing a high-tech entertainment model for their children's ministries, others are seeking spiritual practices that invite children into quiet community and contemplation. This chapter tells the story of a children's minister who implemented contemplative practices in her Wednesday night program for first through fifth grades. Data were generated through interviews with the children and the children's minister; observations of the weekly gatherings; and samples of the children's work. The findings support the view that children are capable of engaging meaningfully in contemplative practices.

> The goal is to create an aesthetic that is inviting, engaging, and screams to a Generation M, "Welcome! You matter!" (Ellis, Baumgart, and Carper, 2006, 247)

> Generation M kids have media in their homes, in their bedrooms, in their classrooms, in their minivans, in their backpacks and in their pockets. Why not at church? (Ellis, Baumgart and Carper 2006, 230)

> The adult is like the matchmaker who wants to encourage the child to get to know God better. So the adult creates a place and time for them to meet and fall in love, but then backs away so that the two can encounter each other on their own terms. (Garrido, 2008, 12)

. . . a space where the only Teacher is Christ; both children and adults place themselves in a listening stance before his Word and seek to penetrate the mystery. (Caveletti, 1992, 134)

The above represent two very different views on how to welcome children in the context of a faith community. One advocates energy, excitement and entertainment and the other calm contemplation. The perspective that children must be entertained often guides churches in efforts to attract children and their families (Beckwith, 2004; May et al., 2005). Entertainment-driven models are based on the belief that it is necessary to utilize technologies used in day-to-day life in order to connect with a media-savvy generation and to compete with other forms of high tech entertainment (Ellis, Baumgart, and Carper, 2006).

Others have raised concerns about increased focus on media and entertainment in children's ministries (Beckwith, 2004; Beckwith, 2010; May 2006; May et al., 2005; Mercer, 2005). One concern is the disproportionate focus on fun. While "fun" is not an evil to be avoided, neither should it be the primary guiding framework for ministry with children. May (2006) asks what might change if we replace "fun" with "meaningful" asserting that "children are eager to be involved in things that are meaningful to them, things that may not always be categorized as fun" (209).

Concerns include the belief that children must be entertained to draw them into the biblical story, which implies a limited view of both the power of the text and of the spiritual capacities of children. There is a lack of awareness of "children's ability to encounter God and experience his presence and the inherent attraction that children have to awe, wonder, reverence and mystery" (May, 2006, 252). Entertainment-focused, media-driven environments provide little space for wonder and reverence and can overshadow the true purpose of our children's ministries—the spiritual formation of our children (Beckwith, 2004).

Is the spiritual formation of children nurtured by the search for the amusing, fun and exciting? Is doing what kids "like" or "want" an appropriate measure for choosing our practices? Children like and want many things that they do not need and they need many things that they do not yet realize they want.

> It is a challenge to distinguish children's needs and yearnings from their wants. Marketing through various media creates wants that are obvious, resulting for many children in a form of impoverishment—a poverty of affluence—since many parents desire to meet children's wants. Yet children also have yearnings and needs for belonging, feeling welcome, being secure, having quietness, understanding, meaning, and connecting with God. (May, 2006, 66)

Rather than mirroring the media-driven culture, might churches instead provide space for children to step out of the fast-paced world and enter into meaningful community? In this kind of community, adults spend time *with* children, rather than doing things *to* or *for* them (Westerhoff, 2008).

This chapter will tell the story of one children's minister and a small group of volunteers who, along with the first through fifth grade children in their church's Wednesday night program, created a space for this kind of community. For several years Sarah Nixon (all names of people and places are pseudonymous), children's minister at Windway Church, had begun to question current trends in children's ministry. She questioned the wisdom of using the "bells and whistles" of technology and media to entertain children in faith community contexts. Guided by what she describes as a "formational theology," she began exploring contemplative models such as Godly Play (Berryman, 1991; Stewart and Berrryman, 1989) and Catechesis of the Good Shepherd, (Cavalletti, 1992). Eventually, she felt compelled to implement aspects of these models in her ministry. Through conversations with the children about their hurried lives and months in prayer, she was convinced that "these children will be called to something that means they will have to know how to find stillness and quiet in the midst of chaos and confusion. If we do not provide them with this, we will have failed this generation."

A JOURNEY INTO THE MYSTERY

And so began a journey—now five years long—into a new way to be with children and with God. Beginning with Sunday morning children's worship for ages three to five and later in the Wednesday evening program for first through fifth grades, Sarah began "exploring ritual, liturgy, and contemplative practices," despite the fact that the church she serves is part of a cognitive, rather than liturgical or contemplative tradition. Her foundational theology claims "that God is working in the lives of children independently of what the adults in their lives are doing." She describes the approach as respectful of children and trusts that God will speak to and through the children as they enter the story together. She does not feel compelled to control the process but trusts that God is at work, drawing the children into relationship with him. This means that time in this Wednesday night setting "is not always predictable and that it is sometimes messy, but there are holy moments almost every week that surprise us—it is the mystery of the journey" (Sarah). Sarah and her team are comfortable with this sometimes messy, mystery.

One practice Sarah first began using with the three- to five-year-olds in Sunday morning children's worship was "wonder questions"—open-ended questions that allow children to listen, reflect and respond as they make sense of God's story (Stewart and Berrryman, 1989). While "dwelling together in the story of the annunciation," Sarah posed this wonder question, "I wonder how Mary felt when the angel came to her?" Several children responded with the expected answers. "She was happy." "Mary felt scared." But then Amy, a little girl who had just turned four, said something quite surprising, "I bet she was mad. It wasn't her plan." Sarah described this as a critical moment for her.

That was the turning point for me. If a barely four-year-old can ask that question, what are we missing in the minds and hearts of our older children? If a four-year-old is thinking those thoughts, the older kids entering those higher levels of abstract thinking must have the opportunity to explore the text in ways that make it real—that allow them to listen and respond. I knew then that I had to find ways to continue these practices of dwelling in the word, wondering and finding quiet with the older children in our church family too. I had thought about it for a long time but couldn't figure out a way to do it, but I felt compelled by the Spirit. It was really an act of obedience.

There were significant challenges along the way. The contemplative models available are primarily developed for young children rather than upper elementary; require very specific materials, space, and time; and don't allow for large groups (Garrido, 2008). In contrast, the Wednesday evening program at Windway Church includes, on any given night, seventy to ninety children in first through fifth grades in a less than ideal space. Actual time available each evening is about fifty minutes. The population is diverse with children of active church members and those whose families do not attend; children whose parents have high levels of education and income and those living on welfare; and children with giftedness and those with disabilities. "One night I (Sarah) looked at the children gathered and realized that over half of them had some significant challenge. Learning disabilities, alcoholic parents, autism, parents in prison, English language learners, Down Syndrome—these are all there in our classroom and more." Despite these challenges, Sarah and her team persisted in the "sometimes messy" process of calling the children to community and quiet contemplation.

For an entire school year (the Wednesday program does not meet in the summer), Sarah worked with the children to "find the quiet space that God put inside them. We began with thirty seconds which was actually more like fifteen after the children were able to calm down." As the children discovered that they could indeed find quiet together, they began asking for more. "We can do three minutes tonight!" "Let's do five minutes." When time came for the summer break, the children were able to sit in communal silence for seven minutes. This time dedicated to practicing the spiritual discipline of silence was the first step. When the children returned the following August, Sarah had developed a vision for a more extensive implementation of contemplative practices for the Wednesday night program.

This vision included the intentional use of repeated rituals, quiet engagement and contemplative practices. Sarah values repetition and ritual as a way to "provide security for the children and establish a collective identity. It helps them know how to enter the space, defining the purpose for gathering there—taking ordinary space and time and turning it into sacred space and time." The children are often reminded that their classroom is "holy ground—a gift from God and a gift to God."

Within the limits of the space available, Sarah worked with her volunteers to create a calm, welcoming environment that invites quiet engagement with each other and with the biblical text. The spiritual purposes of their weekly practices are frequently repeated for the children. Sarah guides her team to use formational language intentionally—providing the children with a vocabulary to describe their spiritual journey. This language is evident as the children describe their experiences and understandings. This chapter will now focus on the children's responses to selected communal practices that are part of the weekly experience.

The Prayer Wall

As the children enter the classroom they engage in quiet gathering activities (puzzles, books, and blocks) until it is time to begin. This calm welcome is followed by a brief time of singing. Songs are chosen to provide opportunity for movement and child-appropriate worship, but songs are avoided "that get the children too revved up" (Sarah). The team chose to sing acapella, finding that the children participated more fully and intently without the apparent distraction of the contemporary instrumental music commonly and successfully used in their Sunday morning setting. Following the singing, it is time to enter into communal prayer with the Prayer Wall—a large wall that has been transformed into a floor to ceiling chalkboard. The children anticipate this time and know how to enter prayer together using this weekly ritual.

Before the prayer time begins, Sarah leads the children in remembering how they will "practice spiritual discipline" during the Prayer Wall experience. The children respond with an evident seriousness and respect as they restate the principles that guide this weekly ritual. "Write small so everyone has room to put their prayers on the wall." "Tall kids should write high so little kids can reach." "You don't have to write a lot—just a word or a name. God knows our prayers." "Keep your quiet place while you wait." They know the purpose of these principles and recognize the importance of "doing the hard work of spiritual discipline" during their weekly time of prayer.

Children are invited a few at a time to write on the wall names of those that God has put on their hearts while a contemporary musical version of Psalm 23 plays softly in the background. Each week, three to four children assist by holding baskets of chalk for their peers. This is a job the children clearly want to do and take seriously with an obvious sense of reverence. As groups of children move to the wall, it is striking to see how they help each other. The older children assist the younger children in finding places on the wall that they can reach. There is rarely any pushing as the children patiently wait on each other.

The children were asked to describe this time of communal prayer. The responses below are representative of the children's perspectives and reveal important insights about the children's spiritual needs and their understanding of themselves and others.

It (the Prayer Wall) is like a silent prayer in your mind. Sometimes it is hard to pray because you might get embarrassed but you can express your feelings on the wall. (Nick—7)

It is really special. I am glad we do it. Pretty much every week I have someone I want to pray about. I know God will help them and I think He feels glad that we do it—write their names up there. Before I go to the wall, I just sit and think about people in my life. Usually names come to me, you know, like ___, ___, and ___ (three children in the church battling cancer). (Kate—8)

Everyone can see the names you wrote so they can pray for them too—even if they don't know them—they see the names and they can pray. (Jessica—8)

It lets you get out your feelings. Sometimes it helps to write them 'cause sometimes it is hard to talk about. (Ryan—9)

Dwelling in the Word

After communal prayer, the children are challenged to "stay in the quiet" as they move into Dwelling in the Word. Sarah affirms again that this is "hard work" and the children have learned to describe this practice of quiet listening as "a spiritual discipline."

Sarah believes that in order to meaningfully join children in discovering the truths of God's word with any real depth, the adults in their world must spend time in the biblical text themselves. Preparation is not making materials and planning activities. Preparation is living in the story. Sarah has been informed by Sonja Stewart's (2000) perspective as she prepares to enter the story with the children.

> The storyteller prepares by prayer and meditation until the story is formed in him or her. God's presence and sense of God's greatness, mystery, and awe in the story need to become part of the storyteller. The storyteller's love for God and trust in the story, the Holy Spirit, and the children help form an atmosphere of expectation and freedom that permits interaction among God, the story and the children. (Stewart, 2000, 24)

Trust in the Holy Spirit's participation in the process is central in this Wednesday night gathering. Unlike entertainment models that work on the assumption that the biblical story must be embellished, broken down and explained in order for children to be engaged and to understand, Sarah trusts that children sense the significance of the God's word and will engage with the text seriously, with a genuine desire to hear from God. "We enter the story together. It doesn't matter if they know the story or if they have never heard it before. They can all enter the story. They can enter the imagination of God" (Sarah).

In order to give children the opportunity to listen deeply to the biblical text, the children will dwell in one passage for several weeks. Sarah has structured the time so that reading the text aloud is part of this process. Each week children eagerly volunteer to read. "We have come to understand that children love to read God's word" (Sarah). This has been a surprising discovery. Despite the level of ability of the reader, the children become focused and attentive during the reading of the text. "They know it is important—that it is holy. They can be distracted and wiggly but when we read the Bible, they get quiet. It is quite amazing" (Sarah). Garrido (2008) asserts that children "quickly become restless when they are given peripheral material, but concentrate and settle down when given what they are hungering for" (12). Sarah believes that the children recognize their need for God's word and so they listen.

On two observed occasions the children offered spontaneous quiet applause after listening to a peer read from the text. Applause is not their normal practice so this was quite unexpected. The first occasion was after a child with developmental disabilities read haltingly through the evening's passage with significant assistance. Despite his struggles, the children listened with quiet respect. "They knew it was important and they applauded. It was a holy moment" (Sarah). The second occasion was after a child new to church, to the class, and to the biblical story, read for the first time. These unsolicited affirmations from the children are evidence of their "understanding that the reading of God's word is special" (Sarah).

In addition to reading the text aloud, Dwelling in the Word often includes simple storytelling techniques similar to those used in Godly Play (Berryman, 2009; Stewart and Berryman, 1989). A blue cloth becomes a sea or lake, a brown cloth a desert. Simple two- and three-dimensional figures are laid upon the cloth as Sarah and the children collaboratively recall the details of the story and engage together in wondering. Sarah had used these storytelling techniques with children ages three to five in the children's worship context and was not sure how the older children would respond. Would they find it unsophisticated and silly? She was surprised by how they engaged. They would lean forward to see what was being placed on the floor, offer possibilities for what the cloth represented, and name with excitement the places and people they remembered. These children did not require technology or media to be drawn into the story. A simple blue cloth will do when they are asked to join their teacher in discovering what God's word has to say to them.

Sarah calls the children to develop a disposition of openness to God's word, reminding them "they can hear something new every time." She models engagement with the biblical story, sharing her own new insights and questions. As they stay with a text for several weeks she challenges them to listen to what God's word might have to say. The following descriptions of their practice of Dwelling in the Word demonstrate the children's growing understanding of God's word and how to listen with an open spirit.

> I think about it—it isn't time to play. It's time to listen. It's hard to explain (pause).
> I feel like (pause) hmm (pause) like I am hearing the Bible, but it is more than just talking about it. It's hard to explain. (Kate—8)

You listen to the story. It's a different kind of listening. (Nick—7)

I think it's a good way to get the verse connection to the brain and then when we hear it and we get old we remember that we heard it. It's like, "Yeah, I remember that." All the kids are listening—like they know how to listen. (Carter—11)

Everyone actually gets in the word that way. Everyone knows how to do it. I think it is like, (pauses) it gives us more time so that we can understand it better and think with different perspectives. It gives us time to actually get in the word and like (pauses again) be part of God. (Melanie—10)

These responses capture the children's understanding that this "listening" is a learned skill of which they are capable. They recognize the distinctive nature of this listening and they value the practice of repeated readings. "The language of 'We have heard this story before!' has almost been eliminated" (Sarah). The emotional quality of their responses—pausing to think, speaking with quiet intensity, leaning forward for emphasis—is not communicated well through simple quotes on a page. However, the seriousness with which they described the practice of Dwelling in the Word was striking.

What Do You Wonder?

The biblical narrative leaves a great deal to the imagination. Many of the details are left untold. Even adults wonder about the lives of the people described in its pages and the purposes of God as he worked through, for and often in spite of his people. "One of the characteristic marks of the biblical storytellers is a certain reticence. There is an austere, spare quality to their stories. They don't tell us too much. They leave a lot of blanks in the narration, an implicit invitation to enter the story, just as we are, and discover for ourselves how we fit into it" (Peterson, 2006, 42). Stewart and Berryman (1989) believe that the "omission of definitions and unnecessary detail provides silences, time and space through which the listener experiences the mystery, awe, and wonder so characteristic of the sacred story" (25). The text itself compels us to wonder.

This wondering is a natural process for children who are inherently curious and comfortable with the knowledge that they do not yet know the answers (Sarah). Perhaps this is something that we as adults can learn from them. We can join them in resting in the mystery—going deeper into the text, discovering together the mysteries God is waiting to reveal.

> Wonder is a very serious thing that, rather than leading us away from reality, can arise only from an attentive observation of reality. Education to wonder is correlative with an education that helps us to go always more deeply into reality. If we skim over things, we will never be surprised by them. Wonder is not an emotion of superficial people; it strikes root only in the person who is capable of stopping and looking. (Cavalletti, 1992, 39)

However, adults often feel compelled to "fill in the blanks" for children. Curricula commonly provide responses that are "prescribed, leaving no reason for personal and communal dialogue with God" (Stewart and Berryman, 1989, 25). Sarah believes that it is important to model for and experience with children the reality that the spiritual journey is one of continual seeking. She holds that caution needs to be exercised in providing quick, simple answers for children as we take this journey together. Instead Sarah invites the children to wonder through the use of open-ended questions that challenge them to reflect on what the passage might mean for them, to speculate what the biblical character might have thought, or to imagine what God was feeling. She is comfortable with silence, even extended silence, as the children contemplate these questions. On rare occasions when the children have no responses to the wonder question, Sarah leaves the question to linger until the following week and invites the children to continue listening until they return next time. When asked to reflect on their experience of wondering, the children communicate an understanding of persistent and personal engagement with the text.

> I had never heard of it before but when I learned about it, it gave me an idea for thinking about the Bible myself—asking myself wonder questions. You know, like when I read by myself. (Melanie—10)

> When Sarah asks wonder questions every kid is thinking something different. It helps the kids kind of, it helps them think of different answers and it helps others understand. It helps when another person says something different. You think in new ways. (Coby—11)

> The wonder questions are interesting questions. It makes me really think about the story. I can't always come up with an answer, but sometimes when I go home I think of something, especially when it gets to me. A wonder question means you really have to listen cause it is a really amazing story. It's like, "What am I going to hear next?" It isn't the same thing every time. You are going to hear if you listen. You can always hear something new. (Kate—8)

God's Word in Color

The children are also given opportunities to visually represent their emerging understandings as part of their communal Dwelling in the Word. Adapting a model for prayer developed by Sybill MacBeth (2007) in her book *Praying in Color*, the children are invited to use line, color, words and images to interact with the text and to share their insights with their peers. They have come to call this practice *God's Word in Color*. An adult volunteer first modeled the process for the children for several weeks. During the reading of the evening's passage, she drew symbols and shapes to represent how the scripture spoke to her and interpreted for the children what her drawing meant—what she was thinking, hearing and wondering.

Each week, following the large group gathering, the children transition to various rooms and are given time to engage in self-selected, open-ended activities (watercolor paints, clay, sand, quiet reading, etc.) for personal reflection and response. Opportunities to practice God's Word in Color were provided during this reflection time using both collaborative and individual structures.

As the children became more comfortable with this method of interacting with the text, they were invited to share their own versions of *God's Word in Color* in the large group gathering. Many volunteered to lead their peers in thinking about God's word in this way. The children prepare for this task by reading and reflecting on the selected text throughout the week.

> I read it in my own Bible too and thought about it at home. What would be good? I thought that instead of a house just built on a rock it could be made all of rock. I kept reading it and reading it and reading it all week. It makes me feel good when I do something like that—a feeling in my heart that I am talking to God. (Kate—8; See Figure 1)

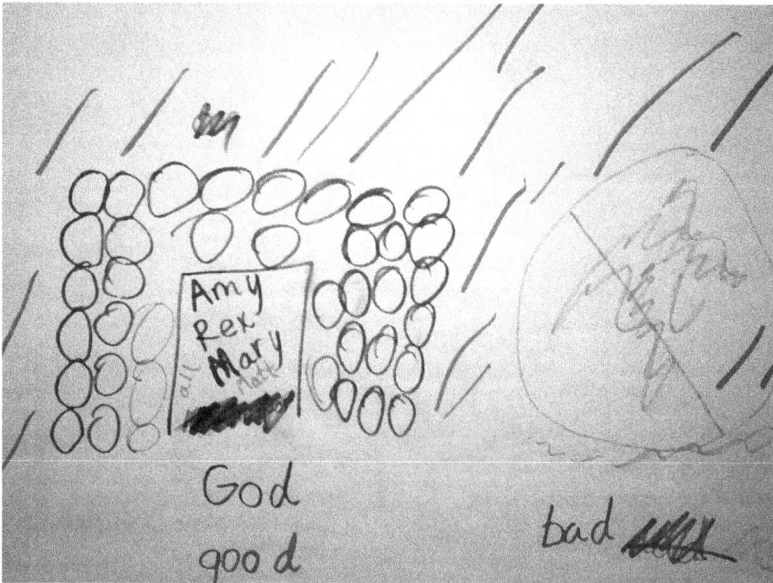

Figure 1: *I read it in my own Bible too and thought about it at home. What would be good? (Kate—8)*

They described repeated readings and even, at times, discussing the passage with friends during the week.

The way I understand it is like drawing it out. To me, it's easier than reading it –it makes a broader picture. I read the story more than 5 times and thought of different things. My story was the potter. I did the puzzle with the potter. He says he molds us—He puts us together, you know. Jessica (her friend) reminded me at school about the puzzle. I did that at the beginning of the week and had forgotten about it. I put those together. (Melanie—10; See Figure 2)

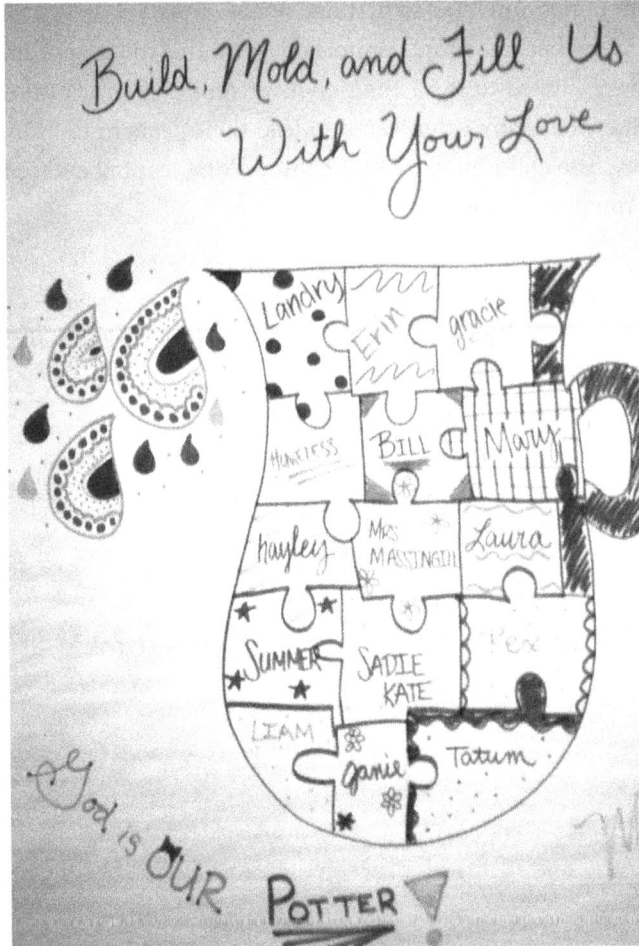

Figure 2: *Jessica reminded me at school about the puzzle. (Melanie—10)*

Parents at home and teachers in Bible class often tried to guide the children in making a plan, but they rarely used these suggestions. Instead, the children's drawings represented their personal responses to the scripture—what it meant to them, what questions they had or how it related to their lives. On one Wednesday evening when the class had been dwelling in the Parable of the Prodigal Son, Nick, a first-grader, had volunteered for God's Word in Color. What resulted was an opportunity for the class to grapple with significant spiritual questions (see Figure 3).

His drawing included simple classifications of behaviors for father and son. When the son comes back, he tells the truth. This is good. But the son had run away and sinned against God. This was bad. The father loves his son and is hopeful. This is good. But the father let him go. This was bad. Wait! The father was bad? This is not the standard interpretation of the parable.

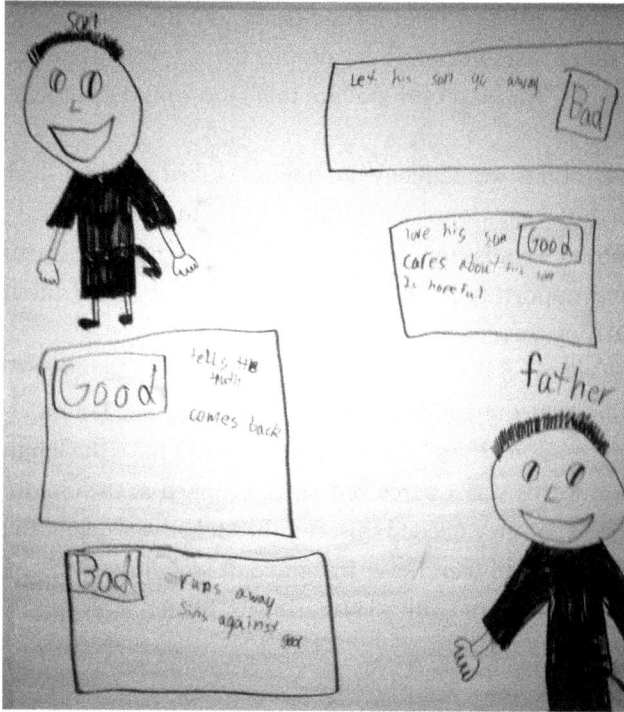

Figure 3: *Why did the father let him go? (Nick—First Grade)*

Nick presented his drawing to the class and then asked with obvious concern, "Why did the father let him go?" What at first seems a childlike question raised for the children some serious questions about God.

First, they recalled that in the parable, the father represents God. What followed was an extended conversation about free will and God's role in the world. "Why does God let people do things that are wrong?" "God should stop people from hurting other people." "But he lets us go sometimes." "But, why? He should stop people. He shouldn't let people do bad things." These are adult questions with deep theological significance—questions with no easy answers that challenge adults as well. Finally, a child said, "It is hard, but God lets us choose. Sometimes he lets us go. But he always lets you come back." The children sat in silence after this final comment as if resting in that assurance, but still wrestling with the unsettling reality of choice.

MORE THAN IMAGINED!

In the context of this quiet, respectful community these children had the opportunity to connect personally with the biblical text, to explore important questions and to acknowledge their confusions and fears. "When you invite children to revisit the text with new questions, acknowledging that answers are sometimes hard to see, you give children a language for difficult times" (Sarah). Together Sarah, her ministry team and the children grappled with understanding God's part in a Tsunami a world away. They shared the pain and confusion of the death of a little boy in their church who died a few days after his seventh birthday despite their fervent prayers. They struggled to understand whom "the least of these" are that God would call them to serve in the name of Jesus.

These conversations would likely not have occurred in a high-tech context seeking to entertain. And that would have been a loss. "In our fast-paced busyness and distraction I'm afraid we miss important insights that we need to learn from our children. And we miss opportunities to help them sort through their questions and fears" (Stonehouse and May, 2010, 23).

As Sarah reflected on the journey that started with an "act of obedience" she felt clear confirmation that the children needed this—they needed quiet so they could listen to God and to each other. "Children don't always have the language to tell you what they need. But this was a perceived need. I looked at the children who are my church. I perceived that they needed this. But the reality was bigger than I ever imagined. It was more powerful than I ever imagined. It truly has communally connected all of us to the imagination of God" (Sarah). It was, indeed, holy ground.

REFERENCES

Beckwith, Ivy. *Formational Children's Ministry: Shaping Children Using Story, Ritual, and Relationship.* Grand Rapids: Baker Books, 2010.

Beckwith, Ivy. *Postmodern Children's Ministry: Ministry to Children in the 21st Century,* Grand Rapids: Zondervan, 2004.

Berryman, Jerome. *Godly Play: An Imaginative Approach to Religious Education.* Minneapolis: Augsburg Fortress, 1995.

Berryman, Jerome. *Teaching Godly Play.* Denver: Moorehouse Education Resources, 2009.

Cavalletti, Sofia. *The Religious Potential of the Child.* Chicago: Liturgy Training Publications, 1992.

Ellis, Tim. et al. "The Media-Driven Active-Engagement Model." In *Perspectives on Children's Spiritual Formation: Four Views,* edited by Michael J. Anthony, 225–277. Nashville: Broadman & Holman Publishers, 2006.

Garrido, Ann. "The Faith of a Child." *America* 199 (2008): 10–13.

MacBeth, Sybil. *Praying in Color.* Brewster: Paraclete Press, 2007.

May, Scottie. "The Contemplative-Reflective Model." In *Perspectives on Children's Spiritual Formation: Four Views,* edited by M. J. Anthony, 45—102. Nashville: Broadman & Holman Publishers, 2006.

May, Scottie, and Beth Posterski, Catherine Stonehouse, Linda Cannell. 2005. *Children Matter: Celebrating Their Place in the Church, Family, and Community.* Grand Rapids: Eerdmans Publishing Company, 2005.

Mercer, Joyce Ann. *Welcoming Children: A Practical Theology of Childhood.* St. Louis: Chalice Press, 2005.

Peterson, Eugene. *Eat This Book: A Conversation in the Art of Spiritual Reading,* Grand Rapids: William B. Eerdmans Publishing Company, 2006.

Stewart, Sonja, and Jerome Berryman. *Young Children and Worship.* Louisville: Westminster John Knox Press, 1989.

Stewart, Sonja. *Following Jesus: More about Young Children and Worship.* Louisville: Westminster John Knox Press, 2000.

Stonehouse, Catherine and Scottie May. *Listening to Children on the Spiritual Journey: Guidance for Those Who Teach and Nurture.* Grand Rapids: Baker Academic, 2010.

Westerhoff, John. H. "The Church's Contemporary Challenge: Assisting Adults to Mature Spiritually with their Children." In *Nurturing Children's Spirituality: Christian Perspectives and Best Practices,* edited by Holly C. Allen. 355–365. Eugene: Cascade Books, 2008.

Chapter 13

Making Faith Their Own

Lessons for Children's Ministry from Kids' Reflections on Their Spiritual Lives

Pamela Caudill Ovwigho and Arnold Cole

Studies purporting that a large percentage of Christian youth "walk away" from the church have raised concerns among the Christian community that teens are entering young adulthood without a firmly established faith. In 2002, the Southern Baptist Convention claimed that 88 percent of youth walk away from the church and never return (Baucham, 2007). An article, "Young Adults Aren't Sticking with Church," appeared in USA Today on August 6, 2007. Reporting on a Lifeway Research survey, the article states that seven in ten evangelical and mainline Protestants adults (eighteen to thirty) who attended church regularly in high school stopped attending by age twenty-three (Grossman, 2007). Some contend that young adults are leaving the church because they have serious doubts about the claims of Christianity (Ham et al., 2009). Developmental theory and research from larger cohort studies, however, suggest that current trends may be simply part of a natural developmental process that each generation experiences.

An understanding of how faith forms across the lifespan is critical for ministries seeking to nurture spiritual growth. Our research center has studied the spiritual lives of more than 100,000 people from around the world. From tweens (eight-to-twelve year-olds) to the oldest old (eighty-to-100 year-olds), people have told us what faith means to them, how they personally connect with God, and how they believe God connects with them. Together their stories show that faith is indeed a journey with common milestones embedded in the unique mosaic of each person's life. An understanding of the different faith stages provides ministry leaders the opportunity to nurture young people at their current level and help prepare and equip them for later stages.

In this chapter, we review Fowler's theory of spiritual development and research on the faith of teens and young adults. We then present qualitative data from interviews with tweens (eight to twelve year-olds) about their spiritual lives. Our findings focus mainly on how church involvement impacts how tweens live each day. Our goal is to inform ministry leaders about what seems to be working in children's ministry and how they can more effectively serve children.

FOWLER'S MODEL OF SPIRITUAL DEVELOPMENT

Based on interviews with nearly six hundred people from a variety of faith backgrounds, James Fowler (1981) proposed a six-stage model of spiritual development. His model starts with preschool children in Stage 1 Intuitive-Projective, when basic ideas about God are impressed from parents and society. In the mind of preschoolers, fantasy and reality comingle.

By the time they reach school age, children move in to Stage 2 Mythic-Literal. Cognitively they are starting to understand the world in more logical ways. Typically they accept their faith community's stories, though they tend to understand them in very literal ways.

The transition to Stage 3 Synthetic-Conventional occurs in adolescence. Young people in this stage move among several different social circles. To accommodate, they often adopt an all-encompassing belief system. Still they typically rely on their parents and institutions such as their church as their authority on faith.

Many people remain in the Synthetic-Conventional stage throughout their life. Others move to Stage 4 Individuative-Reflective. As teens move in to young adulthood, their world expands even more and they often come in contact with other belief systems. They critically examine their own beliefs and may even become disillusioned with their faith.

Wrestling with their beliefs and the paradoxes of life helps people move to Stage 5 Conjunctive Faith. They realize the limits of logic and that life can be full of mystery. They often return to the sacred stories of their youth, although this time they are their own. Some go on to Stage 6 Universalizing Faith and live their lives fully serving others, free of any real worries or doubts.

CURRENT TRENDS AMONG YOUTH

Unfortunately, empirical tests of Fowler's model are limited. The model, however, does provide an alternative interpretation of the current trends regarding young adults' religious participation. Specifically, lower religious affiliation and church attendance may be the natural result of people moving from synthetic-conventional faith to individuative-reflective faith and then to conjunctive faith (Keeley, 2010). Partial support of this hypothesis can be found in data showing similar decline in attendance during young adulthood among earlier generations (Pew Research Center, 2010).

To date, there is little data available that examines youth who appear to walk away and those who actually return after a time of reflection and questioning. In our own studies with mature Christians, the most common pattern observed is involvement in church up to high school graduation, a "drifting away" from faith in young adulthood, and a later return to active involvement in Christianity and church life in later adulthood (Cole et al., 2013).

We hypothesize that an important piece of the puzzle is the extent to which youth engage in private spiritual practices such as prayer and reading or listening to scripture (Ovwigho et al., 2010). While many youth may have professed faith in Jesus and been active in the life of the church, their connection through prayer and engaging the Bible doesn't exist Monday through Saturday. In effect, they enter young adulthood with faith that is essentially mediated through the church and their parents. At this critical juncture, the pressures of adulthood bring new demands, while ties with the formal church and parents weaken. This, in turn, can weaken their relationship with God as well.

Taken together, both development theory and the current trends in religious affiliation and church attendance among young adults suggest that many youth will experience a time of testing and questioning of their spiritual beliefs. For children's ministries, a critical question is how they are preparing children for the challenge of making their faith their own and thus, moving from one stage to the next.

In-depth studies of the spiritual lives of teens are helping to form new models of youth ministry (e.g., Smith et al., 2005). Similarly, we can also learn much about the spiritual lives of children by talking to them directly. As they share how they view God, what spiritual practices are most meaningful for them, their struggles and what they need from the adults in their lives, ideas for improving children's ministries will emerge.

This is the challenge we address in this study. Specifically, we interviewed tweens who regularly attend mainstream Christian churches about what they experience in church, how they connect with God between Sundays, and what they believe will help them grow closer to Jesus. These qualitative data are supplemented with quantitative from our previous national studies of the spiritual lives of tweens, teens and young adults.

STUDY METHODS

Our qualitative data come from semi-structured interviews with twenty-one children who were between the ages of eight and thirteen in the spring of 2012. Table 1 shows that participants were fairly evenly divided in terms of gender and age. In terms of their denominational affiliation, eleven were Lutheran, five Nazarene, four Southern Baptist, and one attended both Catholic and Nazarene churches.

Table 1: *Participant Characteristics*

Participant Characteristics (n = 21)	
Gender	
Male	11
Female	10
Age	
8 years	3
9 years	5
10 years	6
11 years	3
12 years	2
13 years	1
Church affiliation	
Southern Baptist	4
Catholic and Nazarene	1
Lutheran	11
Nazarene	5

Participants were recruited through their churches' Family Ministry Director or Senior Pastor. Dr. Ovwigho met with each participant and his or her parent to explain the purpose of the study, obtain the parent's informed consent, and obtain the child's assent. Children were told that anything they shared in the interview was confidential and would not be shared with their parents, teachers, and/or pastors. They could refuse to answer any of the questions and could stop the interview at any time. As a thank you for participating, families received a set of Bible-based cards for family devotions. Seven general questions provided the framework for the interviews:

1. Did you go to church or Sunday school last week? If so, could you tell me a little about what you learned or remember?

2. Was there anything during the week that reminded you of church or Sunday school? If so, what was that?

3. Outside of church and Sunday school, what do you do that helps you stay close to God?

4. What activities, if any, does your family do together that helps you stay close to God?

5. What kinds of things make it harder for you to stay close to God?

6. If you could tell your Sunday school teacher or pastor anything, what would you say they can do to help you stay closer to God?

7. Now if you could tell your parents anything, what would you say your family can

do to help you stay closer to God?

FINDINGS

Kids Have Trouble Connecting Sunday with the Rest of Their Week

The tweens we interviewed (we are using fictitious names) generally did not remember much of what they heard in church or Sunday school, even just a few days later. In fact, nine of the twenty-one remembered nothing at all. A few remembered general things such as:

> Grace (9)—We talked about forgiving. Then we played a game where you hop up and down with an egg on a spoon.

> Max (8)—We did something quick and then played a fun game.

> Ross (9)—I remember we did a craft. It was about our spirit and body and things we believe about God.

> Andy (9)—It was about Jesus. (*Interviewer: Do you remember what about Jesus?*). Um . . . no.

More substantial memories were often associated with a game or teachers sharing personal stories about their real life experiences. Examples include:

> Sarah (13)—It was about temptation. They gave us peanut butter cups and if we waited to eat them, we got another. (*Interviewer: Oh, so to see if you could resist?*) Yeah. Lots of kids ate theirs right away.

> Marty (10)—It was this story about how the CIA stopped <our teacher> because they thought he was going to hurt the Dalai Lama. That people think he is a god. (*Interviewer: That's quite a story.*) Yeah, it was about how he was afraid to say he was a Christian.

When they considered their daily lives, tweens rarely encountered situations that reminded them of what they had learned in church or Sunday school. Several remarked that "It doesn't seem connected." A few, however, did see a connection. For example, Joseph (10) said he sometimes thinks about Sunday school when he's tempted to do something his teacher told him not to do. Delia (12) and Baily (11) both commented that they had talked to their mothers about the video they had watched in Sunday school. John (10) was reminded of his Sunday school lesson when he was at the swimming pool and noticed that "the water was flat like when Jesus calmed the storm."

Kids Primarily Connect with God through Prayer During the Week

Prayer was the primary way tweens connected with God during the week. Most said that they prayed alone either before bed or before meals. A handful of children reported having a devotional time with their families each day.

Beyond family devotions, few kids spent any time reading or listening to the Bible during the week. Several remarked that they knew they should and yet did not. Some stated that they were too busy with school, lessons and sports. Others said that they just had trouble understanding the scriptures. For example, Leah (12) shared: "Sometimes it's hard to understand. I like stories so that's what I read when I do. I have trouble with the Psalms, but I like stories."

Music was an important way to connect with God for some tweens. Several remarked that they listen to Christian music or sing during the week to remind them of Jesus.

A few also described trying to do those things that they know are pleasing to God. For example, Grace (9) tries to help her little brother and Jamal (9) washes the dishes for his mom. Ross (9) tries to get the kids in his neighborhood to stop saying "Oh my God."

These qualitative findings on tweens' private spirituality reflect trends we have seen in other studies. For example, in a national study of 1,009 tweens, the vast majority said that they pray each day. Few, however, read or listened to the Bible outside of church (Ovwigho & Cole, 2010).

Family Activities to Stay Connected with God Are Limited

When asked about what their families do together to stay connected with God during the week, tweens most often mentioned praying together and attending church.

> Max (8)—We do family devotionals at night with a Jesus book. My dad prays with me & my brothers every night.

> Cash (9)—My family prays at night and before meals.

> Ross (10)—We pray together. My mom has the Bible app on her phone so we listen together sometimes.

> Marty (10)—We go to church on Fridays. We pray before our meals. We go to church and Sunday school. We take family walks and talk about what we are grateful for.

A time where their family gathered for devotions was mentioned by several tweens as well. How helpful tweens found these devotions, however, seemed to depend on how they were structured. When the primary focus was on reviewing biblical accounts, kids often saw little value because they felt as if they were hearing the same stories over and over.

> Joseph (10)—My parents talk about things they listened to. We've tried to do devotionals sometimes. It seems like the same stories all the time.

> Katie (10)—We do a little devotion at night. (*Interviewer: Is that helpful to you?*) Not really. It seems like the same stories over and over.

What seemed to resonate with tweens most was when they spent time discussing what was going on in each person's life. Marty and Joseph both mentioned this type of personal sharing in their responses presented above. Leah (12) felt connected to God during family devotion time when "We talk about what God wants us to do. We support each other. We encourage each other."

Distractions and Peers Who Don't Believe Make It Hard for Tweens to Follow Jesus

Tweens clearly recognized things in their daily life they made it hard for them to make the choices they feel would please God. One obstacle is when they encountered neighbors or peers who aren't Christians. For example:

> Joseph (10)—Our neighbors because they don't follow God. (*Interviewer: How does that affect you?*) Well, we try to tell them about God but we don't know how they will take it.

> Leah (12)—People. Seeing other people not follow God. The world . . . well, media. That can be a bad influence on us.

> Cash (9)—Some people/friends. (*Interviewer: How is that?*) They say bad words or they say God isn't real.

> Michael (10)—Friends who don't believe. Peers in general.

> Hannah (12)—When people badmouth Jesus or cuss. I hate that.

> Marty (10)—Peers. (*Interviewer: How is that?*) Well, they want you to watch shows that aren't good. If you talk about church, they say they don't believe.

Struggles with their own desires and times when others hurt them, also presented challenges to tweens. Several commented that these types of situations made it harder for them to follow Jesus:

Grace (9)—When you don't want to obey. When someone is mean and you want to kick them. When I don't want to listen.

Max (8)—When I fight with my brothers. When I don't get something I want. Sometimes it's hard to give to others.

Emily (8)—Sometimes it's hard to be nice.

Katie (10)—When someone does something bad to you. It's hard to forgive.

Jenny (8) –Today my sister said it was her turn to pick first with the Play-Doh, but she picked first last time. It's hard when she lies and I'm angry.

The older tweens shared they often felt too busy to "fit" God in to their week. Similarly, some participants talked about being too distracted by video games, sports, and media.

Delia (12)—I'm pretty busy. With clarinet, piano, and Girl Scouts, I have something almost every day after school.

Sarah (13)—TV & video games are addicting.

Seth (11)—Well, distractions, like TV or my toys just lying there waiting for me to play with them.

Tweens Want Their Sunday School Teachers to Challenge Them

In thinking about how Sunday school and church could help them connect more with God, tweens offered several ideas. One theme was to give them tools that help them carry their faith over to the rest of the week.

Delia (12)—Give us homework so we don't forget about God during the week. (*Interviewer: What would that look like?*) Just a certain verse that we could look up and think about.

Jenny (8)—Well, they have this thing where if you read six missionary books and answer the questions you get a special prize. (Interviewer: So would you like more things like that?) Yeah.

Adam (11)—Try to read the Bible every day. My Sunday school teacher tells me that. Give us extra activities to do at home.

Another common theme, particularly among the older children, was to add more variety and more challenge to Sunday school. Several children commented that they felt like they were hearing the same stories repeatedly. For example:

> Katie (10)—Tell different stories. (*Interviewer: Bible stories or other kinds of stories?*) Bible stories! We go over the same ones all the time. And tell them with feeling.

> Leah (12)—Don't tell the same stories over and over. (*Interviewer: Is it the same stories or just they are told in the same way?*) Sort of both. We've heard Noah every year. We need more depth. They still treat us like we're little. We want to be challenged. That's what my religion teacher did this year. (*Interviewer: He made you think?*) Yes! But it was still fun!

A final common theme was to allow more time in Sunday school for questions and discussion. Emily (8) thought they should have more variety in the songs they sing, longer stories & more time to ask questions. John (10) felt there should be more time for the teacher to share about his or her life and for the kids to ask questions. Similarly, Michael (10) was interested in open discussions about what they really believe.

Tweens Want to Connect More with Their Families on a Spiritual Level

When asked how their families could help them stay close to God, tweens frequently mentioned praying together. Some talked about reading the Bible together so that they could ask questions and their parents could help them understand more.

> Grace (9)—Do Bible study together. Do devotions together. Give me tools to help me understand the Bible better like stories about people who have done things wrong and now choose to follow Jesus. Or, maybe Bible flashcards. And answer my questions.

> Cash (9)—Send us to church camp. Take time to do Bible study and pray with us, even include my friends.

> Bailey (11)—Spend half-an-hour a day together to read the Bible, pray, and help with Awana homework. Spend family time together.

> John (10)—Read the Bible with them. Pray with them. Come to Sunday school.

Open discussions about how they are living their faith each day were another common theme. For example:

> Katie (10)—Tell personal stories. (*Interviewer: How would that work?*) We should talk about what's hard to us so we can help each other.

Leah (12)—I would love to pray together. To talk about our struggles. To read the Bible together and talk about it. And still go to church together . . . It's important we keep doing that.

Michael (10)—Discuss what their faith means to them.

Marty (10)—Do it first. (*Interviewer: What do you mean?*) Show us how you stay close to God.

MINISTRY IMPLICATIONS

In this study, we've explored tweens' views on Sunday school, family activities and how they connect with God Monday through Saturday. Our goal was to hear from the kids' perspective how they live their faith, what challenges they face, and what they feel would help them grow in their faith.

Much of the previous qualitative research on the spiritual lives of young people has focused on teens (see, for example, Smith & Denton, 2005). From a development perspective, we felt that it was important to study tweens as well to understand how they are being prepared for the stages to come.

Consistent with what we have seen in previous studies, prayer was the primary personal spiritual practice for tweens. Few engaged with the Bible outside of church. Unfortunately, there seemed to be little specific extension of their Sunday school lessons to their everyday life. Future studies, with larger samples, are needed to determine if these findings are generalizable to tweens from different denominations.

In this study, tweens had several ideas for how Children's Ministry leaders can help them connect more with God during the week. Our participants, in fact, loved this question and through the course of the interviews we began referring to it as the "Big Idea" question. In concluding this chapter, we offer to readers the three most common Big Ideas participants shared to help them live their faith each day:

Big Idea #1: Enter Their World

In many ways, tweens asked for their Sunday school teachers to enter their world. They want to be challenged more, whether that means dealing more with the tough topics such as getting along with peers or taking a more active role by bringing something to class or leading a discussion. Entering their world also means allowing more unstructured time in Sunday school when they can just talk about their spiritual lives.

Big Idea #2: Captivate Them with God's Love Letter

Most kids get that praying is how we talk to God. The connection that we hear from God through the Bible is missing for many (Ovwigho & Cole, 2010). For some, opening a Bible never enters their minds as something they would do outside of church. Others have heard that they should read the Bible, but don't really understand why. Although they could repeat many Bible facts and rules, the tweens we interviewed didn't seem to have a good understanding of the relational aspect of scripture. To learn how to engage the Bible as God's love letter to them, tweens say they need simple tools and the ability to ask questions.

Big Idea #3: Mix It Up

A somewhat surprising finding from our study was that kids as young as eight complained that there was too much repetition in Sunday school. The biblical accounts of Noah and Jonah were the two that tweens identified as the most "overdone."

As children move in to third grade and above, the challenge for children's ministry leaders is to vary the curriculum. This could take the form of exploring some of the lesser known biblical accounts. Another option is to use the more popular biblical accounts or topics, but consider them from a different angle. For example, rather than teaching only on the facts of Jesus's life, consider the questions that Jesus asked. Those questions and the circumstances surrounding them provide wonderful raw material for the types of discussions tweens say they are craving as they make the Christian faith their own.

REFERENCES

Bauchman, Voddie. *Family Driven Faith*. Wheaton, IL: Crossway, 2007.

Cole, Arnold, and Pamela Ovwigho. "Truths Learned Along the Way: The Spiritual Journey of Mature Christians." Unpublished manuscript. Lincoln NE: Center for Bible Engagement, 2013.

Fowler, John. *Stages of Faith: The Psychology of Human Development and the Quest for Meaning*. New York: Harper Collins, 1981.

Ham, Kenneth, and Britt Beemer. *Already Gone: Why Your Kids Will Quit Church and What You Can Do to Stop It*. Green Forest, AR: New Leaf Publishing Group/Master Books, 2009.

Keeley, Robert. "Faith Development and Faith Formation: More Than Just Ages and Stages." *Lifelong Faith*. (2010): 20–27.

Ovwigho, Pamela, and Arnold Cole. "Scriptural Engagement, Communication with God, and Moral Behavior Among Children." *International Journal of Children's Spirituality* (2010): 101–113.

Pew Research Center. *"Religion Among the Millenials."* Washington DC: Author, 2010. Available online: http://www.pewforum.org/uploadedFiles/Topics/Demographics/Age/millennials-report.pdf

Smith, Christian, and Melinda Denton. *Soul Searching: The Religious and Spiritual Lives of American Teenagers.* New York: Oxford University Press, 2005.

Chapter 14

How the Psalms Can Be Used to Encourage Faith Formation with Children and Teens

Robert J. Keeley and Laura Keeley

Christians have turned to the Psalms for comfort and for inspiration for centuries. The book of Psalms gives us the language to approach God. The Psalms give us permission to express our feelings to God, *all* of our feelings. We can come to God when we are happy and excited, when we are depressed or lonely, or when we are anxious or sad. The Psalms are written by real people with real feelings to a very real God. As John Witvliet wrote, "the Psalms engage us more personally, more intimately than other forms of biblical literature" (Witvliet 2007, 72). The Psalms help us know that God will take us as we are—sinful, mixed up people.

But the Psalms include words and images that are sometimes difficult for children. Perhaps more importantly, they are emotionally mature pieces of writing. When we bring the Psalms to children we tend to give them just a few well-chosen passages that provide comfort or offer praise. We merely scratch the surface of what the Psalms represent. Many children (and adults) know Psalm 23 ("The Lord is my shepherd . . .") or Psalm 100 ("Shout for joy to the Lord, all the earth . . ."), but few of them know Psalm 22 ("My God, my God, why have you forsaken me?"). The Psalms are a book that, frankly, we've simultaneously praised and ignored.

WHY STUDY THE PSALMS?

As we're considering curriculum choices for children, why should we study the Psalms? We are not suggesting that the stories of the Old Testament, and the stories and teachings of Jesus should be replaced by a study of the Psalms, but we do think that the Psalms have an important place in a balanced curriculum for children.

First of all, the people of Israel knew the Psalms well. The Psalms were an integral part of the way they talked about God and to God. Jesus quoted the Psalms often—there are at least four instances in the book of Matthew alone (Matt 21:16, Matt 22:44, Matt 23:39, and Matt 27:46). Phrases from the Psalms were part of everyday language of the ancient Jews in much the same way that we share common phrases such as "a stitch in time." If we want to make a point that doing something before it's really necessary is often the wisest course of action we can just say "a stitch in time" and our listeners can complete the phrase and get our point. Ann Spangler and Lois Tverberg give examples of Jesus using the first line from a Psalm and expecting his audience to be able to fill in the rest (Spangler and Tverberg, 2009).When Jesus quotes Psalm 22 ("My God, My God, why have you forsaken me") or Psalm 31 ("Into your hands I commit my spirit") on the cross, he likely expected those listening to be able to recall the rest.

Psalms are also the songs of God's people. They have been chanted and sung for literally thousands of years. In the fourth century, Saint Ambrose, the Archbishop of Milan asked, "What is more pleasing that a Psalm?" (McKinnon, 1987, 126). John Chrysostom wrote:

> But from the Spiritual Psalms can come considerable pleasure, much that is useful, much that is holy, and the foundation of all philosophy, as these texts cleanse the soul and the Holy Spirit flies swiftly to those who sing such songs. (McKinnon, 1987, 80)

The Psalms became the primary source of ancient Christian hymnology (Wilson, 1989) and that tradition continues to be vital today with much continued scholarship on the Psalms as well as worship resources making use of the Psalms.

The Psalms give us language that we can use when we want to praise and thank God for his goodness. They also give us words to use to get at some complex faith issues such as depression, the problem of evil and disappointment with God. The Hebrew people were people who did not hide or suppress their emotions (unlike the prevailing Greco-Roman world at the time of Jesus) (Wilson, 1989) and the Psalms give ample evidence of that. In his book on the Jewish Roots of Christianity, *Our Father Abraham*, Marvin Wilson notes that, "the book of Psalms—especially those penned by David—allows us to peer into some of the deepest emotional crevices of the human heart" (Wilson, 1989, 139).

The Psalms are a place where we can be fully human, fully people with a wide range of emotions, joys and sorrows that can be brought to God. The Psalms remind us that God can handle our expressions of those feelings. He is big enough to be with us when we cry out "How long Lord? Will you forget me forever?" (Ps 13:1) and also welcoming when we affirm, "But I trust in your unfailing love" (Ps 13:5).

The Psalms also remind us that God takes us as we are and gives us examples of how to talk to God. Col. Herman Keizer, retired Army chaplain and co-director of the

Soul Repair Center at Brite Divinity School in Fort Worth uses the Psalms as a way to address what he and his colleagues call "moral injury."

> Distinct from physical injuries or even PTSD (post-traumatic stress disorder), moral injury is damage to the soul. It occurs when war combatants violate deeply held moral beliefs in the conduct of war. Not limited to people of faith, moral injury results from heinous acts of war that "unmake the character" of soldiers. (Calvin Institute of Christian Worship, 2012)

Keizer says,

> The psalmist is really angry at God, and some soldiers are really angry with God. I ask them to read the Psalms out loud, read the emotion and anger in the Psalms. They'd look at the binding to see which version of the Bible I was using and ask, 'Is this in my Bible?' There's grief and sorrow and anger to God, but the Psalms show a resolve to get through it. (Calvin Institute of Christian Worship, 2012)

As these soldiers realized, the Psalms show us that God expects to hear from us—not some sanitized always happy version of us, but he expects to hear from the real people that we are. The Psalms help us to be real with God . . . and with ourselves.

This is quite different from the sometimes merely happy version of Christianity that is presented to children and teens (Keeley, 2008). The Christian life is filled with times of trial and disappointment as well as times of peace and joy. The spiritual lives of children and teens are no different. They know what real life is like. They are immersed in a culture that pursues happiness. They are numbed to violence through the news and TV. But many of them are given a God who hears our praise but not our sorrows. The Psalms help us to show children and teens that these feelings of distress are not indicators of failure in the Christian life but are a normal part of what it means to live in a sinful world. We forget that God's people were called the people of Israel—a name that means they wrestle with God. God expects us to wrestle with him and the Psalms show that in action.

The oft-presented happy version of Christianity could be responsible for what Christian Smith refers to as Moralistic Therapeutic Deism (Smith and Denton, 2005). This type of Christianity sees God as a creator who wants people to be good, happy, and to whom we turn when there is a problem. This type of Christianity is pervasive among teens and young adults, according to Smith. The Psalms, with all their raw emotion, are an antidote. They show us a God who cares about us, a God who wants to hear from us in all of our circumstances.

Finally, seeing the Psalms as serving merely as words for us to reflect our feelings is missing part of their usefulness. John Witvliet applies this notion to the Psalms when he writes that a familiarity with the Psalms helps "each of us express our particular experience, but they also help us practice forms of speech that we are still growing into" (Witvliet, 2007, 12). The Psalms do much more than just reflect how we feel—they help us know how to approach God. Just as a person rehearses for a concert or practices for an athletic event, rehearsing the language of the Psalms gives us the vocabulary that we need when our own words fail us.

Our goal for ourselves and for the children and teens we work with is for all of us to know the Psalms well enough that we can use them, sing them, speak them in much the same way a jazz musician uses melodies and riffs. We want to be able to improvise on the Psalms so that we can use this language to enrich our interactions with God and with each other. In Luke 1:46–55, Mary sings the *Magnificat* based on the song of Hannah from 1 Samuel 2. Mary knew Hannah's song so well that she was able to use it as the basis for her own song, adjusting it and adapting it to her particular circumstances. This is a model for what we would like to see children and teens (and adults!) do with the Psalms. This improvisation happens with a deep engagement with this book, something that takes both intentionality and practice. Giving children authentic access to this rich text not only helps the children now, but also plants the seeds for better adult practices.

CHALLENGES

It is hard to find adult Christians who don't speak of the Psalms with great warmth and affection. Even with nearly universal praise many adult Christians are only familiar with a handful of Psalms. On the one hand, this is surprising. Why would this part of scripture be so mysterious to so many? On the other hand, there are some clear reasons why this might be the case.

First of all, there are a *lot* of Psalms, 150 to be exact! It is hard to know 150 of anything well but here is a wealth of riches. Additionally, Psalms are not titled like stories. If we say the story of Jonah and the whale you can probably quickly remember it. If we say Psalm 87, however, there is no clue in the title about the content of the Psalm. It is also easier to remember narratives because of the ready flow of one event into the next. There are few Christians who could not easily give the basic outline of the story of Noah and the ark, but asking them to recite even a well-known Psalm, such as Psalm 150 is more challenging.

Some of the Psalms were specifically written to include poetic devices to aid in memorization. Some of them, for example, follow the alphabet so that each verse or section begins with the next letter. Unfortunately, this is a system that does not translate from one language to another well so that method turns out to be less useful in English.

Psalms also use abstract ideas, many of which are difficult to explain to children. Psalm 2, for example, begins with "Why do the nations conspire and the peoples plot in vain?" Just that sentence has at least two abstract ideas. Even some phrases that adults don't think twice about, Psalm 62:2 for example which says, "He is my fortress,

I will never be shaken," can be met with wonder by children. When Laura read that verse to a group of children, one of the younger ones responded with "A fortress? How can a man be a building?"

It is also true that the even if the words and concepts are challenging, the Psalms can be emotionally mature and children might not relate to them well. The most obvious example is Psalm 137:9, "Happy is the one who seizes your infants and dashes them against the rocks." How do we explain this to children? (Some might ask how to explain it to adults!) There are less obvious examples though, like Psalm 51, "For I know my transgressions and my sin is always before me." This Psalm shows a heart that is broken and laid bare before God.

So our challenge is this: how do we make the Psalms concrete, child friendly, bite sized, and approachable but still retain the Psalm's intent, meaning and beauty? If we really think the Psalms are worth learning for children we don't want to just make this another example of happy Christianity with a focus on the Psalms of comfort or praise like Psalm 23 and Psalm 100. We don't want children to think that the Psalms are little more than a book where you can read nice things about God. We want children to engage with the scriptures, to be aware that God hears them, and to give them language that they can use when they feel like singing a praise chorus or when their world has been shattered.

ONE APPROACH

By taking a Psalm that is not well known, Psalm 107, we developed specific ideas and responses to help children and teens engage the Psalm in an authentic way. We considered four age groups: very young children (ages three to five), early elementary aged children (ages six to nine), upper elementary and middle school children (ages ten to fourteen), and high school teens (ages fifteen to nineteen).

Children: Three to Five Years old

Description: The vocabulary of children three to five years old is growing rapidly so this is a good time to introduce some of the vocabulary of the Psalms. Children this age also enjoy rituals and taking part in repeated behaviors such as hearing the same book read over and over. They also like repetitious songs and poems. They are not able to understand metaphors so we are mindful to be concrete in the way we approach a Psalm.

Using Psalm 107: By age three many kids are trained or are being trained to say, "Thank you." Psalm 107 reminds them to give thanks to God. By hearing and saying the words for Psalm 107:1, children make it part of their vocabulary. This helps them to understand how to respond to God.

Ideas for Psalm 107:

1. Memorize the first verse, "Give thanks to the LORD, for he is good. His love endures forever" (NIV). Talk about what the word "endures" means ("stays forever"). Ways to memorize might include.

   a. Divide the verse into smaller sections and have the child repeat the phrases:

   Give thanks to the Lord (Give thanks to the Lord)
   For he is good (for he is good)
   his love endures (his love endures)
   forever (forever).

   b. Say the verse repeatedly. Work on repeating the verse throughout the day and then once a day for a while.

2. Together, draw pictures of three people for whom the child is thankful. Point to the first picture and talk about how wonderful it is to have that person in your lives and pray for him or her. Repeat verse one. Do the same pattern for the second and third person.

3. At home before a meal, say Psalm 107:1 together. Then ask everyone to say one thing for which they are thankful. Continue until everyone gathered has had the opportunity to speak. End by repeating Psalm 107:1.

These simple activities focus on the main theme of the Psalm (thankfulness) while keeping the focus of this gratitude concrete. We also introduced some of the language of this Psalm.

Children: Six to Nine Years Old

Description: A child who is six to nine years old sees the world in concrete terms. Things are either good or bad. They like to voice their opinions even though their opinions may be a repetition of their parents or other important adults. They are eager for approval from adults.

Using Psalm 107: Kids at this age can easily visualize people being lost, wandering hungry and thirsty. They could draw pictures of these scenes from the Psalm. Extending the notion that wandering people could also represent people who lack focus and are wandering in their lives will not usually work since children this age don't handle abstractions well. A leader can talk about that idea to help the children start to think about others but don't expect all of the children to come up with suggestions. Work with the words or with the images that are in this Psalm, especially the in-distress and the out-of-distress contrast.

Ideas for Psalm 107:

1. Memorize the first verse using some of the ideas mentioned previously for younger children.

2. Write Psalm 107:1 in a large circle on a sheet of paper. List things to be thankful for inside this circle. Place the paper in a visible place and add to the list throughout the week.

3. Read Psalm 107:1–9. If the child can read, take turns reading the verses.

4. Talk about why the people in these verses were sad and miserable. What did God do for them? Talk about what makes you sad. What does God do for you?

5. Select one verse from Psalm 107:1–9. In that verse, pick one word that seems the most important. Then write the verse, making your selected word larger and more colorful than the other words. (You might want to look at some of the artwork of Timothy Botts for examples of how this can be done well. One example is in the book, *Portraits of the Word*.)

6. Learn and sing the song "Forever" by Chris Tomlin. Print out the lyrics and highlight all the words in the song that are also in Psalm 107. This song can be found on the albums *The Noise We Make* by Chris Tomlin, *Worship* by Michael W. Smith, or in the hymnal, *Lift Up Your Hearts* (Faith Alive Christian Resources 2013, 578).

7. Notice the connections between verse four and verse seven, and between verse five and nine. What happened to make that change? Draw two pictures, one with the people in distress and one with the people out of distress. Find other pairs of verses with contrast (4 and 7, 5 and 9, 10 and 14, 17–18 and 20, 23–27 and 29–30, 33 and 35, 39 and 41.)

These activities extend the idea of thankfulness and include a larger portion of the Psalm. It begins to get at the structure of the Psalm and shows that the words to this Psalm show up in songs as well.

Children: Ten to Fourteen Years Old

Description: Kids in this age group can begin to understand metaphors and think logically. They relate new things to personal experience. They are beginning to think about how others may experience life. At this age, many are making a decision to follow the faith of their parents. It is also good to begin to be more explicit about what they believe and to practice articulating their faith. This age child can also talk about how God's people are not always happy but, when we cry out to God, he hears us.

Using Psalm 107: For this age we can begin to work on relating to others. How would it feel to be in distress due to lack of food or water? What does being lost in a storm feel like? What would you do? What does the author do? Reassure the kids that God does respond. Notice how God is acting in their daily lives of the people in the Psalm, just as he is acting in our lives every day. Like the author, our response is to thank him.

Ideas for Psalm 107:

1. Compare Psalm 107:1 to Psalm 136. Talk about why the two Psalms are so similar.

2. Print out Psalm 107. Ask the kids to find the pattern in the Psalm. Highlight the verse using the following color code. Once you've looked at the pattern, write your own section of the Psalm using this pattern.

    a. Blue—trouble

    b. Green—God's response

    c. Yellow—our thanks

3. Look at Psalm 107:1–9. Ask the kids to pick out one verse that summarizes Psalm 107:1–9. If none of the verses work, have them write their own summary verse.

These activities extend the learning to the entire Psalm and ask the students to see the underlying structure in this episodic Psalm. It asks them to bring a higher level of understanding to their study but with significant support and scaffolding.

Teens: Fifteen to Nineteen Years Old

Description: Teens are starting to think abstractly. They can become quite upset about the injustice in the world but often see things either positively or negatively. They also need to know that they are important to God and that God knows them and loves them personally. They may have doubts and questions about their faith. After reflecting on the faith of their parents for many years, they are trying to decide if this faith works for them. The Psalms can be a great assurance to kids as they read that others have had doubts and feelings of loneliness just like they do.

Using Psalm 107: In Psalm 107, the author looks at people in peril . . . no food, no water, no cattle. The people bring these troubles to God. Psalm 107 shows how we can talk to God when we are in distress. Help the teens to recognize that God didn't leave them in distress. Then the author thanks God for his help, just as we should.

Ideas for Psalm 107 with teens:

1. Encourage teens to look for the pattern in the Psalm just as we did with the ten to fourteen year olds but let them discover the pattern themselves. You might want to still give them three highlighters to mark a printout of the chapter.

2. Encourage teens to write their own Psalm using the pattern of Psalm 107. (They don't have to do the entire Psalm to get the pattern—verses 1–9 may be sufficient.)

3. Write a paraphrase of the Psalm. Articulate that God's people are not always happy but God hears them and comes to their aid.

4. Create a readers' theater to illustrate the pattern in the Psalm. (In one we made we used five readers, one of whom introduced each "episode" in the Psalm and in pairs the others alternately showed distress or God's care.)

5. Read Psalm 107 from a paraphrase like *Psalms Now* (Brandt, 1974) or *The Message* (Peterson, 2002). Discuss what you like about the paraphrased version and what you dislike compared to the Bible translation you used.

6. Select one verse from Psalm 107 that summarizes the Psalm.

7. These activities review the entire Psalm but with fewer learning supports. It also reinforces the notion that the Christian life is not just fun and games but includes times of distress. Even in those times, however, we are always in God's care.

ACCESS POINTS

There are other approaches for introducing the Psalms to children and teens as well. We want to make the Psalms part of our lives and the life of our children and teens. Our model has been to give them access points to the Psalms, ways that they can gain entry to these texts and see their truth and the beauty. These ideas can be used in church settings, schools or in the homes. Some of the examples in this section take some significant effort, others could be done very easily.

1. *Make the Psalms part of everyday life.* Read them often, when you get up, at the table, waiting in the car or at bedtime. Don't feel as if you must always read the entire Psalm; select verses to read carefully, being true to either the thrust of the whole Psalm or true to that section of the Psalm.

2. *Memorize Psalms.* Repetition is enjoyed by children (and adults) so feel free to re-read Psalms you've spent time with before. Don't feel overwhelmed by the amount of chapters! Work on a handful each year. One idea to try with a group is to assign a phrase to each child and recite it with each person contributing their phrase at the appropriate time. This can be a great way to take attendance at Sunday school or on the bus for a service project. Soon the whole group will know the entire Psalm.

3. *Sing Psalm songs.* Many of the songs that are used in worship or in other settings are based on the Psalms. "Shout to the Lord" is based on Psalm 98. "Step by Step" is based on Psalm 63. The list goes on . . . As you sing them, read a few verses from which the song is based. This reinforces the notion that the Psalms are the songbook of God's people. A great resource is the newly published collection of Psalms called *Psalms for All Seasons* (Faith Alive Christian Resources, 2012).

4. *Combine a song with a reading of a Psalm in worship.* One fine example is to combine a reading of Psalm 46 with the simple song "Don't Be Afraid" written by John Bell (Faith Alive Christian Resources 2013, 429). Sing the song after reading verses three, six and nine.

5. *Use Vertical Habits to organize your study of the Psalms.* The Vertical Habits (Witvliet 2007, 11–12) are simple language for the feelings expressed in the Psalms.

The vertical habits are:

- I love you

- I'm sorry

- Why?

- I'm listening

- Help

- Thank you

- What can I do?

- Bless you

These simple phrases can form the basis for a study of a particular Psalm. For example: Which of these phrases best describes the feelings in this Psalm?

6. *Connect Psalms with Bible stories.* Psalm 51 has been associated with the story of David and Bathsheba for a long time (and it may actually have been written as a response to those events.) But other Psalms can be paired with stories as well to help us explore the thoughts and feelings of those characters in the story. Reading Psalm 3 when telling the story of David fleeing from Absalom, for example, gives insight into what David might have been feeling. Psalm 116 might actually be what Jesus and the disciples sang at the end of the last supper. These stories add extra poignancy to the Psalm and enhance the story as well.

7. *Use dramatic readings.* One simple way to create a reading is to take two different translations (or a translation and a paraphrase) of a Psalm and read them together. For example, the first reader reads Psalm 13, from the New International Version and the second reader Psalm 13, from the Message. The first reader reads verse 1, and the second reader reads verse one, and so on (we first came upon this idea in a presentation by the theater company, Friends of the Groom).

8. *Write your own Psalm.* There are a number of ways for children and teens to do this. Note the structure of a particular Psalm and build one similar, like we demonstrated in our Psalm 107 example, above. Play with the synonymous or antithetical structure of many Psalms (where a sentiment is repeated with similar words or the opposite of an idea is expressed in negative terms). Invite children to build an ABC Psalm, like Psalm 119 except in English. After telling older children or teens the story of David and Bathsheba, have them write what they think David might write. Then compare their version to Psalm 51.

9. *Encourage art based on the Psalms.* Children and teens can create pictures or other art work based on a phrase or a whole Psalm. Publish pictures of the artwork in a book using Snapfish or some other on-line photo book vendor.

10. *Focus on special sections of the Psalms.* One way to reduce the number of Psalms in your study is to only look at the Psalms of Ascent (Psalms 120–134 used as the Hebrews walked to Jerusalem for the Passover) or the Hallel (Psalm 113–8 used in the celebration of the Passover meal).

By using some of these access points children and teens can develop a love and appreciation for the Psalms that allows them to begin to understand the riches that are included in this wonderful collection of writings.

REFERENCES

Botts, Timothy. *Portraits of The Word.* Carol Stream, IL: Tyndale House, 2002.

Brandt, Leslie F. *Psalms Now.* St. Louis: Concordia, 1974.

Calvin Institute of Christian Worship. "Soul Repair, Moral Injury and A 'Third Conversion.'" 2012. http://worship.calvin.edu/resources/resource-library/soul-repair-moral-injury-and-a-third-conversation.

Faith Alive Christian Resources. *Psalms For All Seasons.* Grand Rapids, MI: Faith Alive Christian Resources, 2012.

Faith Alive Christian Resources. *Lift Up Your Hearts.* Grand Rapids, MI: Faith Alive Christian Resources, 2013.

Keeley, Robert J. *Helping Our Children Grow in Faith.* Grand Rapids, MI: Baker, 2008.

McKinnon, James. *Music in Early Christian Literature.* New York: Cambridge University Press, 1987.

Peterson, Eugene H. *The Message.* Colorado Springs: Navpress, 2002.

Smith, Christian with Melinda Lundquist Denton. *Soul Searching: The Religious and Spiritual Lives of American Teenagers.* Oxford: Oxford University Press, 2005.

Spangler, Ann, and Lois Tverberg. *Sitting at The Feet of Rabbi Jesus.* Grand Rapids, MI: Zondervan.

Wilson, Marvin R. *Our Father Abraham: Jewish Roots of the Christian Faith.* Grand Rapids, MI: Eerdmans, 1989.

Witvliet, John D. *The Biblical Psalms in Christian Worship: A Brief Introduction and Guide to Resources,* 2007. Grand Rapids, MI: Eerdmans.

Chapter 15

The End of the Story
Why and How to Teach Children About the Second Coming of Christ

Sharon Warkentin Short

I once asked my fourth and fifth grade Sunday school students what they knew about the second coming of Christ. They unanimously responded that this event occurred when Jesus rose from the dead and came out of the tomb. It dawned on me then that I had very rarely seen a lesson about Jesus's promised return in any of the Sunday school curricula that I had used over the years, nor had I included it in the comprehensive three-year curriculum I had written for my own program.

My suspicion that instruction about Christ's second coming is conspicuously absent from most children's Sunday school materials was confirmed in an informal survey of popular publishers. I identified fifteen well-known companies and scanned the Scope and Sequence charts that they provide online for their Sunday school programs. I expected that stories about Jesus's return would most likely be found in the Sunday morning curricula, since these programs generally provide the most basic or core Bible teachings of a church's children's ministry. This curriculum survey was limited to materials written for children in the elementary grades, that is, grades one through five or six, depending upon the publisher.

Of the fifteen programs I reviewed, six did not appear to include any lessons at all about the return of Christ. One program offered one lesson per year; one included one lesson per three-year cycle; three had one lesson every six years; three included two lessons every six years; and one provided three lessons in its six-year cycle. The *most frequently* that a Sunday school student in a church using any of these curricula might receive formal instruction about Jesus coming back to earth was one class session per year, and that was in only one of the fifteen programs. Oddly, these lessons often appeared on low-attendance Sundays such as Memorial Day weekend or the last Sunday of the summer quarter. Children who happened to miss that week might receive no exposure to this doctrine at all.

During a conversation in which I contrasted this paucity of references to Christ's return with the multiple lessons that most curricula include *every* year about Jesus's birth, death, and resurrection, a listener immediately responded, "Yes, but those are important events!" And that is precisely the point. The second coming of Christ does *not* appear to count as an important event in the minds of most church education leaders, Sunday school teachers, and Bible lesson writers. In this chapter I will explore (a) why teaching about Jesus's return is imperative in a comprehensive Bible teaching program, (b) what constitutes the essential content of such teaching, (c) why this doctrine has not received widespread inclusion, and (d) how to teach children more effectively about the end times.

WHY SHOULD WE TEACH CHILDREN ABOUT THE SECOND COMING?

Central to my argument that children (and all Christians) need a lively awareness of Christ's promised return is my conviction that the Bible as a whole tells one coherent story. Understood this way, the Bible is more than a large anthology of various genres of literature written by many different authors and compiled over a long period of time. Although these facts about the Bible are true, it is also true that this collection as a whole constitutes one overarching narrative. The Bible in its entirety has the shape of a story.

Any fully developed story consists of six basic elements: (a) setting and (b) characters, which define an initial situation; (c) a problem, which disrupts the original context; (d) events, which consist of attempts to solve the problem; (e) the resolution, which describes the effective solution to the problem; and (f) the conclusion, which summarizes a return to stability comparable to the circumstances with which the story began. Mandatory story tension is created by the uncertainty about which events will eventually succeed in solving the problem, and in the best stories the precise nature of this resolution comes as a surprise.

Viewed as one continuous story, the metanarrative of the Bible incorporates these same six basic story elements. In the beginning, God created a perfect world (setting) populated by humans whom he made in his own image to partner with him in tending and developing this beautiful creation (characters). Through human rebellion, sin entered this idyllic setting, ruining the flawless harmony of the created order, distorting human administration of the world, and spoiling the divine-human collaboration that God desired (problem). God initiated a strategy to restore his damaged creation and to reclaim a relationship with alienated humans through his choice of one man, from whom he built a nation. God's purpose from the beginning was that this nation would mediate his blessings to the rest of humanity, but this plan was frustrated time and again through human failure (events). Ultimately God accomplished the redemption of his broken world through the birth, ministry, death, and resurrection of his son, Jesus, whose earthly life span was situated within that chosen nation (resolution). These momentous events effectively destroyed the power of sin over humanity and over all of creation. But what is the conclusion to the Bible's grand story? It seems that a great deal of Bible teaching misses the mark here.

In terms of story shape, the point of the conclusion is to demonstrate how the resolution reverses or repairs the problem that initially disrupted the setting and characters. In other words, the conclusion is the "happily ever after" ending that corresponds to the "once upon a time" beginning of the narrative. In the great story of the Bible, the conclusion demonstrates how the resolution (the life, death, and resurrection of Jesus) re-establishes the conditions that prevailed in the opening setting of the story, showing how all of creation—including humanity—will ultimately be restored to its original purity, beauty, harmony, and purpose. This outcome is the already-revealed happy ending toward which the plot of the entire Bible is directed. This great "re-creation" began with the resurrection of the Lord Jesus and will be completed when Jesus returns to earth in all of his glory.

That is why boys and girls, and all believers, need to hear the story of Christ's second coming as frequently as they hear stories about Jesus's first visit to planet earth. They need to hear how God's great story will end! Children desperately need the "blessed hope" (Titus 2:13)—the confident expectation—that Jesus is coming back to make everything in the world right again. In our Christian education efforts, when we bring hearers right up to the resolution of the story but then fail to tell them how it ends, or offer them only an incomplete or intermediate ending, we are leaving out the very best part.

WHAT IS THE ESSENTIAL CONTENT OF TEACHING ABOUT THE SECOND COMING?

Biblical scholarship concerning "End Times" has generated a spectacular and bewildering variety of theological systems that attempt to incorporate the available scriptural evidence into some consistent doctrine. However, within this impressive diversity concerning the details, several core truths remain constant.

The Certainty of Jesus Coming Again

First of all, Jesus is definitely coming again! As Hoekema (1979) claims, "Every book in the New Testament points us to the return of Christ and urges us to live in such a way as to be always ready for that return" (109). The expectation that Jesus would certainly come back dominated the preaching, teaching, and writings of the New Testament church (Hoekema, 1979), and it continues to be the common hope of Christian believers today.

The Literalness of Jesus Coming Again

Secondly, Scripture stresses the literal, visible, physical return of the Lord Jesus to this earth. When Jesus discussed his coming again, he was not referring to his spiritual presence with his followers in the person of the Holy Spirit, as true and wonderful as that reality is. He meant he was really, bodily coming back to stand on this ground again (Pahl, 2011).

In his letter to Titus, Paul referred in the same passage to the already-accomplished first appearance of the Lord Jesus and to the joyful hope of his future appearance (Titus 2:11–13). If Jesus's first coming was literal, visible, and physical, it seems logical to conclude from this passage that the second coming will be the same (Hoekema, 1979).

The Purpose for Jesus Coming Again

Simply stated, the purpose for Jesus's return to earth is to complete the redemption of humanity and all of creation that he inaugurated at his first coming (Goheen n. d.). Jesus by his death and resurrection decisively defeated the power of sin that has devastated planet earth since the days of Adam and Eve. Sin and Satan have already been conquered. The battle has already been won. However, we are currently living in the span of time between that victorious battle and the end of the war. When Jesus comes again, evil on earth will be banished for good (Walsh and Middleton, 1984).

Christians are generally very familiar with the belief that Jesus died and came back to life to save *us* from sin, but we speak far less frequently of how Jesus by his death and resurrection saves *all of creation* from the catastrophic consequences of sin (Goheen n. d.). The ministry of Jesus during his first advent provided a sort of down payment—a first installment—of what God will accomplish thoroughly and comprehensively when Jesus comes again: storms were stilled, disabled people were made whole, the dead came back to life, demons were banished, illness was cured. At that time, however, not *every* sick person became well, not every dead person was raised, and not every natural disaster was averted (Walsh and Middleton, 1984). That was just the beginning of the glorious consummation that is still to come, for which all the earth desperately sighs and groans (Rom 8:19–22). The cosmic scope of the salvation that will be completed when Jesus returns is emphasized in such Scripture texts as Acts 3:19–21, Ephesians 1:7–10, and Colossians 1:19–20 (Middleton, 2006).

When Jesus comes again, all of humanity and all of nature and the entire universe will be restored to their original created perfection (Vang and Carter, 2006). Jesus is coming back to complete the marvelous, miraculous work that he began when he was here two thousand years ago (Pahl, 2011).

THE OUTCOME OF JESUS COMING AGAIN

The ultimate outcome of Jesus's return to earth will be the establishment of a new heaven and a new earth. This expectation is mentioned in several key Scripture texts. In the prophecy of Isaiah, the Lord declared, "Behold, I will create new heavens and a new earth. The former things will not be remembered, nor will they come to mind" (Isa 65:17). Then, in his second epistle, Peter discussed the prospect of "the day of the Lord," and he summarized his explanation with the encouraging words, "in keeping with his promise we are looking forward to a new heaven and a new earth, the home of righteousness" (2 Pet 3:13). Finally, in the concluding chapters of the visions entrusted to the Apostle John, he wrote, "Then I saw a new heaven and a new earth, for the first heaven and the first earth had passed away, and there was no longer any sea" (Rev 21:1). This is how the story will end when Jesus comes again: with a re-creation of both the heavens and the earth, resulting in a restored earth in which God's redeemed people will relate in perfect harmony to him, to each other, and to the natural world (Goheen n. d.).

Parallels between Genesis 1–3 and Revelation 20–22

Further evidence for the future renovation of the whole earth can be found in the structure of the Bible's grand narrative. It begins with the creation of the heavens and the earth (Gen 1:1) and ends with the appearance of a new heaven and a new earth (Rev 21:1). The first three chapters of Genesis establish the initial setting and characters of the story, and introduce the problem. The final three chapters of Revelation demonstrate restoration to stability after the problem has been resolved. If Genesis 1–3 constitute the Bible's "once upon a time," then Revelation 20–22 correspond to its "happily ever after." The following table, which summarizes some of the parallels between the very beginning and the very ending of God's great story, is adapted from Alcorn (2004) and Pate et al. (2004).

Table 1: Parallels between Genesis and Revelation

GENESIS 1–3	REVELATION 20–22
Serpent deceived humanity (3:13)	Serpent will be bound to prevent him from "deceiving the nations" (20:2–3)
Satan introduced sin into the world (3:1–5)	Satan will be finally judged (20:7–10)
Death entered the world (2:17; 3:3; 3:6)	Death will be eradicated (20:14)
Water symbolized unordered chaos (1:1)	There will no longer be any sea (21:1)

Sin brought tears and suffering into the world (3:16–19)	There will be "no more death or mourning or crying or pain" (21:4)
Sinful humans were banished from the presence of God (3:23)	"The dwelling of God [will be] with men, and he will live with them" (21:3)
Sinful actions devastated human flourishing (chapter 4 and following)	Sinful actions will be banished (21:8, 27)
Sinful people were prevented from eating from the tree of life (3:22, 24)	People will have free access to the tree of life (22:2, 14)
The ground was cursed (3:17–19)	"No longer will there be any curse" (22:3)
Sinful people hid from God's presence (3:8)	"They will see his face" (22:4)
God created light and separated it from darkness; God called the light "day" and the darkness "night" (1:3–5, 14–19)	"There will be no more night. They will not need the light of a lamp or the light of the sun, for the Lord God will give them light" (22:5)

NEW EARTH WILL BE OUR HOME

The most important point of this entire discussion is that New Earth will be the eternal home of God's people. Every individual who has expressed saving faith in the Lord Jesus in this life will someday live forever in a solidly resurrected physical body on a firmly material resurrected earth (Bartholomew and Goheen, 2004). This incredible truth was the most surprising discovery of my study of the great story of the Bible. I was familiar with the Bible texts about "the new heavens and the new earth," but somehow it never occurred to me that this new earth would be populated by God's redeemed people. I don't know who I expected would be occupying New Earth, but I simply assumed that in the life to come Christians would be someplace else.

The hope of eternal life on New Earth contradicts a great many of our implicitly held and explicitly expressed beliefs about life in the "hereafter." The tacit expectation of many Christians is that at death our essential, spiritual selves escape from our imperfect bodies and our flawed planet to dwell in "a better place." As I will explain, this anticipation is true and valid as far as it goes, but it is not the end of the story. God's ultimate intention has always been to heal our bodies and mend our world so that we can experience life on planet earth according to his original design (Alcorn, 2004).

Life on New Earth

The reader will have noticed by now that I have begun to capitalize the phrase *New Earth*. I got this idea from Randy Alcorn (2004) who writes the name this way to emphasize that it will be a definite geographical reality—like New Mexico or New Orleans. The place name New Earth positively sparkles with possibilities!

Of immediate significance to believers who live on this side of New Earth is the incredible promise that "there will be no more death or mourning or crying or pain" when the earth is made new (Rev 21:4). We will experience human life on this planet free from all the anguish that sin introduced into the original perfect environment that God designed.

One aspect of life on New Earth that seems certain from Scripture is that work and cultural development will continue (Bartholomew and Goheen, 2004). God's command to the first humans to care for and develop the natural world preceded humanity's catastrophic fall into sin. Meaningful, creative labor that fills the worker with a sense of pride and accomplishment is part of the "very good" world that God made (Gen 1:28, 31), and can reasonably be expected to continue in the renewed earth—but completely free from the frustrations and disappointments that often accompany work in the present fallen world.

Furthermore, the cultural advances that have already been achieved even in this broken world will probably endure. Lawrence (1995) speculates, "Surely the finest and most liberating achievements of the ages, those aspects of human endeavor that have been in harmony with God's desire for this world, will be retained and assimilated into life on the new earth" (112). The incredible expectation that all the good things accomplished in this life will endure into eternity means that everything we do here and now matters, and it means that we do not need to grieve like those "who have no hope" (1 Thess 4:13) when a believer's contributions are curtailed due to illness, disability, or death. Those accomplishments will all still be there—with limitless time, energy, and resources to continue building upon them.

In addition, life on New Earth will mean a reunion with all of God's people who have died. Even though we cannot comprehend the details—will people be different ages? Will I recognize my grandmother if she is no longer old and frail? Will the child who died in infancy always be a helpless baby?—it seems clear that people will retain their identities and will be recognizable by others, just as Jesus was recognizable to his friends in his glorified body after his resurrection (Alcorn, 2004; Lawrence, 1995). Our separation from loved ones who died in Christ is only temporary; when Jesus returns, we will have all the time in the world to enjoy them again.

However, these incredible blessings pale in comparison to the most amazing feature of life on New Earth: that those who belong to Christ will see him face to face and will abide forever in the very presence of God (Alcorn, 2004; Carson, 2010). We will experience the kind of intimacy with God that he intended from the beginning.

One of the most stunning images in Revelation depicts "the Holy City, the new Jerusalem, coming down out of heaven from God" (21:2). Accompanying this magnificent vision is the astounding declaration, "Now the dwelling of God is with men, and he will live with them" (Rev 21:3). This city represents the very presence of God (Carson, 2010), and it is pictured as descending to earth. As Pahl (2011) explains, "'heaven' will be much more 'earthy' than Christians typically think. We are not brought up to some spiritual heaven; rather, heaven comes down to earth" (84). Understood this way, we really will spend eternity in heaven—because the breach between heaven and earth that was caused by sin will be closed (Alcorn, 2004). Life on New Earth will quite literally be . . . heavenly.

WHY ISN'T THE SECOND COMING WIDELY TAUGHT?

We as God's people are heading toward a thrilling future in which everything that is currently wrong with our world will be made right, and everything that is currently missing from our human experience will be restored. *Why on earth are we not telling our children about these events?* Several possible explanations for this widespread failure to instruct children about Christ's return come to mind.

Emphasizing Present Blessings

One reason may be that in our Christian education efforts, we are overemphasizing the present blessings that Jesus brings into our lives and minimizing the future benefits. Contemporary Bible preaching and teaching tend to depict the conclusion of Scripture's great story in terms of *current personal experience*, asserting that people who express saving faith in Jesus receive from God the resources they need to enjoy successful and fulfilling lives right now. The benefits accruing to individuals who receive salvation are often defined predominately in terms of their individual lives today, such as harmonious marriages, insights for child-rearing, sound financial decisions, emotional stability, wise career decisions, and so on. This perspective is obvious in many children's Bible curricula in which the lesson "applications" stress such daily-life issues as getting along with family, making friends, telling the truth, being kind to others, not being afraid, sharing with the needy, and showing respect to those in authority.

Even though these outcomes for present human thriving are defensible from Scripture and are certainly an aspect of authentic Christian experience, they do not accurately represent the conclusion of the Bible's grand narrative.

Misunderstanding the Intermediate State

Another possible explanation for the dearth of instruction about Christ's return is that many Christians confuse the believer's temporary condition after physical death with the eternal condition that God has planned for them. When Christians die, their souls definitely leave their bodies and reside in heaven with God, while their lifeless corpses remain on earth. Paul, for example, contrasts the conditions of being "at home in the body" with being "away from the Lord," and conversely being "away from the body" with being "at home with the Lord" (2 Cor 5:6, 8) (Middleton, 2006).

It is this immaterial heavenly existence that is popularly (although inaccurately) depicted in cartoons, paintings, literary allusions, and song lyrics. However, this disembodied existence, or in formal theological terms, the *intermediate state*, is only temporary (Lawrence, 1995). Believers who have died in Christ experience joy and peace in heaven right now, *and* they eagerly anticipate the day when they will receive new, resurrected, glorified bodies (Alcorn, 2004). Paul's words again:

> While we are in this tent, we groan and are burdened, because we do not wish
> to be unclothed but to be clothed with our heavenly dwelling, so that what is
> mortal may be swallowed up by life. (2 Cor 5:4)

This incredible, permanent transformation of our bodies will occur when Jesus comes back (1 Cor 15:51–52). Thus the idea of "going to heaven when you die" is true for Christians for the present time, but it is not the end of their story.

Christian teachers and parents who are uninformed about the distinction between the present heaven (the dwelling place of God that is disconnected from earth because of sin) and the future heaven (the dwelling place of God that will once again coincide with earth) (Alcorn, 2004) may expect that bodiless existence in another realm is the end of the line for Christians. In that case they are not likely to teach children about the wondrous complex of events surrounding the return of Jesus to our world. They are simply not expecting anything more to happen!

Focusing on the Details

Perhaps the primary reason why teachings about Jesus's return are missing from many children's Bible curricula is that devout Christians differ considerably in their understanding of the details surrounding this great event. The biblical evidence has been synthesized in a remarkable variety of ways, and Christians have been known to become quite defensive and argumentative in promoting their system of choice. Too often, formal study of eschatology in Christian colleges and seminaries concentrates much more on comparing the systems and defending a preferred one than on celebrating the end result of whatever is going to happen. Curriculum publishers may understandably shy away from promoting a particular perspective in order to sell their materials to as large a market as possible. Volunteer Sunday school teachers in a particular church may represent a range of viewpoints, and rather than confusing children with contradictory teachings may avoid the issue altogether. The end result may be that children learn nothing about the second coming.

Author David Lawrence (1995) compares this fascination with the chain of events surrounding Christ's return to a fixation on labor pains that overrides excitement about the baby who is being born. Believers can become so passionate about defending a particular doctrinal construction that they miss the essential point on which all Christians have historically agreed—namely that Jesus is coming again to restore all things.

In this chapter I have intentionally presented the second coming as one construct, without attempting to separate discrete components such as the rapture, the tribulation, the millennium, the first resurrection, the second death, the judgment, and so on. This does not imply that these separate events are unimportant or unnecessary to study, but my purpose has been to keep the focus on the big picture, which is that Jesus is coming back to establish a new world in which his people will dwell bodily. On this essential fact all orthodox Christians agree, and this basic truth is what children desperately need to know.

HOW SHOULD WE TEACH CHILDREN ABOUT THE SECOND COMING?

Since teaching about Christ's return has not been emphasized with children, parents and church leaders may wonder how to proceed. In this final section are some suggestions for incorporating the doctrine of Christ's expected return into the regular Christian education of children.

Pray for His Return

In the final chapter of the Bible, Jesus assures his beloved church, "Behold, I am coming soon!" (Rev 22:7, 12) and at the end he adds, "Yes, I am coming soon" (Rev 22:20). In response, the aged Apostle John earnestly prays, "Amen. Come, Lord Jesus" (Rev 22:20).

When is the last time you heard a parent, children's pastor, or Sunday school teacher pray with a group of children, "Lord Jesus, please come back soon"? It seems to me that this would be an excellent place to start. Christians in Peter's second letter are described as people who "look forward to the day of God and *speed its coming*" (2 Pet 3:12; emphasis added), a characterization that must surely include fervent prayer for the great day to arrive. In the context of our prayers with children for their help and healing, safety and protection, strength and provision, we as Christian leaders could routinely add something like, "And thank you, Lord Jesus, for your promise that a day is coming when people will not be hurt or sick, afraid or lonely, hungry or cold any more. Please come back soon to make everything right in our world again."

Eagerly Anticipate His Coming

In addition to praying for Christ's return, all of us who minister with children must converse regularly about this marvelous event. As we are applying a Band-Aid to a scraped knee, we could mention, "Won't it be great when Jesus comes back and nobody ever gets hurt again?" As we are collecting offerings to provide food for needy children, we can reiterate, "Jesus is pleased that we are helping hungry children in this way. Jesus cares very much about children in need. And someday, when Jesus comes back to earth, he will take away all these problems and nobody will ever be hungry again." When we are counseling a child through a crushing disappointment or a devastating loss, we can assure them, "God did not mean for life to have hard times like this. God's plan for this world was for everyone to be secure and protected, and he is planning to make it that way again. When Jesus comes back, all these terrible troubles will go away forever."

Include the Second Coming in the Festivals of the Church

The liturgical calendar of the church and the major seasonal observances celebrate annually the birth, death, and resurrection of Jesus, as well as major events in his earthly life. But when do we as a church celebrate his certain return? Interestingly, the season of Advent originally recalled not only the first coming of Jesus as a baby in Bethlehem, but his anticipated second coming (Talley, 1986). Perhaps it is time to reclaim this emphasis, and during the weeks leading up to Christmas to simultaneously acknowledge his first and his second advents. The last Sunday of the church year, immediately before the first Sunday of Advent, is called Christ the King Sunday, so named to remember that Jesus will someday return as a triumphant king (Webber, 2004). This day, too, would be an ideal occasion to celebrate Christ's promised return.

Teach About the Second Coming in the Curriculum Cycle

This suggestion should be obvious in light of the survey with which I introduced this chapter. Curriculum planners and publishers must commit to telling children the *whole* story about Jesus—his birth, earthly ministry, death, resurrection, ascension, present intercession, *and* expected return. It is an important event!

Teach Children to Live in Light of the Second Coming

Does it really matter? In light of the substantial disagreement among dedicated Bible scholars about end-times events, Christians may be tempted to question whether these issues really matter. Isn't it enough to know Jesus in this life, regardless how things will play out in the future?

The reality is, our orientation toward the future significantly influences how we live today. If our hope and expectation is that at death, Jesus will remove us from this miserable planet and relocate us to a different and better world, then we will not be particularly concerned about what happens "down here" (Goheen n. d.). After all, we are not planning to stay around. If, however, our hope for the future is bound up with a renewed existence on earth, and if we believe that God will preserve in the New Earth every good achievement we have accomplished in this life, we will work tirelessly to make this world better for everyone *today*. Why not teach our children to do the same?

Maranatha. "Come, O Lord!" (1 Cor 16:22).

REFERENCES

Alcorn, Randy. *Heaven*. Carol Stream, IL: Tyndale House, 2004.

Bartholomew, Craig G., and Michael W. Goheen. *The Drama of Scripture: Finding Our Place in the Biblical Story*. Grand Rapids, MI: Baker Academic, 2004.

Carson, D. A. *The God Who is There: Finding Your Place in God's Story*. Grand Rapids, MI: Baker Books, 2010.

Goheen, Michael W. "(Re)New(ed) Creation: The End of the Story." *Scripture & Worldview*. http://www.biblicaltheology.ca/bluearticles.htm (accessed December 3, 2008).

Hoekema, Anthony A. *The Bible and the Future*. Grand Rapids, MI: William B. Eerdmans, 1979.

Lawrence, David. *Heaven: It's Not the End of the World*. Valley Forge, PA: Scripture Union USA, 1995.

Middleton, J. Richard. "A New Heaven and a New Earth: The Case for a Holistic Reading of the Biblical Story of Redemption." *Journal for Christian Theological Research* 11 (2006): 73–97.

Pahl, Michael W. *The Beginning and the End: Rereading Genesis's Stories and Revelation's Visions*. Eugene, OR: Cascade Books, 2011.

Pate, C. Marvin, J. Scott Duvall, J. Daniel Hays, E. Randolph Richards, W. Dennis Tucker Jr., and Preban Vang. *The Story of Israel: A Biblical Theology*. Downers Grove, IL: InterVarsity Press, 2004.

Talley, Thomas J. *The Origins of the Liturgical Year*. 2nd Edition. Collegeville, MN: The Liturgical Press, 1986.

Vang, Preban and Terry Carter. *Telling God's Story: The Biblical Narrative from Beginning to End*. Nashville, TN: Broadman & Holman, 2006.

Walsh, Brian J. and J. Richard Middleton. *The Transforming Vision: Shaping a Christian World View*. Downers Grove, IL: InterVarsity Press, 1984.

Webber, Robert E. *Ancient-Future Time: Forming Spirituality through the Christian Year*. Grand Rapids, MI: Baker Books, 2004.

SECTION THREE

Engaging Methodologies

Chapter 16

Body and Spirit

The Role of Physical Movement in Children's Spiritual Development

Holly Catterton Allen, Robin Howerton
with Will Chesher and Hannah Brown

Experienced schoolteachers frequently incorporate bodily movement when they teach children. Besides knowing that movement makes learning more fun, these teachers are also aware that educational psychologists recommend movement to enhance learning, that is, they are cognizant of the body/mind connection. In speaking about body/spirit issues, we have asked teachers in faith settings why they use movement when teaching children; their answers have included:

- To get the wiggles out

- To transition to another activity

- To illustrate a song

- To accompany a memory verse

- To regain attention

- For physical exercise (for health reasons)

- To change the pace

- To teach specific information (e.g., Ten Commandments)

- To act out a Bible story

- Just for fun

These responses indicate that many teachers in faith communities use movement for utilitarian purposes but also recognize that engaging the body can aid learning. But our question for this discussion goes beyond the body/mind connection; this chapter addresses the body/spirit relationship. Even teachers in faith settings do not tend to link their use of bodily movement with spiritual development specifically.

Of course, the body, mind, and spirit are interrelated. For example, using movement to teach a memory verse or to teach the Ten Commandments can be seen not simply as a body/mind connection but also as a body/spirit connection—or more holistically as a body/mind/spirit integration. Our purpose in this chapter is not to bifurcate the body/mind/spirit relationship into two disparate pairs (i.e., body/mind and body/spirit); we hope ultimately to bring together all three. However, our predominant focus will be on the neglected relational pair—the body/spirit connection.

We believe that the body/spirit connection has been neglected due in part to the sometimes negative view of the physical body in historical Western Christianity. That is, the body has commonly been viewed as a liability in spiritual formation rather than as an asset. The purpose of this chapter then is to argue that the body can contribute positively to the spiritual growth and development of children—as well as adults.

Exploring the interconnectedness of the body and spirit is a rich cross-disciplinary endeavor. This study draws from the fields of theology, Scripture, church history, spiritual formation, kinesthesia, educational psychology, developmental psychology, and current brain research (e.g., neuropsychology and neurotheology). Given the interdisciplinary nature of the enterprise, it is evident that this chapter will not (and cannot) address all the issues that inhere to the body/spirit relationship. Thus, we propose a limited agenda in the form of three questions:

1. What factors have contributed to the tendency in Western Christianity to see the body as a liability to spiritual formation?

2. How are *body* and *spirit* interconnected?

3. How can the body (movement, stillness, etc.) be utilized to promote, nurture, and foster spiritual growth and development in unique ways?

The following story about Anne will give the phrase *embodied spirituality* a face.

THE INITIAL SPARK: ANNE'S STORY

By Holly Allen

There is a particular moment in my life when the indisputable yet mysterious connection between body and spirit captured my attention. About twenty years ago my family was part of a faith community that began to grow exponentially drawing unchurched and broken people to Christ. A fresh enthusiasm, a sweet spirit of joy and hope permeated the worship, and as we sang contemporary songs (a bit unusual then), many raised their hands, and some (though not many) danced in the aisles.

Anne began coming to these two-hour worship gatherings. After a few weeks, Anne spoke with me about her general discomfort during worship. She said she felt that she was expected to raise her hands, but that she didn't want to, that it didn't feel authentic to her, and that she didn't like the pressure. As Anne spoke she crossed her arms over her chest—her body language adding emphasis to her words. I assured her that many others were not raising their hands, and that most worshipers were very focused on worshiping, not on what other worshipers were or were not doing, and that she should indeed feel free to allow her arms to simply rest at her sides. Anne continued to worship with this faith community over the next year. During these months her family was experiencing intense conflict, and one Sunday evening Anne called me and said:

> I have felt really uncomfortable about everybody raising their hands when we worship, as I told you before. But this morning as we were singing, I was praying and listening to God and crying out to him, and . . . my arms just went up. I don't remember thinking "Put your arms up" or "I should raise my arms"; they just went up.

> All afternoon I have been thinking about this and I realize now that my resistance to raising my hands has been tied to a need to keep myself distant from God—probably part of my strong need for independence; when I raised my arms today, my hands were open, palms facing up. I think it was my body showing that I was at the end of myself, and that I am ready to receive whatever God wishes to give.

Anne's experience, this deep body/spirit moment, has lingered in my memory, awaiting consideration. At the time, I had no tools to process Anne's experience or comprehend its significance—I had not really considered the body/spirit connection. The time for consideration came a few years ago when I was conducting research about children's spirituality; only at that point did I begin to discern the importance of what I had glimpsed that day.

A BODY/SPIRIT DISCONNECT

Due to a deeply embedded dualistic impulse, Christians have tended toward a mixed theology regarding the relationship of body and spirit. Though a few faith traditions view very active bodily movement (e.g., dancing, swaying, raising hands) as an integral part of Christian worship, some have viewed such movement as inappropriate and perhaps irreverent. One could say—only slightly tongue-in-cheek—that many faith traditions can identify with the phrase "the frozen chosen." A typical worship gathering in many evangelical Christian faith communities today would reveal quite a restricted range of bodily movement: standing, sitting, and bowing one's head in prayer. Historically liturgical churches have employed a broader array (though still quite limited) of physical movement to accompany or complement various aspects of worship, for example, the sign of the cross, kneeling, and the blessing of the priest.

According to Father Thomas Ryan (2004), differing views of the physical body and its connection with the spiritual realm come from a difference in the way in which traditions interpret the story of Scripture. Those who hold to a strong theology of redemption, the bodily resurrection, and the re-creation and repopulation of the heavens and the earth tend to have a positive view of the physical body and its role in spiritual formation (Ryan, 2004). In contrast, faith traditions that emphasize body-less escapism to a purely spiritual heavenly existence for all of eternity—in essence, Gnostic eschatology—tend to have a negative view of the physical body and therefore resist the idea of movement in connection with spirituality (Ryan, 2004). The following sections address the sources of somewhat negative attitudes toward the body in Western Christianity and offer a fuller, richer, more biblical understanding of the interconnectedness of body and spirit.

Historical Influences

Plato's dualistic view of human nature has influenced Western thinking about spirituality for millennia (Radford, 2006). Plato considered life to be a battle between the bodily passions that drag us down and the rational/spiritual that can discern truth, beauty, and reality. For example, Plato writes

> It seems that so long as we are alive, we shall continue closest to knowledge if we avoid as much as we can all contact and association with the body, except when they are absolutely necessary, and instead of allowing ourselves to become infected with its nature, purify ourselves from it until God himself gives us deliverance. (Wiseman, 2004, 4)

In the early centuries of the church, some theologians attempted to reconcile the incarnation of Jesus Christ with Greek influences, and taught that Jesus was not really human, but only appeared human, and either did not have a physical body or merely "inhabited" one during his time on earth. These Gnostics also taught that his resurrection, therefore, was the freeing of his spirit from his body of the appearance of his body, and it was this type of "resurrection" that Jesus had in mind for his followers (Cox, 2002).

Later Augustine, though not a Gnostic, in some of his writings described the body as a weapon of sin and man as a soul "using" a body. His comments regarding sexual intercourse between a husband and wife as sinful except for the purpose of progeny (Augustine, *Soliloquies*) have especially contributed to the general body/spirit disconnect that emerged in early Christianity.

Although monks are credited with preserving the Christian faith through the dark medieval period, some monks pursued spirituality at the expense of the body, for example, fasting to sickness or death, self-flagellation, going without sleep, and exposing themselves to the elements. These examples reflect the notion of body as a barrier rather than a benefit to spirituality.

This body/spirit dissonance has wafted down through Christianity to the present day and perhaps still tends to color believers' views of the role of the body in spiritual formation.

Redefining the Role of the Physical Body in Christian Theology

The early Church fathers opposed the body-spirit dualism of Gnosticism, ruling at the councils of Nicaea and Constantinople that Jesus was both divine and human and ascended to heaven with his physical, albeit glorified, body. Just as the early Church fathers tried to resist the mixing of Greek and Christian philosophy so, too, do modern Christians have a responsibility to carefully develop a truly biblical theology of the physical body.

According to Ryan (2004), Christians are in a bind when it comes to theology and the physical body; he puts the dilemma like this:

> Christianity finds itself in the awkward position of trying to develop a positive theology of creation without ever having rejoiced in the human body. In theory, we have the highest theology of the body among all world religions. In practice, we are still dualistic and suspicious of anything too earthly and sensual; we live largely in our heads. And yet we believe that, in becoming flesh, God honors skin, praises skin, enters it, caresses it, embraces it. Salvation for us is not a question of escaping this skin, but of having skin glorified. That is why Jesus never preached simple immortality of the soul, but insisted on the resurrection of the body. (34)

The high theology that Ryan refers to should then check our tendency to view the body as an obstacle to spiritual formation. In fact, Scripture offers numerous examples of embodied spirituality. Below is a partial listing:

- Exodus 15:20: Miriam and the other women danced after being delivered from Egypt.
- Exodus 29:7: "Take the anointing oil and anoint him by pouring it on his head."
- Deuteronomy 26:10: "Bring the firstfruits; place the basket before the Lord your God and bow down before him."
- Judges 5:3: "Hear this, you kings! Listen, you rulers! I will sing to the Lord, I will sing; I will make music to the Lord, the God of Israel."
- 2 Samuel 6:14: David danced before the Lord with all his might.
- 1 Chronicles 16:9: "Sing to him, sing praise to him; tell of all his wonderful acts."

- Psalm 30:11: "You turned my wailing into dancing; you removed my sackcloth and clothed me with joy."

- Psalm 47:1: "Clap your hands, all you peoples; shout to God with loud songs of joy."

- Psalm 95:6: "Come, let us bow down in worship, let us kneel before the Lord our Maker."

- Psalm 149:3: "Let them praise his name with dancing and make music to him with tambourine and harp."

- Psalm 150:4: "Praise him with tambourine and dancing, praise him with the strings and flute."

- Luke 7:38: The woman washed Jesus's feet with her tears and anointed them with ointment.

- John 13:5. 14: Jesus washed the disciples' feet; the disciples washed one another's feet.

- Acts 2:2–4: The Holy Spirit enabled those in the upper room to speak in other languages.

- Acts 2: 38: "Repent and be baptized . . . ."

- Romans 16:16" "Greet one another with a holy kiss."

- 1 Corinthians 6:15, 20: "Do you not know that your body is the temple of the Holy Spirit . . . ? Therefore glorify God in your body."

- 1 Timothy 2:8: "I desire then that in every place the men should pray, lifting up holy hands."

Though some in Christian history have downplayed, ignored, or even condemned employing the body to promote spiritual formation, others have recognized that the body can nurture spirituality. God's people have been known to bow, sing, anoint with oil, greet with a kiss of peace, go on nature retreats, teach children to kneel for bedtime prayers, make the sign of the cross, shake hands, act out passion plays, prostrate themselves, applaud, participate in ropes courses, dance, lay hands on a person, stand, speak in tongues, kneel, close eyes, walk labyrinths, twirl, dress modestly, put motions to lyrics, shout, raise hands, wash feet, bow heads, cry, fold hands, play instruments, fast, feast, slay in the Spirit, baptize, read responsively, dedicate babies, lament, welcome new believers, and take communion, to list many common physical practices with spiritual intentions. Clearly, Christians through the ages have integrated the spiritual and the physical in a variety of ways.

THE BODY/SPIRIT/MIND CONNECTION AND THE SCIENCES

Both the social sciences and the hard sciences have contributed to our understanding of mind/body/spirit connections.

Insights from Educational Psychology and Kinesthesia

Much information exists regarding using bodily movement as a *learning* tool. In the field of educational psychology, persons who learn best when they participate in bodily movement are known as kinesthetic learners; they learn by doing. Kinesthetic learning is in fact very effective for most people; kinesthetic activities are known to increase reading, science, writing, and spelling aptitudes in students, especially among those with learning disabilities (e.g., Weggelaar, 2006; Plourde and Klemm, 2004; Grant, 1985). In general, humans tend to remember things longer when movement is involved.

According to Madigan (2008), "Movement builds the framework for learning. A student's physical movement, emotional, social, and cognitive systems are interactive and interdependent" (2). Though we are not primarily focused on *cognitive* learning in this chapter, we must acknowledge that *separating* cognitive and spiritual isn't necessary either—they too are connected. To paraphrase Madigan (2008): A person's physical movement, emotional, social, cognitive—*and spiritual*—systems are *interactive* and *interdependent*. We will see more of this interconnectedness as we explore findings from current brain research.

Brain Research and Spirituality

In the last fifteen years, the field of neuroscience has been rapidly expanding in its research focus exploring religious and spiritual phenomena. The leading scientist in this field of study is Andrew Newberg (2005, 2008). His work intersects with both neuropsychology and neurotheology.

Newberg is best known for the brain imaging tests he performed on Tibetan Buddhist monks, Franciscan nuns, and Pentecostals by injecting radioactive material in their brains. Newberg and his team took a neural snapshot of the participants at a base level, where they were not involved in any type of religious activity, and then during the peak of their religious activity—the Buddhist monks when they reached their peak of meditation (indicated by the participant), the Franciscan nuns during a centering prayer, which is a type of meditation, and finally, the Pentecostals while they were speaking in tongues.

Newberg (2008) described his findings as follows: at the peak of their meditative practice the frontal lobes (the attention part of the brain) of the Buddhist monks and the Franciscan nuns increased in activity; that is, the results demonstrated that the monks and nuns were focusing attention keenly on their respective types of meditation. At that same peak moment, both groups experienced a decrease of activity in their parietal lobe, which is the orienting part of the brain. The decrease in activity "is part of what is associated with somebody losing that sense of self" (Newberg, 2008). The result is a feeling of oneness with something larger than oneself, a "totally unitary reality" (Newberg, 2005, 6490), a feeling that participants in this study (and other studies) describe as spiritually transcendent.

Although Newberg is not asking precisely the same questions we are asking in this chapter in regards to body and spirit, his research can inform our work. In broad terms, Newberg's work demonstrates that there appears to be specific brain activity associated with religious experience. That is, the SPECT scan brain imagery actually depicted the spiritual change the nuns and monks perceived and reported that had been prompted by meditation and prayer.

In the years since his initial experiments with the nuns and monks (first published in 1993), Newberg (2008) has summarized his understanding of the brain and religious/spiritual interconnectedness with a pithy statement: "what fires together, wires together" (9)—that is, "the more [one uses] a particular pathway of neurons, the more strongly they become connected to each other" (9). Newberg says that regularly worshiping at a church or synagogue, hearing the same stories, saying certain prayers, and experiencing the same rituals stimulate and strengthen neural pathways. As these physical religious experiences create connections to the transcendent, that is, the spiritual, these neural pathways are fortified. Newberg's neurotheological work shows that body, brain, and spirit are undeniably integrally interconnected.

CONNECTING CHILDREN'S SPIRITUALITY WITH THE BODY

The last portion of this chapter will describe ways to employ the body to enhance spiritual formation. What can be done in the body that can especially nurture children (and others) spiritually?

Prayer and the Body

A few years ago, when Holly was addressing a large audience, a sign language expert had been asked to sign for several hearing-impaired attendees. Holly opened the session with a prayer for all who were there, casting her eyes over the assembly as she prayed. Holly was entranced by the sign language linguist as she captured the words of the prayer in visual representation. Later Holly asked her if she would teach all the attendees the signs for a few words. The prayer the group would be praying together was: "Lord, you are holy; God, we give you glory." The sign linguist taught the hand signs for Lord, holy, God and glory. The signs for holy and glory are beautiful and expressive. The signs for Lord and God embody honor and respect and exalt God as

Sovereign Lord. As the group prayed and signed, "Lord, you are holy; God we give you glory," Holly watched a thousand women bestow honor on their Lord with their hearts, souls, and *bodies*. It was a powerful moment.

Others have been aware of this body-spirit prayer connection. Doug Pagitt and Kathryn Prill (2005) in their book *Body Prayer: The Posture of Intimacy with God* have written thirty prayers, describing accompanying physical positions for each prayer. Each of these prayer postures reflects and helps create prayerful attitudes. For example, below is their prayer of hopefulness.

> God of God, Light of Light,
> Holy is our Lord of Life.
> Bless me with hope as one of your own. (Pagitt and Prill, 2005, 32)

The body posture description reads simply: "Stand or sit. Look up to the ceiling or sky. Let the rest of your body relax" (32).

The described postures are not merely physical postures; they are physical reflections of spiritual postures. These same postures can be seen in the emotions of an individual's heart. The spiritual and physical are connected, thus influencing each other in these prayer posture movements.

> From the beginning Christians have recognized that prayer is not simply a matter of words; it is an integration of all of life, through the body. The use of the body in prayer is not just a long-held practice; it is a way of deepening our life of prayer. Just as nonverbal communication relies on gestures, tone of voice, and speed of speaking to reinforce our words, physical acts extend the meaning of our worded prayers. Physical movement and meaning postures indicate more fully what is on the heart of the person who is offering prayers to God. (Pagitt and Prill, 2005, 5–6)

Thus far, we have discussed adding specific bodily movements to prayer. In contrast, another way to consider the body/spirit connection is to *add prayer* to common physical activities such as chores, getting dressed for the day, or preparing for bedtime. Some of the prayers that have been preserved from the days of Celtic Christianity reflect this body/spirit relationship; for example, the following prayer was recited while milking the cow:

> Bless O God, my little cow,
> Bless, O God, my desire;
> Bless thou my partnership
> And the milking of my hands, O God. (Balzer, 2007, 77)

For children today, making their bed offers an opportunity for a specific prayer, and so does unloading the dishwasher, taking out the trash, sweeping, putting on clothes, putting away pajamas, books, and toys, or brushing teeth and taking a bath.

Helping children create short prayers that accompany such ordinary activities can transport these ordinary corporeal activities into the spiritual realm.

Kneeling and Bowing

Most of the world's religious traditions have valued bowing as an effective spiritual practice (Heng Sure, 2010, 60). According to Heng Sure, bowing demonstrates humility and vulnerability, working against pride and arrogance. In Western Christianity today bowing typically consists merely of a slight tilt of the head toward the chest, whereas bowing in some of the world's religions and in historical Christianity has often called for fuller bodily engagement, for example, bending from the waist with the upper body perpendicular to the floor. The proper form for *reverential* bowing (common in Buddhism) requires knees, elbows, and head to touch the ground. Full prostration would be the fullest form of bowing.

Kneeling in prayer can be considered a form of bowing as well. Kneeling is common in most historically liturgical churches, but is strikingly absent from evangelical churches that do not follow scripted liturgical guidelines. Similar to the prayer postures introduced earlier (Pagitt and Prill, 2005), kneeling can be a means of becoming more open to spiritual interaction.

Employing kneeling and other forms of bowing can help children—and adults—acknowledge God as Holy, Sovereign, Most High, Name above all Names, and Lord (Yahweh). The practices of bowing and kneeling nurture humility and function as antidotes to pride (Heng Sure, 2010), thus fostering more effective communication with God. Barbara Myers (1997) in her book *Young Children and Spirituality* says that repeated physical rituals such as kneeling and bowing help "organize" spiritual experience; they promote "leaning beyond the immediate experience" (78). Roehlkepartain and Patel (2005) believe that these physical rituals allow people to connect with the transcendent. Repeated physical patterns that attach to spiritual realities (rituals) preserve pathways similar to Newberg's (2008) insight that "what fires together, wires together" (9).

Dance

Dance is a biblical form of worship. In Psalm 13:3 God commands dancing to glorify him, "Let them praise his name with dancing," and again in Psalm 150:4, "praise him with tambourine and dancing." Not only did King David recommend dancing as a way to worship God, he also practiced what he preached. "As the ark of the covenant of the Lord was entering the City of David, Michal daughter of Saul . . . saw King David dancing . . ." (1 Chr 15:29).

Worshipers in America don't tend to dance (though in charismatic churches it is typically more acceptable). Webber (1994) says that the "church's uneasiness about including dance in worship stems, in part, from the dualism that equates the body with evil and the spirit with good" (728), as has been noted earlier in this chapter. Webber (1994) says that worship that is both physical and spiritual can transcend this dualism and believes that movement and dance are fundamental elements of worship; "they can be used to express the many moods of worship: joy, sorrow, reverence, submission" (719).

Children, music, and dance fit perfectly together, or as Ng and Thomas (1981) say in *Children in the Worshiping Community*, "music and children are a natural combination" (103). Webber (1994) says that to "witness the natural human response of dancing, we need only look at our children. Even before a child has mastered speech, he or she will likely whirl and jump in dancing movements" (729).

Muller (2010) says that "children express their spirituality primarily through behaviors. They use art, dance, song, and movement to express joy, despair, awe, and wonder; to deal with suffering; and to question meaning in their experiences" (199–200). Thus, teachers in Christian settings may wish to create opportunities for children, especially young children, to dance in response to God's work in the world.

Jeanne Broadbent (2004) in her article "Enhancing Children's Spirituality through Creative Dance," describes one such opportunity. Broadbent created a small-scale research project that involved seven- and eight-year-old children in two classes in a Roman Catholic school. Over six dance sessions/workshops the children (with Broadbent's help) created a dance around themes related to the Creation story (the earth awakening from darkness, darkness/sadness turning to joy/light, the earth turning, the ocean/sea/water as waves, etc.). The children's dance moves included "high, medium, and low movements, floor work, a range of jumping techniques, stillness, repetition and varying dynamics" (100). Along the way, children kept journals, wrote poems, and were interviewed by Broadbent in order to track their experiences and glean their spiritual musings. One child wrote: "I felt like I was going to be a new person. Like I was going to be reborn" (102). Broadbent commented that the journals, interviews, and poetry were very revealing and provided "real insight into the children's growing spiritual awareness as it related to the theme of Creation" (102).

Broadbent's premise is that learning through creative dance can enable children to experience feelings of transcendence. Perhaps more than any other suggestion in this chapter, the movement of dance connects in unique ways with children and can be a conduit between the child and God.

Stillness

Another spiritual and physical behavior that we can employ with children to nurture their spiritual development is stillness. General pedagogy has encouraged teachers to use physical *movement*, *activity*, and *busy-ness* to engage children, and indeed physical movement typically does engage children. However, creating opportunities for stillness, places for meditation and venues for listening to God can offer an alternative and unusual (for children) approach to integrating body and spirit. Those who write about spiritual disciplines for adults describe multiple ways to be still before God (e.g., journaling, *lectio divina*, silent retreats, and meditation). However, we rarely employ these "adult" spiritual strategies with children, perhaps because we doubt the ability of children to be still or to hear from God.

But children need space, just as adults do, to discern the work of God in them. Myers (1997) encourages parents and teachers to create "sacred space—a space laden with expectation, transcendence, and mystery" (78).

Children may need help to quiet not only their bodies but also their hearts. In general, most church programs for children have not allowed much space for stillness and contemplation. Typically, few opportunities are provided for children to wonder about themselves or about God. Godly Play is a contemplative-reflective approach to teaching that can help children learn to quiet themselves (Berryman, 1991, 1995). Bible stories are told with softened voice and special textured support materials, and following each story several wondering questions are asked. Most of these questions are designed not to elicit discussion, but rather to provide opportunity for children to wonder internally, for example, "I wonder why the disciples are following Jesus?" or "I wonder how welcoming a child is like welcoming Jesus?"

Godly Play taps into this unique body/spirit process of stillness. In the quietness following the wondering questions, children often sit in silence, considering, listening. Whether we use Godly Play or not, leaving open space—creating sacred space—in our time with children allows them to think, listen, perceive—and to ask, "Who are you, Lord?"

Labyrinths

One interesting way to combine movement with quietness is walking a labyrinth. European Christians in the middle ages would sometimes make the pilgrimage to Jerusalem. This was an exhausting, dangerous, and expensive trip, and some would save and prepare for such a trip for years. The process was viewed as a three-part journey: 1) releasing of responsibilities in one's life such as family and job as one walked to Jerusalem, 2) entering the place of Jesus's earthly existence, walking where he walked, dwelling in a sense in his presence, and then 3) returning: making the long laborious return trip where one would once again take up one's former responsibilities in life.

Because the trip was so costly and long, few could make the pilgrimage. Eventually indoor labyrinths were created so that more "pilgrims" could participate in a representation of the journey. The most famous labyrinth is at Chartres Cathedral in France. A person could "simulate" the trip to the Holy Land by walking the labyrinth: 1) releasing responsibilities as one walked toward the center, 2) "entering" into a sacred space (dwelling in the center of the labyrinth that represented Christ), and then 3) returning to one's responsibilities, walking out of the labyrinth.

Making a labyrinth today can represent just such a journey. Holly has done this several times, most often in a large cleared room utilizing masking tape on the floor, other times using desks, chairs, or other furniture to make the labyrinth. A room full of folding chairs in rows adapts quite easily. Most labyrinths are designed as unguided personal experiences, as aids for an individual.

- to release burdens and leave anxiety behind as they enter
- to walk circuitously to the center where the person rests, waits, and dwells while quietly receiving from Christ
- to then slowly move though the labyrinth toward the exit, returning to their life refreshed and renewed

Children especially enjoy walking labyrinths since it offers a unique and fascinating venue to combine the spiritual with bodily movement. Guided group experiences also work well for children: leading the children into the labyrinth in groups of five or six, sitting at the center with a few whispered encouragements, and walking out together as the guide quietly narrates the process.

CONCLUSION

Christianity in general espouses healthier views of the body than in centuries past. However, our practice has not changed noticeably. In some ways the body is still viewed as suspect. Those who write in the field of spiritual formation are convinced that

> the relationship between the physical body and spiritual transformation is inseparable. Far from being a hindrance to spiritual transformation, the physical body is the instrument and means for exercising spiritual disciplines. These disciplines, done in the physical body, posture an individual to receive and release the indwelling presence of Christ. (Cox, 2002, 281)

Cox further says that all human interactions with God and the natural world in which we live are by default experienced by the *whole person.* Taking Cox's statement even further, Eugene Peterson (2011), speaking at a recent conference, said, "The body is not a barrier to spirituality; indeed it is the only access we have."

Though Cox and Peterson may have been thinking of adults in their comments, their statements are no less true of children. Perhaps they are *more* true for children, since children seem to comprehend that the physical and the spiritual are integrally connected. Generally they are more in tune with their bodies than adults and are typically less inhibited (Moore, 1975). For children, acknowledging the environment through the body is natural. Rather than hindering children in their bodily expression of love for God, perhaps those of us who work with children should be more intentional in nurturing the body/spirit connection by incorporating physical practices with spiritual intentions such as bowing and kneeling, creating labyrinths, allowing opportunities for dance, and providing sacred space and times of quiet and stillness.

Children begin life with a sense of the inexpressible mystery of God. As adults, we are called by God to nurture that sense of the holy in children. It is a remarkably audacious task—to help children seek the ineffable. Creating opportunities for integrating the physical and the spiritual is a surprisingly powerful way to nurture children on their spiritual journeys.

REFERENCES

Augustine. *Soliloquies.*

Balzer, Tracy. *Thin Places: An Evangelical Journey into Celtic Christianity.* Abilene, TX: Leafwood, 2007.

Berryman, Jerome W. *Godly Play: A Way of Religious Education.* San Francisco: HarperCollins, 1991.

Berryman, Jerome W. *Teaching Godly Play: The Sunday Morning Handbook.* Nashville: Abingdon Press, 1995.

Broadbent, Jeanne. (2004). "Embodying the Abstract: Enhancing Children's Spirituality through Creative Dance." *International Journal of Children's Spirituality* 9 no. 1 (2004): 97–104.

Cox, Darrel. "The Physical Body in Spiritual Formation: What God Has Joined Together Let No One Put Asunder." *Journal of Psychology and Christianity* 21, no. 3 (2002): 281–291.

d'Aquili, Eugene G., and Andrew B. Newberg. "Religious and Mystical States: A Neuropsychological Model." *Zygon* 28 (1993): 177–200.

Grant, Marie. "The Kinesthetic Approach to Teaching: Building a Foundation for Learning." *Journal of Learning Disabilities* 18, no. 8 (1985): 455–462.

Heng Sure, Bhikshu. "Reverential Bowing as Contemplative Practice." *Religion East & West* 5 (October, 2005): 73–84.

Madigan, Jean Blaydes. "Action Based Learning: Building Better Brains through Movement," The Primary Conference (2008). Retrieved from The Primary Conference 2008 website: www.muconf.missouri.edu/primary/handouts/preconbbuildingbetterbrains.pdf

Moore, Thomas W. "Transpersonal Education: A Preview." *Journal of Education* 157, no. 4 (1975): 24–39.

Muller, Carolyn R. "Spirituality in Children: Understanding and Developing Interventions." *Pediatric Nursing* 36, no. 4 (2010): 197–208.

Myers, Barabara Kimes. *Young Children and Spirituality.* New York: Routledge, 1997.

Newberg, Andrew. "How our Brains are Wired for Belief." Faith Angle Conference. [Conference Presentation and Forum, May 5, 2008). Retrieved from Pewforum.org.

Newberg, Andrew. "Neuroscience and Religion: Neuroepistemology." In *Encyclopedia of Religion* (2nd edition; Vol. 10) edited by Lindsay Jones, pp. 6488–6492. Farmington Hill, MI: Thompson Gale, 2005.

Ng, David, and Virginia Thomas. *Children in The Worshiping Community.* Atlanta, GA: John Knox Press, 1981.

Pagitt, Doug, and Kathryn Prill. *Body Prayer: The Posture of Intimacy with God.* Colorado Springs, CO: Random House, 2005.

Peterson, Eugene H. "St. Mark: The Basic Text for Christian Spirituality." Keynote Address at the North American Professors of Christian Education Conference, Seattle, WA, October 20, 2011.

Plato, *Phaedo* 66b-67a.

Plourde, Lee A., and E. Barbara Klemm. "Sounds and Sense-Abilities: Science for all." *College Student Journal* 38, no. 4 (2004): 653–660.

Radford, Mike. "Spirituality and Education: Inner and Outer Realities." *International Journal of Children's Spirituality* 11, no. 3 (2006): 385–96.

Roehlkepartain, Eugene, and Eboo Patel. "Congregations: Unexamined Crucibles for Spiritual Development. In *The Handbook of Spiritual Development in Childhood and Adolescence* edited by Eugene Roehlkepartain, E. King, L. Wagener, & Peter L. Benson, pp. 324–336. Thousand Oaks, CA: Sage, 2005.

Ryan, Thomas. "Toward a Positive Spirituality of the Body." In *Reclaiming the Body in Christian Spirituality,* edited by Thomas Ryan, pp. 21–56. Mahwah, NJ: Paulist Press, 2004.

Webber, Robert E. *Music and the Arts in Christian Worship* (Book 2). In *The Complete Library of Christian Worship: Vol. 4B* edited by Robert E. Webber. Nashville: Star Song Publishing Group, 1994.

Weggelaar, Cornelis. "Kinesthetic Feedback and Dyslexic Students Learning to Read and Write." *ETC: A Review of General Semantics* 63, no. 2 (2006): 144–151.

Wiseman, James. "The Body in Spiritual Practice: Some Historical Points of Reference." In *Reclaiming the Body in Christian Spirituality,* edited by Thomas Ryan, pp. 1–20. Mahwah, NJ: Paulist Press, 2004.

Chapter 17

Through the Lens

Film, Ethnography, and the Spiritual Development of Children

Mark Borchert

In her documentary film *Praying for Lior* (2008), director Ilana Trachtman introduces audiences to Lior Liebling, a Jewish boy with Down syndrome, as he prepares for his Bar Mitzvah. Lior struggles with his disability, the loss of his mother, a Rabbi, to breast cancer, and relationships with classmates at his orthodox Jewish school, but he finds meaning and joy in the expression of his faith. This is evident when Lior "davens" or sings and chants daily prayers. Despite his loud and flat voice, his frequent prayers are delivered with such joyful devotion that they become a centerpiece of the film. His religious community, both at school and in the synagogue, embraces Lior's prayers as authentic spirituality. Trachtman's film ultimately presents the Bar Mitzvah as an exuberant and moving occasion for this young man, his family, and his entire faith community.

This film allows audience members to experience a faith community as they encounter the daily life of Lior and his family and friends. The audience comes to know the spiritual practices of the synagogue and religious school, primarily from the vantage point of Lior and classmates. When Lior davens and we see his classmates' respect for and participation in the ritual, we understand the centrality of this type of prayer in this faith tradition. The film shows the values of this faith community, and we learn its distinctiveness and priorities from the perspective of some of its youngest members. One of Lior's friends tells an interviewer, "God makes every person with a different test in this world. When God makes Lior with Down syndrome, I don't know but maybe he thinks Lior can stand this kind of test." He goes on to explain, "It also becomes a test to us. How we treat Lior, if we do things with Lior, that is part of our test." Through the film, audience members come to understand the values of a faith community by hearing about them directly from children.

A well-crafted documentary film often opens up a new world, revealing its values to audiences. As the filmmaker captures the comments and expressions of real people, especially children, and brings the images of daily life to the screen, the viewer is allowed unique access into the experiences, values, and challenges of others. When this new world involves a faith community, the story that is presented in the film makes apparent the deep values and distinctive understandings of a particular religious group. The audience learns what spirituality means for the community in the film.

The portrait presented in a documentary can echo the insights revealed in ethnographic research. Like the cultural anthropologist, the documentary filmmaker is engaged in participant observation and in-depth interviews. Like the ethnographer, the director closely analyzes and organizes material to present meaningful cultural patterns and practices. Both the documentarian and the ethnographer ultimately work to tell the authentic stories of others, particularly the stories of differing groups of people. Noted anthropologist Clifford Geertz (1973) has described this type of work as providing "the answers that others, guarding other sheep in other valleys, have given" (30).

This chapter examines documentary filmmaking as an approach for uncovering the spiritual values of a community as revealed by the children in that group. It explores the ethnographic use of the documentary interview in filmmaking. Film interviews can reveal in a dramatic way the understandings, spiritual practices, and cultural values of children within a specific faith community. Through filming children's responses to questions about their spiritual understanding and lives, and editing the responses into a film that tells the story of a faith community, the meaning of children's spirituality in a particular context begins to unfold. This chapter considers the potential of filmmaking as an analytical approach to the study of children in faith communities. It also examines some of the challenges of this approach and provides some guidelines for practitioners interested in employing this methodology. Documentary filmmaking is a tool for presenting rich images and descriptions of life. Through sights and sounds, the filmmaker interprets the stories of others. It can be a key to explaining the spirituality of a group in a new way.

CHILDREN'S SPIRITUALITY AND ETHNOGRAPHIC RESEARCH

An understanding of our spiritual journey is closely related to the stories that we tell, particularly the stories about our families, our communities, and ourselves. These stories disclose our hopes and fears, values and priorities, and even our images of the God. Stories can create expectations, empower action, and give meaning to past events. Stories are shared experiences that foster community and build relationships. One learns much about a group of people by listening to their stories.

Scholarship in the area of communication increasingly focuses on the concept of story. James Carey (1989), in his seminal work in communication studies, considers two types of communication scholarship. He suggests that in the past, American communication research and discourse have emphasized notions of communication associated with sending or conveying information, often with an eye on the effects of this information on recipients. Carey labels this approach as a transmission view of communication. Like postal deliveries, messages primarily are seen as being sent for informational purposes, transmitted from one point to another, often with the intention of influencing the receiver.

As an alternative to this approach, Carey describes a ritual view of the communication. From this perspective, communication is about sharing an understanding or building a common framework. From a point of view emphasizing the communal nature of communication, much of this sharing is not about transmitting new information; rather it is about building, maintaining, or transforming a common understanding or shared identity (Carey, 1989, 56). Communication often is related to continuing rituals that embody the core values of a group. As people tell stories, write books, produce art, and engage in ceremonies, they are communicating a shared set of values. Even children's games often represent the inherent cultural values of their social group. The bedtime stories, the daily rituals, the art projects, and the conversations on the playground and the school bus are all communication routines that can reveal the identity and values of a group.

In this context, spirituality can be seen as the shared understanding of a community of faith. The rituals and stories of a religious community are often reflected in the words and activities of its children. While the spirituality of children has connections to the way young people interpret religious texts, the dynamics of their families, their own developmental stages, and many other factors, it also expresses the distinctive values of their faith communities. Children interpret and embody those values, often as they participate in the rituals and stories of the group. This shared understanding, as it is revealed in the communication of children, is the focus of the ethnographic studies of spirituality.

In the book, *When I Was a Child*, Susan Ridgely Bales (2005) offers an ethnographic study of Catholic children's understanding of their first communion. Through in-depth interviews with children and participation observation, she gained insights into how children themselves understand their first communion. Her book is filled with stories and pictures created by children explaining their understandings of this sacrament. Her study provides an interpretation of the meaning of this spiritual ritual and its connection with the children's wider understanding of life. Bales describes how her status as an outsider helped her to have a unique role in the children's eyes. For them, as a researcher she was a representative of the adult world but different than their parents or others adults because she did not have children herself and was a Protestant that had not experienced the ritual in which they were about to partake. They explained their perspective to her, and in the book Bales presents new insights into the rich sensory experience that children anticipate as they approach this sacrament. Her ethnography unlocks the meaning of the experience for the children involved.

In recording and analyzing the children's understanding of the ritual, Bales employs an interpretive approach as described by ethnographer Clifford Geertz, a pivotal figure in anthropology. Geertz (1973) argues that in approaching culture "the road to the general lies through a concern with the particular" (53). Specific descriptions of culture, like those provided in Bales's study, give rise to more general conceptions. When Geertz discusses "the general," it is never in the sense of an abstract set of rules generalizable across all cultures. The "general" must be found through the particular case. He writes that the interpretive approach provides an understanding of relationships "in which biological, psychological, sociological, and cultural factors can be treated as variables within unitary systems of analysis" (Geertz, 1973, 44). Description and analysis are interconnected within the particularities of a specific context. Ethnography reveals the specifics and connections within a unified cultural setting. Geertz suggests that with an understanding of specifics, the student of culture can begin analyzing and building theory, grounded in the realities of lived experience.

Through ethnography, Geertz (1973) advances a semiotic analysis of culture, an understanding that focuses on "systems of constructible signs." He describes culture as "webs of significance" and its analysis as "not an experimental science in search of laws but an interpretive one in search of meaning" (5). In what Shankman (1984) describes as the core of Geertz's intellectual program, the anthropologist aims at replacing what he views as a reductionistic, mechanical social science with an alternative approach, one that focuses on the socially-constructed realm of the sign (263).

Geertz (1973) argues, "Between the basic ground plans for our life that our genes lay down . . . and the precise behavior we in fact execute . . . lies a complex set of significant symbols under whose direction we transform the first into the second, the ground plans into the activity" (50). According to this interpretive approach, the transition from a multitude of possible lives to a person's actual life is based upon a symbolic system governing social behavior. This argument suggests a central role for what anthropologists describe as "emic" understandings in the unfolding of personal and social histories. Emic perspectives are, as Harris (1979) notes, the categories, rules, or symbolic understandings that one must know in order to think and act as a native. The great appeal of an interpretive approach resides in the central place that it offers to questions of meaning, to the realm of the symbolic. For Geertz, the study of symbolic interaction is crucial in an understanding of culture. His work continually emphasizes the exploration of the shared mental world of his ethnographic subjects, the "story they tell themselves about themselves" as he writes of the Balinese, a group on which he focuses much of his ethnographic research (Geertz, 1973, 30).

Like Geertz, any contemporary ethnographer, especially one seeking to understand children's notions of spirituality, is concerned with systems of signs, the emic understandings that give meaning to lived experience. It is through understanding this web of significance, as it is revealed in people's words and actions, that we can know what spirituality means for an individual in a particular group. This type of understanding is not only the quest of the cultural anthropologist; it is also the realm of the documentary filmmaker.

ETHNOGRAPHY AND DOCUMENTARY FILMMAKING

Ethnographic studies and documentary filmmaking have long been connected. As Marks (1995) indicates, anthropologists were developing the field of ethnography at the same time filmmakers were fashioning early documentaries. In 1922, for example, Bronislaw Malinowski published *Argonauts of the Western Pacific*, about Trobriand people of Papua, New Guinea. This was a key work in establishing fieldwork as a centerpiece of anthropological research. Participant observations and in-depth interviews played a key role in documenting culture for Malinowski (Malinowski, 1961). His study of tribal people established many of the practices that continue to be used in anthropology for discovering and interpreting the symbols, stories, and perspectives of native people.

In the same year that Malinowski published his seminal work, Robert Flaherty produced *Nanook of the North* (1922), one of the earliest documentary films. In a way that had never been done before, the director carted the bulky silent film cameras of his time far into the Canadian arctic to tell the story of an Inuit family and their traditional life and cultural practices. The film shows Nanook and his family hunting, kayaking, building an igloo, visiting a trading post, and engaging in other aspects of daily life. It purported to reveal the true story of native people. Both Malinowski's and Flaherty's works were foundational in developing a methodology for recounting the emic understandings of a cultural group. Fieldwork and filmmaking appeared to give direct access to native lives and stories.

In later years, the works of both Malinowski and Flaherty came to symbolize the troubling challenges of authorship in this type of storytelling. On careful analysis, ethnographic film and writing could not be considered "merely" the documenting of culture. As Murphy notes, Flaherty created many scenes in *Nanook of the North*, emphasizing only the traditional aspects of Inuit culture, like walrus hunting, while ignoring many of the more modern features, like the use of rifles in the hunts. Often this was done in collaboration with his subjects who not only staged scenes for the benefit of the audience but also maintained and helped to operate some of Flaherty's camera equipment (Murphy, 2008, 271). In a similar way, the posthumous publication of Malinowski's diaries revealed the problem of authorship and authenticity. Diary entries revealed the ethnographer's surprising contempt for native people, a feeling that might have shaped his field research and writing (Murphy, 2008, 270–271).

Contemporary documentary filmmaking still holds many similarities to ethnographic research. Schensul and LeCompte (2012) write, "Essential ethnographic skills are relating, listening, explaining, observing, questioning, communicating, recording, discussing, and revising" (2). As documentary filmmaker James Marsh suggests, these same skills are needed to shape a documentary film, "I don't just randomly sit down and ask questions," says the director of the academy award-winning film *Man on Wire* in an interview for the book *Documentary Storytelling* (Bernard, 2011, 315). He describes the comprehensive research, detailed planning, careful listening, and interactions that are essential to the interview process. "The rhythm of the film gets established at the very point of the interview," says Marsh (Bernard, 2011, 315). Then just as a cultural anthropologist carefully analyzes and revises the ethnographic document, the filmmaker skillfully edits interviews to present a compelling and authentic documentary story. In the same way ethnography reveals the cultural beliefs and practices of others, a well-done documentary film brings the experiences and values of others to life on the screen.

The documentary, *Born into Brothels* (2004), presents the life of children in the squalid red-light district of Calcutta. The film tells the story of a New York photographer who develops a relationship with the young sons and daughters of the prostitutes in one of the poorest parts of India. She gives the children cameras and teaches them how to take pictures, and then their photographs of street life are used to raise funds for their education. In the story, the audience is confronted with the stark realities of urban childhood in the third world, the determination and at times futility of the kids' efforts, and the values and culture in which they live. The words and images of the children help the audience to know and experience their world, at least in some small way. Just as an ethnography might do, the film points to the understanding, identity, challenges, and values of a particular group.

DOCUMENTARY INTERVIEWS WITH CHILDREN IN FAITH COMMUNITIES

Since they reveal cultural values and practices, documentary films have the potential of expanding our understanding of children's spirituality. They can provide a window into the patterns and beliefs of a community of faith and the perspectives and concerns of its young members. In the controversial documentary *Jesus Camp*, filmmakers present the story of a Pentecostal children's ministry and summer camp program. In the words and images of children, the film presents a community's understanding of religion and its conservative political agenda and activism. While the filmmakers are clearly presenting their critique of this belief system, the perspectives of children are articulate throughout the film. Their words disclose their hopes, fears, and motivations, allowing the audience to understand what their faith means to them. Although the film is crafted to tell a particularly critical story, *Jesus Camp* (2006) gives audiences insights into one group of children's religious values and actions

The professional documentarian is not the only one that has access to filmmaking tools for exploring children's spiritual values. Religious practitioners, Christian ministers, and scholars of children spirituality now have the ability to use video to discover, interpret, and present children's understanding of religious experience, perhaps with even greater insights and authenticity than some professional filmmakers. High-definition video cameras are now readily available, even on some cell phones. Editing software is accessible on multiple platforms. Some training is required to understand the basics of digital editing, but these skills are relatively easy to acquire. Using these tools and with access to children within a faith community, it is possible for ministers and scholars, with very little technical experience, to tell the faith stories of these children in effective and compelling ways. These stories are likely to reveal new insights or at least open discussions about children's spirituality.

Just as it is critical for the ethnographer to find helpful research informants, it is important to locate articulate and open interviewees in order to create a film exploring the spirituality of children within a faith community. As representatives of that community, the children should be open to sharing issues of faith. They and their parents or guardians should agree to interviews, understanding that some of the responses will be used in a film. Parents should sign a release agreement that indicates how the children's words and images will be used and distributed. With the widespread popularity of YouTube, Vimeo, and other video-sharing websites, it is important to clarify if the film will be distributed via the Internet. Some parents may not want their children's images accessible in that form. Perhaps the video is intended for use within an educational setting in a church group or an academic conference. In other cases, the film may be created for film festivals or other venues. Whatever the method of distribution, it should be specifically agreed upon in writing prior to the interview process.

Interviews are likely to be the building blocks of a film that addresses issues of spirituality, and the explanations of the children often reveal much about the implicit values and understanding of a faith community. Asking the right questions is a key to effective interviewing. The interviewer should carefully prepare questions that can open up lines of discussion, but she or he must be ready to deviate from this inquiry when new insights or other areas of discussion emerge. Surprising responses should give rise to new questions and further investigation.

In the 1950s and 1960s, a television program, *Art Linkletter's House Party,* featured a segment entitled "Kids Say the Darndest Things." In this segment, the host asked young children questions, sometimes related to religious subjects, and the children's responses were used for humorous effect (*The Best of Art Linkletter,* 2005). But an unusual response by a child should be more than a cause for a chuckle. In fact, ridiculing or laughing at children's religious understanding might be embarrassing for children or even destructive to their spiritual life and development. Unusual responses, in fact, can provide new insights into how children within a faith community understand their religion and interpret their world. Rather than a momentary laugh, they can lead to new questions about how children interpret spirituality. An interviewer always should seek to place a child's answers within a context to understand their significance and meaning.

The interviewer's questions also should be open ended, formulated in such a way as to promote explanations. Rather than asking if a child liked a religious ceremony, a better question explores the sights and sounds that he or she remembers from the experience. Excellent interviewers are able to elicit stories and cause people to reflect on their experiences. They listen closely, formulating appropriate follow-up questions and providing positive non-verbal feedback. (Verbal feedback can create a distracting off-camera voice.) The interviewer may learn much by just asking the child to "say more" about a topic. In the editing process, it is best if the answers make sense without hearing the interviewer's questions. By being silent and allowing a person to talk, a segment of the response might stand on its own. An interviewer also might ask a question in a particular way. For example, an interviewer might say, "Can you *repeat* and finish this sentence? 'If someone asked me to describe God, I would say . . .'" which allows the audience to understand the response without hearing the question.

Establishing a rapport with the child is one of the most important aspects of the interview process. Interviews should begin with questions designed to set a child at ease, even if they have nothing to do with the topic of spirituality. The interviewer can move to more sensitive, challenging, or more personal topics after a level of comfort has been established. The goal is for the interviewee to relax, forget about the camera, and freely share thoughts and feelings.

Cinematography is critical in crafting a film that can reveal spiritual values and practices. In most cases, a cameraperson can focus on cinematography, while another person poses the questions. This allows for the best interview process. Following these guidelines can ensure that a cinematographer shoots engaging material for the film:

- Place the camera on a tripod to ensure a steady shot without distracting movement;

- Select a quiet setting and a background that enhances the interview;

- Make certain that there is plenty of light, especially for indoor interviews;

- Use an external microphone rather than one available on the camera;

- Test the sound levels and quality before beginning the interview;

- Frame the interview subject in a head and shoulders shot, avoiding too much or too little headroom;

- Zoom in as the shot is framed; most novice videographers do not position the subject tightly enough within the frame;

- Shoot over the shoulder of the interviewer; he or she does not need to be visible in the shot;

- Have the subjects look directly at the interviewer rather than the camera;

- Avoid a profile shot by making certain both eyes of the interviewee are visible to the camera.

In interviewing children, positioning them on chairs or stools can minimize movement, though the cameraperson always needs to be attentive to maintain a well-framed shot. The focus is on acquiring shots that can be used in the final film.

The interview responses become the raw material for the creation of the story. The filmmaker can develop transcriptions of the interviews and like an ethnographer look closely for themes and patterns that emerge in the comments of children in a particular faith community. These transcriptions can form the basis for a documentary script, which can be shaped on paper before the editing process. By grouping the statements of interviewees thematically in the script, the filmmaker can create a more engaging story as the film moves quickly from one person's response to another person's perspective. In this way, the script draws attention to connections and shared beliefs. This technique also avoids "jump cuts" or springing from one point in an interview to another place in the same interview.

The script then forms the basis for the editing process. Most films use short sound bites and move quickly from one idea to the next. Not only are the words in the responses important, but the visuals are equally if not more essential to a film. Segments that are poorly shot may be more distracting than useful in a film, regardless of the words that are said. The script provides the framework, but in editing together shots, the filmmaker must consider not only the words, but also the pacing and sequence of images. Poor images, jump cuts, or lengthy comments can be covered by cut-aways. These sequences of shots illustrate the ideas that are being described by interviewees. The voices of interviewees are heard, while images depicting their ideas are seen.

Film offers the opportunity not only to tell a story, but to show a story as it unfolds. Visually engaging films are more compelling and tend to hold their audiences' attention in more significant ways. Music and narration can be used to create continuity and tie together different interviews. Music can also underscore the emotional significance of a segment in a film. The process of editing is an art form in which words, images, music, narration, pacing, and a storyline all can come together to create a powerful shared experience.

In the experience of editing documentary interviews, authenticity should be the filmmaker's guide. Too easily the words and images of others can be manipulated in ways that might distort the meanings or misrepresent the original intent. The filmmaker should seek to not only remain faithful in presenting the perspectives of their interview subjects, but also to be truthful in presenting the values and priorities of a faith community. Too often filmmakers tell stories motivated by their own political, economic, or entertainment agendas rather than seeking and presenting the emic understandings of others.

CONCLUSION

Films can present the spiritual practices and beliefs of children in powerful ways. As audience members, we not only hear the words but we can see the faces, gestures, and emotions of children. We can watch them live life within a faith community and experience their triumphs and challenges. Film reveals life in a rich and detailed way, allowing people to speak for themselves.

As this chapter has suggested, practitioners in children's ministry can find in documentary filmmaking the means of exploring the shared values of a faith community. Film allows the opportunity to present those values to the group for self-reflection or to share the spiritual identity of a group with others. A documentary in which children in their own faith setting speak about their spiritual understanding and values offers a vehicle for both spiritual growth and discovery. The technology for this approach to spiritual understanding is available, and this chapter has presented a methodology for crafting such a project.

Filmmaking can be a very effective ministry tool in a variety of settings including Sunday school and Bible studies, with young people discussing baptism or approaching confirmation, and with children seeking to understand prayer or to explain worship. Picking up a camera can begin an ethnographic journey, an experience filled with rich stories and surprising insights.

REFERENCES

Bales, Susan Ridgely. *When I Was a Child: Children's Interpretations of First Communion.* Chapel Hill, NC: University of North Carolina Press, 2005.

Bernard, Sheila Curran. *Documentary Storytelling: Creative Nonfiction on Screen,* Third Edition. New York: NY: Focal Press, 2011.

Born into Brothels. Directed by Ross Kauffman. 2004. Thinkfilm, 2006. DVD.

Carey, James W. *Communication as Culture: Essays on Media and Society.* Boston, MA: Unwin Hyman, 1989.

Geertz, Clifford. *The Interpretation of Culture.* New York, NY: Basic Books, 1973.

Harris, Marvin. *Cultural Materialism.* New York, NY: Random House, 1979.

Jesus Camp. Directed by Heidi Ewing and Rachel Grady. 2006. New York, NY: Magnolia Pictures, 2007. DVD.

Malinowski, Bronislaw. *Argonauts of the Western Pacific: An Account of Native Enterprise and Adventure in the Archipelagoes of Melanisian New Guinea.* New York: NY: Dutton, 1961.

Marks, Dan. "Ethnography and Ethnographic Film: From Flaherty to Asch and After." American Anthropologist 97, no. 2 (1995): 339–347.

Murphy, Patrick D. "Writing Media Culture: Representation and Experience in Media Ethnography." *Communication, Culture & Critique* 1, no. 3 (2008): 268–286.

Nanook of the North. Directed by Robert Flaherty. 1922. Criterion Collection, 1999. DVD.

Praying for Lior. Directed by Ilana Trachtman. 2008. New York, NY: First Run Features, 2009. DVD.

Schensul, Jean J., and Margaret D. LeCompte. *Essential Ethnographic Methods: A Mixed Methods Approach, Second Edition.* New York, NY: Rowman & Littlefield, 2012.

Shankman, Paul. "The Thick and the Thin: On the Interpretive Theoretical Program of Clifford Geertz." Current Anthropology 25 (1984): 261–279.

The Best of Art Linkletter's Kids Say the Darndest, Vol. 1. Time Life Records, 2005. DVD.

Chapter 18

Strategies for Engaging Children at the Deepest Level in Spiritual Formation

Gary C. Newton

To see the phenomenal growth of children's ministries all one has to do is visit a large church, a regional or national children's ministry conference, or the many websites geared towards children's ministry curriculum. Yet the challenge for us as Christian educators committed to the spiritual formation of children is not to let the consumer driven trends of our culture replace spiritual depth with superficiality. That would undermine what we know to be true about the nature of children's spirituality, how children learn, and how God works in the lives of children.

A CAMP "AHAH"

Children have always amazed me with their deep thoughts and questions when they are given a safe place to talk and a listening ear. Last summer, while teaching children at a camp in northern Minnesota, I had a chance to see this in a powerful way. I was asked by a counselor to share the bedtime devotions with a cabin of eight rambunctious eleven-year-old boys. Rather than taking the usual approach of simply reading and talking about a passage of Scripture, I started with a brief story from my childhood when I wrestled with spiritual questions. Then I simply asked them to share some of the questions that they had been thinking about during their week at camp. To my amazement, these usually rowdy boys began to share some very deep philosophical, theological, and personal questions. Issues emerged and grew as the boys affirmed and disagreed with each other's comments. Some even brought in relevant biblical texts to shed light on their friends' questions. The topics of discussion were more typical of a seminary dorm room discussion than bedtime devotions for junior campers. The progression of the questions and discussion went something like this:

> If God really created everything good, then where did Satan come from?
>
> Did we come from monkeys? . . . . .That's what my teacher says.
>
> How can God be good if He created the Devil?
>
> If God is good why did he let my dad leave our family?
>
> What will happen to Satan in the end?
>
> How do we know there is a real Hell?
>
> Does Hell last forever or do people just burn for a while and then go?
>
> Who goes to Hell and what is it like there?
>
> How can a good God send people to Hell?
>
> Will my dad go to Hell? I don't like that at all!
>
> How can anyone ever be good enough to get to heaven? Everyone I know, including myself, sins all the time. It is impossible not to sin. Life would be no fun!

The boys talked non-stop for over an hour and fifteen minutes until the cabin checker knocked on the door and told us that we had to put the lights out and hit the sack. In closing, I thanked the boys for their honesty and depth and reaffirmed the importance of their questions and the wise biblical principles that they brought up in answer to their own questions. The next morning I began our large group Bible teaching time by having the whole cabin line up and share the different questions they brought up and discussed the night before. With no preparation each boy recited their questions clearly. Those questions became the catalyst to ignite the minds of the children to reflect upon the series of camp Bible lessons on a deeper level during our closing Bible lesson time.

THE HEART DIAGRAM AND A CHILD'S JOURNEY TOWARD SPIRITUAL DEPTH

The purpose of this chapter is to help those working with children to understand and appreciate the nature of "heart-deep teaching" and to become more familiar with strategies of engaging with children at the deepest possible level in their spiritual formation. "Heart-deep teaching" is a concept that I have developed more fully in a book of the same title based on biblical, theological, educational and social science research (Newton, 2012).

Before we examine the various strategies for encouraging children to wrestle with biblical principles at a deep level, we must define the nature of "deep teaching and learning." While educators have traditionally built upon Bloom's taxonomy related to the sequencing of depth in learning, we must realize that this original taxonomy related primarily to the cognitive dimension of the person. In planning an accurate map of what depth looks like in the spiritual journey of children, we must develop a more holistic picture.

Spirituality in children must integrate all dimensions of the person including the mind, the emotions, the will, and behavior at the deepest possible level. Both the Old and New Testaments refer to this deepest part of the person as the "heart." Rather than a separate ontological part of the person, the heart is simply the deepest unified core integrating all of the parts of a person. Thus the heart, contrary to what we hear in most love songs, includes all of the dimensions of the person or child.

Before we can design strategies to help children in their spiritual journey, we must gain as much wisdom as possible about this journey to the heart. Based on our definition of the heart as the focal point of our cognitive, affective, and volitional functions, we will map out the process of going deeper in each of these domains. We will attempt to show the inter-relationships of these domains in our journey to the center of the heart. Equipped with a better understanding of the process of the journey to the heart, we will be able to design wiser approaches to engage children in the spiritual formation process.

The journey to the heart can be compared to a journey descending the steps of a ladder, each step representing a different domain—cognitive, affective, and volitional—toward the core of the heart. Each of the steps represents the sequential stages that a child takes toward heart-deep learning in each domain. While the Bible is the key source in understanding this process of going deeper in spiritual formation, we can also clearly see the order and sequencing of the steps toward the heart from the collective observations of years of social science research. By integrating biblical and social science research, we can formulate a theory of how to respond to the Holy Spirit and His Word at progressively deeper levels towards the heart.

The journey of depth in the spiritual formation of children can be pictured as a process of moving from external to internal in each of the dimensions of the person. The deepest level of children's spirituality would be embodied in the child's heart or the center of the child's being. Throughout the Old and New Testaments the term, heart, represents the innermost part of the whole person, including the core of a person's emotions, volition, thinking, and intention. While different passages and contexts in Scripture may focus on one of these parts of the heart over another, there is no warrant to limit the term heart in Scripture to any one dimension of the person. Rather, the heart is the center of all domains of the person. This concept is essential to designing holistic strategies to engage children in their journey to experience the depth of the knowledge of God.

It is clear that New Testament writers use the term heart to depict the deepest part of the person, the inner man, or what some call "the real person." In the New

Testament, the heart is the place at the core of the person where the most important dynamics of one's life originate. Thoughts, understandings, desires, perceptions, reasoning, imaginations, intentions, conviction, purpose, meaning, and faith all have their roots in the heart. True transformation of the heart affects every part of the person including behavior and lifestyle.

Henri Nouwen (1981) reaffirms the nature of the heart as the center of our quest for intimacy with God. In his thoughtful book, *The Way of the Heart*, he suggests that understanding the nature of the heart and submitting it to God is at the core of intimacy with the Father. From the heart arise hidden impulses, as well as conscious feelings, moods, and wishes. The heart is also the center of perception and understanding. Finally, the heart is the seat of the will: it makes plans and comes to good decisions. Thus, the heart is the central and unifying organ of one's personal life. The heart determines personality, and is therefore not only the place where God dwells, but also the place to which Satan directs his fiercest attacks.

From a theological perspective, the heart is the place where the deepest spiritual activity takes place. As the center of a person, the heart is where God connects with those He created and they respond to His calling. While this is true for all God's people, adults and children alike, it is especially descriptive of children. After all, Jesus used a child as an example for adults of exemplary faith (Matt 18:1–4). While children have obvious developmental differences from adults, those differences, according to Jesus, do not affect the essence of faith. Children have a unique capacity to trust others and to connect with them on a deep level.

The following "Heart-Deep Diagram" depicts the dynamics of a model I have constructed to illustrate the process of how children progress deeper in the journey of spiritual formation. Issler and Habermas (1994) have defined the ladders in the "Heart-Diagram" that I am referring to as "levels of learning." We will be looking at four domains through which social scientists and educators explain the various taxonomies of the different types of learning. The Cognitive Level refers to knowledge and intellectual skills, the Affective Level to emotions and attitudes, the Dispositional and Volitional Level refers to values and tendencies to act, which intersects with all the domains, and the Behavior Level refers to physical skills and habits. While it may be helpful to separate these levels for purposes of analysis, we must realize that learning is "holistic and interrelated" (Issler and Habermas, 1994).

For this reason we will depict our journey to the center of the heart as a descent, passing down through the four levels. This journey will progressively circle deeper into the depths of the person as the Holy Spirit acts as a catalyst within each of the areas of a child's heart. His role is to initiate and direct the whole range of learning as children respond to experiences, stories and principles from God's Word. Working together with a parent/teacher, other fellow learners, and the environment, the Holy Spirit initiates and directs this process of heart-deep learning. Thus the Holy Spirit acts as a primary agent of spiritual formation through each of the domains.

Heart Deep
Teaching and Learning

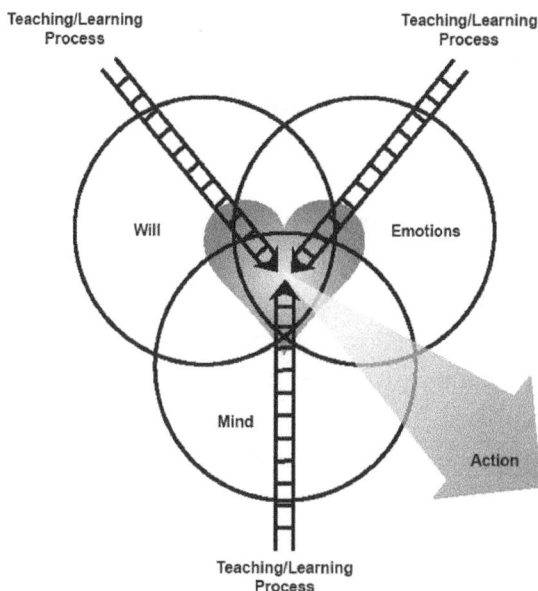

The "heart-deep diagram" represents this journey to the center of the heart of the child. The journey passes through each of the dimensions of the heart including the mind, the emotions, and the will. The closer the journey progresses to the center of the heart, the more integrated the learning becomes. As the journey progresses deeper through the various taxonomies toward the center of the heart, the more difficult it becomes to differentiate between the various domains. Thinking, feeling, and deciding merge as both teachers and children become more sensitive to the Holy Spirit in their journey toward transformation of the whole person. Obedient action based on the integration of thinking, feeling, and choosing becomes both the result and the catalyst for continued integration and deeper learning toward transformation. Obedient action or behavioral change reflects the continual transformation process within the heart. Good works, godly behavior, and fruitfulness proceed from the heart to affect the child's life, family and community.

STRATEGIES OF ENGAGING CHILDREN IN SPIRITUAL FORMATION THROUGH INTERACTIVE, ACTIVE, AND INDUCTIVE LEARNING EXPERIENCES

Although I have worked extensively with children from both churched and un-churched backgrounds, I am always amazed at the intuitive theological depth that comes from the hearts of children who have had little or no formal theological training. While working with at-risk children as Director of the Huntington Kid's Club in Huntington, Indiana, I became more and more convinced that when children are given a rich opportunity to experience the love of Jesus and the security of a godly community they are intuitively drawn to Him.

I remember one learning experience in particular that demonstrated this principle. In order to introduce our unit theme, the Life of Jesus, we wanted to understand the children's initial concepts of Jesus. Sixty children were divided into groups of three to five around the large room with a large poster board and markers. They were asked to draw as many pictures, images, or symbols representing Jesus that they could on their poster boards within their small groups.

The leaders of each group were instructed to not interpret or instruct the children, but simply to encourage their creativity and insights. After about twenty minutes the leaders asked the kids to tell them what their pictures meant to them personally. At the end of this learning activity we were astonished at the breadth, depth, insight, and detail found in the children's pictures and explanations. To our surprise many of their comments related biblically accurate ideas about God, Jesus, and the Holy Spirit with the events they were experiencing in their everyday lives. They depicted both Jesus and God as powerful, yet sensitive to their problems and needs.

What impressed our leadership team was that without formal religious training at home or church, these children were able to identify many details about the nature of Christ and the essence of how much He loved and cared for them in practical ways. We used their images and illustrations from these initial insights to examine more closely the life of Christ from Scripture.

Strategies to engage children in their journey to deeper levels of spiritual formation are based on the concepts of "Heart-Deep Learning" discussed in the first section of this chapter. To summarize what we discussed earlier, the concept of "heart-deep" spiritual formation is based on a Hebrew understanding of the "heart" as the innermost essence of a person that involves the mind, emotions, and will. When the heart is engaged by the power of the Holy Spirit within the context of God's Word, both character and behavioral changes occur. While the foundation for this model comes directly from biblical and theological research, it is reinforced from recent social science research in children's spirituality, transformational learning, experiential learning, and deeper learning. Such research clearly indicates that actively engaging emotions, mind, will, and body in learning experiences results in deeper learning.

Institutional religious education traditionally has failed to understand the dynamics of how children learn spiritual values at a "heart-deep" level. When religious educators focus predominantly on deductive teaching—telling and preaching—children often fail to engage the full capacities of their brains. Brain research reinforces the fact that children learn in all dimensions through their experience with their environment. As Marilee Sprenger (2008) explains:

The brain is the only organ in the body that is shaped through its interaction with the environment. If the brain is the organ that is dedicated to learning and memory, educators need to be familiar with brain-compatible practices and those that are brain antagonistic. Based on what we currently know about the structure and function of the brain, brain-compatible teaching emphasizes the way the brain naturally learns. (2008, 2)

While the ontological nature of Truth does not depend on experience, a child's understanding of Truth is directly related to a positive experience of Truth in as many dimensions of as possible. The younger the child, the more it is necessary to provide such significant positive experiential interaction with Truth. Learning activities are simply the ways and means that effective teachers help students to not only hear the Word, but to experience it at a deeper, multi-sensory level. By incorporating multidimensional learning activities, involving as many of the domains as possible related to the learning goals, good teachers engage their students in accomplishing their goals. Kurt Lewin (1951) wrote that learning must actively integrate thinking, feeling, and doing within a learning experience. While people learn through their senses, experience itself is not enough for purposeful learning. Processes of thinking, feeling, and doing must be activated at the heart of the person.

David Kolb describes a four-step process by which people learn. The process begins with *concrete experience* for the learner in which the learner is involved in an experience related to the goal of the lesson. In the next stage, *reflective observation*, the learner thinks through his observations about his experience. Next, in the *abstract conceptualization* stage he attempts to think through his observations for generalizations or principles related to his experience. Then, finally, in the *active experimentation* stage he puts into action his generalizations of principles based on his reflections of his experience. Kolb suggests that this cycle of learning integrates all of the aspects of the person in learning by focusing not just on the experience, but on thinking about it, reflecting on it, sharing feelings about it, and determining to act upon what was learned (Kolb, 1984). This cycle of learning has become a model for many lesson plans implementing a more holistic approach to learning. Kolb's four steps of a learning experience provide a good conceptual model for the process of engaging children in deeper levels of spiritual formation and learning.

This approach was first popularized within the evangelical church in Larry Richard's *Hook, Book, Look, Took—Method*, which appeared in the first edition of *Creative Bible Teaching* (Richards, 1973). Kolb's four steps of the learning experience also provided the fundamental framework for much of the writing in the area of learning styles (LeFever, 1995).

The key elements in Kolb's Learning Cycle include engaging the learner in concrete experience, interacting and reflecting on that experience, combining those observations together into generalizations, and then designing and implementing an active response to the principles learned. The distinctive focus of such learning activities is that the learner is always engaged in the experience. Engaging learning activities should be used whenever possible to involve children in deeper levels of learning and spiritual formation.

There has been a lot of research evaluating a wide spectrum of resources to design effective learning experiences. Rather than use research findings as a "bag of tricks" to help us find the easiest and quickest path to learning, we need to use research to provide us with wisdom and insight into how to build more effective strategies to help children move to deeper levels of spiritual formation and learning. Christian educators must avoid the temptation to simply use educational research to help their teaching become more stimulating, entertaining, or compelling for children. We must use the insights from Scripture, theology and social science research to help children become engaged at deeper levels in the spiritual formation process of becoming Christ-like.

When all dimensions of the child are actively engaged in a spiritual formation learning activity, they are much more apt to experience the presence and power of the Holy Spirit in their lives and move to deeper levels of learning. In order to set an optimum learning environment for this to happen, teachers must intentionally set clear goals and objectives related to the objective content and principles in the biblical text and the needs of the students within each of the four domains identified earlier: cognitive (mind), affective (emotions), volitional (will), and behavioral (action). Clearly defined goals and objectives then become the basis of choosing learning activities. Starting with goals and objectives rather than methodology keeps Christian educators from drifting into a superficial, entertainment-focused strategy of children's ministry that often fails to propel children towards deeper levels of spiritual formation.

After brainstorming all the potential learning activities that could be used to help children accomplish the goals of a particular lesson, the next step is to prayerfully choose the most effective learning activities and sequence them in an order that would provide variety, continuity, and clarity to accomplish the purpose of the lesson. While it may be a temptation for some more analytical teachers to simply design their lesson according to the structure of the statement of goals, dealing with one domain at a time, it may be wiser to integrate the various domains at each step in the lesson. Goals from the various domains should be woven together in a seamless journey toward cognitive, affective, volitional, and behavioral depth. Every attempt should be made to integrate the goals from the various domains as students wrestle with the meaning, implications, and applications of the main lesson principle to their lives.

Novelty and spontaneity can spark deep levels of learning in the most surprising situations. Last summer while teaching children in a camp setting, I asked one of the children who was obviously engaged in the lesson to come up front to participate in an "on-the-spot" role-play related to a point I was making from the biblical text. His informal comments did more to take the group to a deeper emotional commitment than anything else I said. While I did not actually plan to have that child participate in the role-play ahead of time, getting him involved was directly related to a goal I had set for the lesson, to help the campers to apply the principle of the lesson to their lives. Implementing creative learning strategies in a class can radically change the involvement of learners in heart-deep learning. By learning to take risks and be creative, a teacher can unleash a whole new dimension of learning to the classroom.

After spending most of her life training teachers to be creative, Marlene LeFever defines a creative teacher as a person "willing to break out of the mold and risk failure because he or she believes God can use a new idea" (LeFever, 1985). While the Holy Spirit definitely uses creative teachers and ideas to accomplish his heart-deep intentions in children's lives, even creative ideas and strategies must be based on clearly defined goals and objectives.

In her book, *Creative Teaching Methods*, LeFever suggests the following categories of learning experiences to help teachers engage their students in more effective learning: drama, role-play, mime, simulation, story, discussion, case study, creative writing and speaking, art, music, and web-based learning. Creative teachers skillfully use a variety of learning activities to engage children in deeper experiences of spiritual formation and learning (LeFever, 1985).

I have become more and more appreciative of Jerome Berryman's approach to the spiritual formation of children through imaginative play related to stories from the Bible. Rather than simply tell children what the stories mean, Berryman engages the children in the story by having them act it out, manipulate the physical characters in a story, wonder, and simply play and experience the story as it is written in Scripture. Berryman explains the dynamics of Godly Play in this way:

> Godly play is an effort to give room and permission for existential questions to arise. It is a way to give children the means to know God better amid the community of children and with caring adults as guides. The theology of childhood is about a kind of knowledge. Godly play is about how to identify, name, and value it. (1995)

Children have the ability to reflect on, wonder about, wrestle with, and question deep issues related to life. They just need to be given an opportunity to do so within a godly community with the proper support, structure, freedom, challenge, and listening ears of adults.

Catherine Stonehouse and Scottie May (2010) reinforce this principle from their lifelong research and ministry with children. While they hold to a solid belief in the propositional nature of God's Word, they do not think that the most effective method for children to know God's truth is always auditory. Instead, children should make God's story their own by connecting that story with the story of their lives. Parents and teachers can help children find meaning as they wonder with them, ask children questions, and allow children time to reflect (Stonehouse and May, 2010).

Often by simply telling children the meaning of a story or the answer to their questions, we rob them of the opportunity to exercise their own creative imaginations and problem-solving abilities. By helping children to connect the biblical story to their own experience through questions, illustrations, and discovery activities, parents and teachers can encourage deeper personal connections to God.

DEPARTING QUESTIONS TO PONDER

Tomorrow I will be traveling with my wife from Minneapolis to Northern Montana to be the Bible teacher at a children's camp. The theme is "Knowing Jesus." It sounds simple; I know the Bible verses by memory. Yet how will I teach the children? What will be my goals? How will I know when I have met my goals? Will kids be so excited about knowing Jesus that they have no choice but to get saved? Will the invitation at the last campfire for children to accept the Lord demonstrate the effectiveness of my lessons? What will I do if the camp director and the counselors have a completely different idea of how to accomplish spiritual formation for children in this particular setting?

Wrestling with these questions helps me to think more intentionally about teaching. May we teach with such purpose . . . that the Word of God reaches deeply into our children's hearts!

REFERENCES

Berrymann, Jerome W. *Godly Play: An Imaginative Approach to Religious Education.* Minneapolis: Augsburg Fortress Press, 1995

Issler, Klaus and Ron Habermas. *How We Learn.* Grand Rapids: Baker Book House, 1994.

Kolb, David A. *Experiential Learning: Experience as the Source of Learning and Development.* Englewood Cliffs: Prentice-Hall, 1984.

LeFever, Marlene D. *Learning Styles: Reaching Everyone God Gave You to Teach.* Colorado Springs: David C. Cook, 1995.

———. *Creative Teaching Methods.* Elgin: D.C. Cook Pub. Co., 1985.

Lewin, Kurt. *Field Theory in Social Science: Selected Theoretical Papers.* 1st ed. New York: Harper, 1951.

Newton, Gary C. *Heart-Deep Teaching: Engaging Students for Transformed Lives.* Nashville: Broadman & Holman Publishers, 2012.

Nouwen, Henri J. M. *The Way of the Heart: Desert Spirituality and Contemporary Ministry.* New York: Seabury Press, 1981.

Richards, Larry. *Creative Bible Teaching.* Chicago: Moody Press, 1973.

Sprenger, Marilee. *The Developing Brain: Birth to Age Eight.* Thousand Oaks: Corwin Press, 2008.

Stonehouse, Catherine and Scottie May, *Listening to Children on the Spiritual Journey: Guidance for Those Who Teach and Nurture* (Grand Rapids: Baker Publishing, 2010), 88.

Chapter 19

Adapting the Ignatian Spiritual Exercises for Children

Andrew S. Kereky Jr.

For over 450 years, the *Spiritual Exercises* of St. Ignatius of Loyola has helped adults deepen their prayer life and relationship with the Lord Jesus Christ. Its various approaches of praying with scripture, praying backwards through one's day, and praying with the imagination demonstrate the beauty of this methodology. Now, the same disciplined approach to prayer can be applied to children as young as ten and eleven-years-old. This chapter explains the effective methods from my doctoral research which hypothesized:

> The Spiritual Exercises of St. Ignatius of Loyola can be adapted for children. When a child seriously undertakes the exercises, as measured by the student and his/her parents, he/she can have a greater appreciation of scripture, a more vibrant prayer life, a deeper relationship with the Lord, and improved moral behavior.

CHILDLIKE FAITH

> He called a child, whom he put among them, and said, "Truly I tell you, unless you change and become like children, you will never enter the kingdom of heaven." (Mt 18:2–3)

> Then children were brought to him that he might lay his hands on them and pray. The disciples rebuked them, but Jesus said, "Let the children come to me, and do not prevent them; for the kingdom of heaven belongs to such as these." (Mt 19:13–14)

Children hold a special place in Jesus's heart, and he reminds us of the importance of becoming childlike in our faith life. We must become as children, filled with awe and wonder, open to new experiences and trusting of God and others as we battle a culture and life that often opposes us. While we are invited to embrace a child-like attitude in our faith journey we must remember to encourage young people to recognize, nurture, and be thankful for this in their own lives. We can greatly assist them by using our role and gifts as disciples to foster children's spirituality.

The *Spiritual Exercises* of St. Ignatius of Loyola utilizes the knowledge of faith already possessed by children and engages this knowledge to deepen the child's relationship with God and the Lord Jesus Christ. It is not primarily catechetical, although it includes a catechetical component that is structured and disciplined. This "how to" guide for a retreat program uses a disciplined approach to prayer developed for adults and adapts it for children in the fifth and sixth grades. The retreat facilitator is invited and encouraged to "make it your own."

PROBLEM AND OPPORTUNITY

Our children are growing up in a world that is more and more secular and less and less godly. One need only look to current television shows, movies and music lyrics to see what our children face. At the same time, fewer Christians are attending weekly worship services and too many Christian parents are under-informed or not knowledgeable about the faith. Helping our children draw closer to God through the *Ignatian Spiritual Exercises* will have an effect on their families, on others with whom they come in contact, and on the children themselves as they mature. According to Thomas Aquinas, "Grace is no respecter of age; the habits (capacities and tendencies) of the theological virtues are infused in even the tiniest infant at baptism," (Trania, 2001, 110).

Note: While this program has a distinctive leaning toward the Catholic faith tradition, it will equally benefit our brothers and sisters in other faith traditions. Deepening one's prayer life, stronger connection to the worship experience, and love of scripture are universal Christian aspirations. Therefore, non-Catholics also will find value in this retreat program and its approach.

MY APPROACH

In this study, fifth and sixth grade students participated in this retreat, which actually took place in their classrooms. Weekly, I visited three fifth grade classes (approximately thirty students in each) during their religion period (thirty-five to forty-five minutes). The task for the week was presented; students prayed the *Exercises* at home for at least fifteen minutes per day. This format may easily translate to a weekly Sunday school class or even be incorporated into a home-schooling setting.

Students were invited to offer their input before, during, and after the nine-week retreat. Here are some of their comments:

- The retreat made me feel like a better person. I am now thinking about the way I treat others and if it's the way I would want to be treated. I am now participating in Mass more than I did before. (Sixth-grade girl)

- The retreat made me think twice before I did something. I felt I was a better person and closer to Jesus when I did it. (Sixth-grade girl)

- I am praying even more after I did these exercises. It was a good experience and I feel like a better person. I feel more [of] Jesus in my life. (Sixth-grade girl)

- I am different because I feel a lot closer to God, also holyier [sic] . . . I read the Bible more often, treating others better, praying more at Mass. I talk to God with things going on in my life. (Sixth-grade girl)

- Because of the Spiritual Exercises, I feel like a better person. I listen at Mass more than I used to, and I try to participate. Also, I pray more at night time than I used to before I did the Spiritual Exercises. It really helped! (Sixth-grade girl)

- The retreat made me feel like a whole new and better person. I feel that I am closer to God because I pray more. (Sixth-grade girl)

I also invited their parents to share observations of their child's behavior, attitudes, and "spirituality" (i.e. Bible reading, Catholic Mass attendance and participation, prayer life). Examples of reports from parents are:

- [Name] has always had a compassionate nature and this retreat helps him to feel good about himself when he does nice things for others. [Name] hands me the Bible in church and murmurs the songs we sing. He asks to go to church and what the family plans are. (Fifth-grade boy's parent)

- [Name] can often be heard asking, 'Is there anything I can do to help?' His younger sister is also imitating this generous behavior. (Sixth-grade boy's parent)

- We find that she asks more questions about the readings at church, [she] sits quieter at church and pays more attention. [And she] reminds family members to do good and make good choices. (Fifth-grade student's parent)

Students who more fully entered into the retreat experience responded with a greater awareness of and inclination toward treating others more respectfully. The following are outcomes of the program.

Scripture Reading

While most Catholic children believe the Bible is the inspired word of God, many are content to be scripturally nourished only at Sunday Mass. This retreat program is fully immersed in scripture, especially the Gospels, and the retreatant is encouraged to make scripture an important part of her/his spirituality and prayer life. Therefore, the child should have a greater appreciation of and attraction to the Bible by the end of the retreat.

Prayer Life

Many years ago I found a definition of prayer that I invite retreatants to ponder: "Prayer is a two-way conversation between two persons that love one another, and one of them happens to be God" (source unknown). A vibrant prayer life is more than just reciting memorized formal prayers each day. A person can have a conversation with God throughout the day by responding with a quick prayer of "thanks" upon seeing a beautiful sunset or offering up a request for strength in a moment of temptation.

Retreatants are invited to widen their understanding of communicating with God. They may not only pray formally more often, but also speak with God more often throughout the day. In addition, some children increase their focus on the needs of others when they pray rather than asking for "things" for themselves. Very importantly, a goal of the program is to encourage children to embrace God/Jesus as a friend who is always present and who desires to share all of life's experiences.

Mass/Worship

As one draws closer to God through a deeper prayer life and connection to scripture, the result is a greater awareness of and appreciation for God's presence and love. This is most evident in one's abiding affection for the Lord Jesus Christ through his Incarnation, life, Passion and death, and Resurrection. No response on our part can ever be sufficient to measure up to God's infinite love, so we respond in the only way we can: with gratitude.

There is no greater way for Catholics to manifest this response than through the Eucharistic Liturgy. We come together in community at Mass to offer praise and thanksgiving for God's abundant blessings. This retreat program guides the retreatant to "full, conscious, and active participation" during Mass as part of the deepening relationship with their loving God. Students who experienced the adapted Ignatian *Spiritual Exercises* experienced a deeper prayer life, and enjoyed a greater connection to scripture. They engaged in a greater worship experience and demonstrated improved moral behavior.

ADAPTING THE IGNATIAN SPIRITUAL EXERCISES FOR CHILDREN

Ignatius of Loyola designed the *Spiritual Exercises* to be adapted according to the "dispositions of the persons who wish to receive them, that is, to their age, education or ability ..." (Elder, 1914, 19). Based on my experience with and knowledge of children's spirituality, designing and leading children's retreats, and guiding others through the *Spiritual*

Exercises, I was confident that the adapted *Exercises* would have a positive impact on children's faith development while maintaining the integrity of the *Spiritual Exercises*.

Praying the gospels with the imagination is a major area of adaptation. While adults tend to be arguably more logical in their use of imagination, children have limitless creativity and can more readily enter into a gospel scene, for example. Their playful imagination, along with their innocent openness, allows the Holy Spirit to touch and influence their encounter with Christ.

The daily Examen (Examination of Consciousness or praying backwards) is another area adapted to be more sensitive to children's emotional and spiritual development. In the adult Examen, the retreatant is faced with her/his actions/words that may reveal shortcomings and failure to love with the heart of Christ resulting in "good guilt." For children, however, the Examen invites the students to prayerfully enter into their daily experiences with a non-judgmental, non-angry Jesus who is present to them to help them grow as disciples (less emphasis on guilt).

Finally, the use of a child-friendly Bible is another adaptation. Adults are free to choose their own Bible, but all of the children used the same Bible which provided consistency. When the retreat ended, children were able to keep their Bible.

PROGRAM OVERVIEW

Suggested Length

Visiting with students once-a-week for an 8 or 9 week program/retreat works well. This allows students to enter deeply into the various dimensions of the *Spiritual Exercises* and gives students ample opportunity to develop prayer habits that may be the foundation of a lifelong meaningful Christian spirituality. However, even in a retreat with less than 9 weeks, this program still offers significant spiritual benefits to retreatants.

Program Structure

Major components of the retreat program are:

- The retreat journey itself
- Praying with the Bible
- Praying with the imagination
- Daily *Examination of Consciousness (Examen)* (praying backwards through one's day)
- Small group faith sharing
- Structure of each session

Section Three: Engaging Methodologies

The chart below depicts the retreat journey, accompanying themes, and the prayer components/tools introduced along the way. The arrow at the top represents the retreat "journey" over the nine-weeks. Below the journey are the various prayer/ retreat "tools" that the retreatant receives to incorporate into their prayer life.

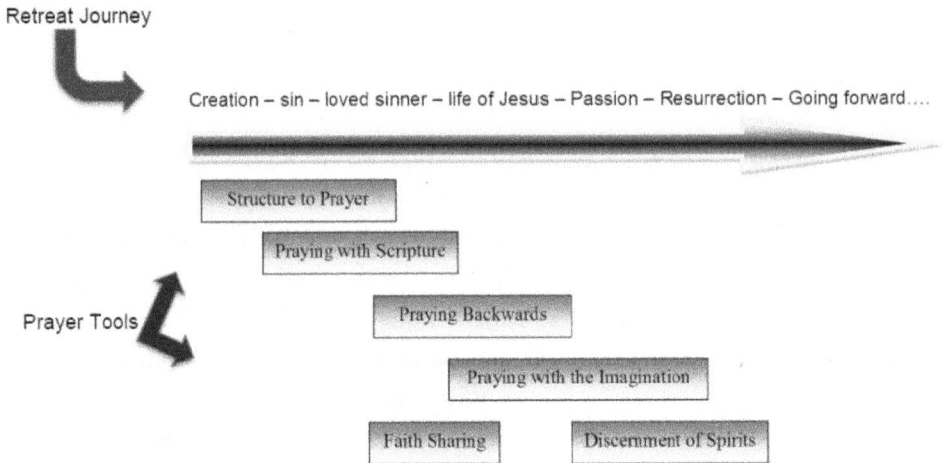

Retreat Journey

Creation – sin – loved sinner – life of Jesus – Passion – Resurrection – Going forward....

Prayer Tools

Structure to Prayer

Praying with Scripture

Praying Backwards

Praying with the Imagination

Faith Sharing

Discernment of Spirits

CONSIDERATIONS AND CONSTRAINTS

Teacher/Facilitator

Teaching how to ride a bike would be very difficult if I hadn't already struggled to learn, fallen off, and finally experienced the joy of finally removing the training wheels. Similarly, guiding others through the *Ignatian Spiritual Exercises* is more spiritually "effective" if the facilitator has experienced them. A full 8-week program will provide a spiritual journey similar to what the children will experience. It will also expose the teacher to the disciplined prayer methods that will be shared with the children (praying with scripture, the *Examination of Consciousness*, praying with the imagination).

If a long retreat is not possible, a weekend retreat based on the *Spiritual Exercises* is helpful though it may be insufficient to gain the depth of understanding to effectively guide children. Reading books on the *Spiritual Exercises* may enhance the experience, but the full retreat is always the best alternative, especially if you wish to lead others. (And it will probably be a life-changing experience for you!)

Importance of Family

Since religion is a central force in many families, the support of families for the retreatant going through the *Exercises* can deeply enhance the retreat experience. While an adult retreatant can benefit from familial support, children benefit to an even greater degree when family members, especially parents, reflect an active interest in their child's retreat experiences. "The family is probably the most potent influence—for better or for worse—on children's spiritual and religious development" (Boyatzis, Dollahite, & Marks, 2006, 305).

One of the themes of the *Exercises* is "finding God in all things." The child will encounter this dimension of the *Exercises* more deeply when the family helps to examine the myriad ways God is present in daily activities. Since "every human relational event can be viewed as spiritual and . . . this is particularly true for intergenerational family relationships," (Boyatzis, Dollahite, & Marks, 2006), all family members have an opportunity to contribute to the retreatant's spiritual growth through their active support.

A very effective method is a single-page, eye-catching newsletter that includes a summary of the week, a brief preview of next week's topic, and ways to encourage parents to be involved in their child's journey through the retreat. Parents may be given the task of asking the child to read her "assigned" scripture passage and sharing what God might have been saying to her. Or, if the student prayed the passage using his imagination, the parent may inquire about the character that the student imagined, or did he enter the passage as himself?

With the Examen (praying backwards) the entire family might do this together and share an example where each person felt God was present during the day. How did they respond to that presence? Were they Jesus for others? If so, the family shares a prayer of thanks/gratitude. If not, the person prays a prayer of contrition/sorrow and the family joins with their prayerful support.

STRUCTURE OF THE PROGRAM

Individual gifts and creativity are important to the "success" of this program. Releasing these talents within a flexible structure provides the best environment for retreatants to grow in their spirituality. This means the retreat experience described here utilizes a workable yet flexible structure/organization that is spiritually beneficial to retreatants in achieving results. The organization allows and invites an individual approach while maintaining the integrity of the *Spiritual Exercises* as St. Ignatius designed.

Materials Needed

Binder with tabs

- Child-friendly Bible
- Weekly handouts
- Props

While the directed part of the retreat is very important (weekly presentation, questions/answers to help clarify, sharing of experiences, small group faith sharing, etc.), for many, the daily individual praying with scripture and praying the *Examination of*

Consciousness may provide the greatest spiritual growth. Therefore, it is important to make this individual prayer time easy for the retreatant. If it is too difficult to identify what is to be prayed today or too challenging to find the page with the helps to praying with the Bible, some retreatants simply may give up. It is worth the investment to purchase binders and exciting for children to receive colorful handouts every week as they build their binder.

The *Breakthrough Bible* from St. Mary Press is designed for 10–13 year olds. Many adults prefer this Bible because:

- They enjoy using the same Bible as their child. This provides another connection between parent(s) and their child(ren) in their retreat journey together.

- Many parents' knowledge and comfort with their own (Catholic) Christian faith is not diminished using this Bible, and they are comfortable with both the drawings and language level.

Overview of the Retreat Structure

The chart provides an overview of the retreat by week. The theme of the week is presented along with the content.

Ignatian Spiritual Exercises for Children
Plan

Week/Tab	Theme	Content (In Class)
1	• Background and Retreat Goals • Ways of praying: unstructured vs. structured	• Introduction: Ignatius; *Spiritual Exercises* • 6 P's of Prayer
2	• Immensity of God's creation • God is present in my daily life: every moment and experience	• Hubble Telescope re infinite universe (video or poster) • Praying Backwards (*Examination of Consciousness*)
3	• God speaks to me through the Bible • God's creation is beautiful but sin has marred it...sin has a history...all the way to me However, I am a loved sinner	• Praying with the Bible • Rose Reflection • "Forgiveness" Holy Card
4	• God becomes one of us • I want to deepen my intimacy with Jesus	• Praying the Gospels with the Imagination
5	• God speaks to us through others in their sharing • I am known by my "fruit." The "success" of my retreat will be noticeable by others in my words and behavior	• Small group faith sharing • Rotten fruit reflection
6	• God Speaks to us through others in their sharing • Helping form an image of the human Jesus	• Small group faith sharing • Sketches of Jesus (www.keatonprints.com)
7	• Being with Jesus during his Passion	• Passion Reflection (use props)
8	• Resurrection	• Small group faith sharing
9	• Maintaining the spiritual momentum	• Review how retreatant can re-do some or all of retreat

Creation – sin – loved sinner – life of Jesus – Passion – Resurrection – Going forward....

Prayer tools in bold

Description of Retreat Components

"6 P's of Prayer"

Praying daily through the *Spiritual Exercises* may require time away from television or playing. Students are encouraged to increase their prayer time to at least 15-minutes per day. Providing structure to this time is accomplished by using the "6 P's of Prayer" method.

1. PREPARE the assigned scripture passage by having it marked in the Bible.

2. PLACE—Find somewhere to be alone away from distractions.

3. POSTURE—Sit relaxed and peaceful, upright in comfortable chair rather than lying in bed.

4. PRESENCE OF GOD—Become aware of God's love and presence. Respond to him. Ask God to speak through scripture.

5. PASSAGE—Read/pray the passage slowly and listen with the heart. Is God speaking? Have a conversation with Jesus.

6. PAUSE—When finished, don't rush off. Sit with the Lord. Offer thanks for the time together. Write one's thoughts, questions, or words of thanks.

Praying Backwards (Examination of Consciousness)

A very important component of the *Ignatian Spiritual Exercises* is becoming more aware of God's presence in daily events, people, and experiences. The student is encouraged to spend time prayerfully reflecting back on their day at mid-day and in the evening to examine how God was present with them and evaluate how they responded to his presence. This reflective prayer time can be part of praying with scripture using the "6 P's of Prayer" method (PAUSE) above. This figure offers the method I invite students to use which incorporates their wonderfully vibrant imagination.

Examination of Consciousness (Exãmen)

Do this LAST in your prayer time.

This can be part of the *"6th "P" of Prayer"* – "PAUSE"

1. Ask Jesus to light up my day so I'll remember.

2. Imagine being in a quiet room with a TV and DVD player.

3. Jesus comes in and sits down right next to you. Tell Jesus how glad you are that he is with you. Jesus picks up the remote and hits "PLAY." You both watch as your entire day begins to play on the TV.

4. When a scene shows where you were very loving or patient or kind, Jesus hits the "PAUSE" button. You both talk about what happened and Jesus tells you how happy he is that you were very loving to the other person. Notice your feelings.

5. If a scene shows where you were unloving (teased, gossiped, disobeyed, hurtful, etc.), Jesus again hits the "PAUSE" button. You both talk about what happened. Share with Jesus how sorry you are. Tell Jesus how you will do better with his help. Notice your feelings.

6. Do this with Jesus (#4 and #5) for your entire day.

7. LOOK TOWARD TOMORROW. What are my plans? What are my desires? How will Jesus be a part of tomorrow?

8. Jesus and you pray an *Our Father*.

Praying With the Bible

God speaks to us through the inspired words of scripture. The challenge for us is to effectively hear our Lord's voice through all the distractions and "noise" in our mind, heart, and environment. It takes patience, practice, and the development of a listening, sensitive heart to hear the "gentle whisper" of the Lord's voice (1 Kings 19:11–12 NIV). Praying with the Bible takes place in the 5th "P of Prayer" (PASSAGE). Here are the steps to guide the student in developing a spiritually sensitive frame of mind and heart to God's voice.

1. Read the entire passage slowly and prayerfully as though God were speaking the words directly to you.

2. Notice any words or phrases that might have stood out from the rest. It's almost as if they were in bold or that God was speaking them louder to you than the other words.

3. When finished, sit quietly and think about any words or phrases that might have stood out. It's OK if nothing stood out.

4. Go back and read/pray the passage again. Did the same word or phrase still stand-out? If so, have a conversation with Jesus about it. Talk to him. Ask questions. What is he saying to you? What is your response? If nothing stood out, sit quietly with Jesus and thank him for this time together.

Praying With the Imagination

Young people have vibrant, active imaginations, much more than do adults. A major component of the *Ignatian Spiritual Exercises* is deepening one's intimacy with the Lord Jesus Christ by praying the gospels with the imagination. More than simply fantasizing or imagining as we would about on a character in a good novel or movie, praying with the imagination uses the gift of imagination in prayer, thereby having an encounter with Jesus through the help of the Holy Spirit.

When praying a scripture PASSAGE in the "5th P of Prayer," the student uses the method, praying with the Bible, for any passage in scripture. If the passage is from one of the Gospels, it contains a setting, characters, and action (miracle, argument, healing, etc.). Here is opportunity to pray with the imagination! The student is encouraged to slowly read/pray the passage to get an idea of the story and details of the scene such as location and surroundings, characters, and action.

Then, and most importantly, the student is invited to enter the story either as himself/herself or as one of the existing characters and have an encounter with Jesus. As the story unfolds, the student interacts with Jesus through prayerful imagination. To conclude, the student is encouraged to spend time speaking with Jesus (during the 6th "P of Prayer"—PAUSE) to reflect further on what occurred. This way of praying becomes a powerful tool to hear the Lord's voice while deepening a relationship with Jesus.

CLOSING COMMENTS

These are suggestions for starting the program:

1. Experience the *Ignatian Spiritual Exercises* yourself. If you are able to fully enter into the experience, I promise it will be life changing.

2. Adapt the *Spiritual Exercises* to the spiritual and emotional needs of the children to whom you minister.

May our Lord Jesus Christ bless you and your efforts to help our children become closer to him!

REFERENCES

Boyatzis, C., et al. "The Family as a Context for Religious and Spiritual Development in Children and Youth." In *The Handbook of Spiritual Development in Childhood and Adolescence*, eds. Eugene C. Roehlkepartain, Pamela E. King, Linda Wagener, & Peter L. Benson. 297–309. Thousand Oaks, CA: Sage, 2006.

"Constitution on the Sacred Liturgy (Sacrosanctum Concilium)," in Vatican Council II, Rome: Catholic Church, 1963.

Mullan, Father Elder, S. J. "The Spiritual Exercises of St. Ignatius of Loyola." P. J. Kennedy & Sons, New York, 1914.

Traina, Cristina L. H., "A Person in the Making: Thomas Aquinas on Children and Childhood," in *The Child in Christian Thought*, ed. Marcia J. Bunge. 110. Grand Rapids, Mich.: W.B. Eerdmans, 2001.

Chapter 20

Applying Contemporary Early Childhood Theory & Pedagogies to the Process of Intentionally Scaffolding Children's Emergent Spiritual Awareness

Sandra Ludlow

This chapter reviews literature on contemporary early childhood theory and pedagogy and uses it to suggest implications for best practice in nurturing children's spiritual awareness and faith formation in faith-based early childhood settings. Also recommended are alternative pedagogies to traditional approaches' overreliance on whole group Bible story pedagogy for three-to-five-year olds. Reflections on lived experiences will be used to illustrate the findings of the literature review.

Children's spirituality is viewed as an inner experience of the sacred through personal awareness, a sense of awe, and mystery sensing, together with the process of wondering, and meaning making (Hay & Nye, 2006). Such a spiritual awareness speaks to the child's heart as it develops within them an understanding of just who God, and Jesus are, and how they work in his/her life. This type of spirituality is always empowered by the Holy Spirit.

THEORETICAL FOUNDATIONS OF METACOGNITION AND SPIRITUAL AWARENESS

The faith-based curriculum in Christian early childhood contexts should be based on a careful consideration of the wisdom and beliefs of contemporary theories of child development and decisions about the best pedagogical approaches to use to scaffold emergent spiritual awareness. Nurturing faith formation and spiritual awareness has its roots in cognitive development, neuroscience, social emotional development, and socio-cultural theory. Theories of development and implications for practice can be found in early childhood development textbooks (Berk, 2006). A number of Christian researchers—Westerhoff (2008), Hay & Nye (2006), Stonehouse & May (2010), Allen with Adams, Jenkins, & Meek (2012)—have also posited suggestions about spirituality and character development in young children. All teachers in faith-based classrooms need to take these factors into consideration when they work with the child, the child's parents, and the Holy Spirit to nurture spirituality, and faith formation.

A careful perusal of the writings of the authors listed above leads to the recognition that the development of spiritual awareness is in fact a multidimensional and multimodal process, occurring over time, through the active engagement and interaction of the child's senses, thinking, feelings, emotions, and morality within a cultural setting. The use of a variety of approaches in combination with the technique "reflective engagement" is recommended (Stonehouse & May, 2010, 86).

One facet of a multidimensional approach is to engage children's emotions and feelings through "experiential awakening" (Hammond, Hay et al., 1990, 179). Bible stories, like all stories, draw children into a world that is outside of their reality (Trousdale, 2007), evoking the "felt sense" of spirituality (Hyde, 2010, 510). As they listen to the narrative, they begin to imagine it, experiencing it through their own lens of familiarity, identifying with the characters, settings, and situations. This entails sensitizing children to their own emotions and relationships, using questioning and insights from their own lives to unpack the intentions of the characters within the stories with the result that this also awakens children to the spiritual truths within each Bible character's experience. It is at this moment that children begin to encounter God. Hay & Nye (2006) frame this spiritual moment through the lens of relational consciousness, defining it as an unusual level of perceptiveness that manifests itself through awareness sensing, value sensing, and mystery sensing. Awareness sensing is defined as an intense felt sense of a situation; mystery sensing is the sense of awe, wonder, questioning, and fascination, while value sensing is defined as moral sensitivity.

There is a rich and long history of theories and beliefs about how young children learn and develop. It is to this history that we turn to shed light on best practice for scaffolding spiritual development in young children. There are a number of notions upon which most early childhood theorists appear to agree. Children are capable and competent. They are active agents in constructing their own knowledge either alone or with the help of adults or more competent peers. Their learning is dynamic, complex, and holistic (EYLF, 2009) occurring within a socio-cultural framework. Table 1 summarizes the beliefs and implications for practice of a number of influential early childhood theorists. These can be used by educators to support learning, development, and spiritual awareness.

Table 1: Theories of Development and Implications for Practice

Theory	Major beliefs	Implications for practice
Piaget Cognitive Development Theory (1962)	Children develop spontaneously due to interaction with, and exploration of, physical, and social environment—assimilation, and accommodation Universal stages of development	1. provide age/stage appropriate experiences 2. treat children as individuals 3. scaffold concrete active discovery learning 4. use close observation 5. use a play based experiential program 6. use open-ended questions
Vygotsky Socio-Cultural Theory (1978)	Cognitive development not universal Relationships, and learning through interactions within zone of proximal development	1. encourage scaffolding by more capable peer, and adults to support learning, and development 2. engage in co-construction
Bruner (1983)	Scaffolding	engage in guided participation
Rogoff (1990)	Development occurs during cultural activities and through using cultural tools	Influenced by: 1. physical, and social setting 2. historical customs 3. practices/rituals
Bronfenbrenner (1979)	Culture and a web of relationships influence knowledge, skills, attitudes, and values Environment — layers of influence	1. influences of relationships bi-directional, dynamic 2. need a cohesive approach between layers of influence
Brian Research	Pruning, and hard wiring Environment—Positive, and negative potential on learning, and development Negative effects of high cortisol levels Increasing capacity for sustained attention, and language development (Berk, 2006, 294)	1. critical periods when negative experiences can have a sustained impact, (Shore, 2003, 37) 2. stress inhibits learning 3. hardwiring 4. responsive caregiving 5. sustained shared thinking
Bowlby Attachment Theory	Attachment—long term meaningful relationships	1. engage in warm consistent care 2. quality of early attachments influence all future relationships
Hay & Nye	Relational consciousness –awareness, sensing, mystery sensing, value sensing, (Hay & Nye, 2006)	Discovery through "self-conscious reflective attentiveness," (Stonehouse, 2001, 3)
Stonehouse & May	Nature of children's spiritual experiences—emotional connectedness through story, prayer, worship within a faith community, sense of belonging, (Stonehouse & May, 2010)	1. scaffold awareness, reflection, wondering, and the expression of feelings, and moral insights (Stonehouse & May, 2010, 86)

NURTURING SPIRITUALITY THROUGH THE INTENTIONAL APPLICATION OF EARLY CHILDHOOD PEDAGOGIES

A consideration of a range of twenty-first century pedagogical approaches (based on notions of the nexus between theory and practice) further suggests age appropriate strategies for nurturing spirituality and faith formation in early childhood settings. They include: Developmentally Appropriate Practice, Multiple Intelligences, Godly Play, Curtis & Carter's Curriculum Framework, High/Scope Approaches to Pedagogy, and the Montessori, and Reggio Emilia Pedagogical Approaches. Table 2 summarizes these approaches and their implications for practice in early childhood classrooms.

Table 2: Approaches to Pedagogy

Approach	Major beliefs, and practices	Implications
Montessori	Learning occurs through active involvement with the physical, and sensory environment. Independent problem solving skills	Combining direct instruction, and careful observation with play based curriculum Self-paced learning
Gardner (2003)	Learning occurs through multiple intelligences	Plan a variety of learning experiences across a broad range of intelligences
Curtis & Carter (2008)	Teachers coach children to learn about learning	Foster dispositions to learn Teacher's role: stage /prop manager, coach, model Designing aesthetically stimulating environments, create a sense of community Open ended hands on materials (Curtis & Carter, 2008)
DAP (2009)	Learning occurs through • Individual, age, and cultural appropriateness • Individual, and small group experiences • Planned, and flexible curriculum	Play-based curriculum based on close observation of children's strengths, needs, and interests
High/Scope (2007)	Intentionality of teacher behavior Teacher's role: facilitator, model, scaffolder	Share control of the curriculum Celebrate the learning Plan–do–review
Berryman	Learning occurs through Godly Play	Set aside a special place to be with God Time, and quiet to be with God Stories told with concrete items Availability of props for child re-telling, and play "Wondering together" about God (Stonehouse, & May, 2010, 89)

Reggio Emilia	Pedagogy of relationships—co-construction Pedagogical documentation-visible listening Environment the 3rd teacher Teacher's role- scaffold, co-construct, reflect, evaluate "100 languages" (Rinaldi, & Moss, 2004)	Co-constructed short, and long term projects, aesthetic environments Teachers role: provocateur, model 100 languages bring depth, and new insights to curriculum Documentation
Siraj—Blatch-ford (2009)	Sustained shared thinking Balance of child, and teacher initiated	Small group, and individual sustained shared thinking Child-centered, adult guided, play based curriculum (2006)
Stonehouse, and May (2010)	Implement reflective engagement approach	Active participation, wondering, and questioning Space for the Holy Spirit's guidance
Habernicht & Burton (2004)	Prayer model—praise, thanks, petition, confession, forgiveness, thanks (Habernicht, & Burton, 2004, 368)	Model praise behaviors Model Christian rituals

Play-Based Curriculum

Twenty-first-century early childhood pedagogies are strongly grounded in play-based curriculum approaches which offer a combination of both free, and or guided play opportunities (Golinkoff & Sharp, 2009) where children can demonstrate learning, metacognition, autonomy, and choice (Arthur et al., 2012) through a curriculum that provides "extensive opportunities for children to direct their own learning in a well-resourced, well-facilitated environment," (Lawrence, 2009, 6). These approaches are favored because, during play, "children willingly work in their zone of proximal development at a level not usually seen in their non-play activities," (Hirsh-Pasek, Golinkoff, Berk & Singer, 2009, 14).

Through play-based experiences children assimilate, and accommodate (Berk, 2006) information in a hands-on concrete manner. This strengthens and develops children's cognitive competence through "countless opportunities for sustained attention . . . symbolic representation, memory development, and hypothesis testing," (Hirsh-Pasek, Golinkoff, Berk & Singer, 2009, 36.)

At the same time, they also develop dispositions to learn such as "enthusiasm, curiosity, commitment, persistence, confidence, cooperation, and reflexivity," (Arthur, 2010, 4). The disposition to be reflective is pivotal in the development of spiritual awareness. It may be seen in the four year-old child who asks you for a box so he can collect money from his peers to *pay* for the building props he wants to barter from other players, to repair the church for Josiah. Or in the child who, having just participated in a role play of Jesus, and the storm, tells you that his dad can't stop a storm, only Jesus can!

Both during, and at the end of play of this nature, it is appropriate for an adult to intentionally (i.e. deliberately, thoughtfully, and purposefully) scaffold the children's reflections (EYLF, 2009) extending, and deepening the play by joining it or asking questions such as, "I wonder why that happened?" "Tell me about . . .?" "What did you discover?" These types of question help children to build knowledge, to communicate, think critically, problem solve, be creative, recall procedures, and collaborate together. In this way adults scaffold the skills of confident, articulate, and competent learners. Watkins, (2008), cautions against pressing young children into religious cognition at the expense of experience, intuition or the felt sense of spirituality. Feelings are just as vital to maturing the Christian experience as are thoughts, and understandings.

Environment As the Third Teacher

Making the environment the third teacher is a further important element in the process of scaffolding children's play. The environment becomes such:

- When teachers provision it in such a way that children are empowered to locate, use, and return materials independently;

- When diverse items are stored in matching containers in specialist areas, enabling children to focus on the contents and support making choices;

- When materials are positioned in smaller, well-defined spaces to scaffold concentration, independence, and more in-depth investigation;

- When materials are presented aesthetically to invite interaction;

- When materials are offered as both individual, and shared experiences;

- When materials used in ongoing projects are able to be left in place rather than packed away at the end of a session (Curtis & Carter, 2008; Epstein, 2007; Walker, 2007).

In environments like this the materials/props act as scaffolds for metacognition, and reframing, deepening children's understanding of the Bible story, and heightening opportunities for them to experience relational consciousness.

Sustained Shared Thinking

A highly useful early childhood pedagogical strategy that teachers can use to scaffold this spiritual awareness involves sustained shared thinking, also called co-construction. It has been defined as:

> . . . two or more individuals working together in an intellectual way to solve a problem, clarify a concept, evaluate an activity, and extend a narrative. Both

parties must contribute to the thinking, and it must develop, and extend the understanding. (Clarke, 2009, 7)

Teachers who use this strategy talk 'with,' and not 'at,' children during their play, and in group times they comment, recall, wonder together, question, and apply connections with personal experience. Children will only enter into this type of thinking when they feel respect, and support for their ideas from the adults and peers in their class. Hand in hand with sustained shared thinking is the gift of time, time to "become engrossed, to work in-depth, to plan, and reflect," (Clarke, 2009, 22.), time to complete their chosen play projects, and opportunities to express their ideas.

One-Hundred Languages

The educators of Reggio Emilia add another dimension to the process of sustained shared thinking that they call the "100 languages" (Rinaldi & Moss, 2004). This teaching approach encourages children to investigate the topic in another language, for example clay, drawing, ICT technologies, collage, drama, or painting thus extending, deepening, and often reframing the investigation. For example, a child may create a complex block construction of the ark or Bethlehem during their play. A teacher using the "100 languages" approach would talk to the child commenting on the construction techniques used and the use of it as a prop in the story retell. They may ask questions, wonder together with the child, perhaps take a photo of it, and suggest that the child might dictate and record a story about their construction; or perhaps suggest as an alternative that the child use drawing materials to record their construction. All of these strategies help to progressively extend and deepen the investigation. The result is sustained shared thinking, ongoing or reframed future understanding, and learning that combines to affirm the child's thinking, creativity, and spiritual awareness. It is a strategy that has the potential to be particularly useful in Christian preschool and school settings.

Pedagogical Documentation and the Pedagogy of Listening

Undergirding play-based curriculum lies the "pedagogy of listening" (Rinaldi, 2001, 80) i.e. adult's active participation in careful observation, documentation, and assessment. When teachers observe the child at play, listen to their conversations, record their actions and conversations and use their professional knowledge to reflect on and interpret what they see and hear, they position themselves to respond to the child's meaning making by supporting the child's learning and development through sustained shared thinking. This process, when supported by documentation, makes the child's learning visible to themselves, their parents and peers. The "pedagogy of listening" (Rinaldi, 2001, 80) also requires teachers to be willing to catch and run with the teachable moment to value these emergent opportunities (Rinaldi, 2001).

Documentation supports this pedagogical strategy through digitally recording children's actions and conversations during their engagement with experiences and using them to "revisit, re-construct, analyze & deconstruct" the experience, to guide future pedagogical decisions, as well as for display and consultation with the child's family, and peers (Rinaldi, 2004, 78). When teachers and parents use these snapshots to discuss the child's learning and development, it "helps them to see things from different perspectives, allowing each . . . to transcend the limitations of their own points of view" (Curtis & Carter, 2000, pxiii).

Process Drama

Grajczonek (2007) cites process drama as a useful pedagogy for helping young children understand in greater depth the events and settings of Bible stories. It also enables them to develop empathy for the character's thinking and feelings. Process drama involves all of the children in the group participating together in role play and improvisation, e.g. building, and provisioning the ark. It enables the teacher to assume the teacher-in-role strategy in order to sustain the play and deepen children's meaning making about the story. In my experience this approach is pivotal in provoking relational consciousness in three-to-six-year olds. It nurtures children's "felt sense" (Hyde, 2010, 510) of God and his character as a three-year old realizes, for example, that God asked Noah to put the food in the ark because he wanted the animals, and Noah to have enough food to eat during the flood.

Godly Play

Yet another pedagogical approach that intentionally supports the child's development of spiritual awareness is Godly Play (Berryman, 1994; Cavalletti, 1992; Lamont, 2007; Stonehouse, 2001). Through its six-step process, this approach "aims to teach children how to use the language of the Christian tradition to encounter God, and to use that encounter to gain direction for their lives," (Lamont, 2007). Warm supportive environments that engage the senses and are provisioned with a rich array of materials available for child choice, together with the practice of intentionally using religious language and opportunities for the child to participate in weekly Communion experiences, comprise the pedagogies of Godly Play.

The strength of the Godly Play approach lies in the space and time it gives children to use the props to explore, make meaning, revisit, and internalize the Bible story. Each revisit deepens the child's understanding and scaffolds the child's awareness, mystery, and value sensing. The responding and prayer time of this approach also act as scaffolds to a child's encounter with the Godhead while the creating step in the approach enables children to work at Bloom's taxonomy's highest level of cognition as they use yet another language to encounter God, and deepen their spiritual awareness. When combined with process drama and the pedagogy of listening, Godly Play has the potential to add another powerful layer to the multidimensional process of scaffolding relational consciousness in young children.

REFLECTIONS ON LIVED EXPERIENCE

I have trailed a number of these pedagogies in my work with three-to-five-year-olds in faith-based preschools as well as in children's ministry. What follows is a reflection on my experience as a pedagogical leader in these faith-based early childhood settings.

Re-Imaging Godly Play

My classrooms have been intentionally set up so that the environment acts as the third teacher. Bible story, felt for crafts, true to life props, Bible time dress-ups in a "home-corner," construction materials, Bible story books, puppets, items from nature, play dough, art materials and such form part of the provisions. This was done because I understood the importance of children constructing their own knowledge with the support of peers, siblings, teachers, and parents, and the significance of using these props as a provocation for working in the child's "zone of proximal development" (Berk, 2006, 260).

In children's ministry settings, it has been my experience that three-year-olds often find walking into a session based on whole group instruction, a challenge. When the children arrived with their parents, I warmly greeted them and encouraged them to choose from one of the available activities set up for the day. In these settings, I deliberately chose to move away from the Godly Play format for several reasons. This initial free play model was familiar to many of the children because it mimicked their arrival at preschool. It allowed the children to enter quietly and to settle without overt adult guidance and interaction with peers. It calmed them and supported them to immerse themselves in their own play, in their own way, and at their own pace (Lubawy, 2009). Teachers quietly and respectfully moved throughout the room engaging with the children in parallel play, co-operative play, and conversations, switching between the roles of provisioner, mediator, leader, and relationship builder with children, parents, and grandparents (Arthur et. al., 2012).

Moments of awe and wonder were provoked in children by stimulating their senses through the use of the "100 languages," (Rinaldi, 2001, 30) by engaging in visual arts, song, dance, drama, interactive materials, and audio visual technologies. I made props and resources available to the children after the story time so they could revisit the story. During the children's ministry time, attempts were made to balance free play with direct instruction, whole group singing, Godly Play, and process drama.

I ensured that worship routines were consistently predictable and occurred in a warm caring environment with familiar adults.

Questions were used during the Bible story and free playtime to help unpack character's thought, feelings, and actions, as well as God's character and his role in the story. Wondering together in sustained shared conversations was pivotal in the Bible story time because I wanted the children "to both wonder about the unfolding actions of God's story but also to be filled with wonder for our awesome God" (Stonehouse and May, 2010, 89).

In response to children's questions and comments, we explored notions of God's care for Noah and his family and compared this with the way he cares for us today. One child was amazed to discover that God actually chooses people to do special jobs for him. Throughout the entire process I guided them in prayer and praise while role modelling worship behaviors, reflection, and Christian character. Sustained, shared thinking appeared to provoke a mystery-sensing moment in individual children.

I noted a number of interesting results of this model. Most children quickly settled to focused play upon arrival and either ignored their parents or jointly interacted with them and the provisions. Some parents quietly talked with their child about the provisions and took the opportunity to talk about God's goodness and creative power or retold Bible stories. As the year progressed, the children began to interact with each other and to play together in parallel and co-operative play. Older siblings often dropped by before and after their own program to play with their younger sibling in this re-imaged Godly Play environment.

In children's ministry settings, (after about thirty-five minutes of free play), we packed away most of the provisions and transitioned the children to the mat for a time of interactive praise songs and a Bible story. One or two provisions were always left out for the less settled child to engage with, while the other children participated in the story and songs. The story was usually told using process drama and concrete props. Occasionally we told the story using felt crafts, or by using a Bible story picture book or DVD. Whichever method of storytelling was used, it was always accompanied by moments of sustained shared thinking.

The pedagogical strategy process drama appeared to be pivotal in raising children's consciousness to the "felt sense" (Hyde, 2010, 510). In the middle of their engagement in the action of the story, they appeared to be more attuned to the feelings and thought of the characters in the Bible story. It was at this point that spiritual awareness emerged and deeper insights were scaffolded by listening to their thoughts and talking *with* them rather than *at* them. After the story, the children who wanted to engaged in a craft activity based on the Bible story while others retrieved the provisions from the shelves and returned to free play. Both types of activities enabled the children to revisit the Bible stories in another of the "100 languages" (Rinaldi, 2001, 30).

The strength of this approach to children's ministry appeared to lay in the unhurried nature of the session, the familiarity of the provisions and the opportunities for revisiting similar provisions each week. Time however, remained a constraint. Each session could only last for sixty-five to seventy minutes and the sessions occurred only once-a-week.

In Christian preschool classrooms, this time constraint did not exist. Children's emerging spiritual awareness could be more robustly and emergently scaffolded. Requests and conversations could be followed up immediately. Closer respect for, and attention to, moments of felt sense could be made through the use of pedagogical documentation. Teachers and children could use these documentations to revisit, reconstruct, and reframe understanding, and awareness, either later in the day or the next time the child attended preschool. The documentations could also be shared with peers and parents offering renewed opportunities for metacognition of the Bible story, God character, and role in our lives. The opportunities for sustained shared thinking were much more frequent and deeper because of the lack of time constraints and the ability to share the action and thinking with well-known adults and peers. Through these emergent curriculum pedagogies, teachers were able to shape a more meaningful and responsive faith-based curriculum for the children in their care.

An example of this occurred a number of years ago in my preschool classroom. At that time, the children's favorite thing to do at rest time was to view a video of Peter Spier's book "The Great Flood" (1979). Each time the children watched it, they discussed the narrative in detail. It appeared that each time the children re-visited the story they deepened their understanding of the plot, setting, character's actions, and the character of God. Teachers co-constructed the children's thinking in their "zone of proximal development" (Berk, 2006, 260).

Throughout the year, on numerous occasions, these same children were able to experience and reframe this same story in a variety of mediums. They read about it in a number of children's Bibles and Bible story picture books during whole group story times and revisited these books, individually and with peers, during their free play. They used dress-ups and building props to tell and re-tell personally meaningful sections of the story through co-operative, parallel, and solitary dramatic play. During this play, they could often be heard singing the songs about Noah that they had learnt in Bible story time. Occasionally, one of the children sat in the teacher's chair and role-played Bible story time with a group of peers. From time-to-time individual children spontaneously used play dough provisions or drawing and painting provisions to make or draw Noah's ark (Ludlow & Fisher, 2010). Teachers documented these experiences and displayed these documentations as part of an emergent "pedagogy of listening" to the children, their peers, and parents (Rinaldi, 2001, 80).

As I reflected back on these experiences, it occurred to me that the theories and pedagogical approaches that were used to inform my curriculum worked together to support children's emerging spiritual awareness. I noticed that spiritual awareness occurred individually in children during multi-sensory re-imaged Godly Play strategies such as process drama and dramatic free play, or when children engaged with the paint and clay provisions. These pedagogical practices gave the child time to feel a part of the experience. It was then moments of felt sense emerged. Entertainment was consciously avoided. Rather, children's ways of knowing were used to make meaning and to heighten opportunities for relational consciousness to emerge. Scaffolding and nurturing in the child a thinking response to who God is and how he works in their life became the goal. In this moment of spiritual awareness, it was important for me to put my ego and agenda aside and to respectfully leave time for the Holy Spirit to act on the child's heart, following up later with an opportunity for the child to express his or her emerging relationship with God and Jesus through prayer and songs of praise.

REFERENCES

Allen, Holly, et al. (2012). "How Parents Nurture the Spiritual Development of Their Children: Insights from Recent Qualitative Research." In *Understanding Children's Spirituality: Theology, Research and Practice*, edited by Kevin E. Lawson. 197–222. Eugene, OR: Cascade, 2012.

Arthur, Leonie. "The Early Years Learning Framework: Building Confident Learners." *Research in Practice Series* 17, no. 1. Deakin West, ACT: Early Childhood Australia, 2010.

Arthur, Leonie, et al. *Programming and Planning in Early Childhood Settings*. South Melbourne, Vic: Cengage Learning Australia, 2012.

Australian Government Department of Education, Employment & Workplace Relations. *Belonging Being & Becoming: The Early Years Learning Framework for Australia*. Barton: Author, 2009.

Berk, Laura. *Child Development*, 7th ed. Boston MA: Pearson Education, 2006.

Berryman, Jerome. *Teaching Godly Play: The Sunday Morning Handbook*. Nashville, TN: Abingdon, 1994.

Cavalletti, Sofia. *The Religious Potential of the Child*, Chicago, IL: Liturgy Training, 1992.

Cavalletti, Sofia. "Discovering the Real Spiritual Child," *The NAMTA Journal*, 24, no. 2. (1999): 6–16.

Clarke, Jenni. *Key Issues: Sustained Shared Thinking*. London, UK: A&C Black, 2009.

Copple, Carol & Sue Bredekamp. *Developmentally Appropriate Practice in Early Childhood Programs Serving Children from Birth through Age 8*, Washington, DC: National Association for the Education of Young Children, 2009.

Curtis, Deb & Margie Carter. *Learning Together with Young Children: A Curriculum Framework for Reflective Teachers*. St Paul, MN: Redleaf, 2008.

———. *The Art of Awareness: How Observation Can Transform Teaching*. St Paul, MN: Redleaf, 2000.

Epstein, Ann. *Essentials of Active Learning in Preschool: Getting to Know the High/Scope Curriculum*. Ypsilanti, IL: High/Scope, 2007.

Fisher, Barbara & Sandra Ludlow. "Understanding Children and Their Faith Development," In *Developing A Faith-Based Education: A Teacher's Manual*, Barbara. Fisher. Terrigal, NSW: David Barlow, 2010: 44–65.

Golinkoff, Roberta. & Sharp, H. Rodney. "The Power of Play: Preparing 21st Century Children for a Global World." Paper presented at NAEYC 18th National Institute for Early Childhood Professional Development. Play Where Learning Begins. Charlotte, North Carolina, June 14–17, 2009.

Grajczonek, Jan. & Ryan, Maurice (eds.) *Religious Education in Early Childhood: A Reader.* Hamilton, Qld: Lumino, 2007.

Habernicht, Donna & Larry Burton. *Teaching the Faith: An Essential Guide for Building Faith-Shaped Kids.* Hagerstown, MD: Review and Herald, 2004.

Hammond, J., David Hay, et al. (1990). *New Methods in RE Teaching: An Experiential Approach.* Harlow: Olver & Boyd cited in *Religious Education in Early Childhood: A Reader*, edited by Jan Grajczonek and Maurice Ryan. 179. Hamilton, Qld: Lumino, 2007:179.

Harris Helm, Judy, et al. "Documenting Children's Spiritual Development in a Preschool Program." *Christian Education Journal*, 4, no. 2 (2007): 268–279. Online: http://proquest.umi.com/pqdweb?index=17&did=1374248161&SrchMode=2&sid=1.

Hay, David and& Rebecca Nye. *The Spirit of the Child*, London, UK: Jessica Kinsley, 2006.

Hirsh-Pasek, Kathy, et al. *A Mandate for Playful Learning in Preschool: Presenting the Evidence.* New York, NY: Oxford University, 2009.

Hull, John. "A Gift to the Child," In *Religious Education in Early Childhood: A Reader*, edited by Jan. Grajczonek, and Maurice Ryan. 177–190. Hamilton, Qld: Lumino, 2007.

Hyde, Brendan. "Godly Play Nourishing Children's Spirituality: A Case Study, Religious Education." *The Official Journal of the Religious Education Association*, 105, no. 5 (2010): 504–518, accessed May 26, 2012: On-line: http://dx.doi.org/10.1080/00344087.2010.516215.

Lamont, Ronni. *Understanding Children Understanding God.* London, UK: Society for Promoting Christian Knowledge, 2007.

Lawrence, Debra L. "Putting Play Back into Practice." Paper presented at NAEYC 18th National Institute for Early Childhood Professional Development. Play Where Learning Begins. Charlotte, North Carolina, June 14–17, 2009.

Lubawy, Joy. *Visions of Creativity in Early Childhood: Connecting Theory, Practice and Reflection.* Castle Hill, NSW: Pademelon, 2009.

Rinaldi, Carla. "Documentation and Assessment: What is the Relationship"? In *Making Learning Visible: Children as Individual and Group Learners*, edited by Claudia Giudici et al. 78–89. Reggio Emilia: Reggio Children, 2001.

Rinaldi, Carla and& Peter Moss. "What is Reggio"? *Children in Europe*, 6, 2004:2–3.

Saraj- Blatchford, Iram. "Effective Pre-School and Primary Education Project EPPE 3–11 An Associate ESRC TLRP Project." Paper presented at ACER Conference Frameworks and Foundations: "When Only the BEST Will Do." Sydney, NSW, March 26, 2009.

Spier, Peter. *The Great Flood.* Bristol: Purnell & Sons. 1979.

Stonehouse, Catherine. "Knowing God in Childhood: A Study of Godly Play and the Spiritual Development of Children." *Christian Education Journal*, 5, no. 2 (2001): 27–46.

Stonehouse, Catherine and Scottie May. *Listening to Children on the Spiritual Journey: Guidance for Those who Teach and Nurture.* Grand Rapids, MI: Baker, 2010.

Trousdale, Ann. "Black and White Fire: The Interplay of Stories, Imagination and Children's Spirituality." In *Religious Education in Early Childhood: A Reader*, edited by Jan Grajczonek and Maurice Ryan. 83–97. Hamilton, Qld: Lumino, 2007.

Section Three: Engaging Methodologies

Walker, Kathy. *Play Matters: Engaging Children in Learning the Australian Developmental Curriculum: A Play Based and Project Based Philosophy*. Camberwell, VIC: ACER, 2008.

Watkins, T. Wyatt. "Unfettered Wonder: Rediscovering Prayer Through the Inspired Voices of Children." In *Nurturing Children's Spirituality: Christian Perspectives and Best Practices*, edited by Holly C. Allen. 131–145. Eugene, OR: Cascade, 2008.

Westerhoff III, John H. "The Church's Contemporary Challenge: Assisting Adults to Mature Spirituality with Their Children." In *Nurturing Children's Spirituality: Christian Perspectives and Best Practice*, edited by Holly C. Allen. 355–365. Eugene, OR: Cascade, 2008.

Chapter 21

"I Hope that One Day I Can Understand"
Early Adolescents Defining Spirituality Through Their Writing, Artwork, and Discussion

Catherine Posey

The challenge of defining spirituality, and more specifically children's spirituality, is an endeavour that those of us who work with children and research children's spirituality most know well. We understand that even though we may arrive at a tentative definition of the term, we recognize we will likely revisit our conception of it again. Though there are some agreed upon aspects of children's spirituality, there are other dimensions that may reflect divergent viewpoints. Rather than illuminate ideas about children's spirituality from the perspective of researchers, educators, or church ministers, however, in this chapter I investigate the voices of early adolescents concerning their perceptions of the term spirituality, and more specifically, the difference between spirituality and religion.

Due to my own research interests, much of my time has been spent talking to children and young adults about their ideas about literature. Since researching the response of readers is significant for my own work, I began to consider that it would be beneficial to ask children and young adults how they perceived the notion of spirituality themselves. Rather than develop my own definition of spirituality from the child or early adolescent's perspective, perhaps, I considered, I might conduct a study in which I explored spirituality from the perspective of the young person. For this particular study, I wanted to know how is spirituality defined from the perspective of the early adolescent? How do twelve and thirteen year olds perceive spirituality as reflected through their explicit defining of the term through their writing, artwork, and discussion?

LITERATURE REVIEW

Little research exists focused on early adolescents defining spirituality in their own terms through their writing, artwork, and discussion. However, research by Wintersgill (2008) and Roehlkepartain (2012) explored the perspectives of young people concerning spirituality. Wintersgill published a research report on teenagers' perception of spirituality in the *International Journal of Children's Spirituality* and intentionally explored the voices of teenagers for producing a definition of the spiritual (2008). Wintersgill was particularly interested in how teenagers' perceptions of spirituality were similar to or different from the "many academic theories of spirituality-in-education that have influenced policy makers" (371). She used both questionnaires and interviews with 385 students in four comprehensive schools over five years. One question asked students to identify school subjects from a list that they consider as helpful for their spiritual development. Additionally, the study included students between the ages of twelve and eighteen, of any faith or none. Though Wintersgill discovered that "no two sets of responses were the same," there were themes that were generated through the data.

One theme included the idea of spirituality as a "dynamic force," as something that "makes you" and "helps you" (Wintersgill 2008, 372). Another theme included the notion of identity, of spirituality as "the real me inside" (373). The responses also referred to spirituality as connection, holding beliefs, and as an aid for people to understand themselves. After discussing the various themes that were generated from the data, Wintersgill concluded by pointing out that students considered "that a number of contrasting subjects (often a humanities and creative/active subject) provided the best basis for spiritual development" (377). This perspective on the relationship between spirituality and the arts complements the perspectives of other researchers in the area of children's spirituality and literature (Pike, 2002; Trousdale, 2006).

Roehkelpartain's research project (2012) looked at how young people around the world conceptualize and engage with spirituality. His study intentionally considered the voices of young people themselves in relation to spiritual development. Using focus groups, Roehkelpartain investigated the perspectives of 171 youth from all over the world. Using grounded theory analysis, he discusses four themes that were generated out of the data that played a role in the direction of the research project. These included the ideas that "young people believe that a capacity for spiritual development is natural and readily available to all young people," "being actively spiritual is an individual choice," "active spirituality shapes a purposeful orientation to life," and "spiritual development is not dependent upon age but is affected by other dimensions of human development" (156). The study also revealed that young people can have difficulty articulating their ideas about spirituality or that sometimes they use religious discourse to express these ideas.

Due to the generating of my own research questions and as a result of the dearth of studies about young people's perceptions of the concept of spirituality, I developed a research study during the spring semester of my first year of teaching at a small private religious school in South Carolina in the United States. My teaching included language arts classes for both the seventh and eighth grade students.

Methodology

With my one class of ten seventh graders, I posed the question: "What do you think of when you hear the word spirituality?" After responding by writing for ten minutes on the computers in our computer lab, the students discussed their ideas in a large group, which included me, their teacher. Some students created drawings of their idea of spirituality using colored pencils and white paper. This data collection phase included gathering the students' writing and artwork, and recording their discussions.

These pre-adolescents attend a private Christian school and as a result, all of them are part of religious families. I consulted Braun and Clarke's (2006) method of thematic analysis in analyzing the data, as the epistemic interest in the study was to produce a conceptual description of twelve and thirteen year olds' perceptions of spirituality as reflected within their writing, artwork, and discussion.

With the time that was available to me, I analyzed the ten journal prompts of the seventh grade students and their artwork. The students did not talk about their responses to their question before they wrote; I simply gave them the prompt question, answered any concerns they shared, and they then wrote their responses on the computers in our school computer lab. No students discussed with one another their ideas about spirituality before responding to it in writing; I specifically waited to have our discussion until after they had shared their ideas through their writing. I also collected nine different drawings, as one student did not turn in a drawing.

Data Analysis

As I explored the written responses of the students, I identified several categories of ideas or of ways of talking about a conception of spirituality. The first category I created was one with passages that related to defining spirituality using sensory details. For example, Anne wrote: "When someone says the word spirituality to me, I think of someone or something that is very calm, quiet, peaceful and very happy." Chloe also wrote: "I guess I think of a flower . . . I think of a white rose. I really have no idea what that means but it seems cool." Chloe often shared pictures God had given her when praying for others in the class. I noticed that Chloe frequently described pictures she had seen while praying and even if she did not understand it, she would still share with me and the rest of the class what she had seen. Sabrina wrote, "I think of things flowing around me and just like the waves of the spirit." Toward the end of her journal prompt, she wrote, "spiritual is like a calm flow of something, like the Holy Spirit, where you are just relaxed." Finally, Diana wrote that when she thinks of spirituality she thinks of a "person doing Taichi on the beach with calm music and the ocean behind him. I imagine it in the fall when everything is just perfect and the wind is blowing behind the person's back."

Several of the students' responses referenced the word "calm," noting that a picture of a white rose might also fit with peaceful, happy, relaxed, and the idea that "everything is just perfect." The references to a "flow" and "waves of the spirit" conjure up an image of peace, relaxation, and calmness. The practice of Taichi further reinforces the notion of peace and calmness.

The second category I created related to the idea of spirituality as certain practices or a way of living. Anne wrote that a spiritual person is "someone who is very strict about what they do, how they do it and how they live their life." Elaine wrote, "It makes me think of Indians. It reminds me of them doing rituals and praying to their gods." Vanessa wrote that she thinks of spirituality, she thinks about "all the different practices and movements in those religions and I think of spirituality." Gwendolyn's writing reflected this idea of spirituality affecting the way you live your life: "I simply think it means spirit. I think spirituality has something to do with your spirit at work; your spirit is controlling your body and not your soul." Eleanor's response echoed this idea: "Being spiritual is more like fasting and praying, taking care of your spirit instead of your physical body." Lucy wrote that a "good spirituality" is "when you're in a relationship with the Lord, and you take care of your spiritual being by not watching, reading, or doing bad things."

I found these comments significant due to the fact that I had not really discussed with the students the notion of attending to the spirit versus attending to the mind or another aspect of our existence. I was impressed with their ability to articulate this idea through their writing. Certainly, these portions of the data point to the understanding of the students that spirituality relates to a certain way of being in the world.

Defining spirituality as connection to God or the Holy Spirit is the third category I developed to explore segments of the students' written responses. After Elaine wrote about spirituality and Indians and their gods, she wrote, "But to me spiritual doesn't mean that. It means to be prophetic and to see things through God's eyes." Vanessa related the definition of spirituality to her own life: "Since I am a Christian, when I think spirituality in the Christian sense I think people filled with the Holy Spirit or very wise prophets." For Chloe, spirituality means many things but especially "something that God has given me or something that isn't from this world . . . I think of it as a picture or word given to someone by God." Chloe continued to write, "I think a spiritual person is someone who knows God better than his best friend." Sabrina also wrote "I think of God and the Holy Spirit." Lucy wrote that when she thinks of spirituality, "I think of the Holy Spirit being in someone."

These segments of the data point to defining spirituality through discourse about God, the Holy Spirit, and a person's relationship with God. Because the students have Christian backgrounds, their ideas about spirituality certainly reflect a Christian spirituality and this seems particularly obvious with these segments of the data. I do recognize connections between these portions of the students' written responses about spirituality and the way in which researchers in Christian children's spirituality have articulated a conception of children's spirituality. If we consult the definition of children's spirituality as presented in *Understanding Children's Spirituality: Theology, Research, and Practice* (2012), we can see such connections:

> Children's spirituality is the child's development of a conscious relationship with God, in Jesus Christ, through the Holy Spirit, within the context of a community of believers that fosters that relationship, as well as the child's understanding of—and respond to—that relationship. (p. xii)

My next category relates to a theme that surfaced within the students' discussions about spirituality: the difference between spirituality and religion. One of the additional questions I posed related to the difference between spirituality and religion. In some instances, the students communicated that they recognized a difference between spirituality and religion, but they were uncertain of its exact nature. Elaine wrote, "I think there is a difference between being spiritual and being religious I just have no idea what the difference is." Vanessa at first wrote that spirituality made her think of the "different religions of the world" and that "spirituality and religion are sorta the same" because all religions have "spiritual stuff." Chloe wrote that a spiritual person is "someone who is more than a religious person." Sabrina, like Elaine, articulated difficulty in distinguishing the two: "I honestly don't know the difference between spiritual and religious." Sabrina then wrote, "Spiritual is just like the Holy Spirit and religious is just a religion. . . spiritual is like a calm flow of something, like the Holy Spirit, where you are just relaxed. Religious is just like people with different religions and different laws and stuff." Gwen wrote, "I think there is a difference between a spiritual and religious person."

Finally, Eleanor wrote, "Having a religion is when you just believe something, but you don't have to do anything to show it. I think it is much better to be spiritual than to just have a religion." As the students wrote about the difference between spirituality and religion, they may have expressed uncertainty at first in their writing. However, their comments were insightful and some of them worked through their uncertainty and nevertheless continued to write relevant and significant points about how the two might be different. This reflects that even though early adolescents may not think they have the answer to a question, they might articulate a significant response if they are given the time to reflect, write, draw, and respond using multiple methods.

After considering the ways in which these early adolescents discussed the difference between spirituality and religion I revisited my own ideas about how spirituality and religion can be distinguished. Many researchers of children's spirituality distinguish between spirituality and religion. For example, Hart (2003; 2006) articulates the differences between spirituality and religion clearly. He perceives religion as,

> ... an institutionalized approach to spiritual growth formed around doctrines, rituals, and standards of behavior . . . Spirituality is the very personal and intimate expression of our relationship with the Divine. (2006, 173)

The ways this connection manifests can operate in contexts other than the physical structure of the church. In other words, spirituality is more expansive than religion, fluid and holistic, and concerned with a deep inner connectedness (Priestly, 2005). Hart argues that "children's spirituality may exist apart from adult rational and linguistic conceptions and from knowledge about a religion" (2006, 163).

Some people find it difficult to discuss the "spiritual" without referring to religion. However, Hay posits that human spirituality is older and broader than religious traditions, and that as an "essential human trait," spirituality can manifest outside of religion (1998, 23–24). Though spiritual expression can operate within religious traditions, it is not necessary for the existence of spiritual experience (Hay with Nye, 1998). Hay & Nye contrast spirituality and religion by discussing differences in the style of language used. While some discuss religion with vocabulary such as theology, dogma, and rules, others speak of spirituality as warm, all-encompassing, and liberating (Hay with Nye, 1998).

Jacqueline Watson explores different understandings of spirituality versus definitions in her study of people's descriptions of their conceptions of spirituality (2000). She discovered that the notion of something outside of the self figured heavily in participants' discussions about spirituality, and even atheists and agnostics highlighted this idea of something beyond in their understanding of spirituality (94). Another concept central to many participants' understanding of spirituality included an "inner reality" (Watson, 95). "For some, both religious and non-religious, the 'inner' was understood as the real or true self . . ." (Watson, 95). Additionally, Schneiders distinguishes between religious and secular spiritualities in her article grappling with the tension between the two (2003). She argues that there is no "generic spirituality" but presents a general definition that can then be applied to specific forms of spirituality, such as Christian or Buddhist spirituality (2003, 167). Schneiders conceptualizes the spiritual as an active transcending of the self through assimilating various parts of one's identity and aiming for an "ultimate value one perceives" (166). It is helpful if researchers recognize that the spiritual dimension of life can manifest in a multiplicity of ways, and that there are key differences between religion and spirituality.

Another dominant trend in the data included questions and wonderings related to the difficulty of actually defining the term. Some students voiced that they were not even certain if they were spiritual or not. The last category I discuss includes comments related to this difficulty in defining the term and the students' own situating of themselves within the notion of being a spiritual person or not. Anne wrote, "I wouldn't say that I'm spiritual." Vanessa wrote, "I may or may not be spiritual." Sabrina stated, "I think I am spiritual 'cause I like to sing songs to the Lord and pray to him." Gwen voiced a desire to know more: "I've always wanted to know more about the spiritual realm. It seems so mysterious to me and I want to feel more of it." She also wrote, "I really don't know if I am spiritual or not." Diana concluded her journal entry with "I don't really have a straight idea of spirituality as you can probably see." Anne wrote, "I really don't understand many things in this world, and one of those things is religion . . . I hope that one day I can understand and tell people about the wonderful things about our God."

I was very interested in these comments, since my own definition of spirituality, as a teacher in a religious school, would consider all my students to be spiritual people who engage with their spirituality on a daily basis in my classroom. As I read their writing about spirituality, which pointed to their wondering about their own spiritual dimension, I was particularly drawn to this notion of struggling to understand the idea of the spiritual. It appeared fairly obvious to me as a teacher that these students were spiritual in multiple ways throughout the school day, but their own reflection of themselves as spiritual was not so self-evident.

IMPLICATIONS FOR EDUCATION AND RESEARCH

Through the analysis of young adults' written, artistic, and oral discourse, researchers of children's spirituality might receive greater and richer insight into how students from a Christian religious background perceive the notion of spirituality for themselves. Furthermore, it might inform teachers and ministers to children on how they can make space for young people to share their ideas about spirituality and their own spiritual development.

My analysis of these journal prompts represents the tip of the iceberg with this study, and this kind of work will certainly continue. However, preliminary research with the written responses suggests it is significant to investigate how early adolescents think of spirituality and themselves and its importance within their lives. For example, in beginning to explore the artwork the students created to represent their ideas about spirituality, I am aware of how useful it may be to allow students to respond to the question of defining spirituality through arts-based methods. Drawings can reflect themes, metaphors, and patterns that can add to the verbal and written responses of young people related to spiritual concepts. Thus, another important outcome of this study is that those who research children's spirituality should be open to allowing for children's and young adult's responses to emerge through a variety of methods. Additionally, the questions posed to young people about their spirituality should also be carefully developed. For this kind of research, the questions asked could be more effective were they more implicit in generating responses related to these young people's ideas of spirituality in the context of their own lives.

REFERENCES

Braun, Virginia and Victoria Clarke. "Using Thematic Analysis in Psychology." *Qualitative Research in Psychology, 3*, no. 2 (2006).

Hart, Tobin. *The Secret Spiritual World of Children.* Maui, Hawaii: Inner Ocean, 2003.

Hart, Tobin. "Spiritual Experiences and Capacities of Children and Youth." In *The Handbook of Spiritual Development in Childhood and Adolescence,* edited by Eugene C. Roehlkepartain et al. 163–177. Thousand Oaks: Sage, 2006.

Hay, David with Rebecca Nye. *The Spirit of the Child.* London: Jessica Kingsley Publishers, 2006. (Original work published 1998).

Lawson, Kevin, Ed. *Understanding Children's Spirituality: Research, Theology, and Practice.* Eugene, OR: Wipf and Stock, 2012.

Pike, Mark A. "Aesthetic Distance and the Spiritual Journey: Educating for Spiritually and Morally Significant Experiences Across the Art and Literature Curriculum." *International Journal of Children's Spirituality 7,* no. 1 (2002): 9–21.

Priestley, Jack. "The Spiritual Dimension of the Curriculum: What are School Inspectors Looking For and How Can We Help Them Find It?" In *Spiritual Education,* edited by Cathy Ota & Clive Erricker, 202–215. Eastbourne, UK: Sussex Academic Press, 2005.

Roehlkepartain, Eugene. "'It's the Way You Look At Things': How Young People Around the World Understand and Experience Spiritual Development." In *Understanding Children's Spirituality: Theology, Research, and Practice,* edited by K. E. Lawson, 152–172. Eugene, OR: Cascade Books, 2012.

Schneiders, Sandra Marie. "Religion vs. Spirituality: A Contemporary Conundrum." *Spiritus 3,* (2003): 163–185.

Trousdale, Ann M. "The Role of Literature in Children's Spiritual Development. In *The International Handbook on the Religious, Moral, and Spiritual Dimensions in Education,* edited by Marian DeSouza, G. Durka, K. Engebretson, & R. Jackson, 1225–1235. New York: Springer, 2006.

Watson, Jacqueline. "Whose Model of Spirituality Should be Used in the Spiritual Development of School Children?" *International Journal of Children's Spirituality 5,* no. 1 (2000). 91–101.

Wintersgill, Barbara. *"Teenagers' Perceptions of Spirituality—A Research Report."* International *Journal of Children's Spirituality 13,* no. 4 (2008): 371–378.

SECTION FOUR

Exploring Children At-Risk, Child Porn,
Social Justice, Intercultural Contexts
and Abstinence Education

Chapter 22

Whose Childhood?

Global Experiences of Children-at-Risk and Spiritual Formation

Susan Hayes Greener

New Testament scholar Mark Powell asked seminarians from three regions of the world to carefully read the parable of the prodigal son and then asked them to briefly outline the main points of the story (2007). When asked, "Why does the young man end up starving in the pigpen?," 100 percent of the American seminarians replied because he squandered all the money that had inherited. When Russian seminarians participated in the same exercise, 84 percent replied that the prodigal son ended up starving because of the famine. Armed with those two categories in mind, when the author posed the question to Tanzanian seminarians, he was surprised when 80 percent of the students came up with a third answer: because no one gave him anything to eat.

So, who is right? The text of Luke 15:13–16 reads as follows (ESV):

> Not many days later, the younger son gathered all he had and took a journey into a far country, and there he squandered his property in reckless living (the Americans' focus). And when he had spent everything, a severe famine arose in that country, and he began to be in need (the Russians' focus). So he went and hired himself out to one of the citizens of that country, who sent him into the fields to feed pigs. And he was longing to be fed with the pods that the pigs ate, but no one gave him anything (the Tanzanians' focus).

Each is correct in its own way and the emphasis of each group is grounded in the history, culture, and personal experiences of the persons reading and interpreting the text. Culture matters. Experience and context matter. None of us live outside of our contextual influences, yet we are often completely unaware of what surrounds us. C. S. Lewis, in his *Reflections on the Psalms*, says,

> Between different ages there is no impartial judge on earth for no one stands outside the historical process; and of course no one is so completely enslaved to it as those who take our own age to be, not one more period, but a final and permanent platform from which we can see all other ages objectively. (1958, 121)

I would agree with Lewis, but take the idea a bit further to include culture and the process of socialization. And I am defining culture broadly in this sense to include cultures of ethnicity, race, age, and social class, as well as subcultures, such as academia and varieties of Christianity. In the words of Barbara Rogoff (2003),

> Culture isn't just what *other* people do . . . . The most difficult cultural processes to examine are the ones that are based on confident and unquestioned assumptions stemming from one's own community's practices. Cultural processes surround all of us and often involve subtle, tacit, taken-for-granted events and ways of doing things that require open eyes, ears, and minds to notice and understand. (368)

We who work in the church and in academia are not exempt from these influences that color our perceptions, readings of texts, and interpretations. The primacy of Western academia is being challenged by voices from other places and perspectives. What has typically been regarded as theology for the church universal, "has been, in many respects, Western theology" (Greenman & Green, 2012, 11). And what has been taken as foundational in child development research has been, in many respects, represented a Western childhood. And the study of childhood spirituality follows a similar pattern, including a heavy reliance on stage theorists, such as Piaget. Cross-cultural research suggests that children's everyday experiences mitigate emergence of capacities, particularly in more advanced stages of development (Gardiner & Kosmitzki, 2011). In other words, even if the order of stages is consistent, children across the world do not necessarily perform cognitive tasks in the predicted way or at the predicted time. The cross-cultural findings suggest that theories, such as Piaget's require further exploration in order to accommodate the influence of culture. And if children's spiritual development has been formed on Western childhoods, Western children, and theories rooted in Western experiences and values, we should hold those foundations and their applications circumspectly.

DEFINITIONS OF CHILDHOOD AND CHILDREN-AT-RISK

Before delving into the spirituality of children-at-risk, childhood and children-at-risk need to be defined and explored. The Oxford English Dictionary defines a *child* as "a young human being below the age of puberty or below the legal age of majority" and the United Nations Convention on the Rights of the Child (1989) defines a *child* as "a human being below the age of 18 years unless under the law applicable to the child, majority is attained earlier." Inherent in both definitions is a movable boundary in that the end of childhood is defined by the legal context in which that child lives. Child sociologists recognize that childhood is a socially constructed period and that for children, it is a temporary one; yet, for society, it is a structural category of that society (Cosaro, 2005). "For society . . . . [childhood] never disappears even though its members change continuously and its nature and conception vary historically" (Cosaro, 2005, 3). It is not only history that alters the conceptualization of childhood; cultural context is critical for understanding the world and definition of the child. Because of this variation due to history and context, *childhoods*, in the plural, is a better term for labeling children's experiences of childhood. Childhood trends indicate that childhoods experiences may be increasingly divergent based upon social class, access to resources and cultural understanding of the role of children.

A common descriptor for divergent childhood experiences is 'at-risk,' a term that is rarely and inconsistently defined, yet carries an inherent understanding for most persons. When asked to define children-at-risk, many succumb to the temptation to list categories, such as street child, child sex worker, child suffering due to HIV/AIDS, orphaned child, unaccompanied child, traumatized child, starving child, child soldier, child laborer, and the list goes on. Others argue that all children have risk and resilience factors and that stigmatizing labels are not helpful for setting definitions. As Moore (2006) asks, "Who is at risk? Is it the child or adolescent? Is it the family? Or is it the community?" (1). The level of analysis can be important in determining at-risk status.

However convoluted the conversation, in the global children-at-risk world (and because the purpose of this chapter is to focus on the global experiences of children-at-risk), there is a unifying factor in the lives of the children we serve with and for— extreme poverty, which is commonly understood as living on less than $1–2 per day. Children living in extreme poverty are far more likely to experience any of the labeling situations listed above, as well as experience additive stressors that impact risk status, such as poor health, domestic violence, abuse, addictions, social isolation, etc. (Greener, 2004). The childhoods experienced by children living in extreme poverty and those living with adequate resources would be understandably different. Yet, some children not only survive but thrive in difficult circumstances. And, even less extreme groups experience different childhoods based upon social class distinctions, ethnicity, and cultural contexts. The questions we must ask ourselves, are these: Is the childhood of the West best? And, should it be considered normative and the gold standard by which other childhoods should be assessed?

I have witnessed the strength and resilience of children in especially difficult circumstances around the world. For the first and only time in my professional development work, I was escorted under armed guard through Mathare Valley, a densely populated slum area of Nairobi, where poverty, crime, and disease are rampant. I recall riding past a stone structure about ten by twelve feet and about four feet high. It had a sign on it declaring it to be a hotel and "Under New Management." And I thought to myself, that despite my education, my global exposure, and my seeming resilience to difficult circumstances of my own upbringing, that I would not last a day in this place. I would not have any notion how to obtain food, safe shelter or clean drinking water. I would be helpless. Yet children in Mathare Valley live in homes with their families, attending school and church, perhaps working in the market or in other entrepreneurial enterprises. And they daily navigate a world that would stymie many persons, especially children that we see as competent, mature, developed, and intelligent.

Societies have long held to differing views of children and childhood which are reflected in Christian theology and also in the social sciences. One of the more colorful taxonomies is in the area of childhood anthropology, where Lancy (2008) alliterates concepts of children as "cherubs, chattel, and changelings," noting how societies often simultaneously see children as innocents, little devils, and commodities that either contribute to or drain financial resources of families. Similarly, people hold different views about the childhoods of children-at-risk.

Perhaps you have a photo of a child-at-risk on your refrigerator at home, a sponsored child who is in need of your assistance to meet basic needs. Needy children are often perceived through negative definitions: as victims or objects of pity, as social problems to be solved, and as humans not only needing protection but from whom we need protection. Children-at-risk have been seen as victims, sentimentalized as the noble poor as in Dickens' portrayals of Little Dorritt and Little Nell, children who are good and grateful and wise beyond their years. Each of these views has elements of truth, yet oversimplifies the lives of the children themselves, overlooking their full humanity and complexity. Vestiges of this sentimentality are heard when people are asked about what they learn from short-term missions visits to impoverished countries A frequent response notes that visitors see the smiling faces of children and conclude, not that they may be nervous or polite in the presence of visitors, but that despite lacking material goods, the poor have great joy and deep faith (Powell, Linhart, Livermore, & Griffin, 2011).

Other well-meaning responses to the issues facing children-at-risk are simplistic and unhelpful. I cannot count the number of persons who have expressed a desire to start an orphanage or work in an orphanage or who want to work with trafficked children. When I raise issues about keeping children with families or at least family-like settings or when I focus on prevention programs that address family poverty that leads to the trafficking of children, responses are often less than enthusiastic. Unfortunately, prevention ministries do not have the same prestige; some work with children-at-risk just seems more spectacular or personally gratifying or perhaps, altruistic, even if the assumptions behind the desire are not in the best interest of children.

OVERSIMPLIFICATION OF CHILDREN-AT-RISK: STREET CHILDREN AS AN EXAMPLE

When the child-at-risk is seen as a problem to be solved, the label can become over-simplified and misunderstood when culturally-bound assumptions drive definitions and interpretation. A case in point is the label of 'street child,' a categorization that initially was based on beliefs that street children were either orphans or forced from their homes involuntarily by their families. In 1987 UNICEF classified street children by two criteria: the amount of time spent on the streets and the lack of contact with responsible adults (Aptekar, 2004), criteria which ignored the perceptions of the street children themselves and how their childhood experience fit within the local cultural context. Most street children were seen as either objects of pity, whose childhood had been stolen from them or delinquents requiring punishment—in other words, a social problem to be solved.

As research in this area developed, a more complex view of street children emerged: the vast majority of street children in developing nations are boys; ninety percent of children kept contact with their families; they left their homes with delib-eration and as a positive coping mechanism; their families needed them to move into adult roles earlier than the accepted norm to allow for economic survival (Aptekar, 2004). Their leaving home was often perceived by the children and their families as a positive step for coping with economic realities and family need. In general, street children in developing nations do not see themselves as victims and the vast majority is neither pathological nor delinquent. Although it is beyond the scope of our discus-sion, it is important to note that the characteristics and circumstances of street chil-dren in the United States are quite different from their counterparts in the developing world. We need to be careful not to over-generalize.

In Rachel Burr's qualitative study of street children in Vietnam (2006), non-governmental organizations dedicated to children's rights and well-being perceived the children either as social evils or children whose childhood had been stolen from them. Burr saw them as "tenacious, highly adaptable, and hardworking" (207), yet their childhoods did not conform to acceptable definitions of childhood, which were often set by Westerners. The children saw themselves as connected to their families, contributing to the local economy and their family's economic survival; they desired and when possible engaged in education; they perceived themselves as entrepreneur-ial, and self-sufficient.

Research on street children isn't easy to conduct and biases concerning child-hood can lead to over-romanticizing children and exaggerating their resilience or over-dramatizing them, leading to worst-case scenario descriptions, which focus on the youngest children or the most delinquent or the most pathological (Aptekar, 2004). Aptekar acknowledges that as a researcher, he was often quick to judge programs for street children based upon his understanding of a proper childhood and proper program and that various programs working with street children were equally likely to judge one another's effectiveness or appropriateness in negative terms. Yet, there were far more children in need of support than program resources for supporting them, indicating a need for networking and collaboration rather than undermining the reputation or efficacy of various program models.

RESILIENCE AND SPIRITUALITY OF CHILDREN-AT-RISK

The idea of developing complex views of children is not a new one. Theologian Marcia Bunge has been an important voice in the disciplines of child theology and child spirituality arguing for complex views and theologies of childhood. In her analysis (2006), views of children need to be held in tension, as children can be seen as: gifts of God and sources of joy; sinful creatures and moral agents; developing beings who need instruction and guidance; fully human and made in the image of God; models of faith and sources of revelation; and orphans, neighbors, and strangers in need of justice and compassion. Although it is tempting to place children-at-risk exclusively in this latter category, they, too, are deserving of conceptualization that allows them to be represented in all other theological categories offered by Bunge.

Although there is a dearth of research on or from the perspective of children-at-risk in areas of spirituality, there is research suggestive of impact of environmental factors and experience on children's spirituality drawn from literatures on coping and resilience. Werner and Smith's (1992) longitudinal work on at-risk children identified spirituality across faiths and denominations as an important protective factor associated with resilience. Likewise, Robert Coles's groundbreaking qualitative study of the spiritual life of children (1990) built upon his work on children of crisis in the United States by expanding research to include children of various faiths around the world. This culminating work was partly inspired by Coles's early work trying to understand the spiritual coping responses of children and families walking through the trials and strains of school desegregation in the American South. The seeming well-being of children like Ruby Bridges stimulated questions about resilience and the role of spirituality in coping with stress. And it seems that stress is not necessarily bad and that some stress may be needed to stimulate growth.

The Chinese symbol for stress communicates the combination of crisis and opportunity (Gardiner & Kosmitzki, 206, 247) and it has been noted that some degree of stress is necessary for humans to be challenged to grow and mature. One area of research demonstrating the impact of stress on the development of children's coping skills is found in chronic health issues. They [children] grow not despite the illness but because of it. Hampell and colleagues (2006) showed that children and adolescents with chronic health conditions coped with everyday stressors (e.g., tension with family or friends, school-related issues) "better than their healthy counterparts" (Gardiner & Kosmitzki, 2006, 246). And although the research on health and spiritual coping in children is sparse, it is suggestive that children's response to health stressors can take the form of spiritual/religious coping (Pendleton, Cavalli, Pargament, & Nasr, 2002). A key component to how stress and trauma is experienced is mitigated by the child's perception of events (Aptekar, 2004), which is heavily influenced by cultural understanding of what is normal for life in a specific context.

Aptekar (2004) illustrates his point through research with displaced Ethiopian adolescents, who had witnessed atrocities and lacked basics, such as water and food. Yet, those with strong spiritual beliefs and who were actively religious did not exhibit the psychopathology associated with trauma. The lack of psychopathology was partially attributed to the children's perceptions that they were not as badly off as their parents had been. He also notes research on Eritrean orphans traumatized by war and famine, whose well-being was grounded in an intervention that allowed for an earlier end to adolescence and the adoption of adult roles so that they could care for others who were suffering in their midst and thereby help themselves. "Adolescent caregivers, in caring for and coming to terms with the grim reality of their loved ones, actually found they were also maturing and finding their own meaning in life" (387).

Similarly, the making of meaning was noted as an important part of resilience and spirituality in youth who had experienced traumatic events (Crawford, Wright, & Masten, 2006). For youth who had experienced a single traumatic event, religious beliefs became weaker or stronger; yet, experiencing multiple traumatic events led to stronger religious beliefs, although more research needs to be done to better understand this finding. Certainly, one could argue that children-at-risk are likely to fall into the category of experiencing multiple traumatic events.

THE CHALLENGES OF A WESTERN CHILDHOOD

So, why are Westerners so quick to see children to be at-risk when their childhoods differ from what is acceptable and known? How are Western notions of childhood being understood globally? Research suggests that middle-class childhoods are becoming more similar around the world and that these class distinctions and access to resources are important factors in determining the types of childhoods children experience (Verma & Sta. Maria, 2006). In addition to the emergence of a worldwide materialistic youth culture, exposure to a globalized range of spiritual beliefs and practices may create confusion and tendency to focus on an individualized spirituality (ibid.). It is almost as if more privileged children are paralyzed by their options.

Certainly, privileged childhoods are not without their shortcomings. A critical difference seen between social classes is the compression of the time allocated to childhood and adolescence in impoverished settings where children are required to take on adult roles and responsibilities earlier than their middle class counterparts to contribute to the survival and well-being of their families. With the middle class, the number of years devoted to adolescence has expanded and some suggest the need for a new developmental category described as 'emerging adulthood' (Henig, 2010). Research on emerging adulthood suggests that persons in their 20s in privileged environments are engaging in extended identity exploration, instability, and self-focus and exhibiting delayed maturity, marriage and financial self-support (ibid.). Some more concerning trends for middle class families include:

> . . . greater investment of financial resources, time, and emotional energy in children by many parents . . . with more monitoring and 'oversupervision' of children . . . . [and] increased pressure on adolescents' school performance. Fewer siblings and cousins mean fewer opportunities to acquire spiritual concepts and skills through these relationships, including empathy and spiritual nurturance. In addition, family mobility, dissolution, and reconstitution may impair spiritual socialization. (Verma and Sta. Maria, 2006, 127)

Parents seem to be experiencing similar overload due to exposure to a vast array of parenting choices, leading to strongly expressed opinions for justification of one's parenting style and the anxious desire to be a 'perfect' parent and to protect our children from failure or poor decisions that might forever damage her prospects for material and personal success. Fear for our children's well-being has contributed to: over-supervision so that children's lives are over-scheduled and removed from extended family and community; over-engagement in children as sources of parental fulfillment and affirmation of our success as parents; and removal of stressors from children's experiences, perhaps to the detriment of growth, coping, and maturation. As noted by U.S. psychologist, Madeline Levine, in her book, *The Price of Privilege* (2008), "A child cannot possibly develop resilience when his parents are constantly at his side, interfering with the development of autonomy, self-management, and coping skills" (Levine, 77). As a former dean of students in higher education, I can personally attest to the intrusion of parents in the lives of their children, even when those children are graduate students and well into their twenties.

In Lareau's landmark longitudinal study of American poor, working class, and middle class families (2011), children of poor and working class families saw their children as adults when they had reached the age of majority while middle class twenty-somethings remained heavily dependent on their parents and were treated as children by them. Moreover, the middle class children were unaware of their place of privilege and the advantages that their class had bestowed upon them. Instead, they saw their accomplishments as strictly due to their own gifts and merit.

> The benefits that accrue to middle-class children can be significant, but they are often invisible to them and to others. In popular language, middle-class

children can be said to have been 'born on third base but believe they hit a triple.' (Lareau, 2011, 13)

Once again, the skin of cultural context is too close for personal awareness.

In contrast, the children of poorer families were very aware of the differences in opportunity due to social class. "In a society less dominated by individualism than the United States, with more of an emphasis on the group, the sense of constraint displayed by working-class and poor children might be interpreted as healthy and appropriate. But in this [U.S.] society, the strategies of the working-class and poor families are generally denigrated and seen as unhelpful or even harmful to children's life chances" (13). In other words, both the parenting and the childhood experiences of the working class and poor fail to meet the societal standards for a "good" childhood.

I am in no way arguing that there are no benefits to a middle class childhood. Obviously, having access to resources allows children benefits, such as education, health care, adequate food, and exposure to extra-curricular activities, to name but a few. But, we must remain open to the idea that each type of childhood has advantages and disadvantages and that there is no perfect environment or method or parenting style or society for creating the perfect childhood experience. Removing our cultural blinders allows us to be sensitive to what the research does and does not say and how our myopic view of our own cultural experiences creates positive bias for our own assumptions and negative bias for what we do not fully know or understand. It is also a much-needed reminder that brokenness and sin are always present in every culture, social class, context, and point of history.

THE IMPORTANCE OF BROADENED CONCEPTUALIZATIONS OF CHILDHOOD

You might be thinking that the discussion of the challenges of Western childhood is far more interesting and applicable to you than the worlds of at-risk children. For the persons working in a mono-cultural suburb or a small town, it may seem more important to focus on research done on and for Western children. After all, that is the population many of us minister to and care for, at least for now. But important demographic shifts are taking place around the world and within the United States.

Philip Jenkins heralded the shift of Christianity in population and power to the Global South and East (2007). And building upon the theme of Christian demographic and geographical shifts, Soong Chan-Rah (2009) reminds us that by "2050, African, Asian and Latin American Christians will constitute 71 percent of the world's Christian population," and "the majority of American Christians will be nonwhite" (US Census, 13–14). As of May, 2012, more than one-half of all births are non-white, according to the U.S. Census. Much of this cultural change is due to immigration. At time, voices have raised concerns about the demise of Christianity in the United States, fearing that the influx of people from many cultures is shifting religious practice.

What has been feared as the de-Christianization of American society is actually a demographic shift toward the de-Europeanization of American Christianity. Immigration is creating significant diversity within the American church (Warner, 2004). When combined with the trend of increasing poverty rates in metro suburban areas from 2000–2008, particularly in the Midwest (Brookings Institute, 2010), encountering diverse childhood experiences is likely even for the most historically homogenous churches. Churches must be adaptable and sensitive to changes in childhood experiences and spiritual nurture of these children who are increasingly in our midst.

It is also important to heed the encouragement of other scholars who have noted the need for the church to learn from Christians around the world. Specifically, scholars have suggested the need for global theologies regarding children (Childhood Studies of Religion, 2013); better developed theologies of suffering (Crawford, Wright, & Masten, 2006) and might I add, particularly the suffering of children; further research on ways of spiritual coping in diverse and difficult circumstances (Mahoney Pendleton, & Ihrke, 2006); and research on culturally diverse views of children's competencies. Knowledge and wisdom from deeper exploration of these issues may be helpful in addressing our own cultural issues regarding children's spiritual nurture and may provide fresh insights and an infusion of thought into child theology, development theory, and the practice of spiritual nurture.

RECOMMENDATIONS FOR INCORPORATING CHILDREN-AT-RISK INTO RESEARCH AND NURTURE OF CHILDREN'S SPIRITUALITY

We might feel paralyzed by our cultural embeddedness and its impact on our awareness, attention, understanding and interpretation of our world. So, how to move forward in the face of such complexity and so many possible variations of human experience? Before proceeding, it is right to express gratitude for people who have laid foundations for future research, including the Children's Spirituality Conference, the Child Theology Movement, and the VIVA Network for Children-at-Risk, all of whom have expanded our networks and understanding through their dedicated efforts. Our conversation today is grounded in their work and service. May I offer some suggestions for response?

1. As practitioners and scholars, let us use child development research carefully to suggest and compare, but not to dictate theory and praxis.

2. Let us commit to educating others about the complexity of children and childhoods and not allow stereotypes and shallow understanding to drive interventions and agendas. This includes being careful as donors not to use Western conceptualizations of childhood to evaluate which programs to support or how they

should be implemented without listening to those from the local context. Once we embrace complex understanding, we have a responsibility to become advocates for all children.

3. Stonehouse and May (2010) have encouraged the act of listening to children on the spiritual journey. Let us expand our listening to include all kinds of children in all kinds of places. I would especially request that research on children's spirituality include Christian children in especially difficult circumstances.

4. Let us be more self-aware of how our own experiences, context, and culture frame our understanding. As Jesus prays for the church in John 17, he reinforces the tension of being not of the world, yet in the world. In this way, the church is counter-cultural, in the world, yet testing that world against scripture. A question consistently comes to mind as we navigate issues of cultures and faith, whatever the culture may be: "What is culture and what is Christian?"

5. May we embrace and heed the voices of global theology and biblical interpretation. Approaching scripture with humility, curiosity, self-awareness, and open-mindedness to a critical posture toward our own cultural milieu creates space for the Holy Spirit to work in us and through us.

CONCLUSION

Let me close with a passage from Genesis 21. The reading follows Abraham's decision to heed Sarah's complaint and to send Hagar and Ishmael away from home and into the wilderness.

> Abraham got up early the next morning, got some food together and a canteen of water for Hagar, put them on her back and sent her away with the child. She wandered off into the desert of Beersheba. When the water was gone, she left the child under a shrub and went off, fifty yards or so. She said, "I can't watch my son die." As she sat, she broke into sobs. Meanwhile, *God heard the boy crying.* The angel of God called from Heaven to Hagar, "What's wrong, Hagar? Don't be afraid. God has heard the boy and knows the fix he's in. Up now; go get the boy. Hold him tight. I'm going to make of him a great nation." Just then God opened her eyes. She looked. She saw a well of water. She went to it and filled her canteen and gave the boy a long, cool drink. [And] *God was on the boy's side as he grew up.* (Peterson, 2005, Genesis 21:14–20) [Emphasis is my own.]

God hears the cries of the Ishmaels. And He also cares for the Isaacs, who have their own set of troubles. There is plenty of work for us to do and there are plenty of ways to nurture children's spirituality and address holistic development issues that face children-at-risk. We will always be working in ambiguous places, relying on what we currently know and believe to be true, yet aware that much remains to be explored.

When approached with humility and increased self-awareness of the biases inherent in the cultural skin that we each carry, the Holy Spirit can use our service, offered in love, for the transformation of children and childhoods.

REFERENCES

Aptekar, Lewis. "The Changing Developmental Dynamics of Children in Particularly Difficult Circumstances: Examples of Street and War-Traumatized Children." In *Childhood and Adolescence: Cross-cultural Perspectives and Applications,* edited by Uwe P. Gielen and Jaipaul Roopnarine, 337–410. Westport, CT: Praeger Publishers, 2004.

Brookings Institute. *The Suburbanization of Poverty: Trends in Metropolitan America* 2000–2008. Accessed May 20, 2012. http://www.brookings.edu/research/papers/2010/01/20-poverty-kneebone, 2010.

Bunge, Marcia. "The Dignity and Complexity of Children: Constructing Christian Theologies of Childhood." In *Nurturing Child and Adolescent Spirituality: Perspectives from the World's Religious Tradition,* edited by Karen-Marie Yust, Aostre N. Johnson, Sandy E. Sasso, and Eugene C. Roehlkepartain, 53–68. Lanham, MD, US: Rowman & Littlefield Publishers, Inc, 2006.

Burr, Rachel. *Vietnam's Children in a Changing World.* New Brunswick, NJ: Rutgers University Press, 2006.

Childhood Studies and Religion Group of the American Academy of Religion. *Future Goals.* Accessed on August 13, 2013. http://childhoodreligion.com/about.html,

Coles, Robert. *The Spiritual Life of Children.* Boston: Houghton Mifflin Company, 1990.

Convention on the Rights of the Child. Accessed on May 20, 2012. http://www2.ohchr.org/english/law/crc.htm, 1989.

Corsaro, William. *The Sociology of Childhood,* 2nd ed. Thousand Oaks, CA: Sage Publications, Inc., 2005.

Crawford, Emily, Margaret O. Wright, and Ann S. Masten. Resilience and Spirituality in Youth. In *The Handbook of Spiritual Development in Childhood and Adolescence,* edited by Eugene C. Roehlkepartain, Pamela E. King, Linda Wagener, & Peter L. Benson, 355–370. Thousand Oaks, CA: Sage Publications, 2006.

Gardiner, Harry and Corinne Kosmitzki. *Lives Across Cultures: Cross-Cultural Human Development.* Boston, MA: Allyn & Bacon, 2011.

Greener, Susan Hayes. "The Effects of the Failure to Meet Children's Needs. In *Celebrating Children: Equipping People Who Work with Children and Young People Working in Especially Difficult Circumstances Around the World,* edited by Glenn Miles and Josephine Joy Wright, 130–136. United Kingdom: Paternoster Press, 2004.

Greenman, Jeffrey P. "Learning and Teaching Global Theologies." In *Global Theologies: Exploring the Contextual Nature of Theology and Mission in Evangelical Perspective,* edited by Jeffrey P. Greenman & Gene L. Green, 237–252. Downers Grove, IL: IVP Books, 2012.

Hampel, Petra and Franz Petermann. "Perceived Stress, Coping, and Adjustment in Adolescents.' *Journal of Adolescent Health* 38 (2006): 409–415.

Henig, Robin Marantz. (2010). "What Is It About 20- Somethings?" *New York Times.* Accessed May 20, 2012. http://www.nytimes.com/2010/08/22/magazine/22Adulthood-t.html?pagewanted=all.

Jenkins, Philip. *The Next Christendom.* Oxford, UK: Oxford University Press, 2007.

Johnson, Todd M. *Christianity in Global Context: Trends and Statistics.* Prepared for Pew Forum on Religion and Public Life. Accessed May 25, 2012. http://www.pewforum/org/events/051805/global-christianity.pdf.

Jones, Phil. *Rethinking Childhood: Attitudes in Contemporary* Society. London: Continuum, 2009.

Labberton, Mark. "Some Implications of Global Theology for Church, Ministry and Mission." In *Global Theologies: Exploring the Contextual Nature of Theology and Mission in Evangelical Perspective* edited by Jeffrey P. Greenman & Gene L. Green, 225–236. Downers Grove, IL: IVP Books, 2012.

Lancy, David. *The Anthropology of Childhood: Cherubs, Chattel, Changelings.* Cambridge, UK: Cambridge University Press, 2008.

Lareau, Annette. *Unequal Childhoods: Class, Race, and Family Life,* 2nd ed. Berkeley, CA: University of California Press, 2011.

Levine, M. *The Price of Privilege: How Parental Pressure and Material Advantage Are Creating a Generation of Disconnected and Unhappy Kids.* New York: Harper, 2006.

Lewis, C.S. *Reflections on the Psalms.* London: Geoffrey Bles, Ltd., 1958.

Mahoney, A., Pendleton, S., & Ihrke, H. Religious Coping by Children and Adolescents: Unexplored Territory in the Realm of Spiritual Development. In *The Handbook of Spiritual Development in Childhood and Adolescence* edited by Eugene C. Roehlkepartain, Pamela E. King, Linda Wagener, & Peter L. Benson, 341–355. Thousand Oaks, CA: Sage Publications, 2006.

Mercer, Joyce A. "Spiritual Economics of Childhood: Christian Perspectives on Global Market Forces and Young People's Spirituality." In *Nurturing Child and Adolescent Spirituality: Perspectives from the World's Religious Traditions,* edited by Karen-Marie Yust, Aostre N. Johnson, Sandy E. Sasso, and Eugene C. Roehlkepartain, 458–471. Lanham, MD: Rowman & Littlefield Publishers, Inc., 2006.

Moore, K.A. "Defining the Term At-Risk." *Child Trends: Research to Results Brief.* Accessed May 25, 2012. http://www.childtrends.org/Files/DefiningAtRisk%5B1%5D.pdf. Publication 2006-12.

Nisbett, Richard, and Yuri Miyamoto. "The Influence of Culture: Holistic Versus Analytic Perception." *Trends in Cognitive Sciences* 9 (2005): 467–473.

Oxford English Dictionary. http://www.oxforddictionary.com.

Pendleton, S. M., K. S. Cavalli, K. I. Pargament, and S. Z. Nasr. "Religious/Spiritual Coping in Childhood Cystic Fibrosis: A Qualitative Study." *Pediatrics* 109, PMID: 11773576, 2H002.

Peterson, Eugene. *The Message: The Bible in Contemporary Language.* Colorado Springs, CO: Nav Press, 2005.

Powell, Kara, Terry Linhart, Dave Livermore, and Brad Griffin. "If We Send Them, They Will Grow . . . Maybe." *The Journal of Student Ministries* 3 (2011):1–5. Accessed May 29, 2012. http://davidlivermore.com/wp-content/uploads/2011/03/If-we-send-them.pdf.

Powell, Mark. *What Do They Hear?* Nashville, TN: Abingdon Press, 2007.

Prout, Alan. *The Future of Childhood: Towards the Interdisciplinary Study of Children.* London: Routledge, 2005.

Rah, Soong Chan. *The Next Evangelicalism: Freeing the Church from Western Cultural Captivity.* Downers Grove, IL, US: IVP Books, 2009.

Rogoff, Barbara. *The Cultural Nature of Human Development.* Oxford, UK: Oxford University Press, 2003.

Stonehouse, Catherine and Scottie May. *Listening to Children on the Spiritual Journey: Guidance for Those Who Teach and Nurture.* Grand Rapids, MI: Baker Academic, 2010.

U.S. Census. "An Older and More Diverse Nation by Midcentury," August 14, 2008. http//:www.census.gov/Press-Release/www/releases/archives/population/012496.html.

Verma, Suman and Madelene. Sta. Maria. "The Changing Global Context of Adolescent Spirituality." In *The Handbook of Spiritual Development in Childhood and Adolescence,* eds. Eugene C. Roehlkepartain, Pamela Ebstyne King, Linda Wagener, and Peter L. Benson, 124–136. Thousand Oaks, CA: Sage Publications, 2006.

Warner, R. Stephen. "Coming to America: Immigrants and the Faith They Bring." *Christian Century* 10 (2004): 20–23.

Chapter 23

Courageously Confronting the Dark Reality of Child Porn

Jennifer Beste

> The comprehensive task of a Christian . . . is the acceptance of human existence
> as such as opposed to a final protest against it. But this means that a Christian
> sees reality as it is. Christianity obliges him or her to see this existence as dark
> and bitter and hard, and as an unfathomable and radical risk. (Rahner, 1978,
> 403)

According to Karl Rahner, one of the twentieth century's most influential Christian theologians, faith and divine grace enable Christians to confront reality as it truly is— even its most evil dimensions—and to respond with love. Particularly in the context of this chapter's topic, Rahner's sober reference to a fallen world is apt: opening myself to the radical suffering of child porn victims, seeking to fathom the global reality of porn producers grooming children in order to record and disseminate child sexual abuse (CSA) images, and considering the expanding market of porn users who masturbate to these images, I frequently wanted to flee from the task of writing this chapter.

To some degree, this chapter does in fact flee, for my synopsis of child porn still does not capture adequately the dimensions of evil apparent in all that I have read about the sadistic content on child pornography websites, the rationalizations of child porn producers and consumers, and the ways in which child victims' very selves are deeply harmed and lives are often destroyed. To readers who likewise share an impulse in these pages to speed past the "digital crime scenes" of child sexual abuse (Olfmann, 2008), I would suggest the opposite. The stakes remain too high, and if Christians are indeed graced with the ability to be the body of Christ and transform our world, then fight—not flight—is what the moment calls for.

As for limitations of this chapter, space constraints do not permit a full account of the global child pornography industry and forms of child sexual exploitation such as child sex trafficking and prostitution. As a backdrop for exploring the physiological, psychological, and spiritual impact of child porn on abuse survivors, I begin more simply with a brief overview of the child pornography industry. Next, I consider the question of the presence of God's grace in the context of child sexual abuse, and in conclusion I advance ways that Christian communities can mediate God's grace, foster healing for child sexual abuse survivors, and prevent future child porn.

CHILD PORNOGRAPHY INDUSTRY: A BRIEF SKETCH

In order to understand child pornography, it is important to situate the phenomenon within the wider pornography industry. As of 2006, the porn industry was already worth approximately thirteen billion dollars in the U.S. and ninety-six billion globally. Currently, images of pornified bodies and porn's underlying narrative of sexuality and relationships pervade U.S. media and culture. As of 2009, there were 420 million internet porn pages, 4.2 million porn sites, and sixty-nine million search engine requests daily (Dines, 2010). The porn industry has become a normalized, mainstream business that increases profit for (and thus acceptance and legitimization by) industries and corporations such as credit card, real estate, and PR companies, hotel chains, DirecTV and cable television, the banking industry, Microsoft, etc.

Strong consensus exists among researchers that contemporary porn has become increasingly violent and more misogynistic (Dines, 2010; Jensen, 2007; Paul, 2006). Gonzo—now just a free internet click away—is the fastest growing type of hard core porn, featuring men committing violent, body-punishing and sadistic sexual acts that are, by design, painful and demeaning to women (Dines, 2010). Within the industry, child pornography is the last market to be exploited and has rapidly expanded since 2002 when the Supreme Court ruled in Ashcroft vs. Free Speech Coalition that the 1996 Child Porn Prevention Act was unconstitutional. When, according to the Court, the Act's definition of child porn (any visual depiction that appears to be of a minor engaging in sexually explicit conduct) was deemed too broad, doors opened for the porn industry to legally depict females eighteen and over as girls and to use utilize computer-generated imagery to create an entire pseudo-child porn (PCP) industry.

Typing the search term "teen porn" currently yields over nine million hits (Dines, 2010). Users now can legally masturbate to images of girls being penetrated by any number of men masquerading as fathers, teachers, employers, coaches, child molesters, or fathers who hire babysitters. Users watch online as sweet, cute, innocent girls are coaxed, encouraged, and manipulated by adult men into revealing the whore that lies beneath. A major theme on sites like the one entitled "Bloody Virgins" entails girls' loss of virginity to older men: "[In gonzo teen porn] constant mention is made of the teen's small vagina and anus," the goal of which is not so much to stress her "innocence" as to highlight "the damage that will be done to her body when she is penetrated by an adult male's penis" (ibid.).

As for the types of child porn displayed most frequently, the majority of PCP sites feature sexual activity between children or solo masturbation by a child, penetrative sexual activity between adult(s) and child(ren), and sadism. While the user is watching physical, sexual, and verbal abuse of "girls," the females on the screen appear as though they desire the pain and abuse and find it pleasurable. Pseudo-child porn sites frequently serve as gateway sites for men who have sexual interest in actual children, for the user on these sites is bombarded with a consistent ideology that legitimizes and celebrates sexual desire for children. Any man can enter a virtual community that welcomes him where sadistic sex with children is "hot fun" for both men and children.

Given the desensitization that occurs with porn use, the tendency to desire more extreme porn, and thrill of ongoing sexual arousal, many PCP users begin to seek actual child pornography. The illegality and secrecy of masturbating to "real" children leads to greater erotic thrill and thus increased demand for child porn sites and images. In regard specifically to child porn film content, child and adolescent victims are subjected to sadistic sexual abuse, perversions, rape, torture, and even murder (Flowers, 2001). Moreover, it is not only pedophiles who utilize these sites; a significant percentage of heterosexual men turn to child pornography after violent gonzo porn with adult women no longer arouses them (Trueman, 2013; Dines, 2010). Psychologist David Heffler, who has counseled such men, states: "After looking at adult porn for a long time, they get bored. They want something different. They start looking at children. Then, they can't get enough of it" (Dines, 2010, 160).

In regard to child pornography in the U.S., law enforcement had nearly eliminated the distribution of child pornography via U.S. mail from the early 1980's until 1996. With the dawn of the Internet, however, the volume of images shared between porn users proliferated exponentially (Hughes, 2001). Presently, more than 20,000 child sexual abuse images are posted on line each week. The FBI's Child Victim Identification Program (CVIP) corroborates a significant increase of child porn files. For instance, in 2005 the CVIP reviewed 1,982,486 child pornography files (images and videos); by 2010 that number had become 13,673,167, a 590 percent increase (National Center for Missing and Exploited Children (NCMEC), 2010). Astonishingly, by 2012, NCMEC analysts received law enforcement requests to review more than 19 million child pornography images and videos (National Center for Missing and Exploited Children, 2012). Such increase in demand for child porn images and films obviously results in an increased prevalence of child porn victims globally.

Furthermore, there is substantial research evidence of a strong correlation between masturbation to images of sexualized children and actual child sexual abuse (Bourke and Hernandaz, 2009; Dines, 2010; Kim, 2004; Westenberg, 2013). According to a 2002 FBI congressional statement, "The correlation between collection of child pornography and actual child abuse is too real and too grave to ignore" (Heimbach,

2002). Illustrating this perfectly is the study by Bourke and Hernandaz (2009) of 115 child porn offenders who had no known histories of sexual offense and who voluntarily participated in an eighteen-month intensive treatment program in a federal prison. Eighty-five percent admitted to sexually abusing children and had an average of nearly nine victims. Of the twenty four who denied any child sexual abuse, nine were voluntarily polygraphed and only two passed. Both of these offenders said that, with access and opportunity, they would have been at risk for engaging in hands-on child sexual abuse. Likewise, other studies have found that up to 80 percent of individuals who viewed child pornography and 76 percent who were arrested for online child pornography had molested a child (Kim, 2004; Lanning, 2001).

As for the identities of child porn producers, many are parents, family members, or adult acquaintances who manipulate children into complying with their requests, digitally record acts of child sexual abuse, and silence their victims with threats. Others are child sexual perpetrators who meet children and teens via social media sites, where they develop trusting relationships. Particularly vulnerable targets are children suffering from maltreatment or prior abuse. Such children and teens will often post pictures or videos of themselves and eventually meet offenders who digitally record their acts of sexual abuse. Yet another feeder for child pornography is the global sex trafficking industry. Porn producers and child prostitution pimps are increasingly buying sexually trafficked children for the global child porn and prostitution industries (Lanning, 2010; Hodge and Lietz, 2007; Flowers, 2001). Exposing children to child and adult pornography is a primary strategy for grooming, desensitizing, and manipulating child pornography victims. Porn producers often threaten to show child porn victims' family members pictures of the victim engaging in sexual activities in order to shame them, keep them silent, and perpetuate further child pornography exploitation.

IMPACT OF CHILD PORNOGRAPHY EXPLOITATION ON VICTIM-SURVIVORS

Words simply fail to do justice to the personal devastation, not just in the wake of CSA, but also connected to the additional trauma of child porn exploitation (CPE) based on a victim's knowledge that permanent digital images and video of their abuse are being distributed anonymously on the Internet. In order to physically and psychically survive even CSA, child survivors experience two main defense mechanisms (Herman, 1992). The first, dissociation, refers to separating and splitting off elements of the traumatic experience—emotions, thoughts, sensation, location, time, and meaning—into shattered fragments that defy conscious integration. Second, victims engage in self-blame and take full responsibility for the abuse, concluding that there is something intrinsically bad about them that caused the abuse. This process of self-denigration and self-hatred occurs even in children who experience complete dissociation and retain no conscious memories of their abuse.

Furthermore, CSA survivors develop a host of post-traumatic stress disorder (PTSD) symptoms in response to the traumatic events. First, they continuously re-experience the traumatic event in the form of flashbacks, nightmares, intense bodily or emotional sensations, terrifying sensory perceptions, obsessional preoccupations, and behavioral reenactments. They alternate between experiencing extreme hyper-arousal (reacting to the slightest environmental stimuli as if everything represented potential danger) and emotional numbing (experiencing withdrawal and detachment from emotions and physical sensations). When emotional numbing does not occur naturally, children often resort to forms of autonomic arousal, which include self-mu-tilation, fasting, vomiting, compulsive sexual behavior, and compulsive risk-taking. Such autonomic arousal offers temporary relief from unbearably negative emotions. Lastly, CSA survivors experience an obsessive compulsion to reenact the sexual trau-ma by acting self-destructively, harming others, or becoming re-victimized. Obsessive re-enactment of the sexual trauma, which also includes highly sexualized and high-risk sexual behavior, is even more exacerbated in child porn survivors. A significant percentage of prostitutes and porn actresses reveal that they were child porn victims. Silbert and Pines found that 38 percent of their sample of 200 street prostitutes re-ported that they were child porn victims or were sexual abuse victims of a child porn photographer (Silbert and Pines, 1984).

As if the trauma of child sexual abuse were not enough to endure, the experience of actually having one's experiences of child sexual abuse photographed and filmed results in yet additional layers of traumatization (Klain et al., 2001): "Being photo-graphed while being sexually abused exacerbates the shame, humiliation, and pow-erlessness that sexual abuse victims typically experience," and in these cases "denial of the abuse becomes even more important . . . and is achieved at greater cost" (Hunt and Baird, 1990).

Studies indicate that child porn victims typically experience even higher degrees of dissociation, PTSD, depression, and psychoses than other child abuse victims (ibid.; Leonard, 2010; von Weiler, 2010). Child porn survivors' degrees of shame, humilia-tion, self-hatred, and self-blame are further intensified for many complex reasons. Chief among them are the following two: first, most perpetrators do not physically force children but engage in manipulative strategies to coerce children into smiling and laughing during the photography and filming of the sexual abuse. Survivors fear that this gives the mistaken impression to porn users and the wider public that they participated willingly and enjoyed the experience; second, children often are manipu-lated to engage in sexual activities with other children or even to recruit their friends to meet the perpetrators. Consequently, they experience profound guilt and self-blame for their role in harming others (von Weiler, 2010; Zillman and Bryant, 1989).

Understandably, the process of recovery from traumatization is even more complicated and filled with greater obstacles for CSA survivors who also struggle with CPE (Leonard, 2010; von Weiler, 2010). Trauma recovery literature has stressed the therapeutic value of assisting trauma survivors to construct a narrative that identifies a beginning and end to trauma, ideally a narrative firmly rooted in the past. The next stage, identifying and mourning the trauma's negative effects on one's life thus far, prepares a survivor to forge a new constructive sense of self by engaging the present, reconnecting with ordinary life, and forming healthy relationships. The difficulty with this, however, is that most CPE survivors, whose images and video of past sexual abuse are being circulated and distributed on the internet, cannot locate their abuse solely in the past. They experience continuous re-victimization since they know that offenders are masturbating to their images of abuse presently and forever. They also struggle with the likely prospect that their smiling images are being used to groom further child sexual abuse victims. As a result, porn child survivors experience intense degrees of helplessness and loss of control. Frequently, they withdraw, isolate themselves, and feel unsafe going out in public due to fear of being recognized by child porn offenders and not knowing it (von Weiler, 2010; Wortley and Smallbone, 2006; Martellozzo and Taylor, 2009).

Such post-traumatic stress disorder symptoms and additional negative effects from child pornography exploitation result in a severely fragmented sense of self and agency. Due to the betrayal of trust from adult perpetrators and their extreme self-hatred and worthlessness, adult CSA victims (including child porn victims) are desperate to find care, protection, and external validation of themselves. Simultaneously, they are deeply afraid of trusting anyone, of being abandoned, and of suffering further abuse. Understandably, these conflicting desires and the highly distorted model of sexuality they experienced make it very difficult to establish and maintain healthy intimate relationships (von Weiler, 2010; Wortley and Smallbone, 2006).

In regard to the effects of child sexual abuse on survivors' spirituality and perceived relationship with God, most research studies find that child sexual abuse negatively affects survivors' relationship with God: survivors tend to perceive God as more distant, judgmental, harsh and/or ashamed of them, and they are less likely to feel loved and accepted by God, to have a sense of trust in God, and to be involved in an organized religion (Kane et al., 1993; Manlowe, 1995; Lemoncelli and Carey, 1996). One study found that, although many sexual abuse survivors desire intimacy with God, "their perceived unworthiness prevents this from ever being experienced" (Hall, 1995). While some incest victims feel guilty about their abuse and pray to God to absolve them of their inherent badness, others experience a profound loss of trust and betrayal of a God who did nothing to stop the abuse. I could find no studies that explore the further effects of CPE on survivors' relationship with God. However, given that these survivors usually experience even more profound and negative PTSD symptoms and negative effects regarding their self-concept and perceived sense of agency than CSA survivors, it is reasonable to expect that CPE further damages CPE survivors' spirituality and relationship with God.

GOD'S GRACE IN THE PRESENCE OF TRAUMA AND SUFFERING

The extent of evil involved in the extreme suffering of CSA survivors challenges or "shakes up" our images of God, our understanding of God's relationship with humanity, and assumptions of divine power and love. In the midst of honestly confronting both the mystery of such evil and the mystery of the divine, I do not believe it is possible to resolve questions of theodicy. One might, however, reasonably hope for theological-ethical insights that help us bring neighbor love and the Gospels to life in real-life scenarios like the ones I have introduced. More modestly, then, I seek now to share important lessons from contemporary trauma studies on recovery and healing from diverse forms of trauma, including severe CSA (Beste, 2007).

Trauma research consistently demonstrates that supportive interpersonal relationships are necessary for recovery from traumatization. Studies demonstrate that the duration of trauma and communal response once it is exposed and stopped are two central factors affecting the level of traumatization and the degree to which one's sense of self and agency are debilitated. For instance, studies indicate that children who report incestuous abuse before it becomes chronic and receive therapy and support from their non-offending parents do not experience the same degree of traumatization as those children who lack support (Scheinberg and Grenkel, 2001). The presence or absence of supportive relationships and communities are thus crucial variables in recovering from traumatization.

From a theological and spiritual perspective, one might understand the essential role of interpersonal relationships in recovery and healing as a strong indicator that God mediates profound grace and healing precisely through these relationships. Rather than acting unilaterally and "magically" restoring victims to wholeness, it appears that God is continuously mediating divine love and healing grace though creation, and even depends upon the cooperation of persons to love their neighbor.

Such mediation of divine grace, however, can be substantially blocked by human agents who commit severe acts of interpersonal harm or avert their eyes to such evil and fail to reach out to stop abuses and support trauma victims. The effects of extreme interpersonal harm have the potential to incapacitate or perhaps even destroy a person's capacity to receive and respond to divine grace by loving one's self, God, and others (Beste, 2007). Given that recovery and healing depend on consistent, supportive relationships, it seems that God is continuously "whispering in our ear," urging us to respond empathetically to those most harmed and marginalized by interpersonal evil. In other words, God entrusts the human community with grave responsibility to be significant vehicles of God's mediating grace to one another, which in turn enables one another's freedom to affirm and love self, others, and God.

More research is still needed to determine exactly how, in their unique contexts, religious communities and civic organizations can most effectively support CPE survivors' recovery. Religious communities in particular remain insufficiently informed about the widespread problems of child sexual exploitation and its impact on victims, so education must become a top priority. Certainly many Christian communities could better recognize their potential as vehicles of God's grace by networking with trauma therapists to train members of their community to become CSA and CPE survivor advocates, and by connecting with spiritual companions equipped to accompany and support CPE survivors as they confront their physical, psychological, and spiritual losses.

In her work with CSA survivors, Mari Zimmerman expresses the invaluable impact such support has had on CSA survivors:

> We feel the warmth of God's love radiating from those who love us even when we cannot love ourselves. They show us the faithfulness of God when we pray. We are given hope by those who refuse to let us go even when we slide into the depths of despair. Places of safety become the holy places where we experience God in our lives. (Zimmerman, 1995, 124)

Zimmerman emphasizes, too, that healing rituals and services have also fostered wholistic integration for many CSA survivors, provided that survivors themselves make final decisions regarding the content of such services. Rituals and services that CSA survivors have found life-giving include themes such as: 1) validating one's commitment to the healing process; 2) cleansing one's self from feelings of shame; 3) mourning one's lost childhood; 4) reconciling oneself with God; and 5) celebrating new images of God (ibid.). Accompanying CSA survivors through a process of confronting and mourning the resulting spiritual losses as they rebuild or begin the process of a spiritual journey has played a positive role in many CSA survivors' recovery. Research studies have found that a relationship with a benevolent God 1) fosters healing in regard to the effects of CSA; 2) makes it easier to secure social support; 3) enables self-acceptance and a positive sense of self; 4) is a protective factor against depression, shame, and interpersonal difficulties; and 5) fosters a positive sense of life (Gall et al., 2007; Valentine and Feinauer, 1993).

Of course, one might legitimately raise the question: how can CPE survivors ever experience an adequate sense of safety, create a narrative integrating past traumatic events, and be able to reconnect with ordinary life when they are aware that globally, and perhaps even in their own community, persons may be viewing and masturbating to their child sexual abuse images? There are no simple therapeutic solutions to the added challenges of post-traumatic stress when the child sexual abuse images are not seized and destroyed by law enforcement agencies. Wrestling with considerations unique to these situations, the counseling community is beginning to identify effective ways to address CPE during therapeutic sessions (von Weiler, 2010). Religious communities can seek counsel from specialized CSA/CPE trauma therapists in order to discern how they can create a safe, hospitable environment for CPE survivors and support them through their recovery process.

Given the widespread forms of child sexual exploitation in our society, religious communities need to acknowledge the high likelihood of the presence of both CSA and CPE victims and perpetrators within their own communities. Priority must be given to educate clergy, ministers, religious educators, and religiously affiliated school teachers to be attentive to signs of CSA and CPE and be empowered to courageously report offenders. Furthermore, as part of their commitment to a safe community not just for CPE survivors but for all children in their midst, it is imperative that religious communities implement a zero-tolerance policy in which all employees are strictly prohibited from viewing child pornography (including pseudo-child porn).

It seems as if this would be a matter of fact, and yet in many states, child porn users are currently only prosecuted if they have downloaded actual child porn sites; persons who have child porn sites on their web browser cache but have not downloaded the images are not prosecuted. Since such porn users are not prosecuted, religious communities might inaccurately interpret lack of prosecution as an indication that their employee does not pose a threat to the safety of their community. Given the social scientific and law enforcement data that affirms a correlation between viewing child porn and actual child abuse, however, religious communities cannot take the risk of retaining employees who present a threat to the safety of children and place them at risk for a lifetime of recovery from CSA or CPE traumatization. Even if particular clergy members are not directly involved in children's ministry or religious education, the very fact that they are valued members of the religious community places children in their proximity and thus at risk.

In addition to supporting CPE survivors and creating a safe community for children, there is a great need for Christian and other religious communities to work together and support all efforts to stop CSA and CPE globally as well as prevent all forms of child sexual exploitation in the future. These efforts include lobbying for more resources to identify and track child Internet porn and promoting harsher punishments for child porn producers and users in the U.S. and globally. Given the evidence of a strong association between viewing child porn and CSA and the fact that pseudo-porn creates a greater demand for child pornography, Christian communities should network with other organizations to repeal the Supreme Court's Aschcroft decision and seek to restore the 1996 Child Prevention Act.

In order for religious communities to seek to prevent child sexual abuse and actually create a sexually just culture in which sexual violence and abuse is no longer tolerated, it is crucial to create awareness and critical dialogue among community members. This means, among other things, education about the pornification and sexualization of childhood and the array of threats to children's prospects for healthy sexuality and intimate future relationships (Olfman, 2009; Zurbriggen and Roberts,

2013). Astonishingly, the "porning" of America begins as early as childhood (Sarracino and Scott, 2008), and the multimillion dollar industry of child pageants is but one example of how our media and culture glorifies young children who mimic the sexual appearance and behaviors of adults. According to Gail Dines' extensive research, girls' clothes now mimic sexualized clothes for women to such a degree that

> the majority of clothing available for elementary school girls at the local suburban mall is from the porn industry, which I call porn fashion. Wearing thongs, low-slung jeans, short skirts, and midriff-revealing tops, these girls now appear "hot" . . . This cultural shift toward sexualizing girls from an early age is bound to have real social consequences. Not only does it affect the way girls see themselves, it also chips away at the norms that define children as off-limits to male sexual use. The more we undermine such cultural norms, the more we drag girls into the category of "woman" and in a porn-saturated world, to be a woman is often to be a sexual object deserving of male contempt, use, and abuse. (Dines, 2010, 162)

Besides these detrimental effects on girls' sexual and gender socialization, the widespread access to internet pornography is distorting boys' and girls' sexual desires, altering their overall sexual and gender socialization, and fostering social acceptance of sexual coercion, aggression, and violence (Corne et al., 1992; Hall and Bishop, 2007; Wolak et al., 2007; Flood, 2009; Owens et al., 2012).

Finally, religious communities need to address pastorally the likely widespread use of pornography among their adult and adolescent members and courageously create awareness about the devastating effects of adult and child porn. Unfortunately, such effects reach far beyond the porn user, as the stability and well-being of marriages and entire families are usually at stake. In order to effect change and give members the resources to form and sustain healthy sexuality and intimate relationships, it is essential to focus on educating members and fostering dialogue about how porn actually undermines sexual satisfaction long term, deeply undermines partners' self-esteem about their bodies and sexuality, ruptures intimate relationships, and frequently destroys marriages and entire families.

CONCLUSION

Throughout his ministry, Jesus defied the social norms of his culture by explicitly welcoming and blessing the vulnerable and the marginalized, and children certainly represented one such social group. Teaching about the kingdom of heaven, Jesus calls a child forth and announces to his disciples,

> Whoever receives one such child in my name receives me. But if anyone causes the downfall of one of these little ones who believe in me, it would be better for him to have a millstone hung round his neck and be drowned in the

depths of the sea. Alas for the world that any of them should be made to fall! (Matt 18: 6–7)

Passionately prioritizing the protection, well-being, and flourishing of children deeply resonates with Christian Scripture and diverse sources present in the Christian Tradition. While it is heartbreaking and overwhelming to face the most radical dimensions of evil and suffering present in all forms of child sexual exploitation, the promise and power of God's grace enables Christians to confront these realities and truly become the body of Christ for those most harmed by all forms of child sexual exploitation. In the midst of accompanying child sexual exploitation survivors on their journeys for justice and recovery, Christians might take special encouragement from Philippians 4:13: "I can do all this through him who gives me strength." With an abundance of grace, Christian communities possess the strength to welcome hospitably CPE and CSA victims into their communities and support them in their quest for justice and healing.

Such grace and abundant blessings can also sustain Christians in their work to build effective coalitions with other religious communities and non-governmental organizations to combat and prevent child sexual exploitation. While much more outreach and support is needed for victim-survivors of all forms of child sexual exploitation, many Christians have responded to the needs of child sex trafficking victims and formed organizations such as World Relief's Evangelical Trafficking Program, Christian Trafficking Shelter Association (CTSA), and Shared Hope International. Such groups witness to our rich potential and become potential vehicles of divine love, so that God's grace may abound in the lives of all child sexual exploitation survivors.

REFERENCES

Beste, Jennifer E. *God and the Victim: Traumatic Intrusions on Grace and Freedom.* Oxford: Oxford University Press, 2007.

Bourke, Michael L. and Andres E. Hernandez. "The 'Butner Study' Redux: A Report of the Incidence of Hands-On Child Victimization by Child Pornography Offenders." *Journal of Family Violence* 24 (2009): 183–191.

Corne, Shawn, et al. "Women's Attitudes and Fantasies about Rape as a Function of Early Exposure to Pornography." *Journal of Interpersonal Violence* 7, no. 4 (1992): 454–461.

Dines, Gail. *Pornland: How Porn Has Hijacked Our Sexuality.* Boston: Beacon, 2010.

Enhancing Child Protection Laws After the April 16, 2002 Supreme Court Decision, Ashcroft v. Free Speech Coalition: Hearing Before the Subcommittee on Crime, Terrorism, and Homeland Sec. of the Homeland Sec. Comm. on the Judiciary, 107th Cong. (2002) (statement of Michael J. Heimbach, Crimes Against Children Unit, Criminal Investigative Div, Fed. Bureau of Investigation). Online: http://judiciary.house.gov/legacy/heimbach050102.htm.

Flood, Michael. "The Harms of Pornography Exposure among Children and Young People." *Child Abuse Review* 18, no. 6 (2009): 384–400.

Flowers, R. B. "The Sex Trade Industry's Worldwide Exploitation of Children." *The Annals of the American Academy of Political and Social Science* 575 (2001): 147–57.

Gall, Terry Lynn, et al. "Spirituality and the Current Adjustment of Adult Survivors of Childhood Sexual Abuse." *Journal for the Scientific Study of Religion* 46, no. 1 (2007): 101–117.

Hall, Ann and Mardia Bishop. *Pop-Porn: Pornography in American Culture*. Westport: Praeger, 2007.

Hall, Terese. "Spiritual Effects of Childhood Sexual Abuse in Adult Christian Women," *Journal of Psychology and Theology* 23 (1995): 129–34.

Herman, Judith. *Trauma and Recovery*. New York: Basic Books, 1992.

Hodge, David R., and Cynthia A. Lietz. "The International Sexual Trafficking of Women and Children: A Review of the Literature." *Affilia* 22, no. 2 (2007): 163–74.

Hughes, Donna. "Use of New Communications and Information Technologies for Sexual Exploitation of Women and Children." *Hasting's Women Law Journal* 13 (2002): 129–148. (2002) Hunt, Patricia and Margaret Baird. "Children of Sex Rings." *Child Welfare* 69, no. 3 (1990): 195–207.

Jensen, Robert. *Getting Off: Pornography and the End of Masculinity*. Cambridge, MA: South End Press, 2007.

Kane, Donna, et.al. "Perception of God by Survivors of Childhood Sexual Abuse: An Exploratory Study in an Underresearched Area," *Journal of Psychology and Theology* 21 (1993): 228–237.

Kim, Candice. "From Fantasy to Reality: The Link Between Viewing Child Pornography and Molesting Children. *American Prosecutors Research Institute* 1, no. 3 (2004). No pages. Online: http://www.ndaa.org/pdf/Update_gr_vol1_no3.pdf.

Klain, E., et al. "Child Pornography: The Criminal-Justice-System Response." Washington, D.C.: National Center for Missing & Exploited Children. No pages. Online: http://www.missingkids.com/en_US/publications/NC81.pdf.

Lanning, Kenneth. "Child Molesters: A Behavioral Analysis." Alexandria, VA: National Center for Missing & Exploited Children, 2010. No pages. Online: http://www.missingkids.com/en_US/publications/NC70.pdf.

Lemoncelli, John and Andrew Carey. "The Psychospiritual Dynamics of Adult Survivors of Abuse," *Counseling and Values* 40 (1996): 175–185.

Leonard, Marcella. "'I Did What I Was Directed To Do But He Didn't Touch Me': The Impact of Being a Victim of Internet Offending." *Journal of Sexual Aggression* 16, no. 2 (2010): 249–256.

Manlowe, Jennifer. *Faith Born of Seduction*. New York: New York University Press, 1995.

Martellozzo, Elena and Helen Taylor. "Cycle of Abuse." *Index on Censorship* 38, no. 1 (2009): 117–122.

National Center for Missing and Exploited Children. "Every Child Deserves a Safe Childhood." 2010 Annual Report. No pages. Online: http://www.missingkids.com/en_US.

National Center for Missing and Exploited Children. "Every Child Deserves a Safe Childhood." 2012 Annual Report. Online: http://www.missingkids.com/AnnualReport.

Olfman, Sharna. *The Sexualization of Childhood*. Westport, CT: Praeger, 2009.

Owens, Eric et al. "The Impact of Internet Pornography on Adolescents: A Review of the Research." *Sexual Addiction & Compulsivity* 19 (2012): 99–122.

Paul, Pamela. *Pornified: How Pornography is Transforming Our Lives, Our Relationships, and Our Families*. New York: Henry Holt and Company, 2006.

Rahner, Karl. *Foundations of the Christian Faith*. New York: Seabury Press, 1978.

Sarracino, Carmine, and Kevin M. Scott. *The Porning of America: The Rise of Porn Culture, What It Means, and Where We Go from Here*. Boston: Beacon, 2008.

Scheinberg, Marcia and Peter Fraenkel. *The Relational Trauma of Incest*. New York: Guilford Press, 2001.

Silbert, Mimi, and Ayala Pines. "Early Sexual Exploitation as an Influence in Prostitution." *Social Work* 28, no. 4 (1983): 285–289.

Trueman, Patrick. "Adult Pornography Leads to Consumption of Child Pornography." In *Child Pornography*, 67–72. Farmington Hills: Greenhaven Press, 2013.

Valentine, LaNae and Leslie L. Feinauer. "Resilience Factors Associated with Female Survivors of Childhood Sexual Abuse. *American Journal of Family Therapy* 21, no. 3 (1993): 216–224.

Von Weiler, Julia, et al. Care and Treatment of Child Victims of Child Pornographic Exploitation (CPE) in Germany. *Journal of Sexual Aggression* 16:2 (2010): 211–222.

Westenberg, Megan, "Establishing the Nexus: The Definitive Relationships between Child Molestation and Possession of Child Pornography as the Sole Basis for Probable Cause." *University of Cincinnati Law Review* 81, no. 1 (2013): 337–360.

Wolak, Janis, et al. "Unwanted and Wanted Exposure to Online Pornography in a National Sample of Youth Internet Users." *Pediatrics* 119, no. 2 (2007): 247–257.

Wortley, Richard and Stephen Smallbone. "Child Pornography on the Internet." U.S Department of Justice. 4 (2006). Online: http://www.cops.usdoj.gov/Publications/e04062000.pdf.

Zillmann, D. and J. Bryant eds. *Pornography: Research Advances & Policy Considerations*. Hillsdale, NJ: L. Erlbaum Associates.

Zimmerman, Mari. *Take and Make Holy: Honoring the Sacred in the Healing Journey of Abuse Survivors*. Chicago: Liturgy Training Publications, 1995.

Zurbriggen, Eileen and Tomi-Ann Roberts eds. *The Sexualization of Girls and Girlhood: Causes, Consequences, and Resistance*. New York: Oxford University Press, 2013.

Chapter 24

Contextualized Social Justice
Entering Into Culture to Bring Life to Worthy Children

Rebecca Loveall, Kelly Flanagan, Chelsey Morrison, and Morgan Sorenson

Lord of all being, there is one thing that deserves my greatest care,
That calls forth my ardent desires,
That is, that I may answer the great end for which I am made –
To glorify thee who has given me being,
And to do all the good I can for my fellow men.

(BENNETT, 2009, 22)

God justifies things by restoring them to their
true and full identity in himself.

(ROHR, 2012, 36–37)

A justice focus when working with children is doing good for them (fostering spiritual development), teaching them to distinguish between good and evil (fostering spiritual discernment), and teaching them to choose the good (promoting individual empowerment). Therefore, justice can be seen as the search for, implementation of and facilitation of goodness, which restores personhood. Yet, justice is a direct result of experiencing justice in our own lives. Unjust family systems, social systems and cultures keep the cycles of poverty, abuse and violence active, and limit growth in the distinction between good and evil. We propose expanding our spiritual development models to take into account how unjust contexts that involve trauma may affect children's spiritual development, including their search for and promotion of good in their own lives and for others.

Systems theories of child development posit that development must be understood as occurring within nested ecological systems (i.e., family, parents' work situation, school) and cultural contexts (i.e., cultural beliefs, socioeconomic status) that interact with the child's individual characteristics in a reciprocal fashion over time (Bronfenbrenner, 1979; Lerner, 2002). Development can be either impeded or nurtured by the processes and interactions occurring within particular contexts.

Lerner (2006) writes:

> . . . healthy development involves positive changes in the relationship between the developing person . . . who is both able to contribute positively to self, family, and community and committed to doing so . . . and a community supporting the development of such citizens. (62)

Justice requires positive contribution and a supportive community. However, many children grow up in less than optimal households, communities, and cultures that may not support their development or value their contributions. Bond (2004) describes such an environment:

> Inadequate time for poorer parents to supervise their children, lack of access to legal institutions for redress of grievances, insufficient policing, lack of technical skills training through the educational system may promote a system of unfairness, cynicism about the use of power, frustration of goals relating to the acquisition of material resources, heightened stress leading to increased emotional reactivity, lower perceived costs associated with the risks of undertaking coercive acts against others, lower self-efficacy . . . such is the daunting interrelatedness of processes at work on aggression in the real world. (p. 64)

This describes a system that perpetuates injustice. Acts of injustice against a child or situations of injustice can often be traumatic and result in long term serious consequences. Judith Herman (1997) describes trauma as "fundamentally unjust" (p. 135). Trauma can negatively alter the regulation of affective impulses, attention and consciousness, self-perception, perceptions of the perpetrator, relationships to others, systems of meaning, and may lead to somatization and/or medical problems (Ford, Courtois, Steele, Hart, & Nijenhuis, 2005). Clearly, injustice in the form of trauma can have a deep and pervasive impact on child development. Thus, it is important to consider trauma and its effects on all areas of development, and specifically on the development of child spirituality. Spirituality has been described by Yust, Johnson, Sasso, & Roehlkepartain (2006) as

> . . . the intrinsic human capacity for self-transcendence in which the individual participates in the sacred—something greater than the self. It propels the search for connectedness, meaning, purpose, and ethical responsibility. It is experienced, formed, shaped, and expressed through a wide range of religious narratives, beliefs, and practices, and is shaped by many influences in family, community, society, culture, and nature. (8)

Clearly implied in this definition is that spirituality is embedded in an individual's cultural and social contexts (Benson et al., 2003; Yust et al., 2006). Thus, like other areas of development, the changes inherent in the development of spirituality are either impeded or nurtured by processes and interactions occurring within particular contexts.

However, when taking into account injustice as the primary context for spiritual development, we see limitations in this definition. If self-transcendence is openness to becoming (Benner, 2012; Loder, 1998) then what we are becoming is a process of choice; that is, the individual person chooses how they relate to their environment and others based on identification with something greater than the self. Self-transcendence is fed through a process of identifying with God in circumstances, in attitudes, understanding and beliefs, and then disidentifying contradictory or erroneous messages based on one's personal experience of the divine. Unjust environments are punishing and neither promote nor invite positive contributions. Therefore, spiritual development, which includes the awareness and promotion of good (justice), is undermined in unjust contexts because self-transcendence, "becoming" something beyond one's current self, is not taught or nurtured by the environment. The self becomes lost as survival becomes the solitary goal.

Our models of spiritual development must then be redefined to include an understanding of developing a self. Loder (1998) includes in his definition of spiritual formation this "second side" of development, or the need for self-relatedness. The simplest way in which to understand self-relatedness is as an openness to being (Benner, 2012; Loder, 1998). "Being" involves the ability to examine circumstances and relationships as well as personal attitudes, behaviors, and beliefs. Thus, the process of self-relatedness is a dialogue between one's social identity and one's personal identity, identifying with certain circumstances and messages while also disidentifying with erroneous or harmful circumstances and messages (Webster, 2005). Both self-transcendence and self-relatedness then are necessary capacities for the growth of human spirituality. Loder (1998) defines these as the two halves of the Image of God in humans, impacted by the continuity and contradiction of one's person as they grow and change (6). The development and dialogue between self-relatedness and self-transcendence is the mechanism that facilitates or hampers growth in one's spiritual identity.

AWAKENING, VALUING, MEANING MAKING, CONNECTEDNESS, AND PURPOSE

In consideration of how this process of spiritual development may work in unjust contexts, we draw from our experiences of working with children in Guatemala, attending to issues of injustice, trauma and identity formation in particular. From these experiences and the current literature on trauma and children's spirituality, we present a model that includes five key components crucial to the development of spirituality: *Awakening, Valuing, Meaning Making, Connectedness*, and *Purpose*. Although the semantics vary, some of these components have received much attention in the literature on children's spirituality, whereas others have not. Specifically, the components of *Awakening* and *Valuing* have received very little attention. We think this may be largely due to a lack of attention to trauma as injustice within literature on spiritual development. Although research in psychology examines the impact of trauma on spirituality and personhood, very few models of *spiritual development* have taken into account the effects of trauma or injustice on spirituality.

Trauma uniquely impacts each component in this model. Herman (1997) describes trauma as "an affliction of the powerless . . . Traumatic events overwhelm the ordinary systems of care that give people a sense of control, connection, and meaning" (33). Edgar (2008) describes oppression (the result of injustice) as "denying people their dignity as God's image bearers" (174). Further, trauma has a significant impact on self-development (Pearlman, 2003); that is, traumatized persons lose their basic sense of self, and victims may develop a "contaminated, stigmatized identity" (Herman, 1997; 104). This should be concerning to us, as a sense of self or identity is important to spirituality (Templeton & Eccles, 2006). As will be described in further detail, *Awakening* and *Valuing* are two components intrinsically linked with identity. Therefore, it is crucial to consider their importance especially when working with children who have been victimized by trauma or injustice.

In this chapter, we will briefly outline each of the more recognized components of spiritual development, followed by a more extensive review of *Awakening* and *Valuing*. It is important to note that the processes of these components do not unfold in a successive manner, but rather in an interactional and ongoing manner. However, *Awakening* and *Valuing* could be considered to be prerequisites to the other components, as they are involved in the development of spiritual identity, which is essential to spirituality overall. We will include ways in which trauma can negatively impede spiritual development, and ways in which spiritual development can be nurtured in cultures of injustice.

MEANING MAKING

Tronick & Beeghly (2011) describe *meaning-making* as a process which begins in infancy, in which a child creates representations (or meaning) through ongoing engagement with both internal and external worlds as he makes sense of positive and negative feedback. Webster (2004) describes a crucial aspect of spirituality as engaging the question of the meaning of life, and argues that a child's meaning is largely impacted by their environment or "horizon of understanding." When a child's horizon of understanding includes abuse and injustice, their meaning making about life and spirituality may be negatively impacted. Therefore, it is crucial that children be supported to make meaning in such a way that motivates them to move forward, rather than in manners involving self-loathing, worthlessness, or helplessness.

With regard to trauma, supporting and allowing the child to tell their narrative of stressful or negative experiences, through written or verbal narration and art, is an important step to making meaning and moving forward (Altmaier, 2013; Fivush, Sales, & Bohanek, 2008) because narratives as "forms of communication with others and with oneself create the context in which meaning can develop" (Altmaier, 2013, 106).

CONNECTEDNESS

Connectedness has been identified as a crucial component to positive youth development (Lerner, 2005). It is defined as:

> . . . a positive bond with people and institutions that are reflected in healthy, bidirectional exchanges between the individual and peers, family, school, and community in which both parties contribute to the relationship. (Phelps et al., 2007, 478)

These bonds are especially important in the development of spirituality, as spiritual development occurs in the context of these connections with family, school, and community (Kim & Esquivel, 2011; Schwartz, Bukowski & Aoki, 2006; Boyatzis, Dollahite & Marks, 2006). Research has linked children's perceptions and relationships with others to their perceptions/relationship with God (Bellous, 2006; Dickie, Eshleman, Merasco, Shepard, VanderWilt, & Johnson, 1997; Granqvist, Ljungdah, & Dickie, 2007). For example, positive parent-child relationships, child-rearing practices and parental God concepts are linked to children's perceptions of God as nurturing, caring, and loving whereas strict disciplinary practices are associated with children's perceptions of God as punishing (De Roos, Iedema, & Miedema, 2004; Dickie et al., 1997). Through interpersonal connections and the influence of others' concepts of God, children develop their own image of and relationship with God (Bellous, 2006).

Trauma can have a highly negative impact on its victims' capacity to develop and maintain relationships, which consequently impacts children's spiritual development. In fact, trauma "may impede the formation of healthy relationships, instead patterning ones that are fraught with instability and chaos along with additional abuse, victimization, and loss" (Pearlman & Courtois, 2005). Therefore, it is especially important to provide stable, caring, and consistent relationships for children who have experienced trauma in order to support their spiritual development.

PURPOSE

Miller-McLemore (2003) describes children as "full persons trying to learn how to wield power appropriately and how to have a real say in their lives" (144). Spirituality develops a commitment in children and youth to contribute to others beyond themselves. By motivating young people to contribute to something greater than themselves (King & Benson 2006), spirituality can greatly influence their sense of purpose.

However, trauma and injustice can have a dramatic negative influence on sense of purpose, as it systematically breaks down all aspects of a child's self (Ford et al., 2005; Herman 1997, 93). The experience of trauma may cause a child to question his or her worth and ability to contribute to life or society. Kierkegaard (1989) describes how the loss of one's self can impact the ability to have individual purpose:

> The biggest danger, that of losing oneself, can pass off in the world as quietly as if it were nothing; every other loss, an arm, a leg, a wife, etc. is bound to be noticed . . . such a person [who sees himself surrounded by the multitude] forgets himself, in a divine sense forgets his name, dares not believe in himself, finds being himself too risky, finds it much easier and safer to be like the others, to become a copy, a number, along with the crowd. (Webster, 2005, 62–64)

Because spiritual development involves a sense of purpose, it is essential that children's sense of purpose is cultivated, but it must be recognized that this purpose is directly tied to a sense of identity.

AWAKENING

Awakening is a term used in adult spirituality literature to describe an encounter with or rediscovery of the authentic self, which is usually provoked through a severe "identity crisis" or traumatic event. Benner (2012) describes awakening as a "shift in consciousness . . . [which] will always involve a change in two things: our sense of our self (identity) and our view of life and the world (perspective)" (p. 58). Therefore, in order to understand awakening, trauma and its impact on identity and perspective must be examined. In order to be "awake" one must be present, with an integrated sense of self; aware of environment, self, and the boundary between.

Growing up within a context of injustice and trauma presents challenges to the formation of identity and development of self. In attempts to avoid accepting a "bad-self," which is often assigned to them by society, some children neglect to define self at all, which creates a self-defined passively by their environment. Tragically, in attempts to find "some sort of structure for meaning," other children "will opt for even negative identities in the face of complete nihilism . . . children will seek out a negative universe on the grounds that anything is better than nothing" (Garbarino & Bedard, 1996). In order to counter these negative identities, children may need support as they attempt to navigate identity formation.

The construction of identity model developed by Bamberg, De Fina, and Schiffrin (2011) provides a helpful representation for understanding the basic components of identity. According to this model, there are three identity dilemmas that are navigated throughout the lifetime and are "continuously negotiated and renegotiated" especially as they relate to issues of religion and spirituality (Schwab, 2013, 2). Each identity dilemma is represented as a dialogue between two opposing poles. The first identity dilemma, continuity versus change, "refers to making sense of one's life over time, reconciling that one is the same person . . . while amid constant change and flux" (Schwab, 2013, 2). The second identity dilemma, sameness versus difference, involves discerning how the self is similar to others and how the self is different than others. The third and final identity dilemma, agency versus non-agency, involves identifying that some experiences and events may be actively chosen and pursued, whereas others are viewed as inescapable and beyond one's control.

Prolonged exposure to injustice or trauma in childhood disrupts continuity or stability, inhibits differentiation from environment, and deteriorates sense of agency, arresting each of the three dilemmas at unipolarity. In this state, the child participates in life in a more passive than active manner, as if in hibernation, and may be unable to "wake up" to actively participate in their lives without the assistance of outside caring support.

In order for children to wake up, it is crucial that they be able to differentiate themselves from the environment in order to gain an accurate perspective of themselves in relation to the divine and others. This process requires reflective space. Childhood spirituality literature has begun to recognize the importance of *reflective space* in the development of spirituality (Hay & Nye, 2006). In *The Spirit of the Child*, David Hay and Rebecca Nye (2006) describe the concept of relational consciousness, the understanding that even young children seem to have a "reflective consciousness." This concept is similar to meta-cognition, in that it gives children the ability to participate in the objective parts of their lives, analyzing their interactions (with God, the world, others, and self), and use them to inform their subjective internal reality and add new "dimensions of understanding, meaning and experience," (109).

Winnicott (1971) expands on the concept reflective space, as it relates to spirituality, emphasizing its importance beginning in infancy:

They [God concepts] form an intermediate space between infant and those in the outside world. In this location, between inner and outer reality, 'illusions' form and meaning is created. This third place, which is neither the self nor the world but is influenced by both, is the genesis of the spiritual aspect of human life. The spiritual is an intermediate space between the person and the material. It is a mid-point reality between subjective and objective realities. Objects form here as a child experiences the self and the world. (2)

In caregiver environments of trauma, the caregiver-child relationship is not emotionally reflective and caring, but rather volatile, chaotic, unpredictable and predominantly punishing. Adults who themselves have been traumatized may have limited abilities to nurture their children. Plantinga Jr. (1995) explains that "socially voiceless and powerless parents demand unquestioning deference from their children as a way of compensation" (57). The child is socialized to adjust to all external expectations to such a degree that their ability for self-reflection is seriously damaged, overtaken by their desire to meet external expectations. The focus of the abused child becomes "other-reflection," rather than self-reflection.

Awakening, in its two foci on authenticity of identity and healthy perspective of self, heavily relies on dialogue and interaction. This is evident in Bamberg et al.'s (2011) three continuums of identity, and the process of creating reflective space. With children, reflective space is created in two ways; first, physically creating an environment in which children are cared-for rather than the care-givers; and second, entering into the details and struggles of their lives. It is helpful to allow children to dialogue about the particulars of their lives (e.g. how many brothers and sisters they have, their favorite color, etc.) as well as asking questions that cause children to grapple with each of the dilemmas of identity formation (i.e. "Even though you've changed, what things about you have stayed the same?" "Even though you can't change that, what are things you can change?"). Through creating and providing healthy interactions with children in these ways, we can promote an accurate perception of self and a more authentic identity.

VALUING

"Personality identities are not formed by individuals alone but are socially constructed by others" (Webster, 2005, 6). Oppressive, unjust cultures often assign children negative labels that can perpetuate their internal understanding of themselves as bad (e.g. poor, uneducated, needy, worthless, or burdensome). In an unjust culture, the social identity assigned to a child often lacks both dignity and recognition of individuality, coalescing around a deep internal understanding as "only bad" (Garbarino & Bedard, 1996) and "only worthy of refusal" (Jensen, 2005, 97).

Valuing involves creating a sense of balance between a good-self (gifts, talents, attributes, capable of choosing well) and a bad-self (imperfect, broken, needy, capable of doing harm). We propose three variables involved in creating a sense of value in a child: *mirroring, attunement,* and the focus on *spiritual identity.* To correct children's tendency towards undue negative self-perceptions, children need healthy *mirroring* of their attributes, interactions, emotions and actions. Healthy, specific mirroring over time allows a child to move beyond global negative self-attributions, to a more balanced understanding of their role in context. Valuing is not promoting the idea of excessive greatness or perfection in each child, but a specific process of recognizing children's strengths. Through recognizing and valuing children's strengths, such as intentionally "catching" them demonstrating positive behavior, a sense of inner, specific, God-given goodness can be developed.

Attunement, described by Winnicot as parents' reactiveness to their child, can be used by supportive and caring others to correct broken emotion management systems. The abused child is hyper-sensitive to guilt and may carry an internal sense of provoking abuse (Courtois, 2008). Attuning adults react in a way that validates children's expressions of needs and emotions. For example, if a child has broken a dish, she may be afraid and hide the broken dish from her parent. Upon discovering the broken dish, an attuning parent may react by assuring the frightened child that it is normal for her to be afraid, assuring her of the relative unimportance of the dish and acknowledging the event as an accident. Children who are accustomed to negative or harsh reactions from caretakers (such as guilting or shaming) may display characteristics such as blaming, minimizing, scape-goating, exaggerating, denying and flattened emotion in these situations. These characteristics represent attempts to avoid the reality of negative specific events in the child's life, and are evidence of broken self-relatedness. Such reactions can be countered and new reactions can be learned through attunement.

Developmental theories show us how identity is formed from inside contexts, circumstances, families, and individuals. Creating a sense of spiritual identity focuses on the identity God offers us from outside, transcending earthly contexts. Indeed, the core of spirituality recognizes there is more than a physical being with an awareness of the primacy of spiritual existence (Garbarino & Bedard, 1996). Before the foundations of the world, before our circumstances, before our choices we were chosen in Christ (Eph 1:4, 2 Tim 1:9, Titus 1:2, Col 1:17). Focusing on spiritual identity emphasizes the importance of a restored and transcendent life, because "salvation is not a promise we possess, but a gift to live as God's children again" (Jensen, 2008, 100).

A child's transcendent self with restored spiritual identity transforms the child's self that is embedded in earthly circumstances. As children begin to accept their identity as a child of God, they gain a sense of being worthy of care. Trauma saturated contexts including circumstances of birth, often create unresolved conflicts with identity. For example, a child may have negative self-perceptions if he were "unplanned," abandoned at birth, or the product of a rape or an affair. A person's identity in God is specific, has been planned, and is not accidental. God created each child with purpose, gifts, and personality. Moreover, he placed children within their unique conditions of life and gave them the ability to find him within them. God gives children the ability to choose *who* they want to be within their unique attributes and *how* they relate to their circumstances and relationships.

These three variables of *mirroring, attunement,* and *spiritual identity* help build up a second "good self" to counteract the pervasive sense of "bad-self," which is a common detrimental consequence of childhood abuse. Indeed, children who have experienced abuse during developmentally sensitive periods "see themselves as unworthy of love, affection and fulfillment of their basic needs by others" (Catherall, 2004, 215). Thus, valuing is pivotal to break cycles of neglect, abuse and violence because it restores the necessary balance in a child's sense of worth.

CONCLUSION

Children who are awakened to their relationship with the divine and see their value in light of Him are able to make meaning of their life, connect with others, and develop a sense of purpose that will propel them to nurture similar outcomes for others. Therefore, by seeking justice for children in a culture of injustice, the recipients of that justice seek justice for others, thus creating a cycle of justice in place of the cycle of injustice previously experienced.

Elaine Scarry's (1999) philosophy on beauty helps clarify the process of how experiences of beauty or goodness can promote justice. Scarry posits that "Beauty brings copies of itself into being" (3). This is evident in God's creation of mankind as a copy of Hhimself. Further, Scarry suggests that when encountered, beauty and goodness are life-affirming, life-giving and life-saving (27). This is especially true considering that the search for beauty and goodness *is* the search for God, who is the source of all goodness. Further, encounters with beauty propel self-transcendence, and thus an encounter "invites the search for something beyond itself" (29). Therefore, as we help children to become aware of the goodness and beauty of their creator, and the goodness within themselves as Hhis image-bearers, they then will seek to replicate the goodness they have encountered and promote justice for others.

The model of spirituality presented within this chapter, and its emphasis on identity and self-relatedness, is especially relevant to cultures of injustice, in which traumatic experiences "overwhelm" individuals so that they lose a sense of "control, connection and meaning" with the world. This directly impacts the processes of *Meaning Making, Connectedness,* and *Purpose,* all of which are essential components of children's spiritual development. These are important and necessary constructs, but offer an insufficient or incomplete perspective of the understanding of children's spirituality within unjust and traumatic contexts. The two additional components of *Awakening* and *Valuing* explored within this chapter broaden the typical understanding of children's spirituality, emphasizing the importance of identity and self-relatedness to spirituality. This addition is particularly relevant within cultures of trauma due to the negative impact of trauma on both identity development and self-relatedness. Although there is significant overlap between the constructs of *Awakening* and *Valuing*, there are distinct differences as well; namely, *Awakening* involves children becoming aware of their being, and understanding the relationship between themselves and their environment and God, whereas *Valuing* focuses on the positive and accurate nurturance of the identity "discovered" through awakening.

A unique aspect of this model is not only its emphasis on injustice, but also its emphasis on promoting and perpetuating justice. "From the perspective of an abused, neglected, and hungry child, sin does not give birth to evil; rather evil is the context in which sin arises" (Jensen 2005: 93); likewise, promoting spirituality as outlined in this chapter creates caring and nurturing environments that give rise to goodness and justice. Justice can be understood as a threefold process. First, justice is justification: "God's merciful act of declaring us just . . . and pronouncing us acceptable" (Bosch, 2009, 71). Second, justice is righteousness: a spiritual quality or attribute that God develops in us, which nurtures our ability to choose between right and wrong. Third, justice is action: "people's right conduct in relation to their fellow human beings" (Bosch, 2009, 71). God's justice restores our connection to and understanding of His goodness, and enables us to act in accordance with it to promote the common good.

When children are *awakened* and *valued* for who they are, made in the image and beauty of their Creator, they are introduced to Christ and God's restorative justice. God's free gift of justification and the belief they are acceptable to God becomes adopted as a crucial aspect of their identity. They then can accept the goodness within themselves and replicate the beauty they have encountered in Christ in the world around them through their individual pursuits to promote justice. It is our hope that this model has provided a broadened understanding of children's spirituality that will allow us to address the daunting cycles of injustice, and replace them with cycles of justice through empowering children to acknowledge the goodness, power, and responsibility of being image bearers of God.

REFERENCES

Altmaier, E. M. "Through a Glass Darkly: Personal Reflections on the Role of Meaning in Response to Trauma." *Counseling Psychology Quarterly*, no. 1 (2013): 106–113.

Bamberg, M., et al. "*Discourse and Identity Construction.*" In *Handbook of Identity Theory and Research.* Edited by S. Schwartz, K. Luyckx, & V. Vignoles, et al., New York: Springer, 2011.

Bellous, J. "The Educational Significances of Spirituality in the Formation of Faith." In *International Handbook of the Religious, Moral and Spiritual Dimensions in Education,*. Eedited by M. de Souza, G. Durka, K. Engebretson, R. Jackson, & A. McGrady. New York: Springer, 2006.

Benner, D. G. *Spirituality and the Awakening Self: The Sacred Journey of Transformation.* Ada: Brazos Press, 2012.

Bennet, A. G. *The Valley of Vision: A Collection of Puritan Prayers and Devotions.* Carlisle: Banner of Truth Trust, 2003.

Benson, P. L. "Commentary: Emerging Themes in Research on Adolescent Spiritual and Religious Development." *Applied Developmental Science,* no. 8 (2004):47–50.

Bond, M. H. "Culture and Aggression—From Context to Coercion." *Journal of Personality and Social Psychology Review,* no.1 (2004): 62–78.

Bosch, D. J. *Transforming Mission: Paradigm Shifts in Theology of Mission.* Maryknoll: Orbis Books, 2011.

Boyatzis, C. J., et al. "The Family as a Context for Religious and Spiritual Development in Children and Youth." In *The Handbook Spiritual Development of Children and Adolescents,* 297–309. Thousand Oaks: Sage Publications, 2006.

Bronfenbrenner, U. *The Ecology of Human Development.* Cambridge: Harvard University Press, 1979.

Catherall, D. R. *Handbook of Stress, Trauma, and the Family.* New York: Routledge, 2004.

Courtois, C. "Complex Trauma, Complex Reactions: Assessment and Treatment." *Psychological Trauma: Theory, Research, Practice, and Policy,* no. 1 (2008): 86–100.

De Roos, S. A., et al. "Influence of Maternal Denomination, God Concepts, and Child-Rearing Practices on Young Children's God Concepts." Journal for the Scientific Study of Religion, no. 43 (2004): 519–535.

Dickie, J. R., et al. "Parent-Child Relationships and Children's Images of God." Journal for the Scientific Study of Religion, no. 36 (1997): 25–43.

Edgar, W., "Suffering and Oppression." In *Suffering and the Goodness of God,* 165–182. Wheaton: Crossway Books, 2008.

Fivush, R., J. Sales, & J. G. Bohanek. "Meaning Making in Mothers' and Children's Narratives of Emotional Events." *Memory,* no. 6 (2008): 579–594. doi:10.1080/09658210802150681

Ford, J. D., et al. "Treatment of Complex Posttraumatic Self-Dysregulation." *Journal of Traumatic Stress,* no. 5 (2005): 437–447.

Garbarino, J., & C. Bedard. "Spiritual Challenges to Children Facing Violent Trauma." *Childhood,* no. 4 (1996): 467–478.

Granqvist, P., Ljungdahl, C., & Dickie, J. R. "God is Nowhere, God is Now Here: Attachment Activations, Security of Attachment, and God's Perceived Closeness Among 5-7-Year-Old Children From Religious and Non-Religious Homes." *Attachment & Human Development,* no. 9 (2007): 55–71.

Hay, D., and R. Nye. *The Spirit of the Child: Revised Edition.* Philadelphia: Jessica Kingsley Pub, 2006.

Herman, J. L. *Trauma and Recovery.* New York: Basic Books, 1997.

Jensen, D. H. *Graced Vulnerability: A Theology of Childhood.* Berea: Pilgrim Press, 2005.

Kim, S., and G. B. Esquivel. "Adolescent Sspirituality and Resilience: Theory, Research, and Educational Practices." *Psychology in the Schools,* no. 7 (2011): 755–765.

King, P. E., and P. L. Benson. "Spiritual Development and Adolescent Well-Being and Thriving." In *The Handbook Spiritual Development of Children and Adolescents,* 384–398. Thousand Oaks: Sage Publications, 2006.

Lerner, R. M. *Concepts and Theories of Human Development (3rd ed.).* Mahwah: Lawrence Erlbaum Associate, 2002.

Lerner, R. M. "Promoting Positive Youth Development: Theoretical and Empirical Bases." Lecture, Workshop on the Science of Adolescent Health and Development, Washington, D.C., September 2005.

Lerner, R. M., A. E. Alberts, P. M. Anderson, & E. M. Dowling. "On Making Humans Human: Spirituality and the Promotion of Positive Youth Development." In *The Handbook Spiritual Development of Children and Adolescents*, 60–72. Thousand Oaks: Sage Publications, 2006.

Loder, J. E. *The Logic of the Spirit: Human Development in Theological Perspective. Logic of the Spirit: Human Development in Theological Perspective*. San Francisco: Jossey-Bass, 1998.

Miller-McLemore, B. J. *Let the Children Come: Reimagining Childhood from a Christian Perspective*. Hoboken: Jossey-Bass, 2003.

Pearlman, L. A., and C. A. Courtois. "Clinical Applications of the Attachment Framework: Relational Treatment of Complex Trauma." *Journal of Traumatic Stress*, no. 5 (2005): 449–459.

Phelps, E., et al. "Nuances in Early Adolescent Developmental Trajectories of Positive and Problematic/Risk Behaviors: Findings from the 4-H Study of Positive Youth Development." *Child and Adolescent Psychiatric Clinics Oof North America, no.* 2 (2007): 473–496. doi:10.1016/j.chc.2006.11.006

Plantinga, C. *Not The Way It's Supposed to Be: A Breviary of Sin*. Grand Rapids: Wm. B. Eerdmans Publishing Co., 1995.

Rohr, R. *Preparing for Christmas: Daily Meditations for Advent*. Cincinnati: Franciscan Media, 2012.

Scarry, E. *On Beauty and Being Just*. Princeton: Princeton University Press, 1999.

Schwab, J. R. "Religious Meaning Making: Positioning Identities through Stories." *Psychology of Religion and Spirituality*. (Advance online publication). doi: 10.1037/a0031557

Schwartz, K. D., W. M. Bukowski, W. T. Aoki. "Mentors, Friends, and Gurus: Peer and Nonparent Influences on Spiritual Development." In *The Handbook Spiritual Development of Children and Adolescents*, 310–323. Thousand Oaks: Sage Publications. 2006.

Templeton, J. L., and J. S. Eccles. "The Relation Between Spiritual Development and Identity Prrocesses." In *The Handbook of Spiritual Development in Childhood and Adolescence*, (2006): 252–265.

Tronick, E., and M. Beeghly. "Infants' Meaning-Making and the Development of Mental Health Problems." *American Psychologist*, no. 2 (2011): 107.

Webster, R. S. "An Existential Framework of Spirituality." *International Journal of Children's Spirituality*, no. 1 (2004): 7–19.

Webster, R. S. "Personal Identity: Moving Beyond Essence." *International Journal of Children's Spirituality*. no. 1 (2005): 5–16.

Winnicott, D. W. *Playing and Reality*. London: Tavistock Publications Ltd, 1971.

Yust, K. M, A. N. Johnson, S. Eisenberg Sasso, and E. C. Roehlkepartain. *Nurturing Child and Adolescent Spirituality: Perspectives from the World's Religious Traditions*. New York City: Rowman and Littlefield, 2006.

Chapter 25

Jesus Loves Which Little Children?
A (Canadian) Proposal for Nurturing Children's Spirituality in Intercultural Contexts

David M. Csinos

Several years ago I worked as a children's pastor at a mid-sized suburban congregation. On Sunday afternoons, this predominantly-white church rented its building to a group of immigrants from east Africa who used the space for their worship services. While the church was happy to rent its sanctuary and Sunday school rooms to this congregation, members seemed to express ambivalence about this arrangement through comments that spoke about how wonderful it is that this group can meet in the building and other remarks about how difficult it is to have them use the space because "they let their kids run around and do whatever they want."

This sort of scene seems to be becoming more common among churches in Canada—and in other places that experience fairly high rates of immigration. Comments made by members of my former church demonstrate the ways in which culture confronts efforts to nurture the spiritual lives of children, for this church's expectations regarding how children's ministry ought to happen (children should participate in supervised Sunday school classes) contrasted significantly with those of the African congregation that rented the building (children may move about the building as they please during worship services). Clearly, culture matters to the spiritual formation of children. And in our pluralistic world, we who seek to nurture the spiritual lives of children need to seriously consider culture and cultural diversity. In this chapter, I cultivate an interdisciplinary conversation between children's spirituality and multiculturalism within my home context of Canada in order to explore how to nurture a spirit of interculturalism through ministry with children.

CONSIDERING CULTURE

When considering a term like *culture*, which is used in many different ways, it is helpful to begin with a working definition, particularly one that leaves room for the full breadth of the term. This is what Carl James (2010) does in his definition:

> Simply put, culture is a concept that refers to the way in which a given society, community, or group organizes and conducts itself as distinguished from that of other societies, communities, or groups. Culture consists of a dynamic and complex set of values, beliefs, norms, patterns of thinking, styles of communication, linguistic expressions, and ways of interpreting and interacting with the world that help people understand and thus survive their varied circumstances. Therefore, members of any given society, community, or group will not only be influenced or shaped by the culture of their group, community, and that society, but will also shape it. (26)

Drawing on this definition, my understanding of culture leaves room for the countless number of ways in which language, size, geography, age, history, socioeconomic status, beliefs, values, and ethnocultural heritage—to name just a few factors—continuously influence the culture(s) of a community or group, such as a congregation, which is in actuality a subculture of a broader culture (Ammerman 1998, 78–82). Furthermore, I recognize that cultures are fluid phenomena that are always being contested, challenged, and reformed as identities shift and members and cultures engage one another.

With this working definition of culture at hand, it is important to address a related term often used within discourses of cultural pluralism and diversity in Canada. *Multiculturalism* is a contested term that has multiple meanings. But, speaking broadly, there are at least three ways to define it. First, multiculturalism describes *the fact of diversity*, the reality that people of multiple cultures live side by side and interact with one another. Second, it can also speak of an *ideology*, a belief that in a given society there is no dominant and enforced culture, so people may choose the cultures (including their own) into which they integrate and with which they identify (Jansen, 2005, 32). In Canada, there appears to be a consensus that "some version of multiculturalism—whatever its limitations—is here to stay, lodged deeply at the heart of Canada's national identity both at home and abroad" (Chazan et al., 2011, 1). A third definition focuses on government *policies* formulated as "solutions" to the perceived problem of diversity. In Canada, such policies intend that, in James's words, "all Canadian 'cultural groups' . . . will be able to participate fully in society and realize their ambitions while 'maintaining their culture'" (2005, 13). In reality, however, multicultural policies do not always meet this mark and they remain marginal to federal initiatives.

CHILDREN, SPIRITUALITY, THEOLOGY, AND CULTURE

Although discussions surrounding culture, diversity, and multiculturalism have not been at the forefront of children's spirituality and theology, significant works in these fields refer to the importance of culture in the spiritual and religious lives of children. One might expect that, after having conversations with hundreds of children from across the globe, Robert Coles (1990) would have something to say about culture. While his diverse group of conversation partners may seem ideal for generating insight into children's spirituality and culture, only rarely does Coles address this topic.

One example, however, is found in his thoughts about a boy named Timmy. He states, "As I sit and think of Timmy's childhood, I recognize its psychological contours—the way, in a family of Irish background, race and class and religion and cultural values combine to work their influence on a boy's life" (126). Although not the focus on his phenomenological research, Coles hints that culture is a variable at play in children's spiritual lives.

While Coles generated data through conversations with children in different contexts and cultures, the research sample informing the work of David Hay and Rebecca Nye (2006) is fairly monocultural. However, their findings offer embryonic foundations for building a case for the importance of considering culture in relation to children's spirituality.

Hay argues that although spirituality is a biological phenomenon, it is always culturally-mediated and shaped by cultural contexts (Hay with Nye, 2006, 25, 26). For him, culture is a variable affecting nearly every node of the spiritual life. But it is not a neutral variable; it can "obscure" or "enhance" (Hay with Nye, 2006, 141) the spiritual lives of children and, according to Hay, the culture of contemporary adult society can hinder spiritual flourishing and close off particular areas of one's spiritual awareness (Hay with Nye, 2006, 33, 63).

Ironically, while Hay addresses culture as a variable affecting children's spirituality, the research sample for Nye's groundbreaking doctoral study—which is intimately connected with Hay's arguments—is largely monocultural. Yet, Nye's theory of relational consciousness strengthens understandings about culture and children's spirituality because it recognizes the importance of not only a child's relationship with God, but also her relationships with material things, with herself, and with other people (Hay with Nye, 2006, 109). So if relationships are central to children's spirituality, then a child's relationships with people of other cultures—as well as those with people from one's own culture—can shape that child's spiritual life. A child's awareness of these relationships is part of his "child-people consciousness," a dimension of spirituality that often acts as a bridge to a child's relationship with God (Hay with Nye, 2006, 116). Building on this assertion, one can argue that fostering relationships that nurture intercultural respect and appreciation can enhance a child's relational consciousness, since these relationships are interwoven with the spiritual life.

So culture matters to the spiritual well-being of children. And, according to Hay, different cultures can close children off to different aspects of spirituality (Hay with Nye, 2006, 63). But isn't the reverse also true? Can different cultures open children up to different aspects of spirituality? Hay alludes that this is so, for he asserts that social agreement can lead to dogmatism through "'cultural sedimentation' of a single perspective" (Hay with Nye, 2006, 153). Thus, relationships that children develop across lines of cultural difference can help them avoid forming a spirituality of harmful dogmatism by exposing them to multiple "equally legitimate ways of seeing" (Hay with Nye, 2006, 153).

Joyce Ann Mercer (2005) also offers insights into understanding children's spirituality and culture. In fact, her methodology for building a practical theology of childhood is helpful for forming a foundation for theological perspectives of children within different cultural contexts and within contexts of cultural diversity.

Drawing from Pierre Bourdieu's assertion that practices are shaped by larger "habitus" or social contexts, Mercer assesses how North America's consumption-based society affects practices and beliefs relating to children's religious education. In covert ways, cultures and ways of living are reproduced in individuals, who often see elements of a culture as personal preferences rather than the learned behaviors and beliefs that they are (Mercer, 2005). Her methodology helps name culture as a habitus and it offers a way of understanding how cultural contexts shape different elements of Christian belief and practice, including perspectives of children and childhood.

Mercer goes on to remind us that no habitus is a simple, one-dimensional social context. Habitus are complex milieu made up of elements from multiple cultures and communities that interact to form ways of life into which people are socialized. This understanding is helpful for making sense of habitus marked by cultural diversity, for in such contexts, multiple cultures vie for formative influence and compete for control of cultural reproduction (Mercer, 2005). In fact, cultural reproduction occurs:

> as dominant groups, able to disguise the power relations in such impositions of cultural arbitraries, thereby set the agenda for what other groups aspire to as they seek to alter their status and power positions. In effect, a particular way of doing things comes to be seen as commonsensical, natural, and self-evident. (Mercer 2005, 98)

In habitus characterized by cultural diversity, dominant cultures can exert power in ways that allow people within this context to believe and live as though the way of life of the dominant group is the best way to live. Thus, understanding Mercer's analysis of how habitus shape theologies of childhood and ministry with children offers insight into mechanisms that play roles in determining how ideas and relationships among different cultures affect theological perspectives of childhood and children's spiritual formation.

THE RISE OF MULTICULTURALISM IN CANADA

While diversity in Canada stretches back centuries, official policies of multiculturalism only arose in the latter half of the twentieth century. In 1963, the Canadian government established the Royal Commission on Bilingualism and Biculturalism in order to recommend action for forging an equal partnership between Canada's "two founding nations," the British and French. This report included a volume addressing the one in three persons in Canada who was not of British or French origin, which, in 1971, led to an official federal policy of "multiculturalism in a bilingual framework" (Jansen 2005, 25), the goal of which was to "support and promote the cultural differences of the various ethnic groups in order to achieve 'unity in diversity'" (Elabor-Idemudia 2005, 58). Fifteen years later, the Employment Equity Act was passed, seeking to remove barriers to meaningful employment for marginalized Canadian groups. This year also marked the first time that the federal census allowed Canadians to select multiple identities as their "ethnic group" (Day 2000, 199).

This is the climate in which I was raised—and it was woven into my childhood. My family joined a local Hungarian club in 1990 and throughout the following twelve years, this community became the backbone of my life. I was involved in fundraising ventures for trips to Hungary with the group; throughout elementary and high school, I based countless school projects on the history, food, culture, dance, and music of Hungary; I performed at cultural galas and festivals across North America, playing the Hungarian national anthem on my *citera* (a Hungarian folk instrument). Anyone who knew me when I was a child or teenager knew I was Hungarian—it was foundational to my identity.

Having Canadians appreciate their heritages—such as the way I came to value my Hungarian heritage—was one of the goals of the countless multicultural policies that were initiated and funded by federal, provincial, and municipal governments in Canada throughout the latter decades of the twentieth century and into the twenty-first. In a sense, I was a poster child for multiculturalism—a prime example of the cultural pride that multiculturalism sought to foster among Canadians new and old.

CRITICIZING MULTICULTURALISM

While I was learning to be a multicultural poster child, others were no so happy with how multiculturalism was being shaped and reshaped in Canada. Authors and scholars like Neil Bissoondath (2002) and Himani Bannerji (2000) penned harsh critiques of multiculturalism based on solid research and personal experiences. While there are certainly positive things that can be said about multiculturalism, criticisms like theirs provide cautionary notes for those of us seeking to seriously consider culture as we nurture the spiritual formation of children.

Culture Simplified

We have seen that broad definitions of culture (like that of James, which I offered above) leave room for diversity, complexity, and countless ways that ethnicity, religion, gender, sexuality, age, and social location, and other characteristics of human life blend together in hybrid identities. In multiculturalism, however, this wide view of culture tends to get stripped down to a perspective that is little more than a synonym for one's country of origin or the country of origin of one's ancestors. It leaves little room for the mixing of cultures and cultural elements in the complex realities of human life.

Thus, multiculturalism in Canada tends to promote a narrow view of culture, shortchanging this term from the fullness of its meaning and failing to allow for the multiplicity of ways that the web of culture is continuously spun and re-spun within the lives of human beings. It neglects the complexity that comes with acknowledging that cultures are not closed and fixed systems, but are created and recreated by ongoing hybridity in intentional and unintentional ways.

Culture Sanitized and Stagnant

In his widely-read *Selling Illusions*, Neil Bissoondath (2002) argues that multiculturalism simplifies and essentializes culture, meaning that it makes culture into a static object (77). Culture becomes a commodity put on display for others to have an easily-digestible "taste" without experiencing the potency of its full flavor. Members of non-dominant groups are assigned the role of the cultural "other" who must preserve their stereotyped cultural heritage rather than evolving and adapting to new times and places (Bissoondath, 2002, 222–3). In Bissoondath's words,

> Culture is life. It is a living, breathing, multi-faceted entity in constant evolution . . . Stasis is not possible. A culture that fails to grow from within inevitably becomes untrue to itself, inevitably descends into folklore. (2002, 75)

Since there are no cultures without human beings, cultures are alive. And, like all living things, they change and adapt to different times, places, and circumstances. Cultures not only act on the lives of human beings, but they are also *acted upon* by people. We make cultures. We adapt cultures. We shape and reshape cultures as we live and move and have our being. But multiculturalism tends to ignore this reality, transforming living and messy cultures into sanitized and simplified stereotypes.

Keeping the Dominant Dominating

Sociologist Himani Bannerji (2000) posits that multiculturalism acts as an apparatus of the state for maintaining hegemonic control of those deemed "other." Multiculturalism, she argues, creates a paradoxical category of "insider-outsider," which refers to non-white persons who are part of Canadian society, but, in her words, "we are not part of its self-definition as 'Canada' because we are not 'Canadians.' We are pasted over with labels that give us identities that are extraneous to us" (2000, 65). Bissoondath makes a similar claim, stating that multiculturalism encourages hyphenated identities and per-suades (non-British, non-white) Canadians to self-identify as *something*-Canadian. Canadians of European descent who speak English as a first language are seen as "just Canadian," while those who don't share their skin color or first language are identified as French-Canadian, Chinese-Canadian, or another hyphenated identity. Rather than nurturing a Canadian identity by helping people self-identify as Canadian, the hyphen highlights the invisibility or normalcy attributed to dominant white cultures and the marginalization that the unequal use of the hyphen maintains. In Bissoondath's words, the hyphen becomes "a sign of an acceptable marginalization" (2002, 108).

Bannerji goes on to call attention to multiculturalism as a way for dominant Anglo-Canadian cultures to maintain their control while "tolerating" and managing others as "multiculture." Yet multicultural otherness is only tolerated as long as it does not threaten the status quo. In her view, Canadian multiculturalism is surface-level and is not meant to dig to deeper issues like social justice and equality (Bannerji 2000, 79). In the end, it keeps power in the hands of those dominant cultural groups that have historically held power.

FROM MULTICULTURALISM TO INTERCULTURALISM

The picture of multiculturalism painted thus far can seem grim—more like a propa-ganda poster for controlling the masses than a tapestry woven with many different threads.

But there is hope. Those concerned with problematic aspects of multicultural-ism are responding by imagining what it means to become *intercultural*. Canadian ethicist Roger Hutchinson (2009) states that interculturalism "shifts the emphasis to encounters among persons and groups with cultural differences" (11). It moves the focus from the tolerance and assimilation of multiculturalism to mutuality, respect, and relationships. It recognizes that one single cultural group can no longer dominate a space and that "[t]he public realm is, and should be, both *shared* and *contested*" (Hutchinson 2009, 5). Interculturalism changes the response to diversity from mere coexistence to the sharing of power.

Within congregations, this shift involves moving from inviting people into *our* churches to being willing to shape what it means to be church *together*. Thus, intercul-turalism disrupts socially- and culturally-constructed ideas of what it means to be and do church, empowering us all to work together to find new ways of being the church. It upsets common practices for children's spiritual formation and challenges us to learn from one another and forge new ways of nurturing faith and spiritual vitality in young people. In intercultural ministry with children, "the way we've always done things" is no longer a good reason for continuing to do what we do (if it ever was a good reason in the first place), because we start recognizing that that there are different people who do things in different ways.

NURTURING A SPIRIT OF INTERCULTURALISM

As I reflect on the criticisms made against multiculturalism outlined above, I'm encouraged by ministry leaders, congregations, and denominations that are naming such problems and attempting to chart paths toward interculturalism. But the problematic aspects of multiculturalism can be deeply ingrained into the psyches of individuals and groups, so those on this journey are certainly swimming against the tide.

What will it take for the tide to change? I remain hopeful that young people can come of age not in the throes of multiculturalism, but in an environment that promotes a just vision of diversity in our increasingly pluralistic world. The tide can change as congregations foster an attitude of interculturalism through its spiritual formation initiatives with young people. Ministry with children can become a catalyst for nurturing children as followers of Jesus who don't just *tolerate* cultural diversity, but who *respect*, *appreciate*, and *embrace* it. From this hope, I share ideas for fostering interculturalism through ministry with children. These ideas will be fairly broad, for it feels imperialistic for me to simply tell others how to shape their practices with children. While some practices may be appropriate for particular contexts, they may not be appropriate for other contexts. Thus, I offer these ideas as invitations to join in the adventure of exploring what it means to nurture young members of the intercultural body of Christ.

Recognizing the Cultural Nature of Children's Ministry

As the spiritual lives of children are culturally-mediated, so, too, are the ways we nurture faith and spirituality in the young. Sunday school, educational programs, and practices that we employ in the spiritual formation of young people are culturally-based. For example, do we include children in worship services or create separate programs that run at the same time as congregational worship? Do we teach children to memorize prayers or to pray spontaneously? Every aspect of our efforts to cultivate spiritual growth in children is related to culture. So a first step in nurturing a spirit of interculturalism through children's ministry is to recognize the cultural nature of what we do to foster healthy spirituality in young people.

Mercer's consideration of habitus in relation to children's religious education reminds us that culture is so deeply ingrained into our visions of the world and so deeply shapes how we make meaning that it takes a conscious willingness and concerted effort to step back and ask how what we do to nurture children is bound up with our particular cultural contexts. But when we recognize the cultural nature of children's ministry, we can realize that our practices for nurturing children's spirituality aren't given to us on stone tablets from on high. They are the products of cultures. And naming this reality helps us to re-imagine our assumptions and practices for fostering faith in children. It invites us to forge different responses to diversity than the shallow tolerance of multiculturalism. It calls us to take on a posture of interculturalism and learn from one another as we all—in our own ways and in ways we create together—seek to cultivate faith among the young people in our midst.

Surrounding Children with Diversity

A second idea for moving towards interculturalism through ministry with children is to surround children with diversity. We can expose them to cultures that are not our own through the stories we tell them, the food we share with them, the music we sing and play together, and so much more. Since every aspect of children's ministry is shaped by culture, each aspect can be reshaped to help fan the spiritual flame in each child by enveloping children in diversity.

But criticisms raised against multiculturalism provide us with three cautionary words in our efforts to surround children with diversity. First, they remind us to be careful not to essentialize and simplify the cultures that we are sharing with them. Cultures are never as simple as they seem, so we need to be cautious not to boil the richness of any culture down to a few simple customs. And since cultures are always shifting and changing as they adapt to new times and places, we ought to expose children to diversity in ways that respect and appreciate cultures—and the people who are part of them.

Second, these criticisms call us to model respect for cultures that are not our own, which involves discerning what is and is not appropriate to share as outsiders to particular cultures. For example, playing some musical recordings of songs from another culture could be a great way to begin bringing diversity into ministry with children. But inviting children into sacred cultural practices that are not one's own becomes problematic. While I have been blessed to participate in Aboriginal smudging ceremonies, I do so only because I have been invited by the elders of a community. The smudging ceremony is a gift for me to receive—not one that is mine to give to others. When we see cultures as gifts, we cherish them and are careful not to pass on what isn't ours to give.

Finally, Bannerji and Bissoondath's analyses of multiculturalism encourage us to remember that as we surround children with diversity, we ought to avoid using the dominant culture as an implied norm. When a person belonging to a dominant culture talks about diversity, it is common to use one's own cultures as the assumed norms or reference points. When this happens, there is a hidden curriculum at play that teaches children that what people belonging to dominant cultures do is the norm and those who do things differently are, in a sense, *ab*normal. This is a tendency that we need to intentionally work at avoiding.

These three cautionary remarks are simply that. They are not meant to deter or discourage us from surrounding children with diversity. Rather, they help us share the gift of cultural diversity with the same respect and appreciation we seek to foster in the children with whom we minister.

Moving Toward Deeper Awareness

As Bannerji and Bissoondath have studied and experienced life amidst multiculturalism, they have been led to label it as surface-level, as not allowing the deeper issues embedded within pluralistic societies to be named and addressed. And their accusations ring true for my experiences as a born-and-bred Canadian.

While we Canadians like to think of ourselves as welcoming of diversity (sometimes by comparing ourselves to other nations), we overlook the fact that racism, ethnocentricism, and xenophobia exist within our borders. Using my life as a poster child for multiculturalism as a case study, it was only by moving to another country that I realized that there's a hidden underside (at least hidden to members of dominant cultures) to the peaceful and tolerant facade of Canadian multiculturalism. Upon seeing the hidden underside of a country and context that was not my own, I started to wonder if there were similar problematic aspects of Canada that I had been socialized *not to see*. I gradually learned (and am still learning) that by being enculturated in a nation that likes to focus on the positive aspects of its history, its life, and its diversity, I had been trained to ignore those problematic aspects of multiculturalism that others—because of skin color, accent, country of origin, or another reason—face on a daily basis.

So while the surface-level multiculturalism rampant in Canada might be open to diversity, it avoids dealing with deeper, more complex, and sometimes ugly issues. But interculturalism says that we cannot ignore these issues any longer. It dares us to dig deeper and analyze difficult and complex issues like power dynamics, institutional racism, white privilege, and cultural discrimination. And we can dig deeper into these issues with children, helping them to see what society may wish for them to ignore. After all, Hay (2006) calls our attention to the fact that a child's consciousness of her relationships can be deepened. Children's awareness of their relationships to others, to the societies in which they live, and to the issues involved in a world of cultural diversity can go deeper than simply being aware that other people do things differently.

Of course, this deepening of a child's awareness of issues surrounding cultural diversity should be done in gradual and age-appropriate ways—and maybe conversations surrounding these issues need to be reserved for older children and adolescents. Some children (and adults) in our communities, particularly those belonging to dominant cultures, will have trouble with these conversations. But others, particularly those who have felt the sting of discrimination and prejudice, already know about them all too well.

Clearly, this is challenging work. And we are going to make mistakes along the way. So we ought to be willing to admit when we mess up, to remain open to being corrected by one another, and to apologize and repent for our mistakes. We need to acknowledge the challenges that come with living interculturally. And we need to learn to forgive one another and forgive ourselves as we seek to nurture a spirit of interculturalism through ministry with children. As we do so, we will open ourselves and help children open themselves to receiving the blessings that come with living interculturally.

A Little Child Shall Lead Us

Hay and Nye (2006) remind us that children's relationships with other people can be a bridge to their consciousness of God (116). The relationships that children develop with others can shape their conceptualizations of and relationships with God—which can in turn shape their ideas of and relationships with other people. As children build mutual and respectful relationships with people across lines of cultural diversity, children can become open to the glorious diversity at play in God's world. They can come to see God as a God of diversity, a God who shows up in the world in many different ways. And when they see God in this way, they can in turn see all people—from any and all cultures—as bearers of God's image. And as the cycle continues, this can in turn open them to seeing and imagining God in new and diverse ways.

So intercultural relationships matter to children's spiritual lives and to the meanings they ascribe to God and their relationships with God. But these relationships also matter for moving toward interculturalism in the church and in the wider societies in which children live. Since, as Hay and Nye argue, spirituality can be a powerful force in social cohesion (2006, 30), nurturing the spiritual lives of children in ways that foster positive encounters with difference can be a powerful force in working toward interculturalism. Unfortunately, contemporary western society tends to privatize spirituality, making it more powerful as a source of personal comfort in the midst of chaos or distress rather than a potent catalyst for social cohesion and intercultural relationships (Hay with Nye 2006, 30).

Yet as Robert Coles interviewed children, he noticed that they desired to know about the other; better yet, he witnessed children's desires for unity with the other (1990). So while the adult world may be prone to privatization of the inner life and may tend to build walls to keep difference at bay, Coles reminds us that children want to hear and be heard by those who are different than they are.

This view may seem romanticized, but it reflects the lives of young people with whom Coles spoke. And it reminds us that sometimes the quest for fostering a spirit of interculturalism and of building mutual relationships across lines of difference is not just ours to pass onto younger generations. In many ways, children can be our guides for navigating a path toward interculturalism. So even though we ought to surround children with difference and help them go deeper in their awareness of cultural difference and diversity, in the end, it is children who can lead us in the adventure of the already-but-not-yet intercultural kingdom of God.

REFERENCES

Ammerman, Nancy T. "Culture and Identity in the Congregation." In *Studying Congregations: A New Handbook*, edited by Nancy T. Ammerman et al., 78–104. Nashville: Abingdon, 1998.

Bannerji, Himani. "Geography Lessons: On Being an Insider/Outsider to the Canadian Nation." In *The Dark Side of the Nation: Essays on Multiculturalism, Nationalism, and Gender*, 63–86. Toronto: Canadian Scholars' Press, 2000.

Bissoondath, Neil. *Selling Illusions: The Cult of Multiculturalism in Canada*. Rev. ed. Toronto: Penguin, 2002.

Chazan, May, et al., "Introduction: Labours, Lands, Bodies." In *Home and Native Land: Unsettling Multiculturalism in Canada*, edited by May Chazan et al., 1–11. Toronto: Between the Lines, 2011.

Coles, Robert. *The Spiritual Life of Children*. Boston: Houghton Mifflin, 1990.

Day, Richard J. F. *Multiculturalism and the History of Canadian Diversity*. Toronto: University of Toronto Press, 2000.

Elabor-Idemudia, Patience. "Immigrant Integration in Canada: Policies, Programs and Challenges." In *Possibilities and Limitations: Multicultural Policies and Programs in Canada*, edited by Carl E. James, 58–75. Halifax: Fernwood, 2005.

Hay, David with Rebecca Nye. *The Spirit of the Child*. Rev. ed. London: Jessica Kingsley, 2006.

Hutchinson, Roger. *Ethical Choices in a Pluralistic World*. Camrose, AB: The Chester Ronning Centre for the Study of Religion and Public Life, 2009.

James, Carl E. "Introduction: Perspectives on Multiculturalism in Canada." In *Possibilities and Limitations: Multicultural Policies and Programs in Canada*, edited by Carl E. James, 12–20. Halifax: Fernwood, 2005.

———. *Seeing Ourselves: Exploring Race, Ethnicity, and Culture*. 4th ed. Toronto: Thompson Educational, 2010.

Jansen, Clifford J. "Canadian Multiculturalism." In *Possibilities and Limitations: Multicultural Policies and Programs in Canada*, edited by Carl E. James, 21–33. Halifax: Fernwood, 2005.

Mercer, Joyce Ann. *Welcoming Children: A Practical Theology of Childhood*. St. Louis: Chalice, 2005.

Chapter 26

No More Sex in the City
Abstinence Education for Middle School Girls

La Verne Tolbert

But put on the LORD Jesus Christ,
And make no provision for the flesh to fulfill its lusts.
(ROMANS 13:14 NKJ)

In a normless society, teenagers may remain ambivalent about appropriate sexual behavior, including those who are Christians or who are being raised in Christian families. The biblical mandate for sexual self-control is repeated throughout scripture, but pre-teens and teenagers who attend public schools are exposed to a learning environment that is highly sexualized. In these settings, secrecy in the name of privacy is advised, and parents are often unaware of the lessons their children are really learning in school.

Abstinence, which is considered to be fear-based religious indoctrination by those who favor comprehensive sex education, is usually not taught, especially in California's public schools. Instead, children are given condoms by nurses who run the School-Based Health Center (SBHC)—a family-planning clinic located on school grounds (Scheyer, 1970). Without parental notification or consent, children are taught comprehensive sex education, which includes intercourse, "outercourse," masturbation, same-sex sex, anal sex, contraception, birth-control, and abortion.

Clinics in schools establish cultural norms for sexual behavior that minimize the spiritual, emotional, and physical consequences of sex outside the safe boundary of marriage. Students are intentionally exposed to explicit films and sexual images with the goal of desensitizing them so they are not embarrassed to talk about sex. They are taught that their parents' beliefs are old-fashioned and that the Bible and the church are outdated, judgmental, homophobic, and biased. No matter how young, children are encouraged that they have the right to be sexually active, messages that are vividly touted on the related SBHC websites to which students are referred.

At the same time, there is a cacophony of research documenting the high rates of teen sexual activity and teen pregnancy, especially in black communities, the same communities where SBHCs are concentrated. Monies, both federal and private, make SBHCs a lucrative business.

Society is replete with evidence that God is right about the safe boundary of marriage for sexual intercourse, even as secularism attempts to remove God from human thought and activity. Sexually transmitted diseases (STDs), including HIV/AIDS, are pandemic. So are broken hearts. Mothers are scrambling to protect their daughters from the human papilloma virus (HPV) by subjecting them to the reportedly dangerous series of vaccinations that may be ineffective to prevent cancer and that resulted in hundreds of young women becoming paralyzed or disabled (*The Daily Sheeple*, 2014).

Bombarded with sexual images, children receive conflicting messages—"Don't have sex, but if you do, use a condom"—which they hear in public schools and from some parents, as well as from some pastors (Tolbert, 1996). The result? Children are confused.

This chapter begins with a Christian worldview integration of the theological basis for sexual purity. Next, a historical overview of the development of SBHCs is presented. It concludes with the role of parents and the urgency of the church to be actively engaged in reinforcing the biblical teaching of abstinence.

CHRISTIAN WORLDVIEW INTEGRATION

Sex was God's idea beginning with Adam and Eve (Gen 1:28). As with every aspect of creation, it is good (Feinberg and Feinberg, 1993), even *very* good (Gen 1:31).

God protects his people from the consequences of non-marital sexual intercourse with the Old Testament law, "You shall not commit adultery" (Exod 20:14). Joseph, a handsome, single teenager, was propositioned by an attractive, wealthy woman. Because of his refusal and obedience to God, Joseph was the chosen instrument of deliverance for his family and nation, demonstrating that individual choices of morality affect the entire community (Evans, 1995). Proverbs is replete with reminders that the proper context for sexual activity is within the marriage bed (Prov 5:15; 6:24–29; 7:6–27; 9:13–18 are a sampling). King David's sin with Bathsheba and God's displeasure as proclaimed by the prophet Samuel provides an antithetical example (2 Sam 11–12).

In the New Testament, illicit sexual activity is evidence of moral depravity (Rom 1:18–32). Prevention, not protection or *provision*, is the charge, as Christians are instructed to walk "not in lewdness and lust" but to "put on the LORD Jesus Christ, and make no provision for the flesh, to fulfill its lusts" (Rom 13:13–14). *Provision* means "foreplanning, foresight, forethought, premeditated plan, making preparation for, providing for" (Strong's #4307).

Amid the backdrop of an idolatrous and promiscuous culture, the Apostle Paul reminded believers that the sexually immoral will *not* inherit the kingdom of God (1 Cor 6:9–10). Our bodies are not for sexual immorality but for the LORD (1 Cor 6:13). Because the consequences of non-marital sex harm the individual, like Joseph, we are to run from sexual sin.

> Flee sexual immorality. Every sin that a man does is outside the body, but he who commits sexual immorality sins against his own body.
>
> Or do you not know that your body is the temple of the Holy Spirit who is in you, whom you have from God, and you are not your own?
>
> For you were bought at a price; therefore glorify God in your body and in your spirit, which are God's. (1 Cor 6:18–20 NKJV)

God's will is that we marry, "For it is better to marry than to be aflame with passion and tortured continually with ungratified desire" (1 Cor 7:9 Amplified). Single people are to abstain (1 Thess 4:3–4); married couples are to be faithful (Heb 13:4). There is forgiveness of sin, as 1 John 1:9 assures: "If we confess our sins, he is faithful and just to forgive us our sins and to cleanse us from all unrighteousness." If we are truly "born of God," however, we will not have a lifestyle of sin. Christians cannot habitually, deliberately, continually practice sin because God's seed is in us (1 John 3:9).

Sexual purity is grounded in biblical discipleship defined as the life-long process of becoming like Christ that is "rooted in clear biblical teaching" (Wilkins, 1997, 61).

Nonnegotiable biblical discipleship

- is grounded in a personal, costly relationship with Jesus;
- results in a new identity in Jesus;
- is guided by God's Word;
- is empowered by the Holy Spirit;
- is developed through a whole-life process;
- is practiced in communities of faith; and
- is carried out in our everyday world. (Wilkins, 1997, 61)

Are children also involved in this process? Yes! As they respond to God's love, children begin the "journey of a deepening relationship and a growing understanding—the process of becoming more and more like Jesus" (May, Posterski, Stonehouse, and Cannell, 2005, 72). Parents are to be role-models who disciple their children, teaching them by talking "when you sit in your house, when you walk by the way, when you lie down, and when you rise up" (Deut 6:7). Unfortunately, some adults reflect on their own foolish promiscuity when they were young and, therefore, feel it unfair to expect their children to abstain. But the Bible says, "Train up a child in the way he should go" (Prov 22:6) *not*, "Train up a child in the way you went."

The disregard of biblical principles in our nation's public schools, plus an agenda that lies buried in America's discriminatory and racist past, together form the backdrop for SBHCs. Clinics on school grounds and clinics near schools (called school-linked clinics or SLCs) are spreading under the guise of health provision for the poor. Although they may provide some medical and mental-health services for students, SBHCs are by design family-planning clinics as demonstrated by this history.

POPULATION CONTROL AND THE BIRTH OF SCHOOL-BASED HEALTH CENTERS

On April 4, 1968, Dr. Martin Luther King Jr, who led the nation in a non-violent struggle for civil rights, was assassinated (Carson, 1998). As the walls of segregation were tumbling down, strategy was afoot to limit the growth of the black population (Farley, 1970). Large families, once necessary for the plantation, were now inconvenient and undesirable in the cities. Sub-standard education (Kozol, 1991) and limited employment opportunities for blacks produced a population that became increasingly dependent upon its government.

African American women were perceived to be particularly fecund or fertile (Farley, 1970) and controlling the growth of the black population was the focus of the federal government's national family planning efforts (*Population and the American Future*, 1972). Preserving the quality of life for the elite class (Hellman, 1971), producing children of higher intelligence in keeping with the eugenics philosophy (Sanger, 1922; 1938; Valenza, 1985), and the Malthusian strategy of monitoring one's own fertility (Scheyer, 1970) were shared goals of the family planning movement.

In 1969, the Department of Health, Education and Welfare (DHEW) established the National Center for Family Planning Services in the Health Services and Mental Health Administration (HSMHA) (Scheyer, 1970). The Family Planning Services and Population Research Act of 1970 (Title X) was an agreement to sub-contract Planned Parenthood Federation of America (PPFA) with federally-funded grants and contracts to provide free or low-cost services to minority women who had been identified as women at high-risk of pregnancy (Scheyer, 1970). Contraceptives and services were to be made available through free-standing, walk-in, non-medical family-planning units (Gobble, Vincent, Cochrane, and Lock, 1969). With the PPFA agreement, Scheyer (1970) observed that the federal government had finally assumed "a responsible role in family planning efforts" by developing a "meaningful federal and private partnership among all interested groups" to address "this area of great social need" (24).

The Commission

Further demonstration of federal commitment was the decision by Congress, in response to President Nixon's request, to create a Commission on Population Growth and the American Future to study the effects of population growth and immigration on government, the economy, and the environment (Scheyer, 1970). In 1972, the Commission, chaired by John D. Rockefeller 3rd, issued its report noting that "small differences in family size will make big differences in the demand placed on our society" (*Population and the American Future*, 1972, 45). Stating that family-planning was too important to be left to voluntary organizations or to private efforts, the Commission authorized $225 million in 1973, $275 million in 1974, $325 million in 1975, and $400 million each year after 1975 in Title X grants and contracts to be paid to PPFA to provide fertility-related services for inner-city women.

The Commission also recommended that laws which restricted the availability of all family planning, including laws pertaining to parental notification and consent, be changed. "The Commission urges that organizations, such as the Council on State governments, the American Law Institute, and the American Bar Association, formulate appropriate model statutes" (*Population and the American Future*, 1972, 170). Contraceptives were to be made available to minors in settings considered appropriate for them—their schools.

Eliminating racial discrimination in employment and improving housing were recommended. Also recommended was passage of the Equal Rights Amendment to encourage women to find meaningful work outside the home which would result in fewer babies.

Planned Parenthood's multi-pronged task was to set up family planning centers in neighborhoods and schools (Planned Parenthood of New York City, 1970). In delivery of services, sex education was important and so was decentralization of schools (Planned Parenthood of New York City, 1970). Mary Calderone, medical director of Planned Parenthood, disassociated from Planned Parenthood to establish the Sex Information and Education Council of the United States (SIECUS), which became the national clearinghouse for sex education curricula for all public schools (Guttmacher and Pilpel, 1970).

The First School-Based Clinic

The first comprehensive school-based clinic (SBC) opened quietly in 1970 in a Dallas high school (Kirby, 1989; Kirby, Waszak, and Ziegler, 1991). By 1971, the illegitimacy rates of girls fifteen to nineteen had risen eighteen percent, but the rise was among white teenage girls (Pilpel and Wechsler, 1971).With the legalization of abortion in 1973, laws regarding parental consent for contraceptive services were challenged. The voting age had been lowered from twenty-one to eighteen, not so that teenagers could vote, but so that late adolescents could be recognized as adults to receive comprehensive services (Paul, Pilpel, and Wechsler, 1974).

Attention now turned to deciding which contraception was most effective for teenagers. Because it was widely used, affordable, and available without medical prescription, condoms were the solution (Harvey, 1972).

In 1973, a second school-based clinic (SBC) was established in a St. Paul, Minnesota, junior/senior high school (Edwards et al., 1980; Edwards, Steinman, and Hakanson, 1977). Parents, teachers, and community leaders who objected to policies and practices that violated their parental rights forced a two-year delay (Edwards, et al., 1980). However, clinic staff assured the community that no contraceptives would be dispensed on site, so the Board of Education finally granted its approval. But contraceptives were given to students during special events.

To encourage students to come to the SBC, clinic staff members were given class schedules to facilitate recruiting students personally. For marketing purposes, SBC services were expanded to include athletic, job and college physicals, immunizations, and a weight-control program; a day care facility was added (Edwards, et al., 1980). This strategy proved successful because the combined services attracted more students to enroll in the SBC (Morris, 1974; Zelnik and Kantner, 1974). "Specialized procedures, tests, and consultations [were] arranged at nearby hospitals" (Dryfoos, 1985). School-based clinics were seen as the best hope of reducing the "unwed mother syndrome" among inner-city women (Edwards et al., 1977, 765).

Reversing Parental Notification and Consent

Reversal of parental consent laws occurred in 1977 with the *Carey v. Population Services International* Supreme Court decision, which ruled that contraceptives were to be made available to all minors without parental notification or consent (Paul and Pilpel, 1979). Mahoney (1979) identified those who opposed sex education and SBCs as people who held traditional views of the family. But the family was excluded from decisions affecting African American children. According to Zelnik (1979), black children learned about sex best in schools as opposed to white children who learned about sex best in the home. At the close of the decade, teenage pregnancy was recognized as "one of America's critical personal and social problems" (Dryfoos and Heisler, 1978).

From Clinics to Health Centers and Condoms for HIV

By 1981, the number of sexually active women rose from 3.1 million to 4.1 million (Forrest, Hermalin, and Henshaw, 1981). Ralph and Edginton (1983) compared "live birth rates in West Dallas to those in a matched area in another part of the city" for "eight consecutive years, from 1971 to 1978" (159). There were 85.3 fewer births at the SBC school.

Although birth-rates were declining, inner-city schools were failing scholastically. In contrast, alternative schools had lower fertility rates due to heightened student aspirations and high teacher expectations (Dryfoos, 1984). Other researchers observed that teen pregnancy had to be examined in context with variables such as the "physical, social, psychological, and economic aspects" which impact sexual behavior (Black and DeBlassie, 1985, 228). While researchers grappled for solutions, religion emerged as a significant factor that was successful in delaying sexual intercourse (Kastner, 1984).

By 1985, there were thirteen comprehensive, multiservice SBCs modeled after the St. Paul school (Dryfoos, 1985; Kort, 1984). Parents still objected, so Dryfoos (1985) cautioned *not* presenting SBCs as family planning clinics but as:

> comprehensive, multiservice units that emphasize physical examinations and treatment of minor illnesses. This portrait certainly is valid, considering that only a small portion of all clinic visits are for family planning. (Dryfoos, 1985, p. 72)

Additionally, clinic staff was advised not to dispense contraceptives during the first year of operation but to introduce these services during the second year after the controversy over opening the SBC subsided (Dryfoos, 1985). And, Dryfoos (1985) explained how SBCs work: No matter the reason for the visit, students are given psychosocial evaluations and questioned about their sexual activity. Contraceptives are recommended, and females receive pelvic examinations and Pap smears, usually during morning school hours. For abortions, clinic nurses drive girls from school to nearby Planned Parenthood facilities and transport them back to school in the afternoon before the end of the school day (Dryfoos, 1985). Parents have no idea that their daughter has had surgery.

School-based clinics are expensive operations. Costs for services, primarily for salaries, range from $90,000 to over $300,000 per clinic (Dryfoos, 1985; Kirby, 1985; *School-Based Clinics that Work*, 1993). Even with substantial Title X and state grants, SBCs received additional funding from Medicaid and social services, plus major funding from private foundations (Dryfoos, 1985; Warren, 1987; Glasow, 1988; Jee, 1993). However, even with substantial contributions, the cost-effectiveness of SBCs had not yet been proven (Dryfoos, 1985).

Center for Population Options Becomes Advocates for Youth

To help craft language and develop strategy for community acceptance of SBCs, the Center for Population Options (CPO), an arm of Planned Parenthood, offered technical and advisory support. Their name seemed a bit too controversial, however, so in 1994 the Center for Population Options renamed itself Advocates for Youth. The objective is to solicit community support by citing poverty statistics and the number of poor children in public schools who are without medical coverage as rationale for

SBC expansion (CPO, 1986; Kirby, 1986; Lovick, 1987). By comparing SBC costs to that of private medical care, school-based health centers or SBHCs as they are now called, are promoted as cost-effective vehicles for delivery of services to the poor (Siegel and Krieble, 1987).

By 1986, there were sixty SBHCs throughout the United States with seventy-five in planning stages (Kirby, 1986). Marsiglio and Mott (1986) observed that young adolescent women fifteen to eighteen years old who had taken a course in sex education were more likely to initiate sexual activity. Dawson (1986) similarly demonstrated that contraception education was significantly related to first incidence of coitus among early adolescents, but religiosity measured by "church attendance one or more times a week reduces the odds of first coitus at all ages" among African Americans (166).

Olsen and Weed (1987) evaluated the relationship between family planning clinics and teenage fertility rates and found an increase of 120 pregnancies per 1,000 among fifteen to nineteen year olds. Even proponents acknowledged that SBHCs failed to impact pregnancy rates (Dryfoos, 1988).

As parents and community leaders learned that SBHCs were planned for their schools, they organized and were successful in preventing these clinics from opening in San Diego, Boston, and New York. States began to place limits on state-funded family planning services (Dryfoos, 1988). But to demonstrate the viability of SBHCs, Brindis (1988) advised clinic staff to evaluate effectiveness by counting the total number of visits and students with parental consent forms on file even though parental consent is not required.

By 1988 there were over 150 SBHCs (Dryfoos, 1988; Kirby, Waszak, and Ziegler, 1989). The Annie E. Casey Foundation donated $50 million to five cities to reach inner-city at-risk youth who were identified as African American (Dryfoos, 1988). Benson and Donahue (1989) objected to this broad categorization of African American teenagers as at-risk youth, citing sampling bias as a methodological problem. Religiosity, the number of nights that seniors go out, and whether or not they have plans to attend college have the greatest predictive power for reducing at-risk behaviors. Teenager's future orientation, educational goals, and the presence of both parents in the home are additional contributing factors (Benson and Donahue, 1989).

HIV/AIDS: Condoms or Abstinence?

With national concern about the spread of HIV/AIDS, the Centers for Disease Control (CDC, 1988) suggested abstinence or sexual intercourse with one mutually faithful uninfected partner as the best protection against infection. Teaching abstinence was urged by the National Conference of Catholic Bishops, but Planned Parenthood researchers disagreed (Dryfoos, 1988). Increasing SBHCs and condom distribution were the recommended interventions for inner-city children (CPO, 1988a; CPO 1988b; Dryfoos and Klerman, 1988).

Dalton (1989) objected. Solutions are "imposed without seeking our views, hearing our experiences, or taking account of our needs and desires" (219). Other African American researchers also protested that condom availability would result in increased sexual activity rates and that, for racist reasons, minority students are especially targeted for these services (Allen, 1989). Allen (1989) also noted that white children are taught that abstinence is the only way to prevent HIV infection, but sex education curricula targeted to black children focuses on pregnancy prevention and the use of condoms (Kenney, Guardado, and Brown, 1989).

A National Adolescent Student Health Survey of 11,000 eighth and ninth graders demonstrated that abstinence is acceptable to 94 percent of adolescent females, and 76 percent of adolescent males believe that "saying no" to premarital sexual intercourse is acceptable (de Mauro, 1989/1990). Teaching abstinence and offering contraceptives for those who choose to be sexually active was recommended (Christopher and Roosa, 1990), but Weed et al. (1991) felt the two messages confusing.

Parents agreed. They favored abstinence education and rejected comprehensive sex education (Stackhouse, 1989/1990). Meanwhile, teen pregnancy in Utah declined with the 1980 law requiring parental consent for birth control (Kasun, 1989).

By 1991 there were 239 SBHCs and SLCs targeting a majority of African American and Latino students (Waszak and Neidell, 1991). In 1992, SIECUS (1992) reported that curriculum emphasizing abstinence and heterosexual marriage was inadequate, and a national plan for mandatory comprehensive sex education and SBHCs in all schools by the year 2000 was developed ("Comprehensive School-Health Education Workshop," 1993). Guidelines for articulating the rationale of SBHCs and for obtaining federal funding and state grants were published (CPO, 1993). McGinnis (1993) applauded the government's commitment to providing family planning and health services for the 46 million children in public, private, elementary, middle, and high schools in keeping with the national agenda of population control.

There were 178 SBHCs by 1992, but to receive increased federal funding for services, more students needed to be enrolled. Pizza parties, school dances, and free tickets to sporting events were added as incentives (Feroli et al., 1992). Not every researcher agreed that SBHCs were effective. Griffin (1993) observed that clinics on school campuses might imply "permission for early sexual activity" (5).

Meanwhile, teenagers were embarrassed with condoms in their classrooms (St. Lawrence, 1993), so based on Bandura's theory of self-efficacy Hayden (1993) developed a game called The Condom Race. Students sit in groups, blind-folded, and roll and unroll condoms on and off "anatomically correct erect penis models . . . [or] appropriate-size fruits or vegetables, such as a cucumber, a zucchini, or a banana. Winners receive more condoms," (Hayden, 1993, 134).

SBHC Evaluation: Results are Not Significant

Brindis et al. (1994) evaluated SBHCs and studied 162 female high school students who attended four California SBHC schools. Results indicate that the presence of the SBHC and

> the availability of contraceptives on site, which has been thought to be an important convenience factor contributing to positive contraceptive adoption, was not found to be significant. (160)

Still SBHCs continued to open in school after school, although lawsuits by parents were successful in closing some clinics (Ebert, 1994).

By 1995, there were 607 SBHCs in high schools and middle schools (Berg, 1994; Schlitt et al., 1995). Surprisingly, researchers announced plans to begin comprehensive sex education at the kindergarten level (Kolbe et al., 1995; McKinney and Peak, 1994).

After two decades of family-planning clinics in schools, Dryfoos (1995) acknowledged that SBHCs did *not* impact the teen birth rate. "These are the worst of times" (Dryfoos, 1995, 19).

Role of Religion

Religion as a preventive factor to premarital sexual intercourse continued to emerge as a successful intervention (Parker, 1994). This was supported by my doctoral research which demonstrates that children who attend church are more likely to disagree with the "safer sex" message and affirm they would not have sex even if they had a condom (Tolbert, 1996).

Additionally, the SBHC presence on school campuses may result in increased rates of sexual activity. Among females who entered high school as virgins, 37 percent became sexually active in the comparison school; 60 percent became sexually active in the SBHC school, $p = .008$.

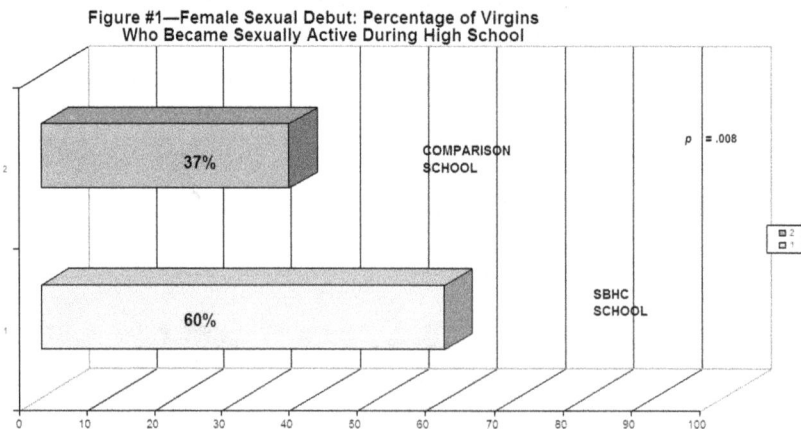

Figure #1—Female Sexual Debut: Percentage of Virgins Who Became Sexually Active During High School

African American males perceived that since condoms are available in their school environment, sexual activity is expected and accepted by parents, principals, and teachers. Despite these and similar findings from other researchers, abstinence education is not taught in inner-city schools in Los Angeles—a decision protested by this researcher when over 14 million in federal abstinence funds was rejected by California legislators.

> Something is wrong with our logic. There are condoms in our schools . . . Studies show that teenagers may not consistently use condoms. Even if they do use them, HIV/AIDS might still result from "imperfect" use. And students may be exposed to other sexually transmitted diseases that are not prevented by condoms. Self-control, self-respect, delayed gratification, planning for the future, building healthy friendships and other values essential to abstinence education are necessary for every area of life, not just in the delay of sexual activity. (Tolbert, 1998, p. B7)

Clinics in Elementary Schools?

By 2005, there were 869 SBHCs. With 195, New York has the largest number in schools K-5. California, with 140, has the second-largest. Thirty-five percent of SBHCs are in elementary schools with plans for expansion to *all* public elementary schools. Pregnancy testing remains a primary service—76 percent (Lear, 2007).

Weed (2009) demonstrated that SBHC strategies are ineffective, noting that "research does not support abandoning abstinence education in favor of a comprehensive sex education strategy that has not been proven to be successful" (2). But by 2011, there were 1,930 SBHCs nationwide, and at annual conventions, strategies are presented to fund and expand clinics throughout the United States (School-Based Health Alliance, 2010–2011; School-Based Health Alliance in Action n. d.)

Websites—What Children and Teens are Learning

The Advocates for Youth (n. d.) website provides resources on how to minimize parental and community objections to open SBHCs in public schools. Included on the website is a link for youth called Amplify Your Voice (n. d.), that has contests to "keep it safe and sexy," a fundraising program for Planned Parenthood, along with videos and content that belittle abstinence-only curriculum.

> "Just Say No" didn't work for drugs, and it won't work for sex. Abstinence-only-until-marriage programs deny our right to honest sex education. These programs censor information about contraception and condoms; make moral judgments students may not share; stigmatize and shame students who have already had sex; and discriminate against GLBTQ students by at best ignoring

us and at worst promoting homophobia. These programs often encourage stereotypical gender roles, use scare tactics, blur religion and science, and contain factual errors, like saying that HIV can be spread through sweat and tears. (Amplify Your Voice, n.d.)

That HIV is spread through illicit sexual activity is never addressed. Condoms proliferate. On one page are pink, orange, yellow, green, blue, and purple candy-colored condoms. Students are instructed how to use condoms for oral sex:

> Cut open this condom and use it as a dental dam! Only use one condom at time (sic) and use a new one for every sexual act! Make sure it looks like sombrero (sic) before you start rolling down! Only use water based lubes. Try putting a drop on the inside too! (Amplify Your Voice, n. d.)

The "Great American Condom Campaign" with a red, white, and blue logo offers this advice: "Do It for Your Country." Also on this website is criticism of the African American church for its stance against premarital sex and homosexuality. False statistical information abounds, such as "95 percent of all Americans have had sex before marriage"; "85 percent of all parents want comprehensive sex education"; "70 percent of teens have had sexual intercourse." There are no sources to support this data.

GOOD NEWS: ABSTINENCE WORKS

There is good news about abstinence education. It works. "Teen sexual activity has decreased significantly . . . even as teens are confronted with an increasingly sexualized culture" (Abstinence Works, 2013, 1). According to the 2006–2010 National Survey of Family Growth, 73 percent of girls and 72 percent of boys ages fifteen to seventeen are choosing abstinence (CDC, 2011).

What is the most frequent reason given for not having sex? Among teenagers who abstain, 41 percent of females and 31 percent of males say it is "against [their] religion or morals" (CDC, 2011, 11). Recent data also demonstrates that abstinence-only education, called sexual risk avoidance (SRA), is successful. For example, the Youth Risk Behavior Survey (YRBS) finds an increase in the number of Mississippi high school students who report always being abstinent—30 percent in 1993; 52.6 percent in 2011 (McAdoo, 2012). In students nationwide, the prevalence of having ever had sexual intercourse has decreased over the past twenty years. "Overall, in the 20-year period from 1988 through 2006–2010, the percentage of teenaged females who were sexually experienced declined significantly (from 51 percent in 1988 to 43 percent in 2006–2010)" (CDC, 2011, 5). Perhaps it's time to empower all students, especially those in the inner-city, with abstinence-only education.

Parents are Pivotal

Parents are pivotal in keeping their children sexually pure (Tolbert, 2007). Setting boundaries, monitoring the Internet, screening friends, and making sure extracurricular activities are wholesome are the responsibilities of mom and dad. And, parents should be educated about the information their children receive in health classes at school. They must ask questions, visit their children's classrooms, and read every form that is brought home at the beginning of the school year. It is especially important for parents to know that they have the right to opt *out* of comprehensive sex education classes for their children (105–108).

There are alternatives to public education such as home-schooling and private or alternative schools. But these are not the only solutions. Being a proactive parent of a child who attends public school—and insisting on parental rights—may help change that school. If it feels like David vs. Goliath, remember, David won!

Parental involvement is especially key in children's spiritual development. In the Roehlkepartain (2012) survey of 7,600 youth ages twelve to twenty-five, family emerged as the most important factor in helping youth in their spiritual life. Family's spiritual involvement and participation makes it easier for the youth themselves to be spiritual. It's understandable. "God designed the home as the primary place for children to receive spiritual instruction" (Bruner and Stroope, 2010, 31). Daily family Bible study results in lively discussions that evaluate the issues of the day based on biblical presuppositions. Unfortunately, many say they don't *understand* the Bible so they leave this vital task in the hands of the "professionals" on Sunday, which isn't what God intended. Thankfully, there are easy-to-read books that explain the Bible so that it is fun to read, understandable and applicable (Tolbert, 2012). Such resources equip moms and dads in providing the spiritual nurture their children crave.

Not to be overlooked is the church's responsibility to sponsor parenting workshops to remind parents of the power they have as role models. Helping parents remember the developmental challenges of growing up and encouraging them about the importance of spending time with their children—especially teenagers—while providing counseling and support are essential (Tolbert, 2007).

ENGAGING THE CULTURE: NO MORE SEX IN THE CITY

When the church is engaged in the culture of the community, teachable moments abound. Many of the children who attend public schools also sing in the choir, and they may also be active in Sunday school and youth groups. Churches that are responsive have an opportunity to intersect the everyday challenges of life with the good news of the Gospel.

> In the midst of these challenges, it is incumbent upon local churches actively to engage the culture and to intervene in the lives of single adults, young

marrieds, and parents in general. Quality and compelling ministries that attract each of these target audiences are specific help that can be provided. Separate ministries for different demographic and affinity groups will ensure that life-stage needs are adequately addressed. Regular interaction with one another in semistructured fellowship environments where mature social competencies can be developed is also imperative. (Cardoza, 2011, 50)

Sex education seminars, guest speakers, Bible studies, youth groups, debates, camps, retreats, and Sunday morning sermons that reinforce abstinence are a sprinkling of the opportunities to share biblically sound, theologically-centered transformative truth in creative ways. One example is the interactive workshop, No More Sex in the City, sponsored by Teaching Like Jesus Ministries (TLJM), Pasadena, CA. Since the first step in providing abstinence education is to train speakers, TLJM developed a five-week Abstinence Training Institute using this curriculum outline:

Session 1—*The Power of Scripture* (the biblical foundation for sexual purity)

Session 2—*The Power of Statistics* (incorporating statistical data)

Session 3—*The Power of Truth* (pregnancy, abortion, and STDs including HIV/AIDS)

Session 4—*The Power of Hooks* (framing the presentation to keep the audience's attention using Nook, Hook, Book, Look, Took, Cook and addressing learning channels) (Tolbert, 2000)

Session 5—*The Power of You* (presentation and evaluation of the abstinence talk)

Among the excellent speakers who emerged from the training were Tegra Little, Founder/Director of No Longer Bound, a post-abortion recovery ministry in Los Angeles, and actress/model, Joy Williams. They participated in a pilot seminar for middle-high school girls during the Daughters of Esther Workshop at Christ Temple Church of Christ Holiness (USA) Pasadena, CA, where Bishop Emery Lindsay is pastor. Mary Bingham, who organized the workshop, invited us for this summer 2011 all-day event. With music, PowerPoint, videos, personal stories, and giveaways, we engaged sixty pre-teen girls and teenagers in a two-hour abstinence session. Ninety-percent of attendees signed the No More Sex in the City Virginity Pledge cards. The seminar was repeated summer 2012 at Crenshaw Christian Center in Los Angeles where Frederick Price, Jr. is pastor during Josie Martin's city-wide abstinence workshop.

Another ideal setting to teach abstinence is a Rites of Passage program for boys where a year-long curriculum of manhood training is taught. For private or Christian middle and high schools, teaching a six-week abstinence curriculum like A. C. Green's *I've Got the Power* reinforces resistance skills equipping students to affirm "Not Yet" or "No More" (Tolbert and Cunningham, 1995).

CONCLUSION

For parents, pastors, youth workers and teachers, the task of imparting biblical values becomes one that is increasingly counter culture. Abstinence education is not prudish, nor is it biased. It is neither the byproduct of religious fanaticism nor the result of fear-based theology. Abstinence is truth, and teaching children how to make right decisions is a loving gift that should be imparted to *all* children.

REFERENCES

Abstinence Works. *Sexual Risk Avoidance (SRA) Abstinence Education Programs Demonstrating Improved Teen Outcomes.* Report. National Abstinence Education Foundation, Washington, DC, 2013.

Advocates for Youth/Center for Population Options. (n. d.) Retrieved from http://www.advocatesforyouth.org/

Allen, W. B. "Target: Minorities." *ALL About Issues.* Stafford, VA: American Life League, October, 1989.

Amplify Your Voice (n. d.) Retrieved from http://www.amplifyyourvoice.com/

Benson, P. L., and M. J. Donahue. "Ten-Year Trends in At-Risk Behaviors: A National Study of Black Adolescents." *Journal of Adolescent Research* 4 (1989): 125–139.

Berg, M. H. "Clinic Considered at Middle School." *Los Angeles Times* [Home Edition, City Times], p. 8., January 9, 1994.

Black, C., and R. R. DeBlassie. "Adolescent Pregnancy: Contributing Factors, Consequences, Treatment, and Plausible Solutions." *Adolescence* 20 (1985): 281–290.

Brindis, C. D. "Evaluating School-Based Clinic Programs." *Clinic News* 4, no. 2 (1988): 38.

———. et al. "Characteristics Associated with Contraceptive Use Among Adolescent Females in School-Based Family Planning Programs." *Family Planning Perspectives* 26 (1994): 160–164.

Bruner, Kurt, and Steve Stroope. *It Starts at Home: A Practical Guide to Nurturing Lifelong Faith.* Chicago: Moody, 2010.

Cardoza, Freddy. "Crisis on the Doorstep" In *A Theology for Family Ministries* edited by Michael and Michelle Anthony, pp. 42–64. Nashville, TN: B&H Publishing, 2011.

Carson, Clayborne, ed. *The Autobiography of Martin Luther King, Jr.* New York: Warner, 1998.

Center for Population Options/Advocates for Youth. School-Based Clinic Policy Initiatives Around the Country: 1986 [Report]. Washington, DC: Author, 1986.

———. *D. C. Teenagers and AIDS: Knowledge, Attitudes, and Behaviors* [Report]. Washington, DC: Author, 1988a. (ERIC Document Reproduction Service No. ED 308 583)

———. *School-Based Clinics: A Guide For Advocates. Developing Policy Statements, Educating Decision Makers, Enlisting Local Support.* Washington, DC: Author, 1988b. (ERIC Document Reproduction Service No. ED 312 784)

———. *Condom Availability in Schools: A Guide for Programs.* Washington, DC: Author, 1993.

Centers for Disease Control. "Condoms for Prevention of Sexually Transmitted Diseases." *Public Health Reports* 16 (1988): 13–20.

————. "Teenagers in the United States: Sexual activity, Contraceptive Use, and Childbearing, 2006–2010 National Survey of Family Growth." Series 23, no. 31 (2011). Retrieved from http://www.cdc.gov/nchs/data/series/sr_23/sr23_031.pdf

Christopher, F. S., and M. W. Roosa. "An Evaluation of an Adolescent Pregnancy Prevention Program: Is 'Just Say No' Enough?" *Family Relations* 39 (1990): 68–72.

Comprehensive School-Health Education Workshop, The [Special issue]. *Journal of School Health* 63, January, 1993.

Daily Sheeple, The. Excerpt from a Story by Sarah Cain. January 4, 2014. Retrieved from http://www.thedailysheeple.com/lead-developer-of-hpv-vaccines-comes-clean-warns-parents-young-girls-its-all-a-giant-deadly-scam_012014

Dalton, H. L. "AIDS in Blackface." *Daedalus* (1989): 205–227.

Dawson, D. A. "The Effects of Sex Education on Adolescent Behavior." *Family Planning Perspectives* 18 (1986): 162–170.

de Mauro, D. "Sexuality Education 1990: A Review of State Sexuality and AIDS Education Curricula." *SIECUS Report* 18 (1989/1990): 19.

Dryfoos, J. G. "A New Strategy for Preventing Unintended Teenage Childbearing [Comment]." *Family Planning Perspectives* 16 (1984): 193–195.

————. "School-Based Health Clinics: A New Approach to Preventing Adolescent Pregnancy?" *Family Planning Perspectives* 17 (1985): 70–75.

————. "School-Based Health Clinics: Three Years of Experience." *Family Planning Perspectives* 20 (1988), 193–200.

————. "From Where I Sit." *Family Life Educator* 14, no. 2 (1995/1996): 1819.

————. and T. Heisler. "Contraceptive Services for Adolescents: An Overview." *Family Planning Perspectives* 10 (1978): 223–233.

————. and L. V. Klerman. "School-Based Clinics: Their Role in Helping Students Meet the 1990 Objectives." *Health Education Quarterly* 15 (1988): 71–80.

Ebert, M. "Will Condoms Land Schools in Court?" *Focus on the Family Citizen* 8 (1994): 10–11.

Edwards, L. E., et al. "An Experimental High School Clinic." *American Journal of Public Health* 67 (1977): 765–766.

————. "Adolescent Pregnancy Prevention Services in High School Clinics." *Family Planning Perspectives* 12 (1980): 614.

Farley, R. *Growth of the Black Population.* Chicago: Markham Publishing, 1970.

Feroli, K. L., et al. "School-Based Clinics: The Baltimore Experience." *Journal of Pediatric Health Care* 6 (1992): 127–131.

Forrest, J. D., et al. "The Impact of Family Planning Clinic Programs on Adolescent Pregnancy." *Family Planning Perspectives* 13 (1981): 109–116.

Glasow, R. D. *School-Based Clinics: The Abortion Connection.* Washington, DC: National Right to Life Educational Trust Fund, 419 7th Street NW, Suite 500, Washington, DC 20004,1988.

Gobble, F. L., et al. "A Nonmedical Approach to Fertility Reduction." *Obstetrics and Gynecology* 34 (1969): 888–891.

Goldsmith, S., et al. "Teenagers, Sex and Contraception." *Family Planning Perspectives* 4, no. 1 (1972): 32–38.

Griffin, G. C. "Condoms and Contraceptives in Junior High and High School Clinics: What Do You Think?" [Editorial]. *Postgraduate Medicine* 93, no. 5 (1993): 16.

Guttmacher, A. F., and H. Pilpel. "Abortion and the Unwanted Child." *Family Planning Perspectives* 2, no. 2 (1970): 16–24.

Harvey, P. D. "Condoms—A New Look." *Family Planning Perspectives* 4, no. 4 (1972): 27–30.

Hayden, J. "The Condom Race." *Journal of American College Health* 42 (1993): 133–136.

Hellman, L. M. "Five-Year Plan for Population Research and Family Planning Services." *Family Planning Perspectives* 3, no. 4 (1971): 35–40.

Jee, M. "School-Based Health Clinics Now Seen as Key Health Site." *Journal of American Health Policy*, (May/June 1993): 53–54.

Kastner, L. S. "Ecological Factors Predicting Adolescent Contraceptive Use: Implications for Intervention." *Journal of Adolescent Health Care* 5 (1984): 79–86.

Kasun, J. "Sex Education: A New Philosophy for America?" *The Family in America*, (July, 1989): 8.

Kenney, A. M., et al. "Sex Education and AIDS Education in the Schools: What States and Large School Districts are Doing." *Family Planning Perspectives* 21 (1989): 56–64.

Kirby, D. *School-Based Health Clinics: An Emerging Approach to Improving Adolescent Health and Addressing Teenage Pregnancy* [Report]. Washington, DC: Center for Population Options/Advocates for Youth, 1985. (ERIC Document Reproduction Service No. ED 277 955)

———. "Comprehensive School-Based Health Clinics: A Growing Movement to Improve Adolescent Health and Reduce Teen-Age Pregnancy [Commentary]. *Journal of School Health* 56 (1986): 289–291.

———. *School-Based Clinics Enter the 90s: Update Evaluation and Future Challenges* [Report]. Washington, DC: Center for Population Options/Advocates for Youth, 1989. (ERIC Document Reproduction Service No. ED 320 209)

———. et al. "Executive Summary: Utilization, Impact, and Potential of School-Based Clinics." In P. Donovan, (Ed.), *An Assessment of Six School-Based Clinics: Service, Impact and Potential*. Washington, DC: Center for Population Options/Advocates for Youth, 1989. (ERIC Document Reproduction Service No. ED 320 207)

———. et al. "Six School-Based Clinics: Their Reproductive Health Services and Impact on Sexual Behavior." *Family Planning Perspectives* 23 (1991): 6–16.

Kolbe, L. J., et al. "The School-Health Policies and Programs Study (SHPPS); Context, Methods, General Findings, and Future Efforts." *Journal of School Health* 65 (1995): 339–343.

Kort, M. "The Delivery of Primary Health Care in American Public Schools, 1890–1980. *Journal of School Health* 54 (1984): 453–457.

Kozol, J. *Savage Inequalities: Children in America's Schools*. New York: HarperCollins (1991).

Lear, J. G. "It's Elementary: Expanding the Use of School-Based Clinics." *California Health Care Foundation*, October, 2007.

Lovick, S. R. *The School-Based Clinic Update 1987* [Report]. Washington, DC: Center for Population Options/Advocates for Youth, (1987). (ERIC Document Reproduction Service No. ED 328 950)

Mahoney, E. R. "Sex Education in the Public Schools: A Discriminant Analysis of Characteristics of Pro and Anti Individuals." *The Journal of Sex Research* 15 (1979): 264–275.

Marsiglio, W., and F. L. Mott. "The Impact of Sex Education on Sexual Activity, Contraceptive Use and Premarital Pregnancy Among American Teenagers." *Family Planning Perspectives* 18 (1986): 151–162.

May, Scottie, et al. *Children Matter: Celebrating Their Place in the Church, Family, and Community*. Grand Rapids, MI: Eerdmans Publishing, 2005.

McAdoo, Larry. "New Data Shows Abstinence Education Works in Mississippi." December 16, 2012. Retrieved from www.ClarionLedger.com

McGinnis, M. J. "Closing Session Comments: Making It Work." *Journal of School Health* 63 (1993): 43.

McKinney, D. H., and G. L. Peak. *School-Based and School-Linked Health Centers: Update 1994*. Washington, DC: Advocates for Youth/Center for Population Options, 1994.

Morris, L. "Estimating the Need for Family Planning Services Among Unwed Teenagers." *Family Planning Perspectives* 6 (1974): 91–97

Olsen, J. A., and S. E. Weed. "Effects of Family-Planning Programs for Teenagers on Adolescent Birth and Pregnancy Rates." *Family Perspective* 20 (1987): 153–195.

Parker, P. H. "An Analysis of HIV/AIDS Related Behavioral Practices, Knowledge, and Beliefs Among Seventh- Through Twelfth-Grade Public School Students in Trenton, New Jersey (Doctoral dissertation, Temple University, 1994. *Dissertation Abstracts International*, 55/08, 22–88.)

Paul, E. W., and H. F. Pilpel. "Teenagers and Pregnancy: The Law in 1979." *Family Planning Perspectives* 11 (1979): 297–301.

Paul, E. W., et al. "Pregnancy, Teenagers and the Law, 1974." *Family Planning Perspectives* 6 (1974): 142–147.

Pilpel, H. F., and N. F. Wechsler. "Birth-Control, Teen-Agers and the Law: A New Look, 1971." *Family Planning Perspectives*, no. 3 (1971): 37–45.

Planned Parenthood of New York City. "Family Planning in New York City: Recommendations for Action." *Family Planning Perspectives* 2, no. 4 (1970): 25–31.

Population and The American Future. New York: Signet, 1972.

Ralph, N., and A. Edgington. "An Evaluation of an Adolescent Family Planning Program." *Journal of Adolescent Health Care* 4 (1983): 158–162.

Roehlkepartain, Eugene C. "'It's the Way You Look at Things': How Young People Around the World Understand and Experience Spiritual Development." In *Understanding Children's Spirituality: Theology, Research, and Practice*, edited by K. E. Lawson, 152–172. Eugene, OR: Cascade Books, 2012.

Sanger, M. *Pivot of Civilization*. New York: Brentano, 1922.

———. *Margaret Sanger: An Autobiography*. New York: W. W. Norton, 1938.

Scheyer, S. C. "DHEW's New Center: The National Commitment to Family Planning." *Family Planning Perspectives* 2, no. 1 (1970): 22–24.

Schlitt, J. J., et al. "State Initiatives to Support School-Based Health Centers: A National Survey." *Journal of Adolescent Health* 17 (1995): 68–76.

School-Based Clinics that Work [Report]. Rockville, MD: Public Health Services, U. S. Department of Health and Human Services, June, 1993. (ERIC Document Reproduction Service No. ED 359 189)

School-Based Health Alliance. *2010–2011 Census Report of School-Based Health Centers*. Retrieved November 20, 2013 from http://www.sbh4all.org/atf/cf/%7BB241D183-DA6F-443F-9588-3230D027D8DB%7D/2010–11%20Census%20Report%20Final.pdf

———. in Action. Retrieved January 12, 2014 from http://www.sbh4all.org/site/c.ckLQKbOVLkK6E/b.8019625/k.7FC9/SchoolBased_Health_Alliance_in_Action.htm

Sex Information and Education Council of the United States. "Future Directions: HIV/ AIDS Education in the Nation's Schools." New York: Author, (1992). (ERIC Document Reproduction Service No. 358 093)

Siegel, L. P., and T. A. Krieble. "Evaluation of School-Based, High School Health Services." *Journal of School Health* 57 (1987): 323–325.

Stackhouse, B. "The Impact of Religion on Sexuality Education." *SIECUS Report* 18 (1989/1990): 21–27.

St. Lawrence, J. S. "African American Adolescents' Knowledge, Health-Related Attitudes, Sexual Behavior, and Contraceptive Decisions—Implications for the Prevention of Adolescent HIV Infection." *Journal of Consulting and Clinical Psychology* 61 (1993): 104–112.

Tolbert, La Verne. "Condom Availability Through School-Based Clinics and Teenagers' Attitudes Regarding Premarital Sexual Activity." (Doctoral dissertation, Talbot School of Theology, 1996). *Dissertation Abstracts International, 57/08A,* 3409.

———. *How to STUDY and Understand the Bible in 5 Simple Steps (Without Learning Hebrew or Greek).* Xlibris, 2012.

———. *Keeping You & Your Kids Sexually Pure: A How-To Guide for Parents, Pastors, Youth Workers, and Teachers.* Xlibris, 2007.

———. "Teaching Abstinence: Legislators Just Said No." [Essay]. *Los Angeles Times.* p. B7, 1998.

———. *Teaching Like Jesus: A Practical Guide to Christian Education in Your Church.* Grand Rapids, MI: Zondervan, 2000.

———. and Shelly Cunningham. *The A.C. Green I've Got the Power Abstinence Curriculum for Middle and High School Students,* 1995. http://www.acgreen.com/abstinence/ curriculum.html

Valenza, C. "Was Margaret Sanger a Racist?" *Family Planning Perspectives* 17 (1985): 44–46.

Warren, C. *Improving Student's Access to Health Care: School-Based Health Clinics. A Briefing Paper for Policy Makers.* New York: Center for Public Advocacy Research, Ford Foundation, (1987). (ERIC Document Reproduction Service No. ED 295 072)

Waszak, C. & S. Neidell. *School-Based and School-Linked Clinics: Update 1991.* Washington, DC: Center for Population Options/Advocates for Youth, 1991. (ERIC Document Reproduction Service No. 341 899)

Weed, S. E. "Another Look at the Evidence: Abstinence and Sex Education in Our Schools. *Institute for Research and Evaluation,* Salt Lake City, UT, 2009.

———. et al. *The Teen-Aid Family Life Education Project. Fourth Year Evaluation Report Prepared for the Office of Adolescent Pregnancy Programs (OAPP).* Institute for Research and Evaluation, Salt Lake City, UT, 1991.

Wilkins, Michael J. *In His Image: Reflecting Christ in Everyday Life.* Colorado Springs, CO: NavPress, 1997.

Zelnik, M. "Sex Education and Knowledge of Pregnancy Risk Among U.S. Teenage Women." *Family Planning Perspectives* 11 (1979): 355–357.

———. and J. F. Kantner. "The Resolution of Teenage First Pregnancies." *Family Planning Perspectives* 6 (1974): 74–80.

Contributor Biographies

Holly Catterton Allen, PhD, is Professor of Christian Ministries at John Brown University in Siloam Springs, Arkansas where she directs the Child and Family Studies program in the Biblical Studies Division. Dr. Allen's areas of interest are children's spirituality and intergenerational issues. Her most recent book (with Christine Ross) is *Intergenerational Christian Formation: Bringing the Whole Church Together in Ministry, Community, and Worship* (InterVarsity Press, 2012). Her first book, *Nurturing Children's Spirituality: Christian Perspectives and Best Practices* (Cascade), an edited volume, was released in 2008.

Jennifer E. Beste, PhD, is College of Saint Benedict Koch Chair in Catholic Thought and Culture at the College of Saint Benedict. Her publications include *God and the Victim: Traumatic Intrusions on Grace and Freedom* (Oxford University Press, 2007), articles in *Sociology of Religion* and *Practical Matters* and chapters in edited volumes, such as *Children in Religion: A Methods Handbook* (2011) and *The Child in American Religions* (2009). She is currently writing a book on college hookup culture and Christian ethics.

Mark Borchert, PhD, is Associate Professor and Chair of Communication at Carson-Newman University in Jefferson City, TN. His research and publishing is in the area of film and religion. He directs the university's film studies program and he is the festival director for the school's Mossy Creek Documentary Arts Festival each spring.

Hannah Brown grew up in Kenya which sparked her love for living overseas and learning about different cultures. She graduated with a BS in Child and Family Studies and minored in Intercultural Studies and Psychology at John Brown University. Currently she is working as Program Assistant for the India Studies Program with Best Semester.

Will Chesher graduated from John Brown University with a B.A. in Intercultural Studies and a Minor in Child and Family Studies. He is currently teaching High School English in Hope, AR with his wife, Brittney, and one day hopes to open an art center focused on creativity, identity, and stories.

Arnold Cole, EdD, is Chief Executive Officer of Back to the Bible, an international media ministry headquartered in Lincoln, Nebraska. His research focuses on developing methodologies, processes, and best practices to instill significant behavioral change. He received his BA & MA in Psychology, and his EdD in Institutional Management from Pepperdine University. His publications include *Unstuck, Tempted. Tested. True,* and the forthcoming *Worry-Free Living: Find Relief from Anxiety and Stress for You and Your Family.*

David M. Csinos is a doctoral candidate and Teaching for Ministry Fellow at Emmanuel College of Victoria University in the University of Toronto where his research focuses on interculturalism and children in Canadian faith communities. He is author of several books and resources about ministry with children and youth, including *Children's Ministry in the Way of Jesus* written with Ivy Beckwith, *Children's Ministry that Fits,* and *Faith Forward* edited with Melvin Bray. He is founder and president of Faith Forward, an organization for innovation in ministry with youth and children.

Benjamin D. Espinoza, M.A., Asbury Theological Seminary, has served in several churches in Michigan, Ohio, and Kentucky. He received the Stonehouse/May Research Scholarship during the 2012 Children's Spirituality Conference for excellence in research and has contributed articles and reviews to *Christian Education Journal, Religious Education, Religious Studies Review,* and *Seedbed.*

Barbara Fisher, Senior Lecturer in the School of Education at Avondale College of Higher Education, Lake Macquarie Campus, New South Wales (Australia) lectures in Religious Education and Early Literacy Development. Her publications include *Developing a Faith-based Education: A Teacher's Manual, Promoting Biblical Literacy in the Elementary School* and *Exploring Worldviews: A Framework.*

James Riley Estep Jr., PhD, is Academic Dean in the School of Undergraduate Studies at Lincoln Christian University. His publications include over 10 books and numerous articles in such journals as Christian Education Journal, Stone-Campbell Journal, and Religious Education, as well as copious academic papers.

Kelly S. Flanagan, PhD, is Associate Professor of Psychology and Director of the Clinical Psychology PsyD Program at Wheaton College. Her publications can be found in *Journal of Psychology and Christianity, Journal of Psychology and Theology, Journal of Adolescence,* and *Journal of Applied Developmental Psychology,* and include an upcoming book, *Christianity and Developmental Psychopathology: Foundations and Approaches.*

Joel B. Green, PhD, is Professor of New Testament Interpretation and Associate Dean for the Center for Advanced Theological Studies, Fuller Theological Seminary in Pasadena, CA. Prior to this, he served at Asbury Theological Seminary as a professor, dean, and provost. He has taught and written extensively on the Gospel of Luke and Acts.

Susan Hayes Greener, PhD, Associate Professor of Intercultural Studies at the Graduate School of Wheaton College, Wheaton, Illinois. Her recent publications include the chapter, "Raising Samuel: Releasing Children to Discover God's Purpose" in *Children and Mission: Recognizing Children and Youth as Strategic Partners in Mission* and she is Editor-in-Chief of *Our Children, Our Being: Christian Reflections and Research on Child Development in an African Context.*

Christopher C. Hooton, M.A., is an ordained Assemblies of God Minister. He has a BA in children's ministry from North Central University and a Masters in Spiritual Formation and Leadership from Spring Arbor University. With a background as a lead pastor and a children and family pastor, he is convinced that his greatest calling is his ministry to his own children.

Robin Howerton is pursuing her master's degree from Dallas Theological Seminary. A graduate of John Brown University in Child and Family Studies, she lives in Northwest Arkansas where she teaches a preteen Sunday school class and an Awana class for toddlers.

Mariana Hwang, PhD, is Assistant Professor and Program Director of Children and Family Studies in the Church Ministry Field at Lincoln Christian University, Lincoln, IL. Her areas of interest are children's spiritual formation and identity formation and she "has reviewed or published articles in the following: *Recovering the Real Lost Gospel: Reclaiming the Gospel as Good News* by Darrell L. Bock for the *Christian Education Journal (2011); Worship for Children's Spiritual Formation, Journal of Christian Education & Information Technology, (2009); Self-Identity in Empathy Development, Journal of Christian Education & Information Technology, (2006); and Understanding Korean-American Children's God-Concept in Relation to their Self-Concept of Development* in the *Christian Education Journal (2005).* She also contributed several articles in the *Encyclopedia of CE* which will be published in 2014.

Rebecca A. Jones, MA, is an Assistant Professor of Communications at Ouachita Baptist University where she teaches courses in speech and mass communication including classes on communicating with children about faith and spiritual topics and family communication. She completed an MA in Interpersonal and Organizational Communication and is currently pursuing a PhD in Communication Studies. Her research interests include family communication and parent-child communication about faith and spirituality.

Jeffrey B. Keiser, MA, Concordia University Chicago, is a Visiting Professor of Education at Concordia University, River Forest IL. He has an early childhood Montessori teaching credential from the American Montessori Society. Before coming to Concordia, he worked as a classroom teacher, as a school principle, and was an executive of a grant-funded accreditation project. Currently, he is pursuing a PhD in early childhood at Concordia University.

Laura Keeley, MA, University of Colorado, is Director of Children's Ministries at Fourteenth Street Christian Reformed Church in Holland, MI. Her publications include *Celebrating the Milestones of Faith* (with Robert Keeley, Faith Alive Christian Resources, 2009) and a number of sections of the intergenerational *We* curriculum (Faith Alive Christian Resources, 2011, 2012).

Robert J. Keeley, PhD, University of Denver is Professor of Education at Calvin College in Grand Rapids, MI and a collaborating partner with the Calvin Institute of Christian Worship. His publications include *Helping Our Children Grow in Faith* (Baker, 2008), *Celebrating the Milestones of Faith* (with Laura Keeley, Faith Alive Christian Resources, 2009) and an edited volume, *Shaped by God* (Faith Alive Christian Resources, 2010.)

Andrew S. Kereky Jr., DMin, is Director of Spiritual Development at St. Raphael Parish in Bay Village, Ohio. He has successfully adapted the *Ignatian Spiritual Exercises* for children, which is part of the fifth grade religious curriculum at St. Raphael School and several other schools in Northern Ohio. He is writing a book to share this unique approach to children's spirituality. He also designs and leads children's and adult retreats throughout the Diocese of Cleveland.

Mimi L. Larson, MA, in Educational Ministries at Wheaton College and MA-Theological Studies at Covenant Theological Seminary has served in vocational children's ministries for over 24 years. This includes local church ministry, curriculum development and teaching. Currently, she is pursuing a PhD in early childhood at Concordia University, River Forest, IL.

Kevin E. Lawson, EdD, is Professor of Christian Education, Director of PhD and EdD programs in Educational Studies at Talbot School of Theology, Biola University, La Mirada, CA. He serves as Editor of the *Christian Education Journal.* His publications include *Understanding Children's Spirituality* (Ed.), and *Associate Staff Ministry.*

Rebecca L. Loveall, MA in Clinical Psychology from Wheaton College is a missionary and the Project Director of Escuela Integrada in Antigua, Guatemala, which focuses on the education and spiritual formation of at-risk youth. Her research interests include culture, trauma, forgiveness and justice. She has published in the *Journal of Psychology and Christianity* and is a contributor in *Children's Spirituality: Theology, Research, and Practice.*

Sandra M. Ludlow B. Ed (EC) is Course Convenor at Avondale College of Higher Education, Cooranbong NSW, Australia. Her current research interests include co-constructed curriculum and nurturing pre-schooler's spiritual awareness and faith formation.

Gary McKnight, ThM, PhD, has served since 2003 in Nairobi, Kenya. He teaches Christian Education and Formation at International Leadership University-Kenya (formerly Nairobi International School of Theology) and Children and Family Ministry at Carlile College. He has recently competed coursework for a DMin in Spiritual Formation.

Shirley K. Morgenthaler, PhD, Loyola University and Erikson Institute, is the Distinguished Professor of Education at Concordia University, River Forest, IL. Her publications include *Right From the Start: A Parent's Guide to the Young Child's Faith Development, Children and Worship: Lessons from Research*, and *Exploring the Spiritual Formation of Children: Foundational Issues.* She served as president of the Chicago Association for the Education of Young Children and the Illinois Association of Early Childhood Teacher Educators.

Chelsey M. Morrison, MA, is a doctoral student in the Clinical Psychology program at Wheaton College with a concentration on Child and Adolescent Psychology. Her clinical and research interests include positive psychology, developmental disabilities, and pediatric psychology.

Gary C. Newton, PhD, is Professor of Discipleship Ministries at Crown College, St. Bonifacius, MN. His publications include *Growing Toward Spiritual Maturity* and *Heart-Deep Teaching: Engaging Students for Transformed Lives.*

Trevecca Okholm, MA, Educational Ministries, Wheaton, Illinois is a Certified Christian Educator, PC/USA. She has been a professional Christian educator and minister to children and families for nearly twenty-five years and is currently serving the church as a children and family ministry consultant. She teaches as an adjunct professor for Practical Theology at Azusa Pacific University, Azusa, California. Her publications include *Kingdom Family: Re-Envisioning God's Plan for Marriage and Family* (Cascade, 2012).

Pamela Caudill Ovwigho, PhD, is the Executive Director of the Center for Bible Engagement, Lincoln, Nebraska. Throughout her career she has researched a variety of topics from welfare policy to family violence to spirituality. Currently she focuses on scripture engagement, spiritual growth, and church health.

Dana Kennamer Pemberton, PhD, is chair of the Department of Teacher Education at Abilene Christian University where she teaches early childhood education. She has presented at numerous regional, national, and international conferences on topics related to children's spiritual development and nurture. She is author of *I Will Change Your Name: Messages from the Father to a Heart Broken by Divorce* (2006) and co-author of *Beautiful in God's Eyes: Building Character, Wisdom, and Faith in Young Women* (2001) and *Let All the Children Come to Me: A Practical Guide Including Children with Disabilities Is Your Church's Ministry* (2008).

Catherine Posey, PhD, is an online instructor in children's literature, writing, and literature at several colleges and universities. She continues to research the area of children's literature and spirituality through studies involving elementary and middle school students sharing their responses to literary texts. After completing doctoral studies in Curriculum and Instruction at The Pennsylvania State University, she taught middle school English for two years at a private creative arts school in South Carolina. She is currently teaching in Northern California where she is writing a children's novel.

Susan B. Ridgely, PhD, is associate professor of religious studies at University of Wisconsin-Oshkosh. She is author of *When I was a Child: Children's Interpretations of First Communion* (UNC Press, 2005) and *Children and Religion: A Methods Handbook* (NYU Press, 2011). She is currently working on ethnography on how families use Focus on the Family childrearing materials.

Sharon Warkentin Short is an experienced children's ministry practitioner. She currently teaches online courses for various Christian colleges and seminaries in the areas of educational ministry and Bible content.

Morgan Sorenson, B.A., is a doctoral student in the PsyD program at Fuller Seminary and alumna of Wheaton College. Her research interests include risk and resilience in high-risk youth populations, social justice, international trauma, and Latin American culture.

La Verne Tolbert, PhD, is president of the Society of Children's Spirituality: Christian Perspectives. She served as a Christian education pastor/director in the local church for over 15 years, and she was assistant professor at Talbot School of Theology where she earned both her masters and doctoral degrees. In 2001, she founded Teaching Like Jesus Ministries, Inc., a parachurch ministry that equips leaders in the local church. Her publications include *Teaching Like Jesus: A Practical Guide to Christian Education in Your Church* (Zondervan), *Keeping You & Your Kids Sexually Pure: A How-To Guide for Parents, Pastors, Youth Workers, and Teachers* (originally published by Zondervan, now Xlibris), *How to STUDY and Understand the Bible in 5 Simple Steps Without Learning Hebrew or Greek* (Xlibris), and *Life at All Costs: An Anthology of Voices from 21st Century Black Prolife Leaders* edited with Dr. Alveda King (Xlibris). With Shelly Cunningham, PhD, she is co-author of A. C. Green's *I've Got the Power Abstinence Curriculum for Middle and High School Students*. From 1975 to 1980 she served on the boards of Planned Parenthood and the Young Women's Christian Association (YWCA) in New York City.

www.ingramcontent.com/pod-product-compliance
Lightning Source LLC
Chambersburg PA
CBHW061958090426
42811CB00006B/974